To scan

STAR WARS™

COMPLETE VEHICLES

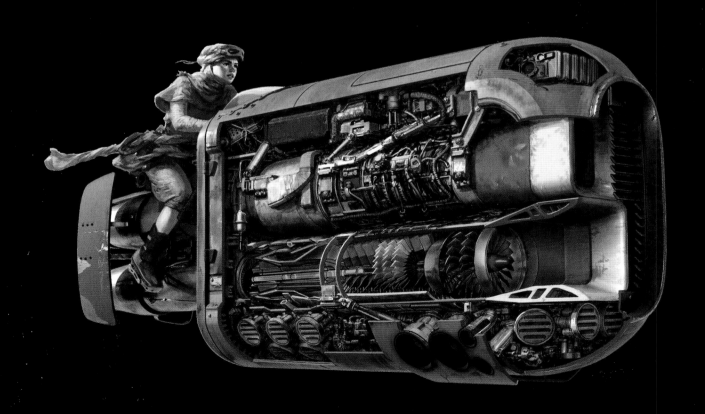

STAR WARS™
COMPLETE VEHICLES

Written by
Kerrie Dougherty
Curtis Saxton
David West Reynolds
Ryder Windham
Jason Fry
Pablo Hidalgo

Illustrated by
Hans Jenssen
Richard Chasemore
Kemp Remillard

Additional illustrations by
John Mullaney and Jon Hall

CONTENTS

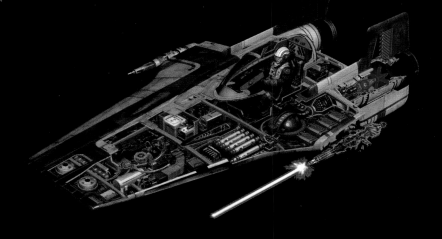

INTRODUCTION

Galactic civilization relies on technologies that have existed for millennia. Faster-than-light communication and travel are routine, and even commonplace devices often boast vast amounts of computing power. Droids serve as cheap and expendable labor on countless planets, taking myriad forms to perform tasks too complicated, dangerous, or tedious for their organic masters. The galaxy's factions also have access to weapons of terrifying power, and defensive capabilities meant to neutralize them. Throughout the long history of the galaxy, war has always spurred technological innovation.

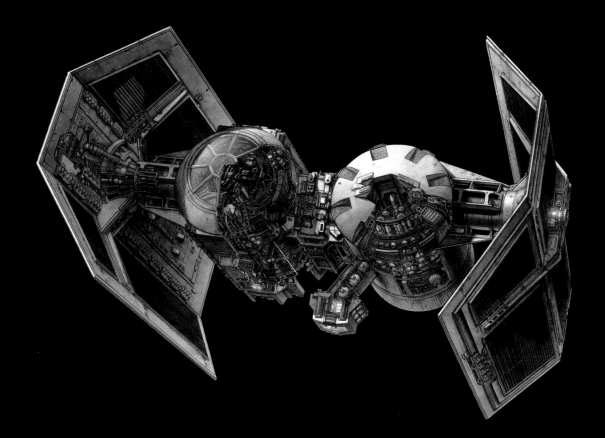

VEHICLE TECHNOLOGY

HYPERDRIVES

Hyperdrives allow ships to travel faster than light, crossing the void between stars through the alternate dimension of hyperspace. Hyperspace fuels, such as coaxium, power a ship into hyperspace while preserving its mass/energy profile, sending it along a programmed course until it drops back into normal space at its destination. Large objects in normal space cast "mass shadows" in hyperspace, so hyperspace jumps must be precisely calculated to avoid deadly collisions.

GRAVITY MANIPULATORS

A number of galactic technologies work by manipulating gravity. Repulsorlifts allow a craft to hover or fly over a planet's surface by pushing against its gravity, producing thrust, while acceleration compensators keep starship crews alive during high-speed maneuvres. Tractor beams manipulate gravitational forces to push or pull objects, while interdiction fields create gravitational shadows that interfere with faster-than-light travel, pinning ships in normal space or yanking them out of hyperspace.

SENSORS

Sensors gather information about the area surrounding a vehicle, highlighting threats and hazards. Passive-mode sensors repeatedly scan the same area, scan-mode sensors have a longer range and collect data by emitting pulses in all directions, and search-mode sensors focus on a specific area for analysis. Data accumulated from scans is then fed into a sensor computer and relayed to a vehicle's operator. Most starships have sensor suites that analyze a wide range of spectra.

ENERGY WEAPONS

Laser cannons and turbolasers are based on the same principle as handheld blasters: energy-rich gas is converted to a glowing particle beam that can melt through targets. The largest such weapons are powerful enough to crack a planet's core. Starships also use ion cannons, which overwhelm electronic systems with ionized energy bursts, and physical ordnance such as concussion missiles and proton torpedoes, whose energy warheads release clouds of high-velocity proton particles.

POWER SOURCES

Vehicles use a range of power technologies, most of which date back to the Republic's earliest days. The most common are chemical, fission, or fusion reactors, which consume a variety of fuels based on local resources. Large starships opt for fusion systems that contain hypermatter-annihilation cores, generating vast amounts of power. Many starship fuels are hazardous to organic beings, circulating in ship systems as corrosive liquids or combustible and poisonous gases.

SHIELDS

Shields are protective force fields that repel solid objects or absorb energy. Concussion shields repel space debris, while two varieties of deflector shield protect craft in battle. Ray shields deflect or scatter energy beams, while particle shields diffuse impacts from high-velocity projectiles and proton weapons. A shield's intensity gradually diminishes with distance from its projector. Most starships use a combination of ray and particle shielding for the most reliable protection.

EPISODE I
THE PHANTOM MENACE

The Galactic Republic is engulfed by turmoil. Thousands of years of peace and prosperity are threatened by the greed of powerful commercial organizations, such as the Trade Federation, which have risen to challenge the authority of the Galactic Senate. To resolve disputes, the Republic must call on the negotiating skills of its guardians of peace and justice, the Jedi Knights. During their efforts to resolve one such flash point—the blockade of the planet Naboo by the Trade Federation—Jedi Master Qui-Gon Jinn and his Padawan Obi-Wan Kenobi become embroiled in a complex plot that ultimately leads them to the desert planet Tatooine. There they discover a young slave, Anakin Skywalker, who shows amazing Force-potential. Qui-Gon believes he may be the "Chosen One" of Jedi lore, destined to bring balance to the Force.

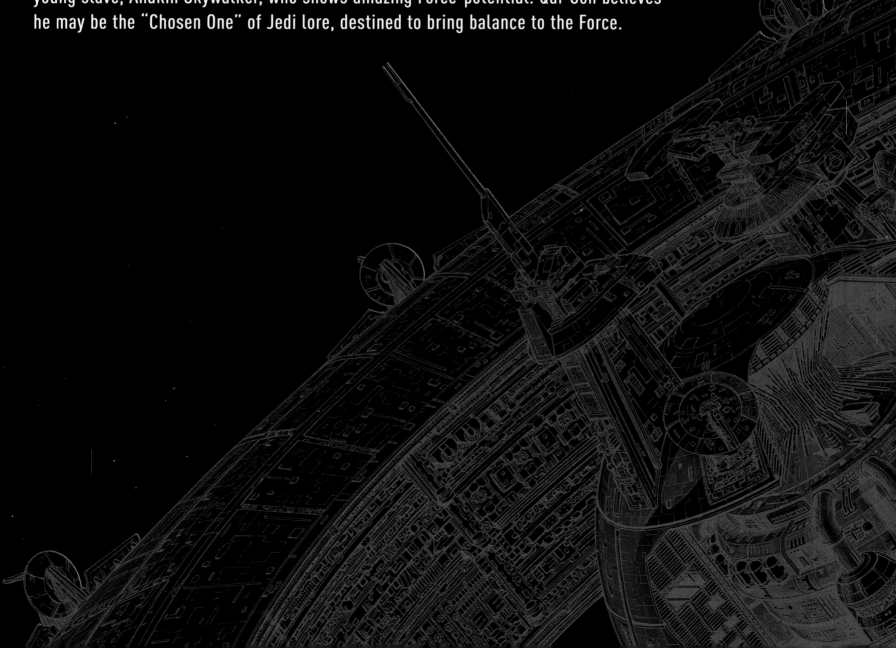

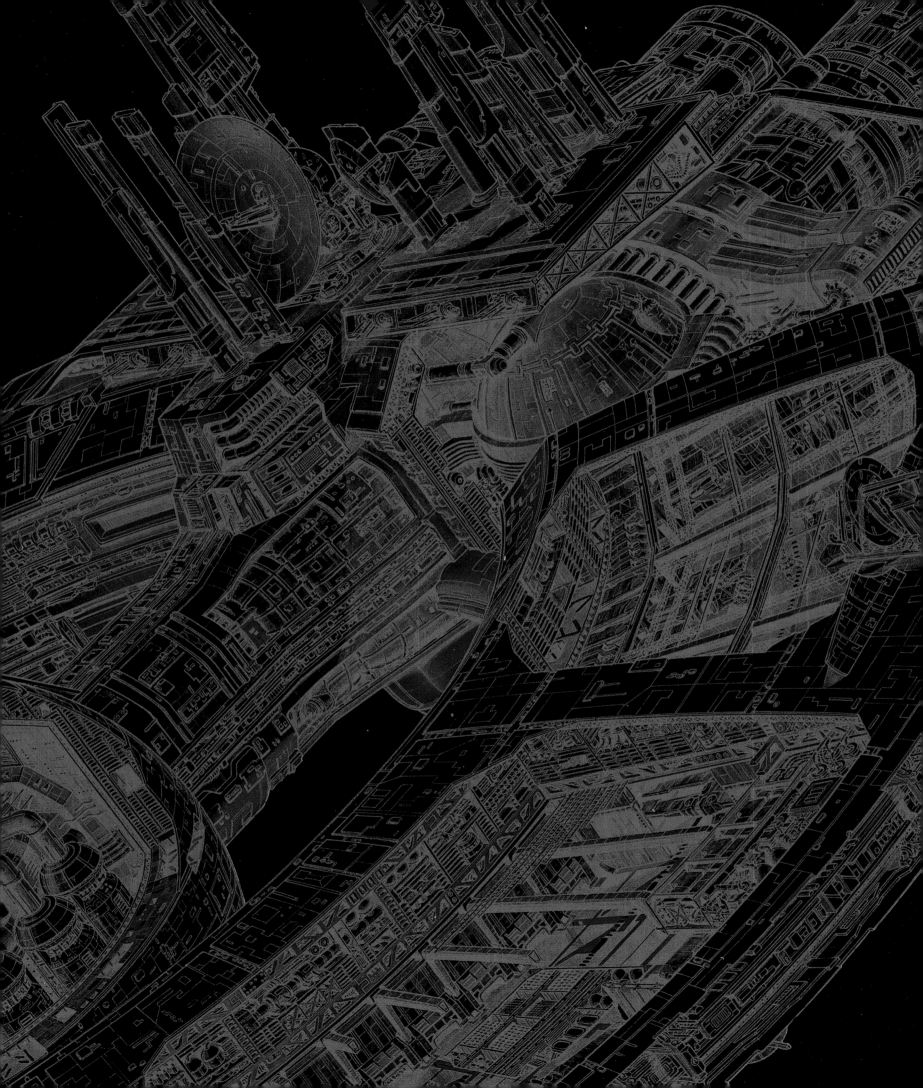

REPUBLIC CRUISER

Carrying two Jedi Knights into the heart of danger, the Republic cruiser is dispatched by Supreme Chancellor Valorum to the blockaded planet of Naboo. The direct predecessor to the well-armed Republic frigate, the peaceful Republic cruiser was assembled in the great orbital shipyards of Corellia, and serves as a testament to the quality and fame of Corellian spacecraft design. The *Radiant VII* is a veteran of 34 years in service of the diplomatic corps of Coruscant itself, capital world of the Galactic Republic. The ship has endured many adventures, bringing Jedi Knights, ambassadors, and diplomats to trouble spots around the galaxy on missions of security and vital political significance. Its interchangeable salon pods are well-armored and insulated against any kind of eavesdropping. In this safe haven, critical negotiations can take place and crises can be averted.

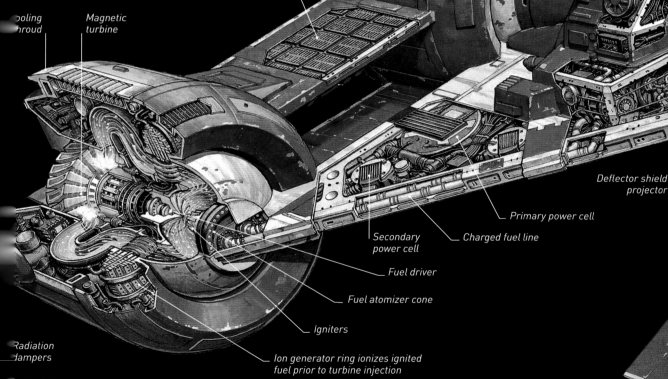

Dyne 577 sublight engine

Deflector shield energizer

Deflector shield generator

Radiator panel wing

Cooling shroud

Magnetic turbine

Deflector shield projector

Standard space docking ring

Primary power cell

Secondary power cell

Charged fuel line

Fuel driver

Fuel atomizer cone

Igniters

Radiation dampers

Ion generator ring ionizes ignited fuel prior to turbine injection

Droid hold

8-person escape pod

COLOR SIGNAL

The striking red color of the Republic cruiser sends a message to all who see it. Scarlet declares the ship's diplomatic immunity and serves as a warning not to attack. Red is the color of ambassadorial relations and neutrality for spacecraft of the Galactic Republic, and has been for generations. The extraordinary full-red color scheme of the Republic cruiser signifies that the ship comes straight from the great capital world of the Republic, Coruscant. The color would eventually be co-opted during the chancellery of Sheev Palpatine of Naboo, whose personal preference for the blue saw it assigned across Republic vessels.

Control Console The Republic cruiser's control console is engineered to allow the captain and co-pilot to share operational duties, or if necessary for just one of them to pilot the ship.

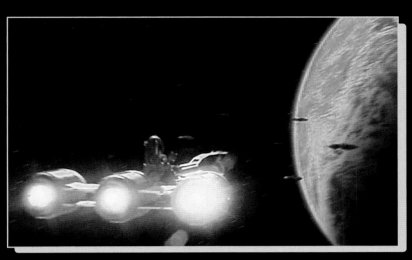

Mission to Naboo Approaching heavily armed Trade Federation cargo ships in orbit around Naboo, the *Radiant VII* maintains full shield power until it lands in a cargo ship's hangar.

COMMUNICATING IN A DIVERSE GALAXY

In order to communicate with any culture it may visit, the Republic cruiser sports a wide variety of dish and other communications antennas. On board the cruiser, two communications officers specialize in operating the communication computers, deciphering strange languages, and decoding the complex signal pulses of unorthodox alien transmissions. Years later, the Empire will standardize communications across the galaxy, making such systems unnecessary.

Upper deck state rooms

Wiring and systems trunk

Formal dining room

Crew lounge

Elevator

Multi-comm station

Salon pod magnoclamps

Navigator's station

Captain's storage

Automated docking signal receiver

Cockpit

Navigational sensor dish

Lounge

Escape pod access tunnel (from lower deck)

Captain's quarters

Salon vestibule

Salon pod breakaway cowling

Interchangeable diplomatic salon pod

Main salon pod airlock doors

Salon pod has seating for 16 beings

Hologram pad

Main forward sensors

Salon pod independent sensors

Mid-deck corridor

TIGHT SECURITY

The *Radiant VII* is a modified Corellian cruiser. Civilian models of the class are used for straightforward transport purposes, but the scarlet Republic cruisers are dedicated to the special objectives of galactic political service. To accomplish their missions, Republic cruisers must often rely on their reputation as absolutely secure vessels for high-level diplomatic meetings and confrontations. For security reasons, crew is kept to a bare minimum, with many ship functions attended by simple utility droids.

DANGEROUS DIPLOMACY

Although the planet Naboo is a member world of the Galactic Republic, it is located near the Outer Rim Territories, where the Republic has little influence. There, worlds without strong military forces are especially vulnerable to attack and invasion. Because the Neimoidian homeworld is also a member of the Republic, and because the Neimoidians rarely take any action that invites trouble with the Republic, the Neimoidian Trade Federation's blockade of Naboo surprises many representatives of the Galactic Senate. When a Republic cruiser delivers a Jedi Knight and his apprentice to a Trade Federation battleship in Naboo's orbit, the Jedi know that if they fail to persuade the Neimoidians to leave the Naboo system, violent conflict could result.

Cruiser Cockpit After successfully delivering the Jedi Knights Qui-Gon Jinn and Obi-Wan Kenobi to a Trade Federation ship, co-pilot Antidar Williams and Captain Maoi Madakor watch helplessly as a droid laser turret targets the *Radiant VII*'s cockpit.

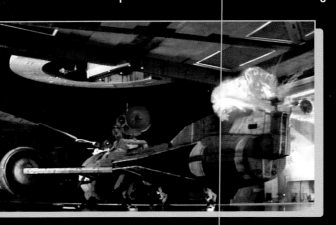

Treacherous Hosts Docked within a Trade Federation cargo ship that has been upgraded with military-grade weapons, the *Radiant VII* becomes vulnerable to attack when the crew lowers its deflector shields.

REPUBLIC CRUISER SALON POD

Republic cruisers often serve as neutral meeting grounds for Republic officials and leaders of groups in conflict. To accommodate the many kinds of alien physiology in the galaxy, customized salon pods are available in the hangars on Coruscant, and the Republic cruiser can be equipped with any of these. In emergency situations, the entire salon pod can eject from the cruiser with its own sensors and independent life-support gear ready to sustain the diplomatic party on board. Unfortunately for the crew of the *Radiant VII*, when their ship is attacked there is no time for such an escape.

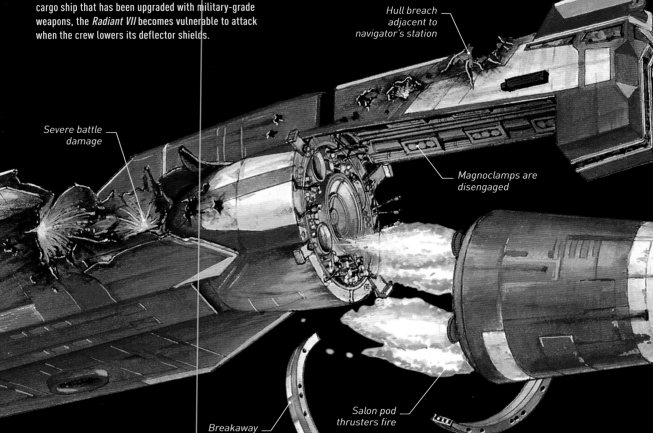

Hull breach adjacent to navigator's station

Severe battle damage

Magnoclamps are disengaged

Independent pod sensors activate

Breakaway cowling releases

Salon pod thrusters fire

DROID INVASION FORCES

The Neimoidian Trade Federation uses a standard plan to invade worlds they hope to dominate. First, an armada of battleships surrounds the targeted world. The battleships deploy Xi Char-manufactured droid starfighters to disable any satellite weapons and communications systems, and send C-9979 landing ships to the world's surface. Each landing ship carries Trade Federation battle droids, tanks, and transports. An orbital Droid Control Ship directs the droids to attack, capture, or destroy the enemy's strategic defenses. Every battle droid obeys orders with ruthless efficiency.

Deployed Landing Ships Each retrofitted Trade Federation cargo ship carries 50 landing ships for transporting war machines and droids to planetary surfaces. Externally, they resemble the Trade Federation's standard commercial cargo barges.

Droid Army Disembarks Operated by the Trade Federation's remote Droid Control Ship, battle droids guide Multi-Troop Transports (MTTs) out of the landing ships and steer them into strategic positions.

Drive unit adapted from civilian cargo sled

Repulsorlift sled

TROOP CARRIER

The Trade Federation troop carrier conveys battle droid units to deployment zones behind the protection of ground armor, in secure conditions, or within occupied areas. A rack similar to that in the MTT contains a full complement of 112 battle droids folded into their space-saving configuration, ready for action on release.

The Conquest of Naboo The droid army descends on the capital city of Naboo, Theed. The force is so overwhelming that no resistance is offered, and the city falls without a battle.

LANDING SHIP

When plans for the ground forces of the Trade Federation secret army had begun to take shape, methods of deployment came under consideration. The Haor Chall Engineering works produced a design for a landing craft that would carry attack vehicles and troops to ground sites from Trade Federation battleships, and, after a period of much-debated development, the C-9979 variant was chosen by the Trade Federation armaments committee. Related in design to commercial cargo barges in the trade fleet, these huge, double-winged ships were built for the sole purpose of transporting AATs (Armored Assault Tanks), troop carriers, and MTTs (Multi-Troop Transports) from orbiting battleships to strategic positions on planet surfaces. The C-9979 offers tremendous antigravity lifting capacity, which is necessary for the heavy, armored cargo. With its defensive laser cannons, the mighty C-9979 presents a bizarre and menacing shadow in the skies of any threatened planet.

MECHANIZED CREW

A relatively small droid crew operates the C-9979, in keeping with the Trade Federation reliance on completely automated soldiery. Droid pilots steer the ship and robot gunners work the cannon stations, which serve to defend the landing ship on its way down. Along the front of the wings are a series of maintenance and repair shops. These are also run by droids, and are used to service and maintain the attack-force components, especially individual battle droids, which need realignment and repair after battle engagements.

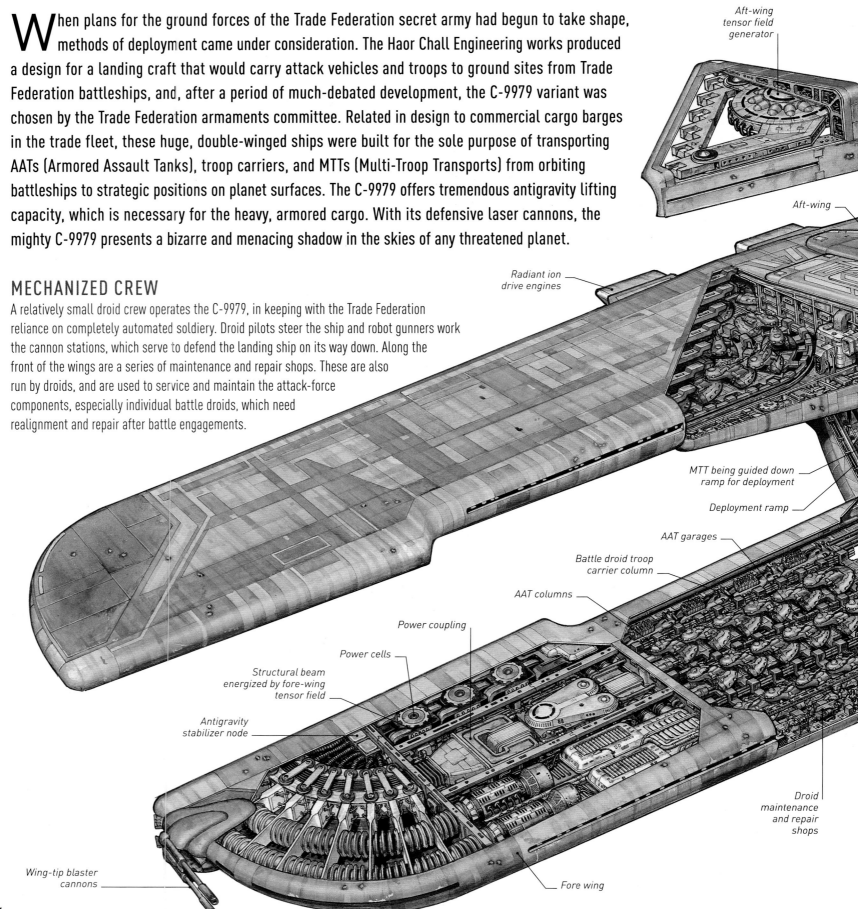

Aft-wing tensor field generator

Aft-wing

Radiant ion drive engines

MTT being guided down ramp for deployment

Deployment ramp

AAT garages

Battle droid troop carrier column

AAT columns

Power coupling

Power cells

Structural beam energized by fore-wing tensor field

Antigravity stabilizer node

Droid maintenance and repair shops

Wing-tip blaster cannons

Fore wing

LOADING

C-9979 landing ships are berthed in hidden hangar areas aboard Trade Federation battleships. Here they are assembled, serviced, and maintained, and when ready for deployment they are loaded with MTTs, AATs, and troop carriers that have been prepared for combat. Landing ships are stored in an unloaded condition, both to reduce structural stress and enable the attack craft to be serviced individually.

Electromagnetic transport clamp-on rail will guide MTT down deployment ramp

Control signal receiver picks up vital signal from the Droid Control Ship

MTT powers up its onboard repulsors in staging area

Control center

Pressure charging turbine atmosphere intake

Deflector shield projectors

Cannon charging turret

Defensive laser cannon

Wing-tip plating is an alloy composite transparent to repulsor effect

Staging area

Fore-wing tensor field generator

Radiator panel for tensor power system

Navigation sensors

Combat sensors

Forward tensor field generator increases load-bearing ability of wing mounts

MTT garage

Antigravity rails support MTTs

Center MTT has deployed and an AAT now follows into position

Doors require clear landing area for opening clearance

Main deployment doors include perimeter field sensors to detect possible land mines, electrical fields, and other hazards

DEPLOYMENT

The wings of the landing ship contain rows of MTTs, AATs, and battle droid troop carriers racked in garage channels for maximum loading capacity. For deployment, the attack vehicles are guided along repulsor tracks to a staging platform. MTTs in particular require the assistance of the repulsors built into these tracks, because their onboard maneuvering equipment is not precise enough to negotiate the cramped confines of the garage zones without risking collisions. At a staging platform, the vehicles are rotated into position and seized by transport clamps, which draw them aft and guide them down the drop ramp in the landing ship's "foot." The great clamshell doors of the "foot" then open wide to release the ground forces. Deployment of the full load of vehicles on board a C-9979 can take up to 45 minutes.

STORING THE TRANSPORT

C-9979s are built with removable wings so they can be stored efficiently. Powerful tensor fields bind the wings to the fuselage when the ship is assembled for use. The huge wings of the C-9979 would tax the load-bearing capabilities of even the strongest metal alloys, making tensor fields vital for the integrity of the ship. Forward-mounted tensor fields bind the wing mounts firmly to the fuselage, while wing-mounted tensor fields keep the span of the wings from sagging.

AAT in escort position

MTT moving out for battle position

MTT

The Trade Federation's Baktoid Armor Workshop has long designed armaments for Trade Federation customers. When called upon to design and build vehicles for the Trade Federation droid army, it easily turned its resources to the creation of deadly weapons made to ensure a long line of future customers. The Trade Federation MTT (Multi-Troop Transport) was designed to convey platoons of ground troops to the battlefield and support them there. Its deployment on Naboo is its first use in a major military action; many transports had seen only training exercises on remote worlds before being used there. MTTs are designed for deployment in traditional battle lines, hence their heavy frontal armor. Reinforced and studded with case-hardened metal alloy studs, the MTT's face is designed to ram through walls so that troops may be deployed directly into enemy buildings (or "future customer buildings," as the Trade Federation often prefers to say). When ready to deploy, it opens its large front hatch to release the battle droid contingents from its huge storage rack, extended on a powerful hydraulic rail. Two droid pilots direct it according to instructions transmitted from the orbiting Droid Control Ship.

Smashing Power The dense forests of Naboo do little to impede the destructive movement of armored MTTs, which are capable of ramming through fortified structures.

HEAVY LIFTING

The MTT's engine works hard to power repulsorlifts that carry a very heavy load of troops and solid armor. The repulsorlift generator's exhaust and cooling system is vented straight down toward the ground through several large vents under the vehicle. This creates a billowing storm of wind around the MTT, which lends it a powerful and menacing air.

Control room escape hatch (at rear)

Lift

Overseer catwalk

Rack operator droid

Deployment rack extensor drive

Rack drive heat exhaust vents

Rack extensor drive engine

Pressure equalizer valves

Power converter grids

Kuat Premion Mk. II power generators

Repulsor motor gas cooling system exhaust

Heavy-duty repulsor cooling fins

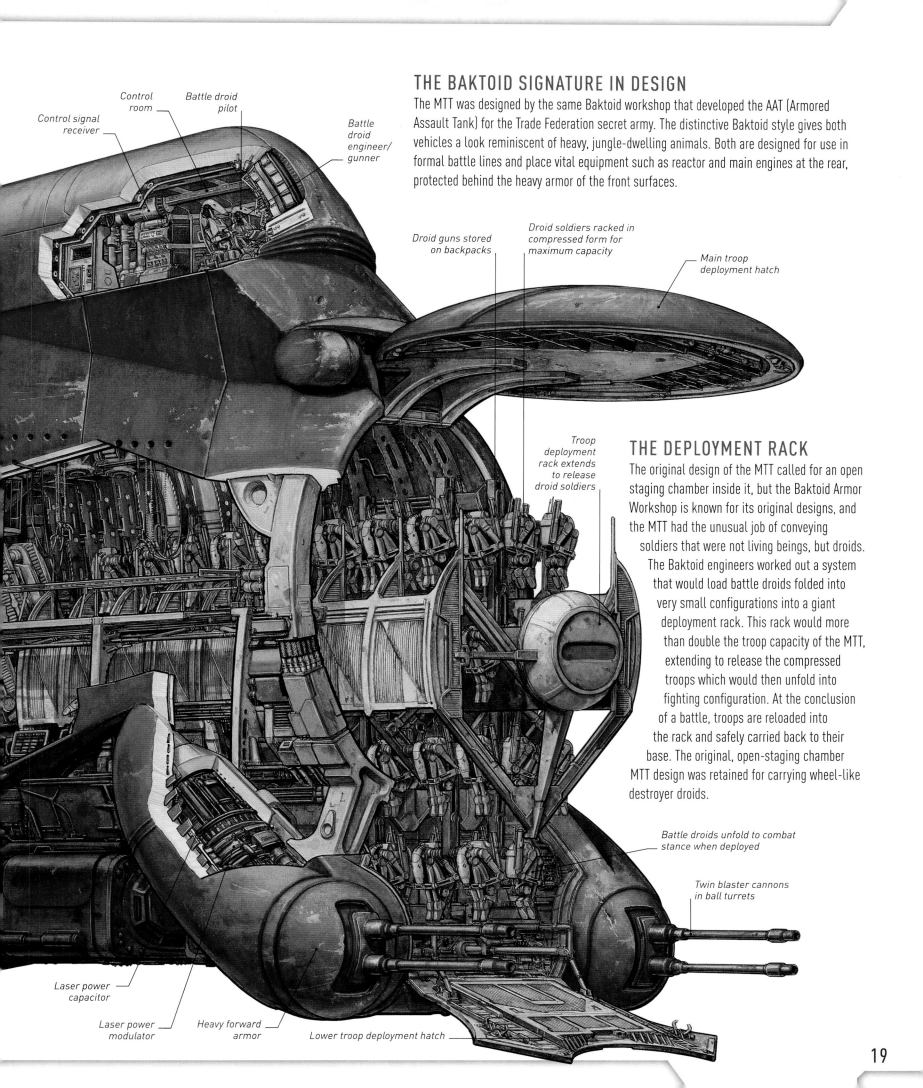

THE BAKTOID SIGNATURE IN DESIGN

The MTT was designed by the same Baktoid workshop that developed the AAT (Armored Assault Tank) for the Trade Federation secret army. The distinctive Baktoid style gives both vehicles a look reminiscent of heavy, jungle-dwelling animals. Both are designed for use in formal battle lines and place vital equipment such as reactor and main engines at the rear, protected behind the heavy armor of the front surfaces.

Control signal receiver

Control room

Battle droid pilot

Battle droid engineer/ gunner

Droid guns stored on backpacks

Droid soldiers racked in compressed form for maximum capacity

Main troop deployment hatch

Troop deployment rack extends to release droid soldiers

THE DEPLOYMENT RACK

The original design of the MTT called for an open staging chamber inside it, but the Baktoid Armor Workshop is known for its original designs, and the MTT had the unusual job of conveying soldiers that were not living beings, but droids. The Baktoid engineers worked out a system that would load battle droids folded into very small configurations into a giant deployment rack. This rack would more than double the troop capacity of the MTT, extending to release the compressed troops which would then unfold into fighting configuration. At the conclusion of a battle, troops are reloaded into the rack and safely carried back to their base. The original, open-staging chamber MTT design was retained for carrying wheel-like destroyer droids.

Battle droids unfold to combat stance when deployed

Twin blaster cannons in ball turrets

Laser power capacitor

Laser power modulator

Heavy forward armor

Lower troop deployment hatch

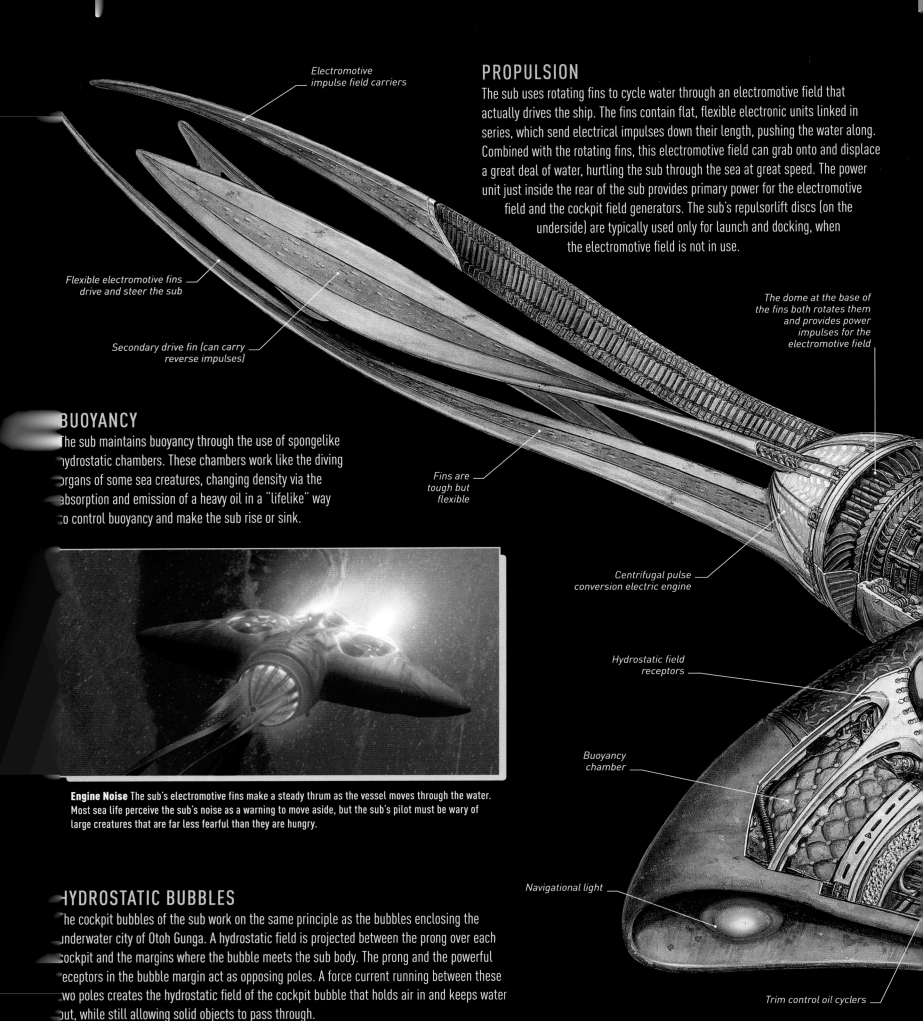

Electromotive
impulse field carriers

PROPULSION

The sub uses rotating fins to cycle water through an electromotive field that actually drives the ship. The fins contain flat, flexible electronic units linked in series, which send electrical impulses down their length, pushing the water along. Combined with the rotating fins, this electromotive field can grab onto and displace a great deal of water, hurtling the sub through the sea at great speed. The power unit just inside the rear of the sub provides primary power for the electromotive field and the cockpit field generators. The sub's repulsorlift discs (on the underside) are typically used only for launch and docking, when the electromotive field is not in use.

Flexible electromotive fins
drive and steer the sub

Secondary drive fin (can carry
reverse impulses)

The dome at the base of
the fins both rotates them
and provides power
impulses for the
electromotive field

BUOYANCY

The sub maintains buoyancy through the use of spongelike hydrostatic chambers. These chambers work like the diving organs of some sea creatures, changing density via the absorption and emission of a heavy oil in a "lifelike" way to control buoyancy and make the sub rise or sink.

Fins are
tough but
flexible

Centrifugal pulse
conversion electric engine

Hydrostatic field
receptors

Buoyancy
chamber

Engine Noise The sub's electromotive fins make a steady thrum as the vessel moves through the water. Most sea life perceive the sub's noise as a warning to move aside, but the sub's pilot must be wary of large creatures that are far less fearful than they are hungry.

Navigational light

HYDROSTATIC BUBBLES

The cockpit bubbles of the sub work on the same principle as the bubbles enclosing the underwater city of Otoh Gunga. A hydrostatic field is projected between the prong over each cockpit and the margins where the bubble meets the sub body. The prong and the powerful receptors in the bubble margin act as opposing poles. A force current running between these two poles creates the hydrostatic field of the cockpit bubble that holds air in and keeps water out, while still allowing solid objects to pass through.

Trim control oil cyclers

GUNGAN SUB

This kind of submersible is a common utility transport in Otoh Gunga. The forward cockpit bubble carries only a pilot and passengers, but the side bubbles can carry either passengers or cargo, depending on whether they are fitted with seats. The sub's distinctive form originates from both the Gungans' construction methods and their love of artistic design. The Gungans produce many of their structures using a secret method that actually "grows" the basic skeletons or shells of buildings or vehicles. This gives Gungan constructions a distinctive organic look, which is then complemented by artistic detail, even on simple vehicles like the sub. Gungan organically generated shells can be combined to make complex constructions, and then modified and fitted with electronic and mechanical components to give them the needed functionality. The organic skeletons are exceptionally strong, though still susceptible to damage by some of the larger sea monsters encountered in deep waters.

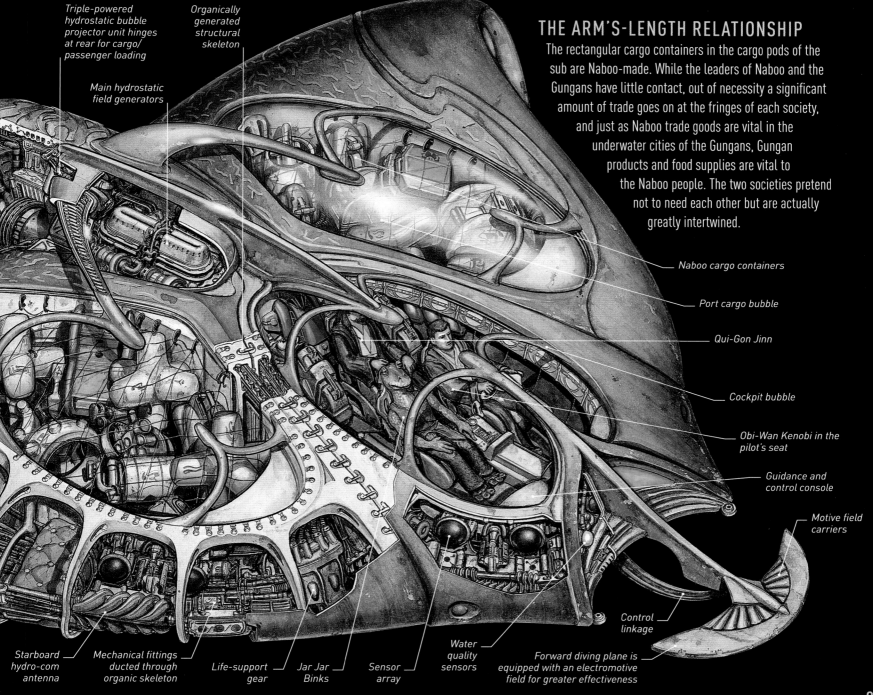

Triple-powered hydrostatic bubble projector unit hinges at rear for cargo/ passenger loading

Organically generated structural skeleton

Main hydrostatic field generators

THE ARM'S-LENGTH RELATIONSHIP
The rectangular cargo containers in the cargo pods of the sub are Naboo-made. While the leaders of Naboo and the Gungans have little contact, out of necessity a significant amount of trade goes on at the fringes of each society, and just as Naboo trade goods are vital in the underwater cities of the Gungans, Gungan products and food supplies are vital to the Naboo people. The two societies pretend not to need each other but are actually greatly intertwined.

Naboo cargo containers

Port cargo bubble

Qui-Gon Jinn

Cockpit bubble

Obi-Wan Kenobi in the pilot's seat

Guidance and control console

Motive field carriers

Control linkage

Starboard hydro-com antenna

Mechanical fittings ducted through organic skeleton

Life-support gear

Jar Jar Binks

Sensor array

Water quality sensors

Forward diving plane is equipped with an electromotive field for greater effectiveness

EXPLORING THE DEEP

While Naboo's landmasses are characterized by lush forests and expansive vistas, the planet's waters are generally considered the stuff of nightmares. Naboo is laced with treacherous underwater tunnels and serpentine caverns that challenge the most experienced pilots of Gungan submersibles, known as bongos. Most of these underwater lanes are filled with monstrous predators, some of which regard wayward bongos as prey. Fortunately, Gungans engineer their bongos with sturdy hulls, powerful electromotive field motors, and headlights that can be adjusted to cut through the murky depths.

Dangerous Tunnels Although naturally formed underwater tunnels offer opportunities for swift travel from one area of Naboo to another, some routes are especially treacherous because of the presence of opee sea killers, whose powerful jaws can rupture a Gungan sub's sturdy hull.

Illuminated Depths While many deep-water fish have naturally evolved phosphorescent appendages to help them lure and locate prey, Gungan subs rely on bright headlights to cut through the murky waters of Naboo.

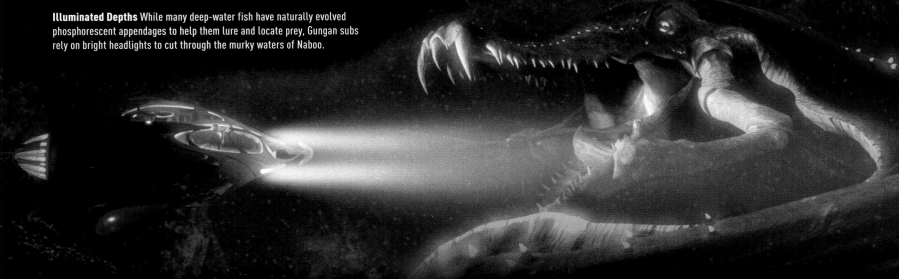

Expansive View Although the Gungan sub's front seats do not offer much elbow room, the sub's large bubble windows give the impression that the cockpit's space is not so limited.

NAVIGATING THE CORE

Naboo is an ancient and geologically unique world that lacks a molten core, and has numerous swampy lakes on the surface leading deep into the planet's structure. Countless caves and tunnel networks permeate the conglomeration of rocky bodies that make up the planet, and the Gungans have explored and navigated these networks for generations. Despite the risk of run-ins with dangerous aquatic beasts, various networks have come to be regarded as time-honored trade routes, and the most expedient avenues for Gungans to travel from one area of Naboo to another. The region known as the Abyss provides a route between Otoh Gunga and Theed City.

Escape Tactic If an opee sea killer attacks a Gungan sub, the sub's pilot may find help in the form of a gigantic sando aqua monster, which is generally more interested in making a meal of an opee than in any small, passing vessel.

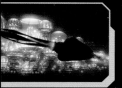

GUNGAN TECHNOLOGY

Thousands of years before the Battle of Naboo, a struggle for territory prompted the Gungans to retreat into the depths of Naboo's seas. There they discovered a strange underwater plant, the locap, which burrows into porous rock and siphons out plasma. The innovative Gungans used subs equipped with front-mounted collectors to harvest plasma from the plant, and discovered many ways to utilize this natural source of energy. The Gungans' distinctive, plasma-based technology is used to generate the hydrostatic fields that surround Gungan cities and submarines.

Adjustable-Strength Bubbles Obi-Wan and Qui-Gon Jinn pass through the bubble walls of the Gungans' underwater city with relative ease, but the hydrostatic fields that separate air from water can be increased to prevent such passage. The hydrostatic fields on Gungan subs are adjusted to prevent wild creatures from breaking through the field.

GUNGAN SUB PEN

To outside eyes a Gungan sub pen might look like an elaborate and beautiful structure of special significance; however, within Otoh Gunga it is just an ordinary docking port. Gungans believe that everything they make speaks of who they are, and that anything they construct should add to the beauty of their world.

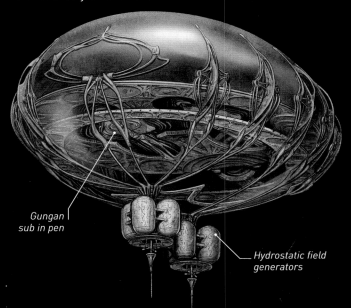

Gungan sub in pen

Hydrostatic field generators

Power Controls Despite the sub's resilient construction, being attacked by a large creature can cause damage to the vessel's power units. The power controls are easily accessible to the sub's pilot, and do not require any special knowledge of Gungan electronics to be repaired.

Strong Skeleton Bursting through the sub pen's bubble wall, a Gungan sub instantly enters the sea. The sub's organic skeletal frame is unaffected by the transition from the air-filled sub pen to the sudden water pressure outside.

NABOO QUEEN'S ROYAL STARSHIP

Queen Amidala's Royal Starship is a unique vessel handcrafted by the Theed Palace Space Vessel Engineering Corps. The gleaming craft, usually helmed by the queen's chief pilot, Ric Olié, conveys Queen Amidala in style to locations around Naboo for royal visits, parades, and other duties. The ship also carries Amidala on formal state visits to other planetary rulers or to the Galactic Senate on the capital world of Coruscant. It is designed for short trips, and features limited sleeping facilities, primarily for the ruler and a customary entourage. Expressing the Naboo love of beauty and art, the dreamlike qualities of the ship, together with its extraordinary chromium finish, make it a distinctive presence in any setting. The starship is made to embody the glory of Naboo royalty—service to the queen is a great honor, and to design a Royal Starship is the highest goal to which a Naboo engineer can aspire. Every centimeter of the ship is laid out with exacting precision, making it a true work of art in every respect.

ROYAL CHROMIUM

A mirrored chromium finish gleams over the entire surface of the Royal Starship from stem to stern. Purely decorative, this finish indicates the starship's royal nature. Only the queen's own vessel may be entirely chromed. Royal starfighters are partly chromed, and non-royal Naboo ships bear no chrome at all. The flawless hand-polished chrome surface over the entire Royal Starship is extremely difficult to produce and is executed by traditional craftspeople, not by factory or droid equipment.

NUBIAN AT HEART

The starship's unique spaceframe was manufactured at Theed, yet the ship makes use of many standard galactic high-technology components that cannot be produced on Naboo. The ship is built around elegant Nubian 327 sublight and hyperdrive propulsion system components, giving it high performance and an exotic air. Nubian systems are often sought by galactic royalty and discriminating buyers who appreciate the distinctive design flair of Nubian components. Nubian equipment is easily acquired on civilized worlds but can be hard to obtain on more remote planets, as the queen discovers during her forced landing on Tatooine.

Starboard sensor array dome

Main hold

Tech station

Jar Jar Binks

Elevator to lower deck

Table

Hyperdrive bay (in floor)

Forward hold

Royal quarters

Navigation light recess

Extension boarding ramp to lower deck

Navigation floodlight

Forward maintenance station

Wiring throughout the ship is laid out with exacting care and precision to honor the queen

Power node

Communications antennas

Forward bulkhead

Navigational sensors

Forward long-range sensor array

Forward deflector shield projector

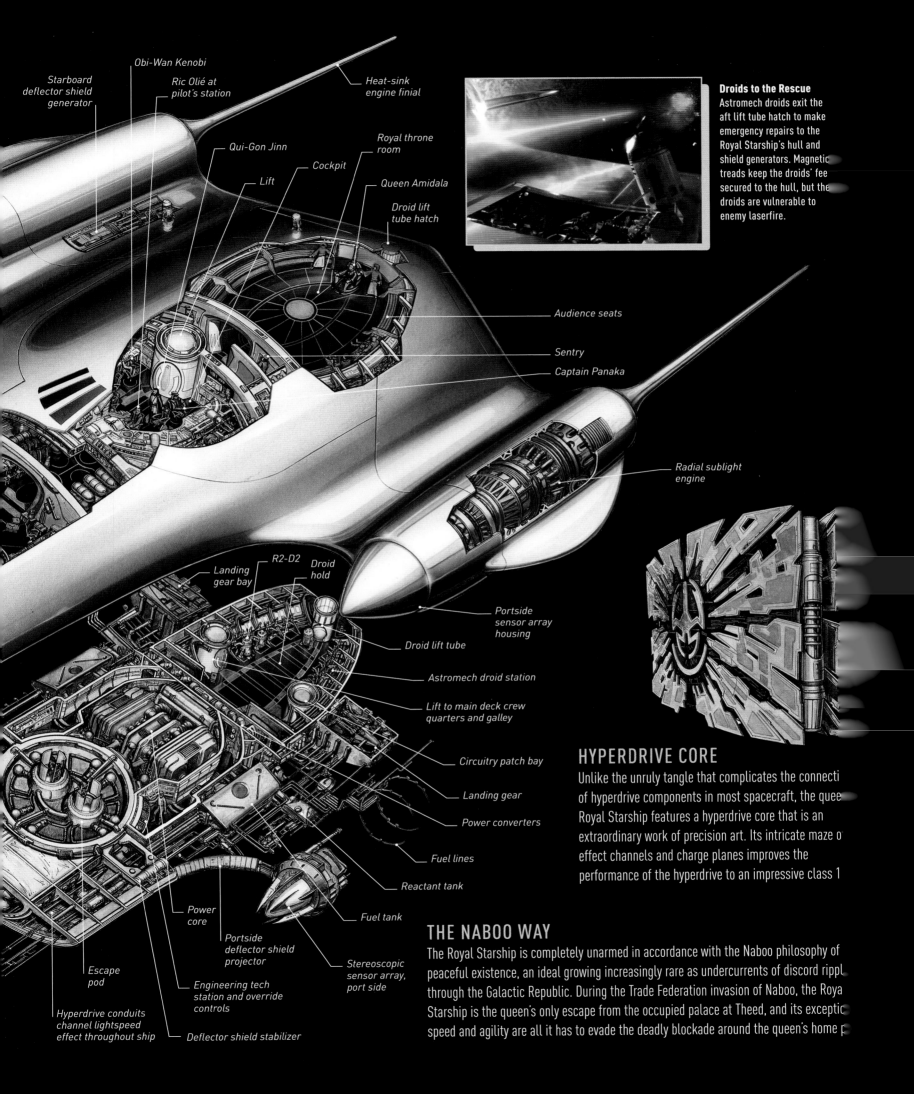

Starboard deflector shield generator

Obi-Wan Kenobi

Ric Olié at pilot's station

Heat-sink engine finial

Qui-Gon Jinn

Royal throne room

Lift

Cockpit

Queen Amidala

Droid lift tube hatch

Droids to the Rescue
Astromech droids exit the aft lift tube hatch to make emergency repairs to the Royal Starship's hull and shield generators. Magnetic treads keep the droids' fee secured to the hull, but the droids are vulnerable to enemy laserfire.

Audience seats

Sentry

Captain Panaka

Radial sublight engine

Landing gear bay

R2-D2

Droid hold

Portside sensor array housing

Droid lift tube

Astromech droid station

Lift to main deck crew quarters and galley

Circuitry patch bay

Landing gear

HYPERDRIVE CORE

Unlike the unruly tangle that complicates the connecti of hyperdrive components in most spacecraft, the quee Royal Starship features a hyperdrive core that is an extraordinary work of precision art. Its intricate maze o effect channels and charge planes improves the performance of the hyperdrive to an impressive class 1

Power converters

Fuel lines

Reactant tank

Power core

THE NABOO WAY

The Royal Starship is completely unarmed in accordance with the Naboo philosophy of peaceful existence, an ideal growing increasingly rare as undercurrents of discord rippl through the Galactic Republic. During the Trade Federation invasion of Naboo, the Roya Starship is the queen's only escape from the occupied palace at Theed, and its exceptic speed and agility are all it has to evade the deadly blockade around the queen's home p

Escape pod

Portside deflector shield projector

Fuel tank

Engineering tech station and override controls

Stereoscopic sensor array, port side

Hyperdrive conduits channel lightspeed effect throughout ship

Deflector shield stabilizer

PODRACERS

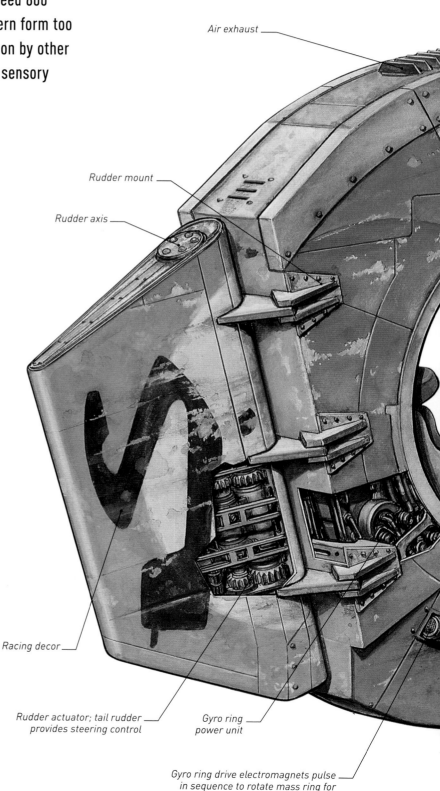

Air exhaust

Rudder mount

Rudder axis

Racing decor

Rudder actuator; tail rudder
provides steering control

Gyro ring
power unit

Gyro ring drive electromagnets pulse
in sequence to rotate mass ring for
stability, keeping pod upright

High-speed podracing harkens back to primitive eras with its traditional podracer designs and the mortal danger seen in racing spectacles. Pulled on flexible control cables by fearsomely powerful independent engines, a small open cockpit (the "pod") carries a daring pilot at speeds that can exceed 800 kilometers (500 miles) per hour. Considered in its lightning-fast modern form too much for humans to manage, podracing is almost exclusively carried on by other species that sport more limbs, more durable bodies, a wider range of sensory organs, or other biological advantages.

"Very fast, very dangerous."

Qui-Gon Jinn

THE STORY OF THE SPORT

Podracing has its origins in ancient contests of animal-drawn carts, of the kind still seen in extremely primitive systems far from the space lanes. Long ago a daring mechanic called Phoebos recreated the old arrangement with repulsorlift pods and flaming jet engines for a whole new level of competition and risk. The famous first experimental race ensured podracing's reputation as an incredibly dangerous and popular sport.

Starting Grid When podracers line up on the arena's starting grid, some pilots deliberately position their vehicles so the heat from their engines will hamper the path or vision of the pilots behind them.

TEEMTO'S PODRACER

Teemto Pagalies' podracer is typical of podracers found in the Outer Rim: a unique design incorporating certain standard features. Its unusual circular shape is designed around an internal metal cycling ring which acts as a gyroscopic stabilizer for the non-aerodynamic pod. Other components are standard: control line anchors, a brace of repulsors to float the podracer safely off the ground, a complex engine sensor and telemetry computer package, and a variety of control levers and switches suited to the particular body shape of the race pilot himself.

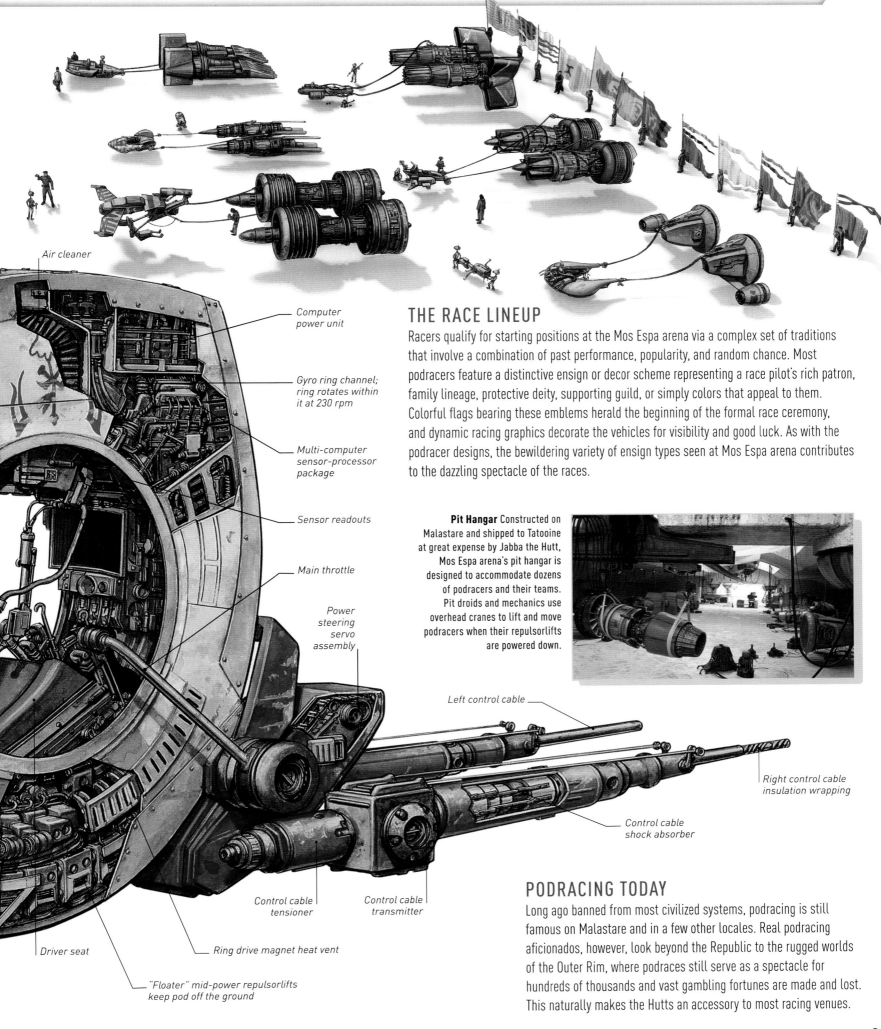

Air cleaner

Computer
power unit

Gyro ring channel;
ring rotates within
it at 230 rpm

Multi-computer
sensor-processor
package

Sensor readouts

Main throttle

Power
steering
servo
assembly

Left control cable

Right control cable
insulation wrapping

Control cable
shock absorber

Control cable
tensioner

Control cable
transmitter

Driver seat

Ring drive magnet heat vent

"Floater" mid-power repulsorlifts
keep pod off the ground

THE RACE LINEUP

Racers qualify for starting positions at the Mos Espa arena via a complex set of traditions
that involve a combination of past performance, popularity, and random chance. Most
podracers feature a distinctive ensign or decor scheme representing a race pilot's rich patron,
family lineage, protective deity, supporting guild, or simply colors that appeal to them.
Colorful flags bearing these emblems herald the beginning of the formal race ceremony,
and dynamic racing graphics decorate the vehicles for visibility and good luck. As with the
podracer designs, the bewildering variety of ensign types seen at Mos Espa arena contributes
to the dazzling spectacle of the races.

Pit Hangar Constructed on
Malastare and shipped to Tatooine
at great expense by Jabba the Hutt,
Mos Espa arena's pit hangar is
designed to accommodate dozens
of podracers and their teams.
Pit droids and mechanics use
overhead cranes to lift and move
podracers when their repulsorlifts
are powered down.

PODRACING TODAY

Long ago banned from most civilized systems, podracing is still
famous on Malastare and in a few other locales. Real podracing
aficionados, however, look beyond the Republic to the rugged worlds
of the Outer Rim, where podraces still serve as a spectacle for
hundreds of thousands and vast gambling fortunes are made and lost.
This naturally makes the Hutts an accessory to most racing venues.

THE BOONTA EVE CLASSIC

Eighteen podracers, many of them well known, qualify for the great Boonta Eve Race in which nine-year-old Anakin Skywalker enters his customized Radon-Ulzer. Also known as the Boonta Eve Classic, the race is held at Mos Espa on Tatooine, and is the largest annual podrace in the galaxy. The Boonta's racecourse features terrifying drops and tortuous curves that pose deadly challenges even to veteran competitors. Notoriously fine-tuned machines, not all the podracers make it as far as the starting line—and several more never make it to the finish—for while mechanical breakdowns are not uncommon, the high-stakes Boonta is also menaced by discreet sabotage.

Ark Roose's Plug-G 927 Ark "Bumpy" Roose is towed by twin-turbined Vokoff-Strood Plug-8G Cluster Array engines with a top speed of 775 kilometers per hour. The open-air channel in the center of each engine cluster provides excellent cooling.

Scale in meters
(5 m = 16½ ft)
0   5

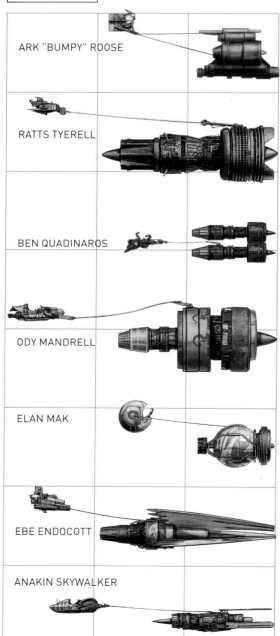

ARK "BUMPY" ROOSE

RATTS TYERELL

BEN QUADINAROS

ODY MANDRELL

ELAN MAK

EBE ENDOCOTT

ANAKIN SKYWALKER

Ratts Tyerell's *Scatalpen* Named after a deadly predator from his homeworld, Tyerell's *Scatalpen* uses twin Vokoff-Strood Titan 2150 rocket engines to tow it to a top speed of 841 kilometers per hour.

Anakin Skywalker's 620C A pair of modified Radon-Ulzer 620C racing engines tows the podracer built by Tatooine native Anakin Skywalker. Although Anakin is strong for a boy his size, he has adjusted his podracer's controls to compensate for his comparatively limited strength.

Ben Quadinaros' BT310 A Toong from the planet Tund, Ben is hoping to turn around a streak of bad luck. Although his rented Balta-Trabaat BT310 podracer can reach 940 kilometers per hour, its power couplings fail just as the race starts.

Gasgano's *Ord Pedrovia* A six-armed Xexto, Gasgano built his podracer from scratch. Named the *Ord Pedrovia*, his pod has customized anti-turbulence vanes and thrust stabilizer cones on the engines, which propel the craft at speeds of up to 820 kilometers per hour.

Dud Bolt's *Vulptereen 327* Dud Bolt pilots a Vulptereen 327 that was manufactured on his homeworld, the planet Vulpter. Identified in some racing manuals as the RS 557, the Vulptereen 327 is very sturdy, has great traction, and can achieve a top speed of 760 kilometers per hour.

Teemto Pagalies' LongTail A Veknoid from Moonus Mandel, Teemto Pagalies pilots an IPG-X1131 LongTail manufactured by Irdani Performance Group. The LongTail has a maximum speed of 775 kilometers per hour, and offers excellent traction on the twisting race course.

Sebulba's Plug-F Mammoth An arboreal Dug, Sebulba is the favorite to win the Boonta Eve Classic, and he is determined to use every dirty trick he knows to make his fans happy. The primary controls for his Plug-F Mammoth are designed so he can operate them with his dexterous feet.

Scale in meters
(5 m = 16½ ft)
0   5

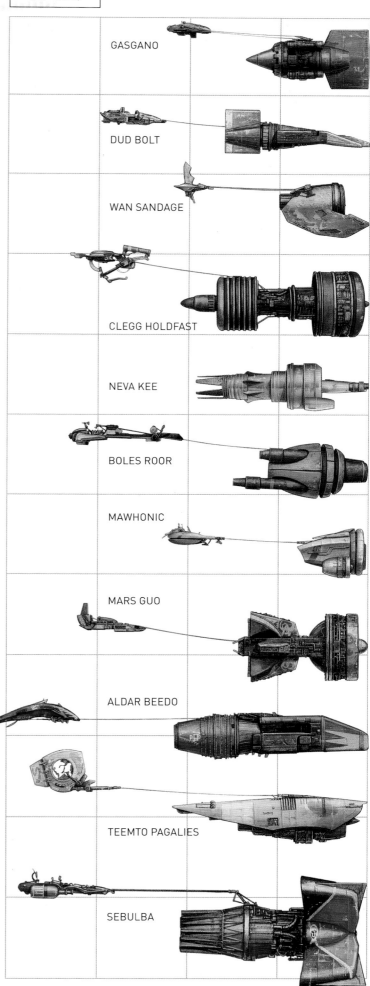

GASGANO

DUD BOLT

WAN SANDAGE

CLEGG HOLDFAST

NEVA KEE

BOLES ROOR

MAWHONIC

MARS GUO

ALDAR BEEDO

TEEMTO PAGALIES

SEBULBA

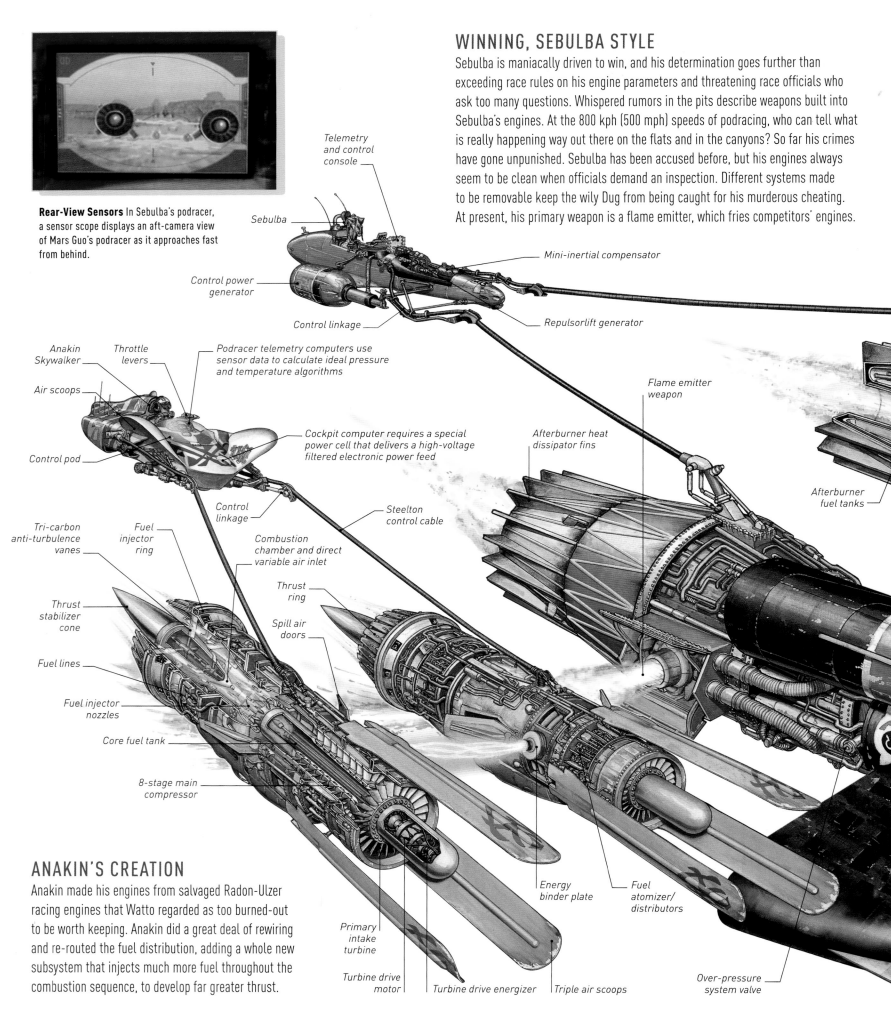

WINNING, SEBULBA STYLE

Sebulba is maniacally driven to win, and his determination goes further than exceeding race rules on his engine parameters and threatening race officials who ask too many questions. Whispered rumors in the pits describe weapons built into Sebulba's engines. At the 800 kph (500 mph) speeds of podracing, who can tell what is really happening way out there on the flats and in the canyons? So far his crimes have gone unpunished. Sebulba has been accused before, but his engines always seem to be clean when officials demand an inspection. Different systems made to be removable keep the wily Dug from being caught for his murderous cheating. At present, his primary weapon is a flame emitter, which fries competitors' engines.

Rear-View Sensors In Sebulba's podracer, a sensor scope displays an aft-camera view of Mars Guo's podracer as it approaches fast from behind.

Telemetry and control console

Sebulba

Control power generator

Control linkage

Mini-inertial compensator

Repulsorlift generator

Flame emitter weapon

Afterburner heat dissipator fins

Afterburner fuel tanks

Anakin Skywalker

Throttle levers

Air scoops

Podracer telemetry computers use sensor data to calculate ideal pressure and temperature algorithms

Control pod

Cockpit computer requires a special power cell that delivers a high-voltage filtered electronic power feed

Tri-carbon anti-turbulence vanes

Fuel injector ring

Control linkage

Steelton control cable

Combustion chamber and direct variable air inlet

Thrust ring

Thrust stabilizer cone

Spill air doors

Fuel lines

Fuel injector nozzles

Core fuel tank

Energy binder plate

Fuel atomizer/ distributors

8-stage main compressor

ANAKIN'S CREATION

Anakin made his engines from salvaged Radon-Ulzer racing engines that Watto regarded as too burned-out to be worth keeping. Anakin did a great deal of rewiring and re-routed the fuel distribution, adding a whole new subsystem that injects much more fuel throughout the combustion sequence, to develop far greater thrust.

Primary intake turbine

Turbine drive motor

Turbine drive energizer

Triple air scoops

Over-pressure system valve

PODRACING RIVALS

The great Boonta Eve Race on Tatooine is a legend among podracers. It is here that racers congregate from widespread star systems to match their skills and their engines against the best, in a setting largely unrefined by civilized society or its rules. Here are to be seen the most determined racers, the most extreme power ratios, the most exciting experimental engines that would be illegal elsewhere, and the most underhanded tactics to be found in the sport. And it is on this stage that a nine-year-old boy named Anakin Skywalker faces the highest possible stakes with a podracer he built himself.

SIZE AND PERFORMANCE

Most podracers go for greater power through greater size, exploiting loopholes in the racing rules to enter larger and more powerful engines with tacked-on subsystems to increase their performance. Sebulba's engines are barely within the rules and would probably not hold up to close inspection, but the race referees know better than to press the issue too hard with the evil Dug. Anakin's engines are remarkable in that he has derived incredible performance from engines smaller than everything else currently used. It all comes from his radical fuel atomizer and distribution system, with multiple igniters throughout the system to get maximum burn from every atom of fuel. In effect, the whole engine is an afterburner once it gets going, but the system works on extremely delicate balances and can be flooded with fuel if pushed before the engines are going full bore, as Anakin finds out early on in the race.

Engine fuel igniters

Annular fuel tank

Compressor

Excess air vent fan

Excess air spill door

Radiator hoses

Energy binder plate

Coolant radiators

Fuel injector

Combustion chamber

Coolant pump

Energy binder arc

Airflow director fence

Split-X repulsor generator housing

Energy binder generator

"It's Skywalker! The crowds are going nuts!"

Fodesinbeed Annodue

Upper Split-X air intake

Split-X stabilizing vane

CATCHING THE WIND

One of Anakin's cleverest engine modifications is the set of triple air scoops ranged around each primary turbine intake. These "air brakes" provide additional control in cornering. Anakin had to wait a long time before he found metal plates and a hydraulic system that would be strong enough to make this idea work. The hydraulic struts are of Tyrian manufacture and came from a military surplus lot that Watto bought from an Outer Rim arms dealer.

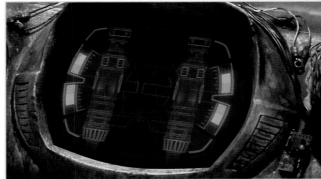

Engine Readout Anakin has modified his podracer's computer to give detailed readouts of energy fluctuations, allowing him to make swift adjustments to his engines.

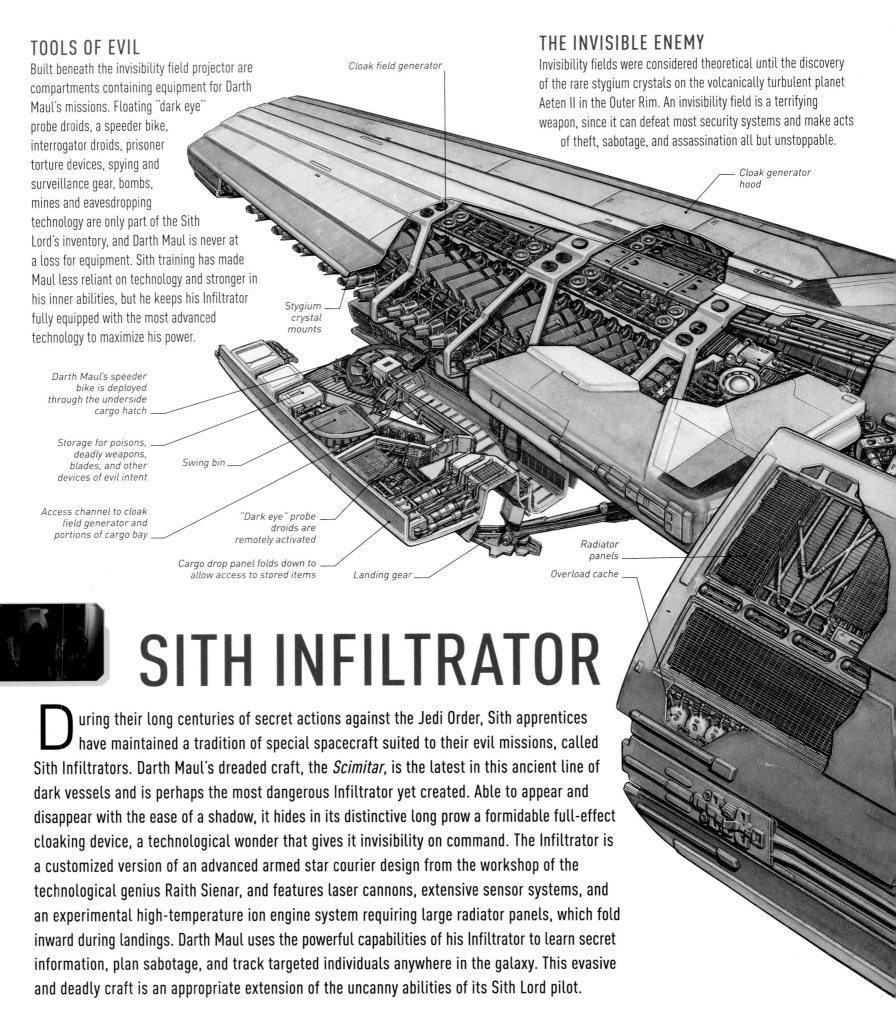

TOOLS OF EVIL

Built beneath the invisibility field projector are compartments containing equipment for Darth Maul's missions. Floating "dark eye" probe droids, a speeder bike, interrogator droids, prisoner torture devices, spying and surveillance gear, bombs, mines and eavesdropping technology are only part of the Sith Lord's inventory, and Darth Maul is never at a loss for equipment. Sith training has made Maul less reliant on technology and stronger in his inner abilities, but he keeps his Infiltrator fully equipped with the most advanced technology to maximize his power.

THE INVISIBLE ENEMY

Invisibility fields were considered theoretical until the discovery of the rare stygium crystals on the volcanically turbulent planet Aeten II in the Outer Rim. An invisibility field is a terrifying weapon, since it can defeat most security systems and make acts of theft, sabotage, and assassination all but unstoppable.

Cloak field generator

Cloak generator hood

Stygium crystal mounts

Darth Maul's speeder bike is deployed through the underside cargo hatch

Storage for poisons, deadly weapons, blades, and other devices of evil intent

Swing bin

Access channel to cloak field generator and portions of cargo bay

"Dark eye" probe droids are remotely activated

Cargo drop panel folds down to allow access to stored items

Landing gear

Radiator panels

Overload cache

SITH INFILTRATOR

During their long centuries of secret actions against the Jedi Order, Sith apprentices have maintained a tradition of special spacecraft suited to their evil missions, called Sith Infiltrators. Darth Maul's dreaded craft, the *Scimitar*, is the latest in this ancient line of dark vessels and is perhaps the most dangerous Infiltrator yet created. Able to appear and disappear with the ease of a shadow, it hides in its distinctive long prow a formidable full-effect cloaking device, a technological wonder that gives it invisibility on command. The Infiltrator is a customized version of an advanced armed star courier design from the workshop of the technological genius Raith Sienar, and features laser cannons, extensive sensor systems, and an experimental high-temperature ion engine system requiring large radiator panels, which fold inward during landings. Darth Maul uses the powerful capabilities of his Infiltrator to learn secret information, plan sabotage, and track targeted individuals anywhere in the galaxy. This evasive and deadly craft is an appropriate extension of the uncanny abilities of its Sith Lord pilot.

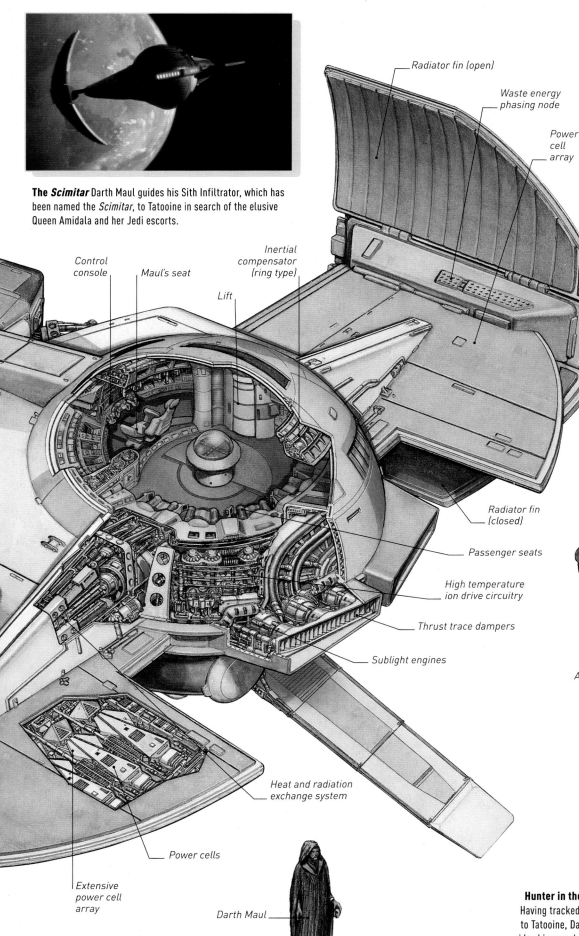

The *Scimitar* Darth Maul guides his Sith Infiltrator, which has been named the *Scimitar*, to Tatooine in search of the elusive Queen Amidala and her Jedi escorts.

Radiator fin (open)

Waste energy phasing node

Power cell array

Control console

Maul's seat

Inertial compensator (ring type)

Lift

Radiator fin (closed)

Passenger seats

High temperature ion drive circuitry

Thrust trace dampers

Sublight engines

Heat and radiation exchange system

Power cells

Extensive power cell array

Darth Maul

UNORTHODOX TECHNOLOGY

The armed courier upon which the Infiltrator was based is a development of Raith Sienar's Advanced Projects laboratory, which continues to experiment with unorthodox spacecraft technologies. Sienar's designs typically incorporate weapons even in craft made for peaceful purposes.

SIENAR: LEGACY AND DESTINY

It is sometimes darkly hinted that Raith Sienar is poised to design the deadly spacecraft of a new space navy that would enforce the law of a new order in the galaxy. In fact, Raith Sienar's operations will eventually become Sienar Fleet Systems, famous and feared throughout the galaxy in the days of the Empire. Sienar's Advanced Projects laboratory will one day create a distinctive TIE fighter reminiscent of the Infiltrator, which will be used by Maul's successor, Darth Vader.

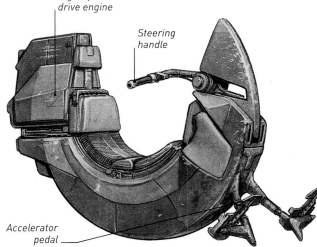

High-speed drive engine

Steering handle

Accelerator pedal

SPEEDER BIKE

Unarmed, this speeder's only special equipment is a high-acceleration engine enabling the bike to reach amazing speeds and cut tight corners. The open design gives excellent visibility.

Hunter in the Desert
Having tracked his prey to Tatooine, Darth Maul rides his speeder bike to confront the Jedi who protect the queen.

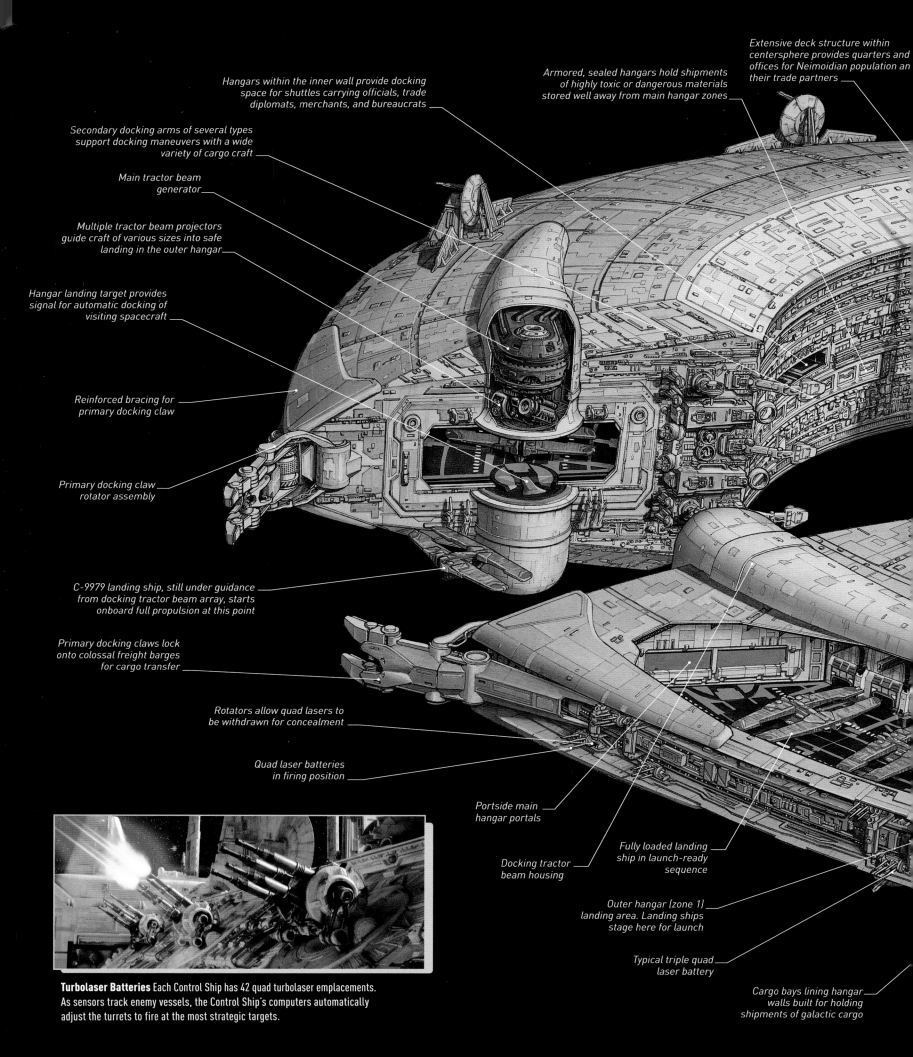

Hangars within the inner wall provide docking space for shuttles carrying officials, trade diplomats, merchants, and bureaucrats

Secondary docking arms of several types support docking maneuvers with a wide variety of cargo craft

Main tractor beam generator

Multiple tractor beam projectors guide craft of various sizes into safe landing in the outer hangar

Hangar landing target provides signal for automatic docking of visiting spacecraft

Reinforced bracing for primary docking claw

Primary docking claw rotator assembly

C-9979 landing ship, still under guidance from docking tractor beam array, starts onboard full propulsion at this point

Primary docking claws lock onto colossal freight barges for cargo transfer

Rotators allow quad lasers to be withdrawn for concealment

Quad laser batteries in firing position

Armored, sealed hangars hold shipments of highly toxic or dangerous materials stored well away from main hangar zones

Extensive deck structure within centersphere provides quarters and offices for Neimoidian population and their trade partners

Portside main hangar portals

Docking tractor beam housing

Fully loaded landing ship in launch-ready sequence

Outer hangar (zone 1) landing area. Landing ships stage here for launch

Typical triple quad laser battery

Cargo bays lining hangar walls built for holding shipments of galactic cargo

Turbolaser Batteries Each Control Ship has 42 quad turbolaser emplacements. As sensors track enemy vessels, the Control Ship's computers automatically adjust the turrets to fire at the most strategic targets.

DROID CONTROL SHIP

From the very first stages, the Trade Federation armaments committee planned to make use of their commercial fleet of giant cargo ships to transport weapons of war. Familiar to millions of officials and civilian personnel, the characteristic Trade Federation cargo ships had been built over many years, plying cargo among the far-flung stars of the galaxy as part of their extensive market. These seemingly harmless and slow-moving container ships would now hide, deep within their hangars, the secret army built to change the rules of commerce. By the end of the project's construction phase the Neimoidians had created from them a frightening fleet of battleships.

WAR CONVERSIONS

The converted battleships bear unusual equipment for cargo freighters, including powerful quad laser batteries designed to destroy opposition fighters launched against the secret army transports. These batteries are built to rotate inward while not in use, concealing their true nature until the Neimoidians wish to uncloak their military intentions to unsuspecting "future customers." While the cargo hangars and their ceiling racks in the inner hangar zones proved sufficient for the carriage of the secret army ground forces, additional large electrified racks were installed in the outermost hangar zones to quarter the dangerous colonies of droid starfighters, which draw power from the racks until launch.

CIVILIAN COMPROMISES

While the Trade Federation cargo fleet was ideal for hiding the existence of the secret army and carrying it unobtrusively to points of deployment, the commercial origins of the battleships leave them with shortcomings as "battleships." Fitted with numerous guns around the equatorial bands, the battleships carry considerable firepower with very limited coverage and so large areas of the ship are undefended by emplaced artillery. The onboard swarms of droid starfighters are thus essential for defense of the battleships from fighter attack.

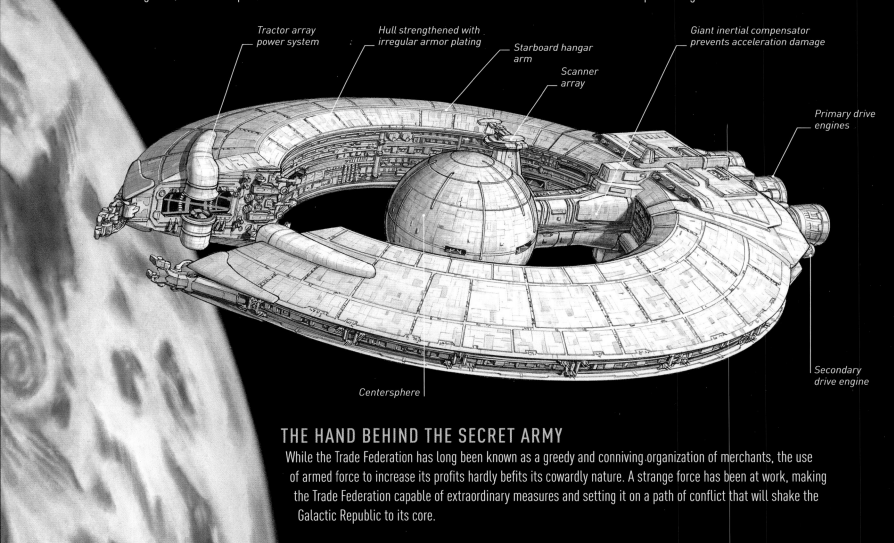

Tractor array power system

Hull strengthened with irregular armor plating

Starboard hangar arm

Scanner array

Giant inertial compensator prevents acceleration damage

Primary drive engines

Secondary drive engine

Centersphere

THE HAND BEHIND THE SECRET ARMY

While the Trade Federation has long been known as a greedy and conniving organization of merchants, the use of armed force to increase its profits hardly befits its cowardly nature. A strange force has been at work, making the Trade Federation capable of extraordinary measures and setting it on a path of conflict that will shake the Galactic Republic to its core.

VULTURE DROID

The space fighters deployed from the Trade Federation battleships are themselves droids, not piloted by any living being. Showered upon enemies in tremendous swarms, vulture droids—also known as droid starfighters—dart through space in maddening fury, elusive targets and deadly opponents for living defenders. They are controlled by a continuously modulated signal from the central Droid Control Ship computer, which tracks every single fighter just as it pulses through the processor of every single battle droid. The signal receiver and onboard computer brain is in the "head" of the fighter and twin sensor pits serve as "eyes."

Composite shell covers antenna that receives control signal

Retracted walk mode claws

Landing repulsor bands

Thrust exhaust nozzles

ATTACK AND FLIGHT MODES

Vulture droids are the most sophisticated automated starfighters ever built, carrying four laser cannons as well as two energy torpedo launchers, which gives them firepower far beyond their size class. To both protect and conceal its deadly laser cannons, the vulture droid retracts its wings in flight mode (above). In this configuration, the droid can hide its military nature, enabling it to ambush the unwary. Covering the weapons when not in use also shields them from micro-particles and atmospheric corrosion. This can improve their accuracy by a tiny degree, an effort at high precision typical of the Haor Chall Engineering company.

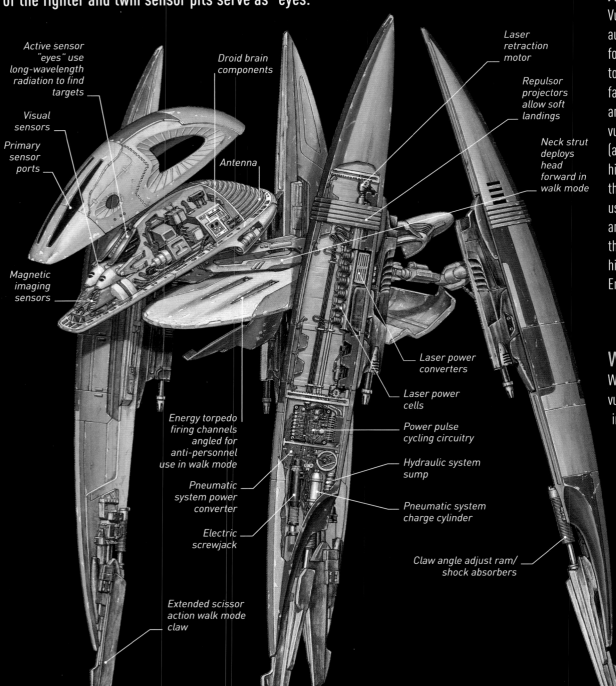

Active sensor "eyes" use long-wavelength radiation to find targets

Droid brain components

Laser retraction motor

Repulsor projectors allow soft landings

Visual sensors

Neck strut deploys head forward in walk mode

Primary sensor ports

Antenna

Magnetic imaging sensors

Laser power converters

Laser power cells

Energy torpedo firing channels angled for anti-personnel use in walk mode

Power pulse cycling circuitry

Hydraulic system sump

Pneumatic system power converter

Pneumatic system charge cylinder

Electric screwjack

Claw angle adjust ram/ shock absorbers

Extended scissor action walk mode claw

WALKING FIGHTERS

When they land on enemy territory, vulture droids reconfigure themselves into walk-patrol mode, using antigravity repulsors to drop safely to the ground. Vulture droids can thus serve as guards to territory they have blasted into submission. In walk-patrol mode they can launch into the air to pursue fleeing ships as easily as they can gun down resisting populations of "future customers." Unsettling, ungainly, and towering, they evoke terror as well as carrying firepower. A vulture droid in walk-patrol mode presents an eerie spectacle: a mindless killing machine directed by a far-off intelligence.

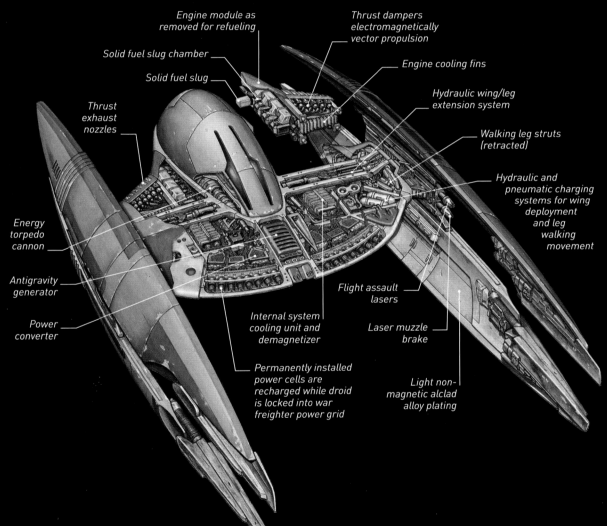

Lethal Precision Weaving across space in tight, rapid formations, vulture droids have a deadly advantage over living opponents.

Engine module as removed for refueling

Thrust dampers electromagnetically vector propulsion

Solid fuel slug chamber

Engine cooling fins

Solid fuel slug

Hydraulic wing/leg extension system

Thrust exhaust nozzles

Walking leg struts (retracted)

Hydraulic and pneumatic charging systems for wing deployment and leg walking movement

Energy torpedo cannon

Antigravity generator

Power converter

Flight assault lasers

Internal system cooling unit and demagnetizer

Laser muzzle brake

Permanently installed power cells are recharged while droid is locked into war freighter power grid

Light non-magnetic alclad alloy plating

VULTURE DROID COLONY STORAGE

Dense ranks of vulture droids hang from ceiling girders in the outer hangar zone of Trade Federation battleships, stored out of the way of hangar activities. Connected to a high-voltage power grid, the vulture droids quietly hum as they are charged to maximum capacity by the reactors of the host battleship. Individual fighters periodically test their systems as they hang, flexing their wings and turning their heads, presenting the uncanny impression of a colony of flying cave predators lying in wait.

AMAZING PRECISION

The flying, walking, shape-shifting vulture droid requires extremely specialized manufacturing, of the kind found in the cathedral factories of the Xi Char, founders of Hoar Chall Engineering. There, ultra-precision manufacturing is a religious practice followed by thousands. The initiates do not concern themselves with the ultimate use of their deadly creations, making the Xi Char ideal pawns of the Trade Federation's dark purposes.

SOLID FIRE FUEL

Unconventional solid fuel concentrate slugs give vulture droids their powerful thrust. Expensive to manufacture, the slugs burn furiously when ignited, allowing the vulture droid to hurtle through space with minimal engine mass. Thrust streams are vectored electromagnetically for steering. The solid fuel system limits the droids' fighting time, but the numerous droids are easily recycled back into their racks for recharge and refueling when spent.

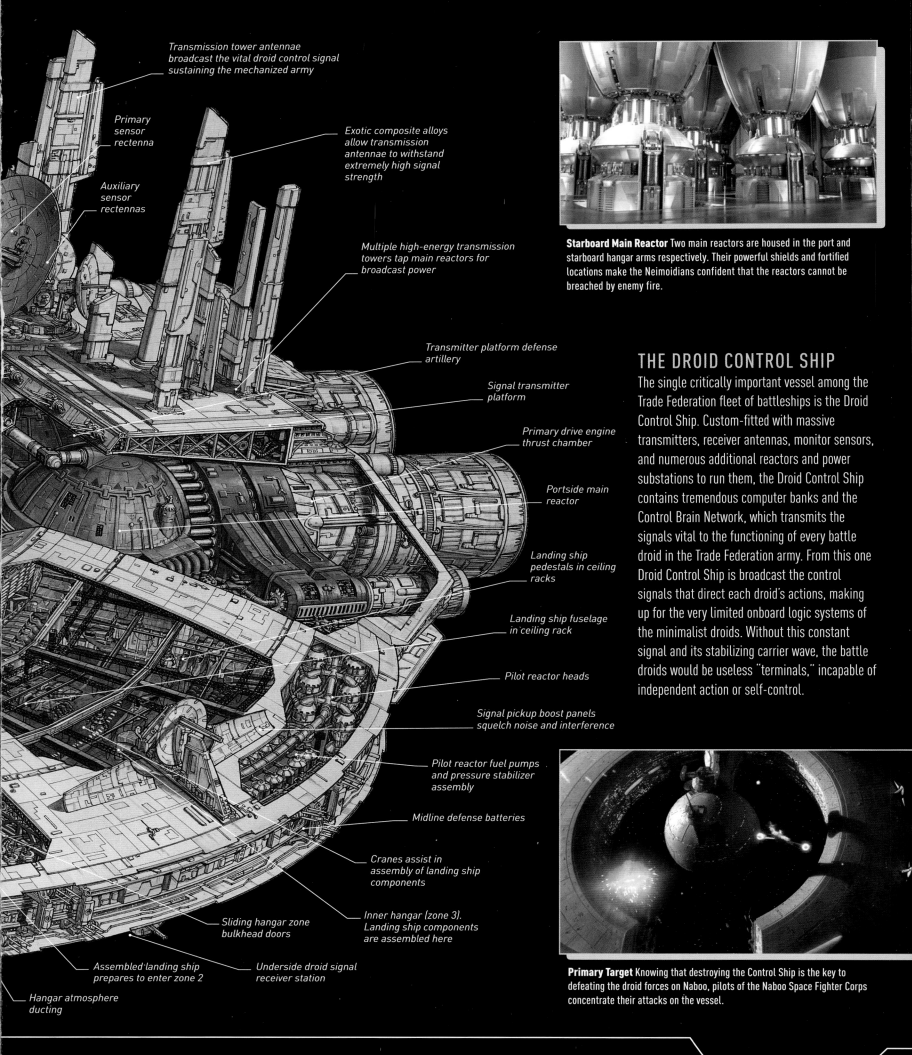

Transmission tower antennae broadcast the vital droid control signal sustaining the mechanized army

Primary sensor rectenna

Auxiliary sensor rectennas

Exotic composite alloys allow transmission antennae to withstand extremely high signal strength

Multiple high-energy transmission towers tap main reactors for broadcast power

Transmitter platform defense artillery

Signal transmitter platform

Primary drive engine thrust chamber

Portside main reactor

Landing ship pedestals in ceiling racks

Landing ship fuselage in ceiling rack

Pilot reactor heads

Signal pickup boost panels squelch noise and interference

Pilot reactor fuel pumps and pressure stabilizer assembly

Midline defense batteries

Cranes assist in assembly of landing ship components

Inner hangar (zone 3). Landing ship components are assembled here

Sliding hangar zone bulkhead doors

Assembled landing ship prepares to enter zone 2

Underside droid signal receiver station

Hangar atmosphere ducting

Starboard Main Reactor Two main reactors are housed in the port and starboard hangar arms respectively. Their powerful shields and fortified locations make the Neimoidians confident that the reactors cannot be breached by enemy fire.

THE DROID CONTROL SHIP

The single critically important vessel among the Trade Federation fleet of battleships is the Droid Control Ship. Custom-fitted with massive transmitters, receiver antennas, monitor sensors, and numerous additional reactors and power substations to run them, the Droid Control Ship contains tremendous computer banks and the Control Brain Network, which transmits the signals vital to the functioning of every battle droid in the Trade Federation army. From this one Droid Control Ship is broadcast the control signals that direct each droid's actions, making up for the very limited onboard logic systems of the minimalist droids. Without this constant signal and its stabilizing carrier wave, the battle droids would be useless "terminals," incapable of independent action or self-control.

Primary Target Knowing that destroying the Control Ship is the key to defeating the droid forces on Naboo, pilots of the Naboo Space Fighter Corps concentrate their attacks on the vessel.

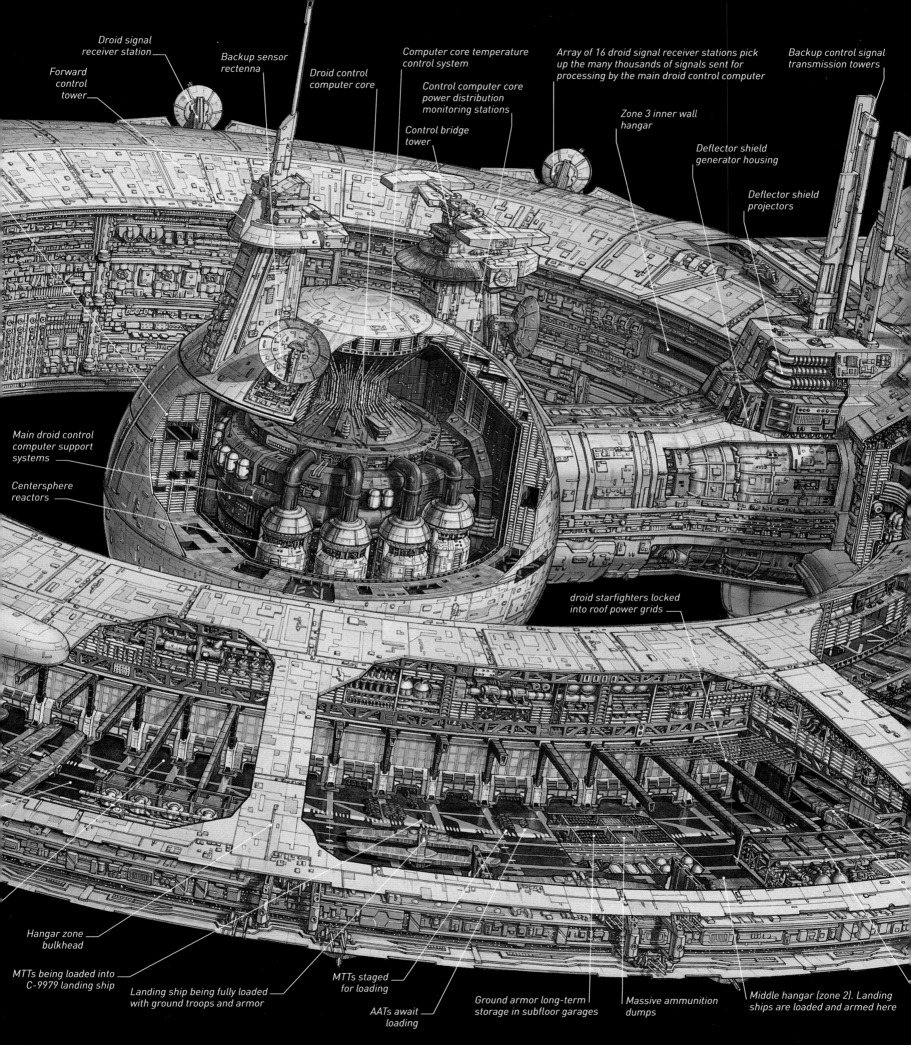

Droid signal
receiver station

Backup sensor
rectenna

Forward
control
tower

Droid control
computer core

Computer core temperature
control system

Control computer core
power distribution
monitoring stations

Control bridge
tower

Array of 16 droid signal receiver stations pick
up the many thousands of signals sent for
processing by the main droid control computer

Backup control signal
transmission towers

Zone 3 inner wall
hangar

Deflector shield
generator housing

Deflector shield
projectors

Main droid control
computer support
systems

Centersphere
reactors

droid starfighters locked
into roof power grids

Hangar zone
bulkhead

MTTs being loaded into
C-9979 landing ship

Landing ship being fully loaded
with ground troops and armor

MTTs staged
for loading

AATs await
loading

Ground armor long-term
storage in subfloor garages

Massive ammunition
dumps

Middle hangar (zone 2). Landing
ships are loaded and armed here

A PILOT'S BEST FRIEND

The onboard astromech droid, a standard R2 type, performs in-flight systems management and flight performance optimization as well as offering limited repair capabilities. The pilot-droid configuration has long proven ideal for small space fighter craft and will continue to do so for generations to come.

ART AND DESIGN

While the long "rat-tail" finials projecting from the engines may look like design flourishes, they are in fact part of the customized engine system developed by the Theed Palace engineers. The finials are actually heat sinks, which circulate coolant and help dissipate the excessive heat of the Nubian engines. The customized Naboo engine configuration burns hotter than normal so as to burn more cleanly, since the Naboo people are very careful not to pollute their planet's environment. The necessary heat sinks were configured into the elegant finials—an example of the inspiring combination of art and engineering found in the best Naboo design work.

Power charge collector

Battle computer interface

Electromagnetic signal receiver

R2 unit computer

R2 astromech droid: the ship's computer and systems plug into the droid's head and body from within

Windshield (slides forward for boarding)

Anakin Skywalker

Power node

Inertial compensator

R2 unit leg clamps

To fit into the small N-1's droid socket, the onboard R2 unit is loaded into the fighter from below. The droid's legs telescope into themselves slightly, and then the droid's head telescopes upward from his body to appear at the back of the fighter

Life-support systems

Power cells

Landing gear

Accidental Pilot Anakin Skywalker takes cover inside the cockpit of a Naboo starfighter to avoid being shot by battle droids. But when the starfighter's autopilot kicks in, Anakin and R2-D2 are whisked into space.

Heat sink finial

Engine heat sink

Customized high-temperature combustion chamber

HIGH-VOLTAGE RAT-TAIL

The center "rat-tail" finial projecting from the rear of the N-1 is a vital component, linking the ship to the palace hangar systems via a plug-in socket found at the rear of each ship's protective revetment area. The primary purpose of this finial is to receive high-voltage power charge energy delivered from the palace generators to activate the ship's systems. Large transformers and converters can be seen on either side of the plug-in sockets in the fighter revetment. The secondary purpose of the center finial is to receive coded information from the palace battle computer. This computer will download information only in the primary security room and through these fighter sockets, preventing any spies from being able to acquire battle information from the palace. The palace battle computer transfers complete battle coordinates and strategic plans into each fighter, allowing the pilots to concentrate on operating their ship's systems while the flight computer automatically directs the ship on a trajectory to the target zone.

Engine-bearing structural member

Fuel lines

Ionization chamber

Sensor lines

Pressure manifold

Binocular rangefinders, targeting, and flight sensors

NABOO N-1 STARFIGHTER

The single pilot Naboo Royal N-1 starfighter was developed by the Theed Palace Space Vessel Engineering Corps for the volunteer Royal Naboo Security Forces. Sleek and agile, the small N-1 faces aggressors with twin blaster cannons and a double magazine of proton torpedoes. Found only on Naboo and rarely seen even there, the N-1, like the queen's Royal Starship, uses many galactic standard internal components in a custom-built spaceframe that reflects the Naboo people's love of handcrafted, elegant shapes. The Naboo engineers fabricate some of their own parts, such as fuel tanks and sensor antennas, but most of the high-technology gear is acquired through trade from other, more industrialized worlds. The Theed Palace engineers developed a customized engine system, however, based on a standard Nubian drive motor but modified significantly to release fewer emissions into the atmosphere.

Laser fire control processor

Laser stabilizing field generator prevents unstable laser bolts from backfiring and damaging the ship

THAT GLEAMING ROYAL LOOK

The N-1 fighter sports a gleaming chromium finish on its forward surfaces, indicating the ship's royal status. Early Naboo spacecraft required a chromelike finish for protection from harmful rays in the planet's upper atmosphere. Now that spacecraft and their pilots are fully shielded from such rays by electromagnetic field technology, the chrome finish is retained for tradition and kept as a royal symbol.

Laser cannon

Communications antennas

Receiver

Royal chromium finish

Fuel pumps and hydraulic system pressurizer

Torpedo launcher assembly

Torpedo magazine (ship carries twin magazines of 5 torpedoes each)

Proton torpedo

Torpedo firing chamber chargers

Infiltrating the Droid Control Ship
After R2-D2 disables the Naboo starfighter's autopilot, Anakin takes evasive action and pilots the fighter into the Trade Federation's Droid Control Ship.

Protective nacelle dome

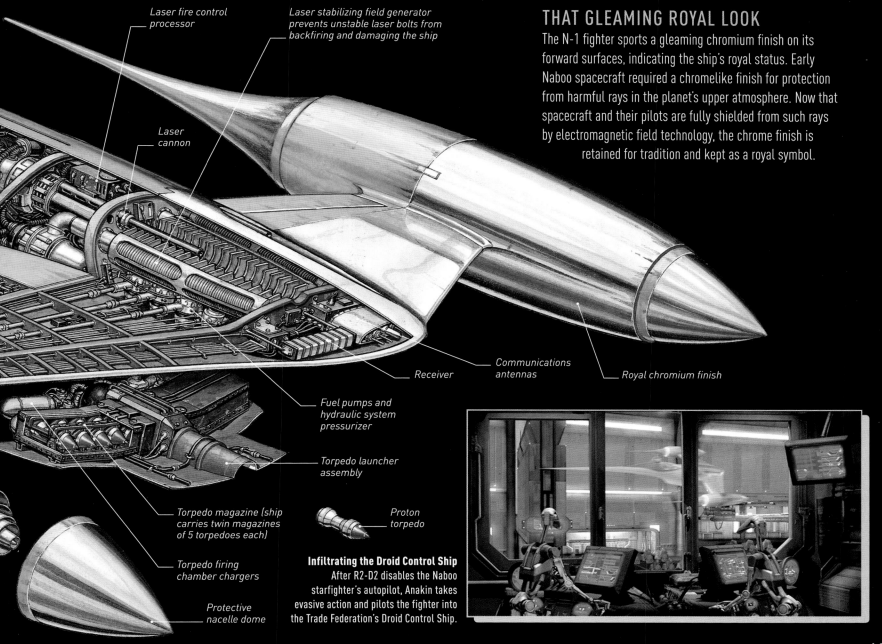

DEFENDERS OF NABOO

Because the Naboo are peaceful people, the Space Fighter Corps is maintained as much through tradition as for military defense, primarily serving as an honor guard for the queen's Royal Starship. Nonetheless, the Royal Naboo Security Forces train in their N-1s on a regular basis, prepared for the honor of serving the queen in combat if necessary, since service to the queen symbolizes service to the great free people of Naboo themselves. When the Trade Federation invades Naboo, the pilots of the Space Fighter Corps know that they must fight against tremendous odds if they are to free their planet.

Chromium Distraction While the N-1 starfighter's chromium finish identifies the ship's royal status, the highly reflective surfaces also serve to "dazzle" enemies, who must adjust their optical sensors to focus on the N-1.

Hyperdrive

Rear center finial plugs into socket in fighter revetment

Fuel tank

Evasive Maneuvers Engaged in their first space battle, Naboo pilots rely on years of training and experience with simulation exercises to avoid being shot down by enemy fire.

STAP

The Single Trooper Aerial Platform (STAP) is an agile flying conveyance designed for Trade Federation battle droids, and outwardly similar to individual repulsorlift "airhooks" used for civilian and military purposes throughout the galaxy. Able to travel swiftly and through dense vegetation, the STAP performs scouting and anti-personnel hunting missions in support of main battle force actions. High-voltage energy cells power the compact machine for limited deployment sorties, after which they must return to be recharged.

Protect the Landing Zone Droid invasion forces are at their most vulnerable as they unload from their invasion transports. STAPs are therefore quickly and easily deployed to patrol the landing zones.

Elevated Position STAP-mounted battle droids serve as roving "eyes" for the Droid Control Ship to help determine battlefield maneuvers.

Battle droid with blaster

B1 Battle Droids After the Trade Federation's invasion of Naboo, battle droid scouts fly STAPs over Naboo's Great Grass Plains to survey the terrain, and transmit data to the Droid Control ship.

Twin blasters

Blaster energizer

Drive turbines

Power cell housing

Footlocks

Antigravity projector

AAT

Designed and built by the Baktoid Armor Workshop for the Trade Federation secret army, the AAT (Armored Assault Tank) carries a crew of four battle droids into combat, presenting the enemy with a heavily armored facade and a blistering hail of assault fire from five laser guns and six energy shell launchers. Their deployment on Naboo is their first use in open combat, but the tanks have seen considerable training action, leaving them scarred and weathered. The AAT is designed for head-on combat in formal battle lines and is accordingly very heavily armored up front. In fact, the nose of the AAT is almost solid armor, designed to crash through heavy walls with impunity.

INSIDE THE COCKPIT

A droid pilot guides the AAT and provides targeting information to the two gunners. The pilot uses a stereoscopic camera that relays information to a periscope scanner.

Secondary laser gun

Rangefinders

Primary laser cannon

Capture of Theed As the most heavily armed ground vehicles in the Trade Federation's invasion force, AATs lead the advance on the capital city of Naboo.

Up to six ground troop battle droids can ride into battle using the three handholds on either side of the tank body

Front hatch: pilot can open it for direct visual sighting if camera damaged

AAT pilot

Short-range blaster

Auxiliary status readouts

Air cooling intake

Shell launcher armor plate

"Foot" section nose ram

ENERGY SHELLS

The AAT's six shell launch tubes can be equipped with a range of ammunition types. As they are launched, the shells are cocooned in high-energy plasma. This speeds them on their way by reducing friction, and dramatically improves their penetrating power. AATs can be prepared for specialized missions with particular shell loads.

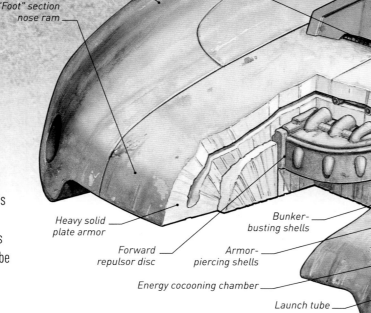

Heavy solid plate armor

Forward repulsor disc

Bunker-busting shells

Armor-piercing shells

Energy cocooning chamber

Launch tube

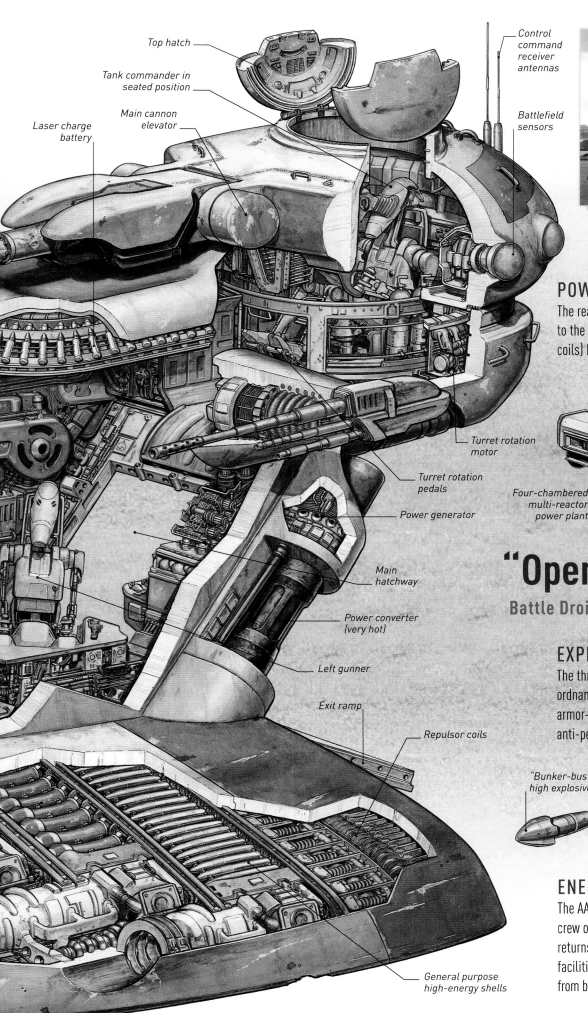

Top hatch

Tank commander in
seated position

Main cannon
elevator

Laser charge
battery

Control
command
receiver
antennas

Battlefield
sensors

Heavy Bombardment AAT laser cannons fire
at Gungan forces during the Battle of Naboo.

POWER PLANT

The reactor and key power and communications gear are kept
to the rear for protection. Heavy-duty repulsors (both disc and
coils) keep the AAT just off the ground and propel it forward.

Turret rotation
motor

Turret rotation
pedals

Power generator

Four-chambered
multi-reactor
power plant

Main
hatchway

"Open fire!"

Battle Droid Commander

Power converter
(very hot)

Left gunner

Exit ramp

Repulsor coils

EXPLOSIVE COMBINATION

The three ammunition types carried as standard-issue
ordnance on the AAT include "bunker buster" high explosives,
armor-piercing shells, and standard high-energy shells for
anti-personnel and anti-vehicle use.

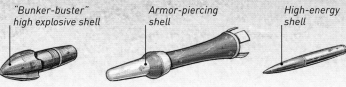

"Bunker-buster"
high explosive shell

Armor-piercing
shell

High-energy
shell

ENERGY SHELL MAGAZINES

The AAT's energy shells cannot be replenished by the droid
crew on board. Instead, the shells are reloaded when the tank
returns to a landing ship or battleship, where mechanical
facilities take the entire contents of the "foot" off the tank
from below. A loaded replacement is then installed in its place.

General purpose
high-energy shells

NABOO SPEEDERS

The small ground craft of the Naboo Royal Security volunteers are lightly armed and armored, since they patrol a fairly peaceful society. They are designed for rapid pursuit and capture of troublemakers, rather than combat with an armed enemy. The Flash and Gian speeders are the most common Naboo ground security craft. Both patrol vehicles are sturdy and reliable and bear mounts for laser weapons that are sent into action only when such force is absolutely necessary.

FLASH SPEEDERS

One of several small ground vehicles used by the Royal Naboo Security Forces, the Flash landspeeder is designed for street patrol and high-speed pursuit of malefactors. The craft normally flies less than a meter off the ground and at maximum height can attain a "float" of a couple of meters.

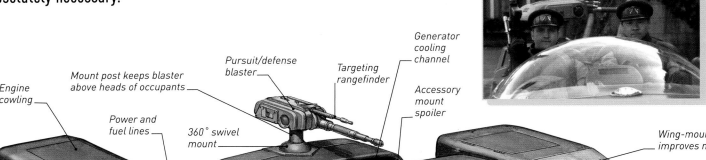

Urban Patrols The Flash speeder is an agile, general-use craft with thrust engines finely tuned to give the pilot good control on narrow city streets.

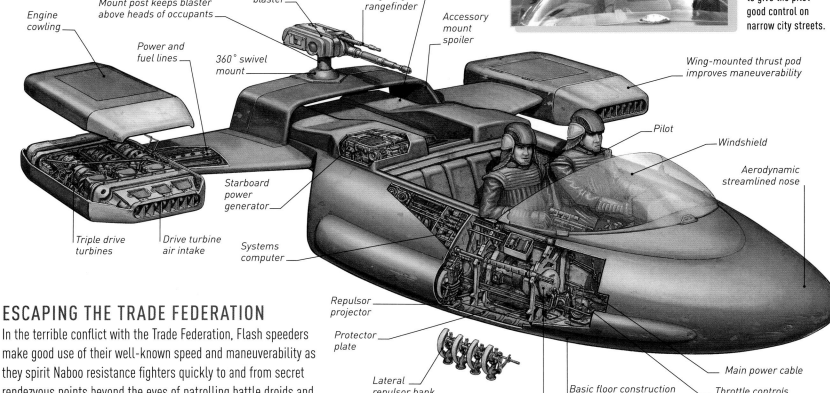

Engine cowling

Mount post keeps blaster above heads of occupants

Pursuit/defense blaster

Targeting rangefinder

Generator cooling channel

Accessory mount spoiler

Power and fuel lines

360° swivel mount

Wing-mounted thrust pod improves maneuverability

Pilot

Windshield

Aerodynamic streamlined nose

Starboard power generator

Triple drive turbines

Drive turbine air intake

Systems computer

Repulsor projector

Protector plate

Lateral repulsor bank

Fuel tank

Basic floor construction designed for urban use

Main power cable

Throttle controls

ESCAPING THE TRADE FEDERATION

In the terrible conflict with the Trade Federation, Flash speeders make good use of their well-known speed and maneuverability as they spirit Naboo resistance fighters quickly to and from secret rendezvous points beyond the eyes of patrolling battle droids and droid starfighters.

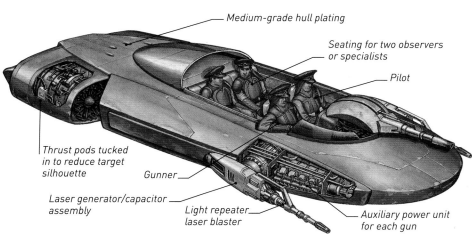

Medium-grade hull plating

Seating for two observers or specialists

Pilot

Thrust pods tucked in to reduce target silhouette

Gunner

Laser generator/capacitor assembly

Light repeater laser blaster

Auxiliary power unit for each gun

GIAN SPEEDERS

Gian speeders are heavier vehicles than the Flash speeders and are called out only for serious situations. Their three laser blasters can easily disable non-military vehicles. They have tougher hulls than ordinary civilian craft and their reinforced bodies allow them to withstand glancing hits. Their compact forward silhouette, with thrust pods tucked in behind rather than out on wing struts, makes the Gian less maneuverable but a harder target for enemies both in front and behind. To assist in tactical deployments, these speeders can be equipped with customized holographic planning systems.

CORUSCANT TAXI

The air taxi shooting through the vast open spaces between the high skyscrapers is one of the most characteristic sights of the famous metropolis world of Coruscant. These air taxis are allowed unrestricted "free travel" and can thus leave the autonavigating skylanes to take the most direct routes to their destination. Skylanes confine most vehicles on long-distance journeys along defined corridors, without which there would be unmanageable chaos in the air. To rate "free travel," air taxi pilots must pass demanding tests that prove their ability to navigate the unique cityscape with skill and safety. They depend on their scanners, keen eyes, and instinct to avoid crashing into other craft, sending their passengers plunging into the street canyons far below.

Convenient Transport Manufactured by the Hyrotti Corporation, the EasyRide passenger airspeeder is the company's most common model.

Communications antenna

Efficient drive engine requires a minimum of fuel

Forward motion engine

Turbine allows rapid acceleration

Seats emit mild tractor field in flight to hold passengers securely inside without belts

Guidance computer balances navigational control between lift repulsors, steering repulsors, and drive engines

Luggage can be stored in crossbar compartments

Headlight circuitry varies spectrum output of beams

Drive engine housing

Simple construction designed for easy maintenance and repair

Multi-spectrum headlights

Side-mounted, low-power repulsors prevent collision and cushion docking

Signal receivers built into body frame pick up air traffic control transmissions

Precision stabilizing and steering radial repulsor array helps taxi navigate in crowded urban skylanes

Lift repulsor carries taxi to great skyscraper heights

WELL-EQUIPPED AIR TAXIS

The standard modern Coruscant air taxi uses a compact, focused, medium-grade repulsor to elevate it to the very highest skyscraper peaks. A radial battery of lower-powered antigravity devices gives it good navigational control in the open air, allowing it to swoop with accuracy around the aerial architecture, docking gently at its final destination. A refined, relatively quiet thrust engine propels the craft with surprising acceleration. Excellent receiver equipment monitors the many channels of Coruscant Air Traffic Control, allowing the pilot to use autonavigation or manual control at any time.

ABOVE AND BELOW

All significant traffic on Coruscant is air traffic—the original ground levels and roads having long ago been abandoned. Sealed tunnels in the lower realms allow for the transport of goods and materials through the city, as bulk shipments are barred by law from the crowded skylanes reserved for travelers.

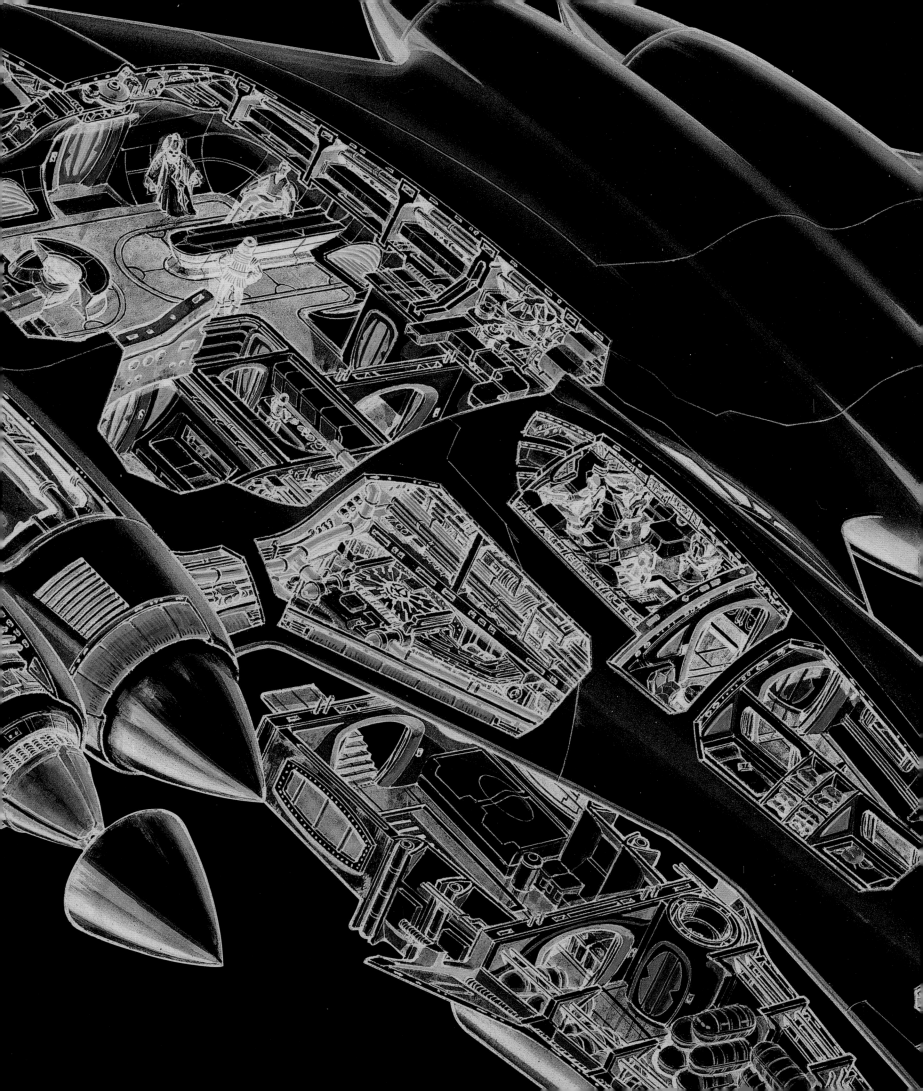

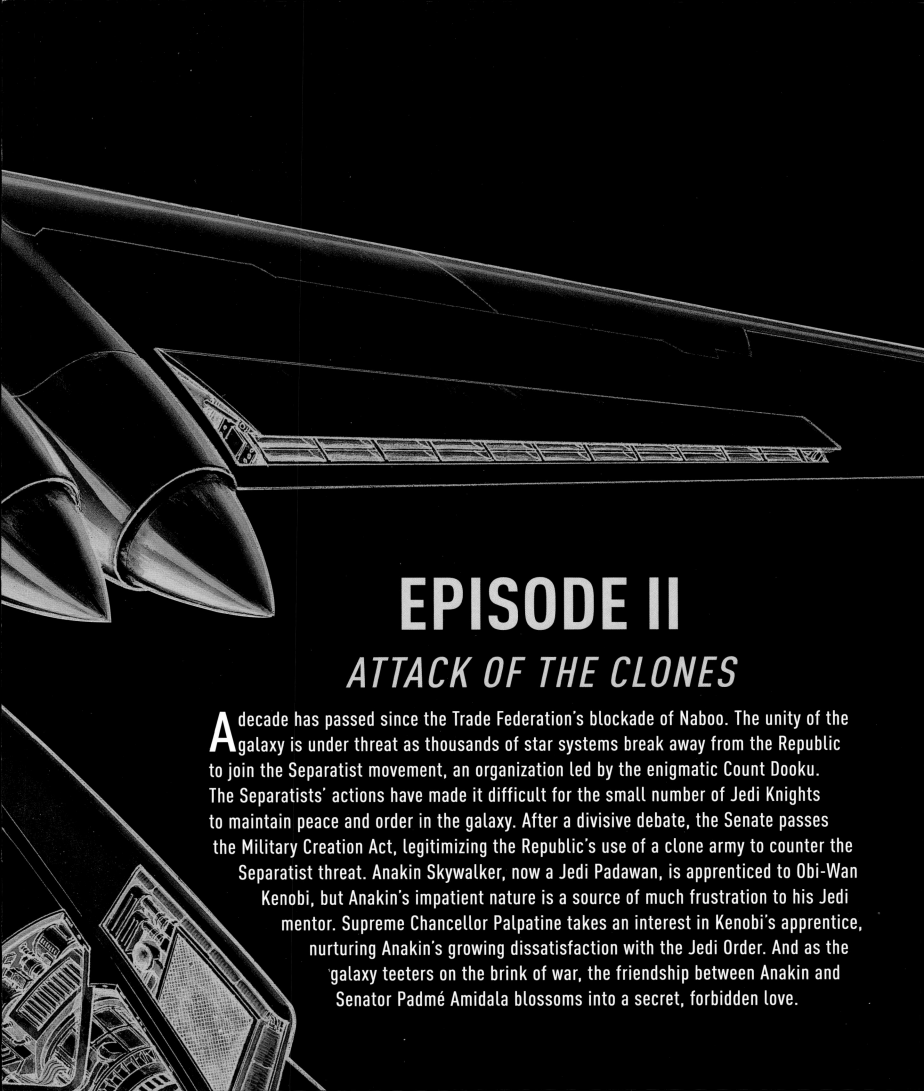

EPISODE II

ATTACK OF THE CLONES

A decade has passed since the Trade Federation's blockade of Naboo. The unity of the galaxy is under threat as thousands of star systems break away from the Republic to join the Separatist movement, an organization led by the enigmatic Count Dooku. The Separatists' actions have made it difficult for the small number of Jedi Knights to maintain peace and order in the galaxy. After a divisive debate, the Senate passes the Military Creation Act, legitimizing the Republic's use of a clone army to counter the Separatist threat. Anakin Skywalker, now a Jedi Padawan, is apprenticed to Obi-Wan Kenobi, but Anakin's impatient nature is a source of much frustration to his Jedi mentor. Supreme Chancellor Palpatine takes an interest in Kenobi's apprentice, nurturing Anakin's growing dissatisfaction with the Jedi Order. And as the galaxy teeters on the brink of war, the friendship between Anakin and Senator Padmé Amidala blossoms into a secret, forbidden love.

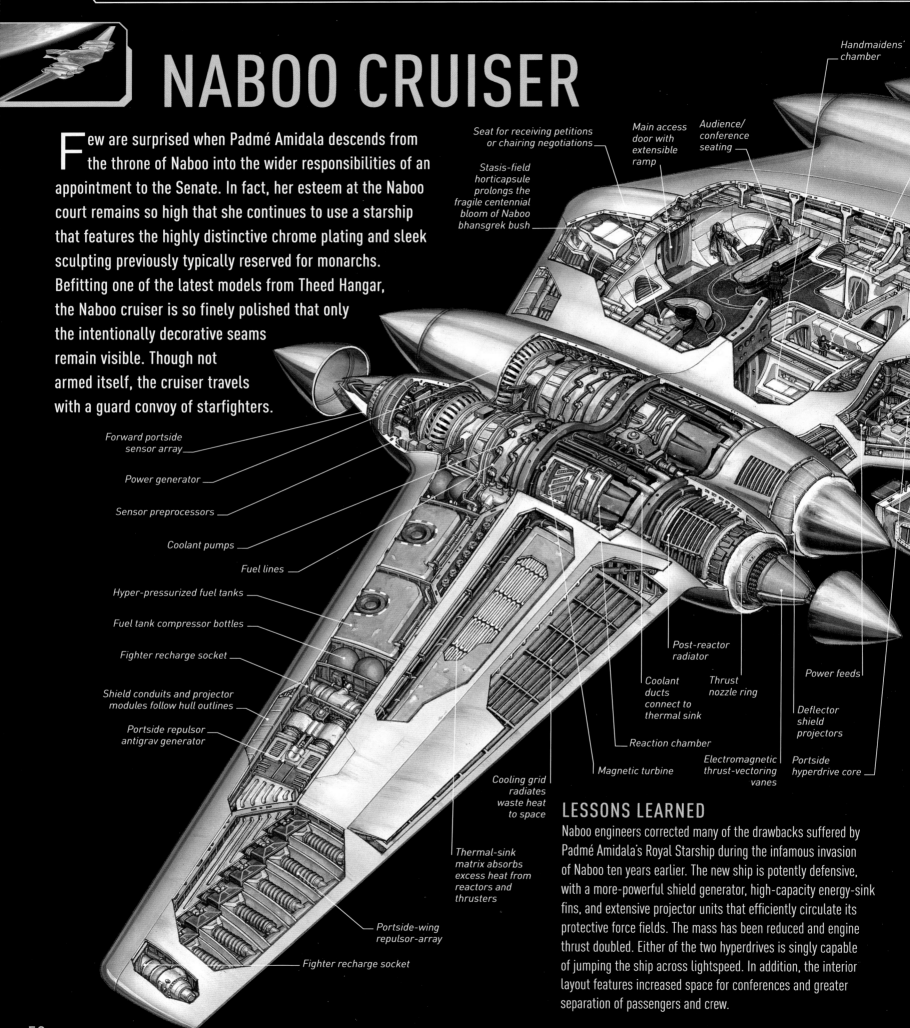

NABOO CRUISER

Few are surprised when Padmé Amidala descends from the throne of Naboo into the wider responsibilities of an appointment to the Senate. In fact, her esteem at the Naboo court remains so high that she continues to use a starship that features the highly distinctive chrome plating and sleek sculpting previously typically reserved for monarchs. Befitting one of the latest models from Theed Hangar, the Naboo cruiser is so finely polished that only the intentionally decorative seams remain visible. Though not armed itself, the cruiser travels with a guard convoy of starfighters.

Handmaidens' chamber

Seat for receiving petitions or chairing negotiations

Main access door with extensible ramp

Audience/ conference seating

Stasis-field horticapsule prolongs the fragile centennial bloom of Naboo bhansgrek bush

Forward portside sensor array

Power generator

Sensor preprocessors

Coolant pumps

Fuel lines

Hyper-pressurized fuel tanks

Fuel tank compressor bottles

Fighter recharge socket

Shield conduits and projector modules follow hull outlines

Portside repulsor antigrav generator

Post-reactor radiator

Coolant ducts connect to thermal sink

Thrust nozzle ring

Power feeds

Deflector shield projectors

Reaction chamber

Magnetic turbine

Electromagnetic thrust-vectoring vanes

Portside hyperdrive core

Cooling grid radiates waste heat to space

Thermal-sink matrix absorbs excess heat from reactors and thrusters

Portside-wing repulsor-array

Fighter recharge socket

LESSONS LEARNED

Naboo engineers corrected many of the drawbacks suffered by Padmé Amidala's Royal Starship during the infamous invasion of Naboo ten years earlier. The new ship is potently defensive, with a more-powerful shield generator, high-capacity energy-sink fins, and extensive projector units that efficiently circulate its protective force fields. The mass has been reduced and engine thrust doubled. Either of the two hyperdrives is singly capable of jumping the ship across lightspeed. In addition, the interior layout features increased space for conferences and greater separation of passengers and crew.

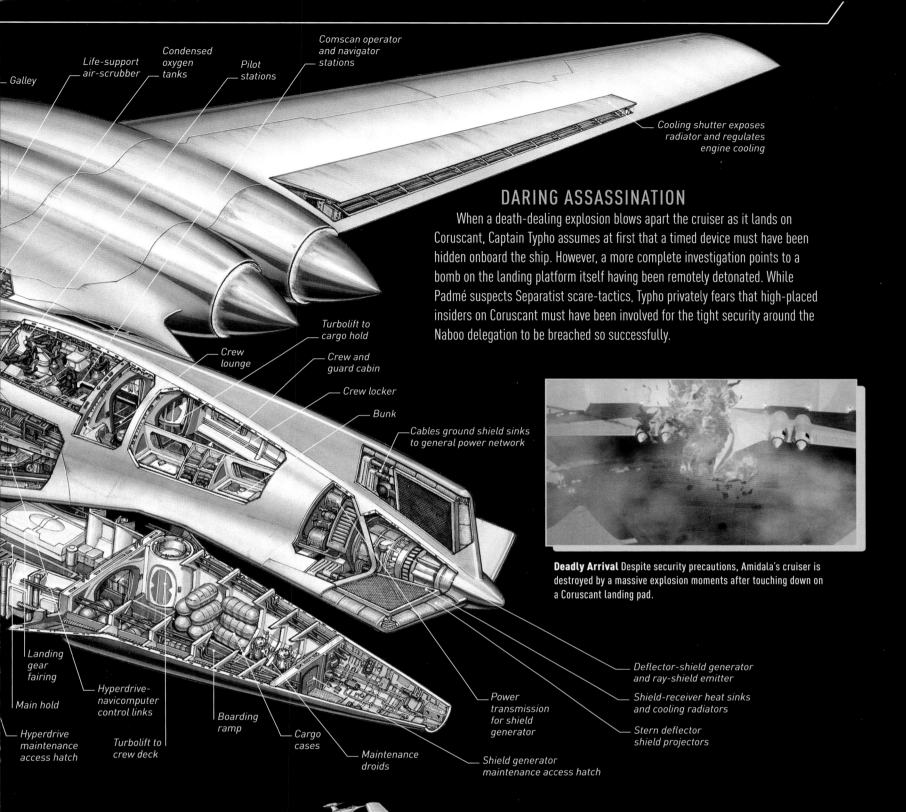

Galley

Life-support
air-scrubber

Condensed
oxygen
tanks

Pilot
stations

Comscan operator
and navigator
stations

Cooling shutter exposes
radiator and regulates
engine cooling

DARING ASSASSINATION

When a death-dealing explosion blows apart the cruiser as it lands on Coruscant, Captain Typho assumes at first that a timed device must have been hidden onboard the ship. However, a more complete investigation points to a bomb on the landing platform itself having been remotely detonated. While Padmé suspects Separatist scare-tactics, Typho privately fears that high-placed insiders on Coruscant must have been involved for the tight security around the Naboo delegation to be breached so successfully.

Turbolift to
cargo hold

Crew
lounge

Crew and
guard cabin

Crew locker

Bunk

Cables ground shield sinks
to general power network

Deadly Arrival Despite security precautions, Amidala's cruiser is destroyed by a massive explosion moments after touching down on a Coruscant landing pad.

Landing
gear
fairing

Main hold

Hyperdrive
maintenance
access hatch

Hyperdrive-
navicomputer
control links

Turbolift to
crew deck

Boarding
ramp

Cargo
cases

Maintenance
droids

Power
transmission
for shield
generator

Shield generator
maintenance access hatch

Deflector-shield generator
and ray-shield emitter

Shield-receiver heat sinks
and cooling radiators

Stern deflector
shield projectors

RELIABLE TRANSPORT

As a leading emissary, Padmé has relied on her graceful diplomatic ship on scores of missions placating disgruntled factions throughout her sector. Even in this sturdy vessel, however, a thorough home constituency tour could last a lifetime in Padmé's lightly populated Chommell sector, which comprises 36 full-member worlds, more than 40,000 settled dependencies, and 300,000,000 barren stars. With more than 1,000 sectors, the galaxy's deceptively fragile harmony depends on efficient divisions of authority within the multi-tiered government, and upon the wisdom of its roving officials and legislators.

Starfighter
docked in
recharge
socket

IN-FLIGHT SUPPORT

Hyperdrive-equipped starfighters of this era are limited in range by fuel capacity. Previously, Naboo N-1 fighters operating far from home could only travel in small steps, accompanied by a tanker. After the invasion of Naboo, designers added innovative recharge sockets to the wings of the new diplomatic barge, thereby enabling the ship to carry its own security escort through hyperspace.

ZAM'S AIRSPEEDER

Hired assassin Zam Wesell flies an airspeeder that is as unusual and exotic as she is herself. The totally self-enclosed craft has no external thrusters and few air intakes because it was built for use on hostile, primitive worlds. Its repulsorlift units provide anti-gravity support, while other mechanisms generate radiation and electromagnetic fields that move the craft by dragging upon the air. This system is versatile enough for use in a huge variety of atmospheres. However, in urban areas, outdoor power lines can snag the propulsion fields and confound the steering— although this merely provides an extra means of traction to a cunning mercenary like Wesell.

WILDERNESS HARDWARE

The *Koro-2*'s forward mandibles operate as an external electromagnetic propulsion system. They intensely irradiate the air around them to induce ionization and make it conductive. Electrodes on each mandible project powerful electric currents across the gap, and the electrified air-stream is magnetically propelled toward the rear, thereby imparting thrust to the speeder. The speeder was designed for scouts exploring the wastelands of worlds lacking complex native life. Zam acquired hers on one of the billions of anonymous, young, highly-metalliferous planets dominated by the resource-hungry Mining Guild in the galaxy's spiral arms. Her use of it in downtrodden urban environments would dismay its designers.

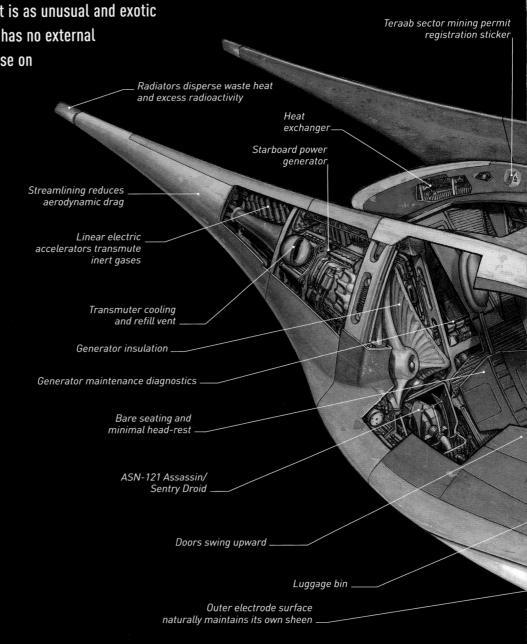

Teraab sector mining permit registration sticker

Radiators disperse waste heat and excess radioactivity

Heat exchanger

Starboard power generator

Streamlining reduces aerodynamic drag

Linear electric accelerators transmute inert gases

Transmuter cooling and refill vent

Generator insulation

Generator maintenance diagnostics

Bare seating and minimal head-rest

ASN-121 Assassin/ Sentry Droid

Doors swing upward

Luggage bin

Outer electrode surface naturally maintains its own sheen

Main radioactive gas delivery and containment shaft

Air dissociator radiation funnel

Prepared for a Getaway Standing on a Coruscant skyscraper's ledge, Zam Wesell takes aim at her target before she leaps into her waiting *Koro-2* airspeeder.

DIRTY TECHNOLOGY

Zam's speeder creates some hazardous side-effects that amuse the callous hunter. Irradiation zones are constrained around the mandibles, but can sicken unknowing innocent bystanders along the vehicle's path. Furthermore, drag-stream ions recombine chemically into unpleasant forms as they pass the cabin. In breathable atmospheres the products can include noxious gases that leave a foul reek in the speeder's wake.

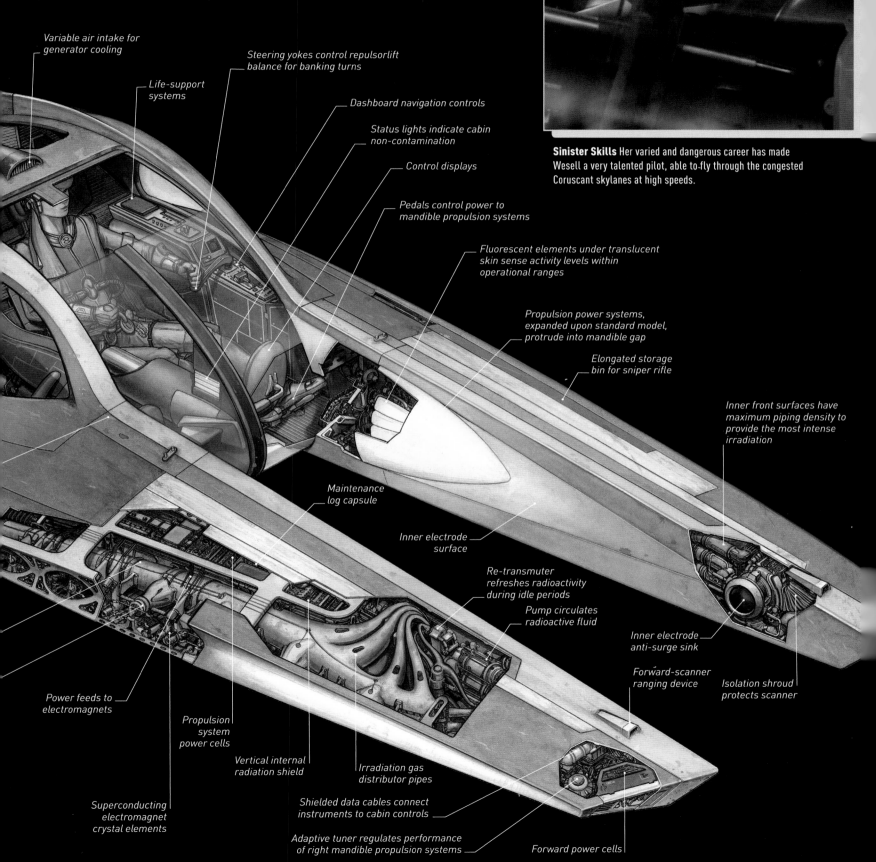

Sinister Skills Her varied and dangerous career has made Wesell a very talented pilot, able to fly through the congested Coruscant skylanes at high speeds.

Variable air intake for generator cooling

Life-support systems

Steering yokes control repulsorlift balance for banking turns

Dashboard navigation controls

Status lights indicate cabin non-contamination

Control displays

Pedals control power to mandible propulsion systems

Fluorescent elements under translucent skin sense activity levels within operational ranges

Propulsion power systems, expanded upon standard model, protrude into mandible gap

Elongated storage bin for sniper rifle

Inner front surfaces have maximum piping density to provide the most intense irradiation

Maintenance log capsule

Inner electrode surface

Re-transmuter refreshes radioactivity during idle periods

Pump circulates radioactive fluid

Inner electrode anti-surge sink

Forward-scanner ranging device

Isolation shroud protects scanner

Power feeds to electromagnets

Propulsion system power cells

Vertical internal radiation shield

Irradiation gas distributor pipes

Superconducting electromagnet crystal elements

Shielded data cables connect instruments to cabin controls

Adaptive tuner regulates performance of right mandible propulsion systems

Forward power cells

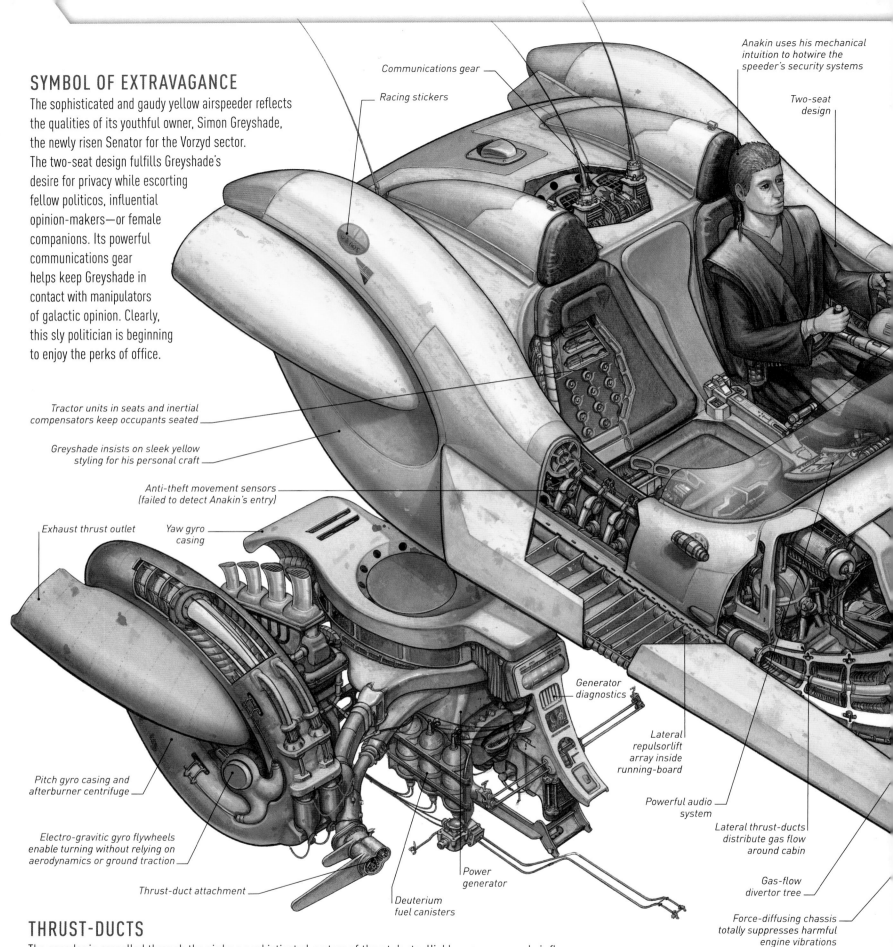

SYMBOL OF EXTRAVAGANCE

The sophisticated and gaudy yellow airspeeder reflects
the qualities of its youthful owner, Simon Greyshade,
the newly risen Senator for the Vorzyd sector.
The two-seat design fulfills Greyshade's
desire for privacy while escorting
fellow politicos, influential
opinion-makers—or female
companions. Its powerful
communications gear
helps keep Greyshade in
contact with manipulators
of galactic opinion. Clearly,
this sly politician is beginning
to enjoy the perks of office.

Communications gear

Racing stickers

Anakin uses his mechanical
intuition to hotwire the
speeder's security systems

Two-seat
design

Tractor units in seats and inertial
compensators keep occupants seated

Greyshade insists on sleek yellow
styling for his personal craft

Anti-theft movement sensors
(failed to detect Anakin's entry)

Exhaust thrust outlet

Yaw gyro
casing

Generator
diagnostics

Pitch gyro casing and
afterburner centrifuge

Lateral
repulsorlift
array inside
running-board

Powerful audio
system

Electro-gravitic gyro flywheels
enable turning without relying on
aerodynamics or ground traction

Thrust-duct attachment

Power
generator

Deuterium
fuel canisters

Lateral thrust-ducts
distribute gas flow
around cabin

Gas-flow
divertor tree

Force-diffusing chassis
totally suppresses harmful
engine vibrations

THRUST-DUCTS

The speeder is propelled through the air by a sophisticated system of thrust ducts. Highly over-pressured air flow
from the turbojets is ignited and hurled through narrow thrust-ducts at transonic velocities. The main ducts pass
through the cabin side walls. Secondary ducts are exposed on the speeder underbelly for cooling by air contact.
Air streams pass through afterburner centrifuges and out of thrust vents at the back. The vents are partly covered
by protective grilles, and have internal shutters to brake selectively or redirect the outflows.

ANAKIN'S AIRSPEEDER

When an attempt is made on the life of the Senator of Naboo and his Jedi Master is whisked off into the night air, Anakin Skywalker needs transport fast. With flawless intuition, he finds the perfect pursuit vehicle in the nearby senatorial parking zone. This overpowered, prized leisure craft, which belongs to a self-indulgent politician, is as quick and agile as any civilian airspeeder or cloud car in Coruscant's sky. Its complex and responsive system of repulsor units, thrust-ducting, and unconventional podracer-like engine arrangement provide one of the galaxy's best starpilots with the balance of superior control and instant familiarity essential for his daredevil pursuit of the assassin, Zam Wesell.

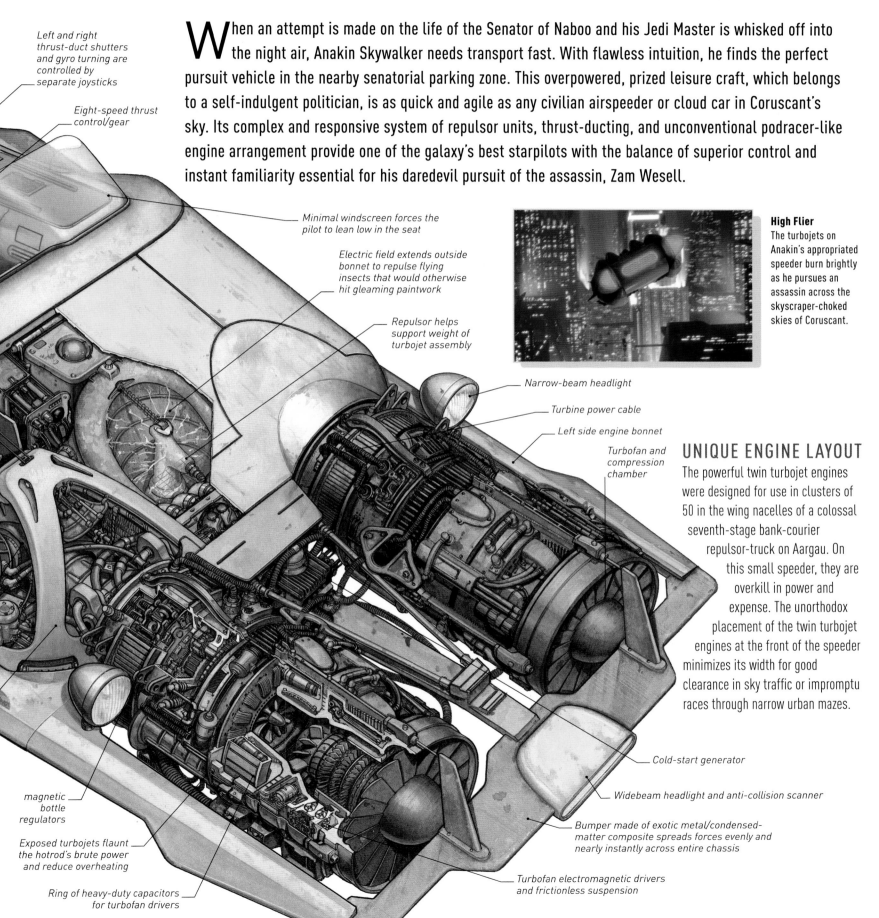

Left and right thrust-duct shutters and gyro turning are controlled by separate joysticks

Eight-speed thrust control/gear

Minimal windscreen forces the pilot to lean low in the seat

Electric field extends outside bonnet to repulse flying insects that would otherwise hit gleaming paintwork

Repulsor helps support weight of turbojet assembly

Narrow-beam headlight

Turbine power cable

Left side engine bonnet

Turbofan and compression chamber

magnetic bottle regulators

Exposed turbojets flaunt the hotrod's brute power and reduce overheating

Ring of heavy-duty capacitors for turbofan drivers

Cold-start generator

Widebeam headlight and anti-collision scanner

Bumper made of exotic metal/condensed-matter composite spreads forces evenly and nearly instantly across entire chassis

Turbofan electromagnetic drivers and frictionless suspension

High Flier
The turbojets on Anakin's appropriated speeder burn brightly as he pursues an assassin across the skyscraper-choked skies of Coruscant.

UNIQUE ENGINE LAYOUT

The powerful twin turbojet engines were designed for use in clusters of 50 in the wing nacelles of a colossal seventh-stage bank-courier repulsor-truck on Aargau. On this small speeder, they are overkill in power and expense. The unorthodox placement of the twin turbojet engines at the front of the speeder minimizes its width for good clearance in sky traffic or impromptu races through narrow urban mazes.

CORUSCANT SPEEDER CHASE

C overed entirely by densely packed skyscrapers, the planet Coruscant maintains a sophisticated global network of computers, sensors, and transmitters to ensure safety for millions of commuters, most of whom travel in droid-piloted vessels on designated aerial paths. However, Coruscant Air Traffic Control does allow Jedi and authorized law-enforcement officers to operate airspeeders relatively independently, enabling such pilots to veer out of the autonavigated skylanes to pursue and apprehend felons. When an assassin uses a droid to target Senator Amidala on Coruscant and flees in a waiting airspeeder, Obi-Wan Kenobi and Anakin Skywalker must chase her across Galactic City.

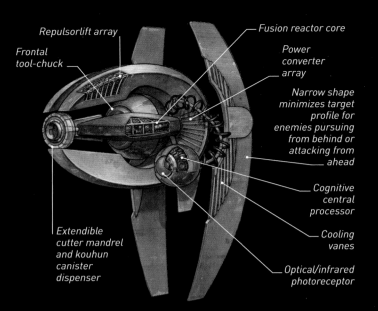

Repulsorlift array

Frontal tool-chuck

Fusion reactor core

Power converter array

Narrow shape minimizes target profile for enemies pursuing from behind or attacking from ahead

Cognitive central processor

Cooling vanes

Extendible cutter mandrel and kouhun canister dispenser

Optical/infrared photoreceptor

ASN-121—ASSASSIN/SENTRY DROID

Assassin Zam Wesell's ASN-121 droid is well-equipped for her deadly missions. Its frontal tool-chucks can wield a variety of implements and weapons, including a harpoon gun, sniper blaster, gas dispenser, spy sensors, flamethrower, and various drills and cutters. A compact fusion generator and modular power-converter array supply the rapidly varying energy demands of this dynamic machine, while independently powered repulsorlift rods work to ensure good balance even under unusual loads.

Maximum Velocity Seated behind the controls of a hastily appropriated airspeeder, Anakin ignores posted speed limits as he pursues an assassin's vehicle, and does little to assuage Obi-Wan's aversion to flying.

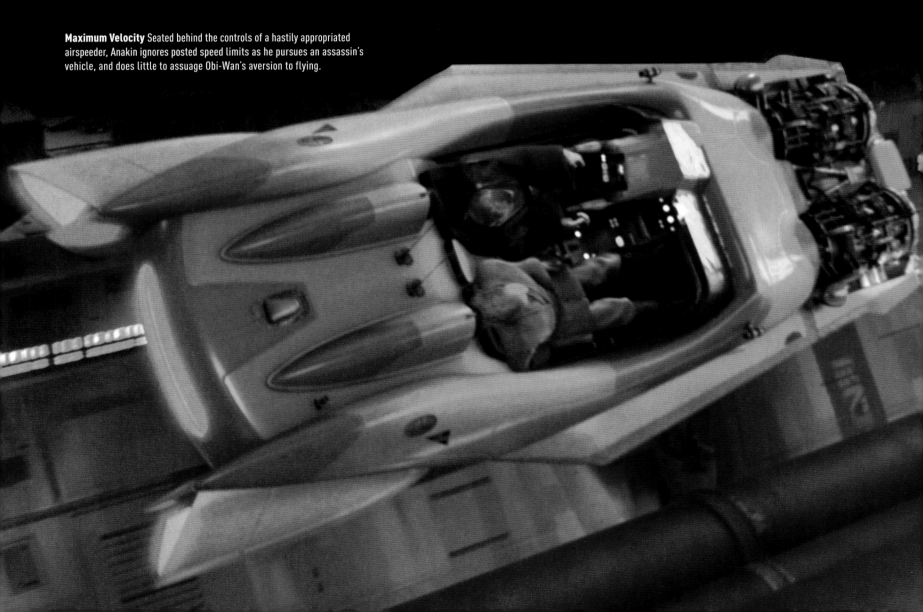

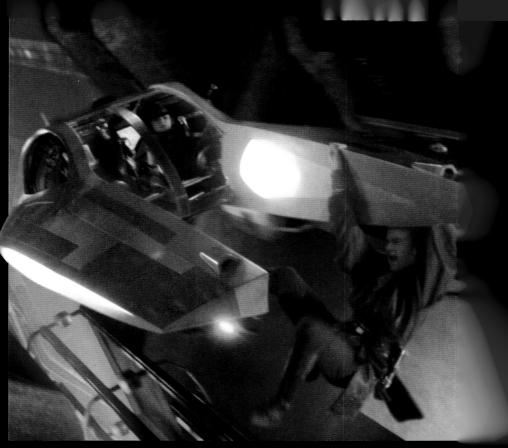

Custom-Made The height of the speeder's customized windscreen leaves the Jedi to assume the vehicle's owner is relatively short.

Holding on Tight After Anakin leaps onto the assassin's vehicle, the assassin swerves and dives in an effort to make the Jedi lose his grip.

FORCED LANDING

Although Coruscant Air Traffic Control's patrol officers, airborne droids, and extensive computer networks constantly monitor Coruscant's skylanes, they can't chase down every airspeeder that breaks away from designated routes, or prevent every shuttle with a damaged repulsorlift engine from crashing. Fortunately, if a Jedi witnesses dangerous or illegal activity in the skylanes, they are fully authorized to intervene. As a result, in an effort to stop an assassin from escaping in a *Koro-2* all-environment exodrive speeder, Anakin Skywalker is compelled to do everything in his power to stop the vehicle. Incredibly, the speeder crashes on one of the lower-level thoroughfares in the Uscru Entertainment District without killing any civilians.

Jedi Intervention Anakin not only manages to cling to the assassin's speeder, but also activates his lightsaber and plunges it into the cockpit.

Crash Site Given the great efficiency of Coruscant Air Traffic Control, a crashed airspeeder is a rare sight on low-level pedestrian walkways.

JEDI STARFIGHTER

When Obi-Wan Kenobi departs on his quest to Kamino, he requisitions one of the Jedi Temple's modified Delta-7 *Aethersprite* light interceptors. This ultra-light fighter is well shielded against impacts and blasts, and is equipped with two dual laser cannons that can unleash a withering frontal assault. Its sleek, blade-like form simplifies shield distribution and affords excellent visibility, especially in forward and lateral directions. A fighter of this size normally cannot travel far into deep space on its own, but the customized Jedi version features a socket for a truncated droid navigator and can dock with an external hyperdrive ring. Its offensively-focused design assumes dominance over any foe—essential for a prescient Jedi or any steely-nerved pilot trained for frontal assaults.

ANCIENT ICON

The starboard wing of Obi-Wan's craft is marked with the symbol of a disc with eight spokes. The ancient icon dates back to a study of numerology, whereby the number nine (eight spokes joined to one disc) signifies the beneficent presence of the Force in a unitary galaxy. After the fall of the Galactic Republic 1,000 generations later, the Emperor will personalize this symbol by defacing the icon with the removal of two spokes.

External Hyperdrive
Because the Delta-7 does not have a built-in hyperdrive, Obi-Wan utilizes a hyperdrive ring to travel through hyperspace. After he reaches his destination, the Delta-7 detaches from the ring, which remains in orbit until it is needed again.

STOICAL DROID

When assigned aboard the Delta-7, astromech droid R4-P17 has a truncated body that allows her to fit within the tight confines of the tiny starfighter. The Delta-7B fighter, with its droid socket located just fore of the cockpit, benefits from a thicker hull structure and allows R4-P17 to use her full-sized astromech shell.

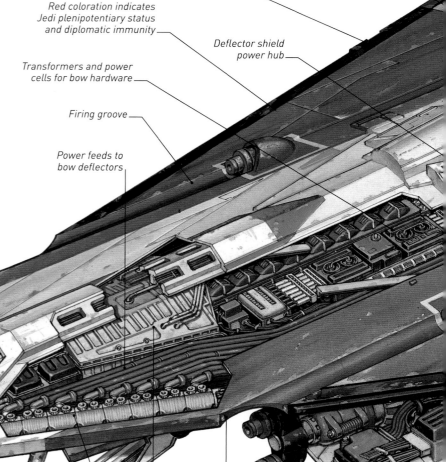

The fighter's tiny profile makes it difficult to detect and easy to hide from long-range sensors

Ancient roundel with eight spokes

Red coloration indicates Jedi plenipotentiary status and diplomatic immunity

Deflector shield power hub

Transformers and power cells for bow hardware

Firing groove

Power feeds to bow deflectors

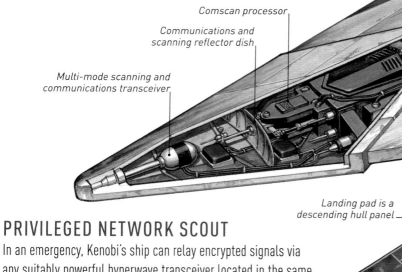

Comscan processor

Communications and scanning reflector dish

Multi-mode scanning and communications transceiver

Landing pad is a descending hull panel

Forward landing gear bay

Port landing light

Forward deflector shield projectors

Ventral landing claw enables docking in zero-gravity environments, such as on planetary ring boulders

Main reactor bulb

Laser cannon capacitors

Forward ventral power tree

Dual laser cannon emitter muzzles

PRIVILEGED NETWORK SCOUT

In an emergency, Kenobi's ship can relay encrypted signals via any suitably powerful hyperwave transceiver located in the same planetary system. During the mission to Geonosis, Obi-Wan uses a powerful interstellar relay station in the Geonosis system to communicate with Anakin on Tatooine.

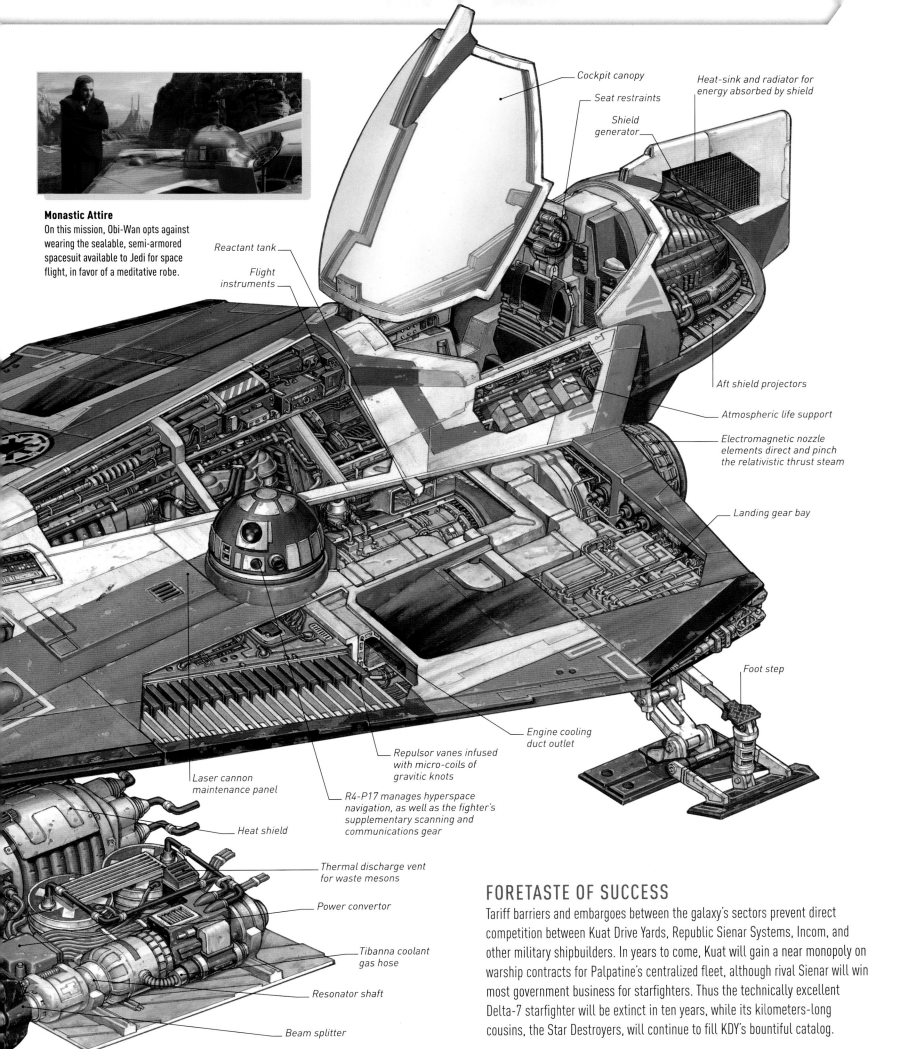

Monastic Attire
On this mission, Obi-Wan opts against wearing the sealable, semi-armored spacesuit available to Jedi for space flight, in favor of a meditative robe.

Cockpit canopy

Heat-sink and radiator for energy absorbed by shield

Seat restraints

Shield generator

Reactant tank

Flight instruments

Aft shield projectors

Atmospheric life support

Electromagnetic nozzle elements direct and pinch the relativistic thrust steam

Landing gear bay

Foot step

Engine cooling duct outlet

Repulsor vanes infused with micro-coils of gravitic knots

Laser cannon maintenance panel

R4-P17 manages hyperspace navigation, as well as the fighter's supplementary scanning and communications gear

Heat shield

Thermal discharge vent for waste mesons

Power convertor

Tibanna coolant gas hose

Resonator shaft

Beam splitter

FORETASTE OF SUCCESS

Tariff barriers and embargoes between the galaxy's sectors prevent direct competition between Kuat Drive Yards, Republic Sienar Systems, Incom, and other military shipbuilders. In years to come, Kuat will gain a near monopoly on warship contracts for Palpatine's centralized fleet, although rival Sienar will win most government business for starfighters. Thus the technically excellent Delta-7 starfighter will be extinct in ten years, while its kilometers-long cousins, the Star Destroyers, will continue to fill KDY's bountiful catalog.

JEDI STARSHIPS

While the Jedi Order typically uses Republic cruisers for diplomatic missions across the galaxy, some assignments require smaller and less conspicuous transports. And because Jedi can't always rely on pilots to reach their destination, Jedi training includes how to fly starships. The Jedi Temple on Coruscant contains hangars for numerous vessels, including single-passenger starfighters. Although most Jedi starfighters are engineered to accommodate humanoid Jedi, some are designed for specific alien species.

In-Flight Support Engineered without a traditional built-in navicomputer, the Delta-7 *Aethersprite* Jedi starfighter utilizes a truncated astromech droid.

Evasive Maneuvers Obi-Wan Kenobi guides his Jedi starfighter through an asteroid belt in a daring effort to evade an enemy missile.

"Blast! This is why I hate flying."
Obi-Wan Kenobi

JEDI TRACER BEACONS
A miniature tracking device, tracer beacons are sophisticated transmitters used to follow starships and pinpoint their exact location. Some tracer beacons, such as the one Obi-Wan Kenobi uses to track Jango Fett's *Slave I*, are magnetic to lock onto a ship's hull, and can even track a ship's journey through hyperspace.

Magnetic Landing Claw The Delta-7 *Aethersprite* light interceptor is equipped with a ventral landing claw, a magnetic gripping device that can adhere to almost any surface, including rocky asteroids.

WEAPON OF A BOUNTY HUNTER

Kuat Drive Yard's *Firespray* patrol craft saw only limited production, as it was too heavily armed for civilian use yet was underpowered by Kuat's home-defense standards. Furthermore, *Firesprays* proved too robust, modular, and user-serviceable to support a profitable post-sale maintenance business. Although bad for the manufacturer, these characteristics make it a perfect starship for an independent bounty hunter like Jango Fett.

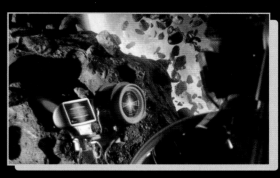

Sensor Scopes *Slave I*'s sensor scopes display readouts for weapons systems as well as navigational and atmospheric data.

INTERIOR REFIT

Slave I has been extensively modified after a few harsh space battles. Jango has added spartan crew quarters for long hunts, since the original *Firespray* was furnished for shorter-term patrols. In addition, the police-regulation prisoner cages have been converted into less-humane, coffin-like wall cabinets to ensure control of captives.

On the Attack Piloting *Slave I* past hazardous asteroids, Jango Fett opens fire on a Jedi starfighter that has followed him from Kamino to Geonosis.

DEVASTATING ASSETS

Slave I's tail blaster cannons are the only overt weaponry retained from the standard *Firespray*, but they have been enhanced with finer aim and variable power. Rapid-fire laser cannons concealed amidships have less control than the tail guns, but deliver powerful energy bolts at a greater rate. Fett has installed physical armaments as well: an adapted naval minelayer deals nasty surprises to hasty pursuers, and a concealed, frontal double-rack of torpedoes fulfils the role of a guided, heavy-assault weapon.

Slave I Originally one of several prototype patrol ships made by Kuat Systems Engineering, *Slave I* is an extremely rare and distinctively designed starship.

JANGO FETT'S *SLAVE I*

Jango fett pilots a viciously effective, customized starship with superior shielding combined with high endurance levels, and a heavy arsenal of overt and hidden weapons. At first glance, the rugged vessel may be unrecognizable, but not alaramingly dangerous. However, closer inspection reveals a montage of patched, rebuilt, and enhanced equipment attesting to its unsavory usage. Jango favors *Slave I* for the element of disguise it affords him; as one of the galaxy's most proficient mercenaries, he nonetheless chooses to work in discreet obscurity, remaining unrecognized by most highly placed security officers and criminals alike. When Jango's son Boba inherits *Slave I*, he will make some changes to suit his greater infamy and more aggressive style, including increased interstellar range and fuel capacity, installation of superior sensor jammers, and other stealth hardware.

Bounty Hunter's Landing Pad The Kaminoans designated a Tipoca City landing platform for Jango Fett's personal use. Accustomed to rapid escapes, Jango makes sure *Slave I* is always prepared for immediate departure.

Fins contain repulsor grilles for landing maneuvers

Jango Fett

Each deck's artificial gravity re-orients depending on flight mode

Flight instruments console

Energy-shield shroud

Ladder to lower level

Corridor segment scavenged from a derelict Corellian starliner

Boba Fett

Expansion grid for future hardware (Boba will install stealth gear)

Upper portside inertial compensator

Sublight communications antenna

Shield generator main power conduit

Forward shield generator destined for relocation to make room for larger power cells and fuel tanks

Forward starboard reactant tank

Jango's bunk

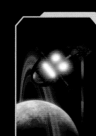

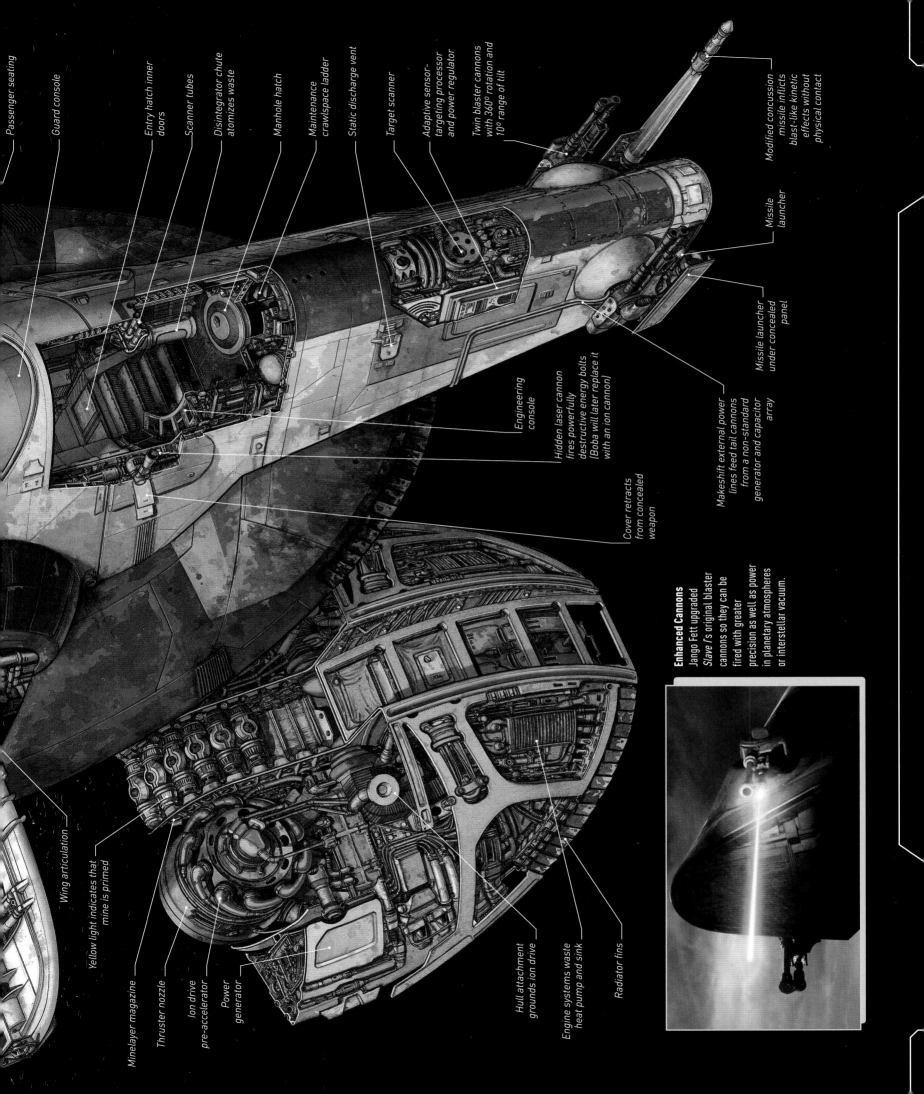

Passenger seating

Guard console

Entry hatch inner doors

Scanner tubes

Disintegrator chute atomizes waste

Manhole hatch

Maintenance crawlspace ladder

Static discharge vent

Target scanner

Adaptive sensor-targeting processor and power regulator

Twin blaster cannons with 360° rotation and 10° range of tilt

Missile launcher

Modified concussion missile inflicts blast-like kinetic effects without physical contact

Missile launcher under concealed panel

Engineering console

Hidden laser cannon fires powerfully destructive energy bolts (Boba will later replace it with an ion cannon)

Makeshift external power lines feed tail cannons from a non-standard generator and capacitor array

Cover retracts from concealed weapon

Enhanced Cannons
Jango Fett upgraded *Slave I*'s original blaster cannons so they can be fired with greater precision as well as power in planetary atmospheres or interstellar vacuum.

Wing articulation

Yellow light indicates that mine is primed

Minelayer magazine

Thruster nozzle

Ion drive pre-accelerator

Power generator

Hull attachment grounds ion drive

Engine systems waste heat pump and sink

Radiator fins

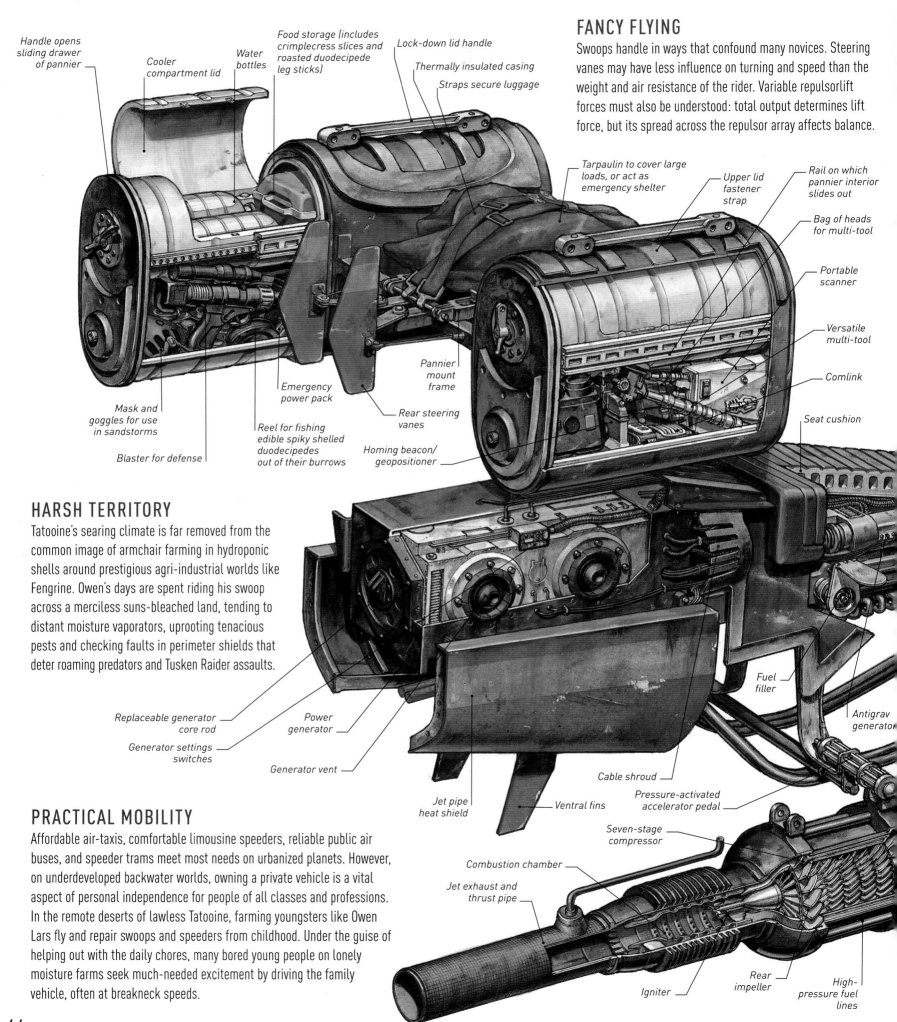

Handle opens sliding drawer of pannier

Cooler compartment lid

Water bottles

Food storage (includes crimplecress slices and roasted duodecipede leg sticks)

Lock-down lid handle

Thermally insulated casing

Straps secure luggage

FANCY FLYING

Swoops handle in ways that confound many novices. Steering vanes may have less influence on turning and speed than the weight and air resistance of the rider. Variable repulsorlift forces must also be understood: total output determines lift force, but its spread across the repulsor array affects balance.

Tarpaulin to cover large loads, or act as emergency shelter

Upper lid fastener strap

Rail on which pannier interior slides out

Bag of heads for multi-tool

Portable scanner

Versatile multi-tool

Comlink

Seat cushion

Mask and goggles for use in sandstorms

Emergency power pack

Reel for fishing edible spiky shelled duodecipedes out of their burrows

Pannier mount frame

Rear steering vanes

Homing beacon/ geopositioner

Blaster for defense

HARSH TERRITORY

Tatooine's searing climate is far removed from the common image of armchair farming in hydroponic shells around prestigious agri-industrial worlds like Fengrine. Owen's days are spent riding his swoop across a merciless suns-bleached land, tending to distant moisture vaporators, uprooting tenacious pests and checking faults in perimeter shields that deter roaming predators and Tusken Raider assaults.

Replaceable generator core rod

Generator settings switches

Power generator

Generator vent

Jet pipe heat shield

Ventral fins

Fuel filler

Antigrav generator

Cable shroud

Pressure-activated accelerator pedal

Seven-stage compressor

Combustion chamber

Jet exhaust and thrust pipe

Igniter

Rear impeller

High-pressure fuel lines

PRACTICAL MOBILITY

Affordable air-taxis, comfortable limousine speeders, reliable public air buses, and speeder trams meet most needs on urbanized planets. However, on underdeveloped backwater worlds, owning a private vehicle is a vital aspect of personal independence for people of all classes and professions. In the remote deserts of lawless Tatooine, farming youngsters like Owen Lars fly and repair swoops and speeders from childhood. Under the guise of helping out with the daily chores, many bored young people on lonely moisture farms seek much-needed excitement by driving the family vehicle, often at breakneck speeds.

OWEN LARS' SWOOP BIKE

O f all people on desolate Tatooine, the implacable moisture farmers have the most pragmatic appreciation of vehicular technology, upon which they depend for daily survival. Young Owen Lars epitomizes this principle, as he patrols the family property on his fast, sand-beaten swoop. Though not especially reliable, this farm vehicle is used more heavily than the homestead's dozen other semi-restored craft because it is fuel-efficient and easy to repair using Jawa-supplied parts. Owen bought his high-powered swoop from a Revwien merchant at an auction in remote Mos Nytram. Originally a racing vehicle, he immediately saw its practical use. Townsfolk might scoff at the sight of a one-time sports vehicle hauling water trailers or vermin traps, but as far as Owen is concerned, utility is the true essence of grace.

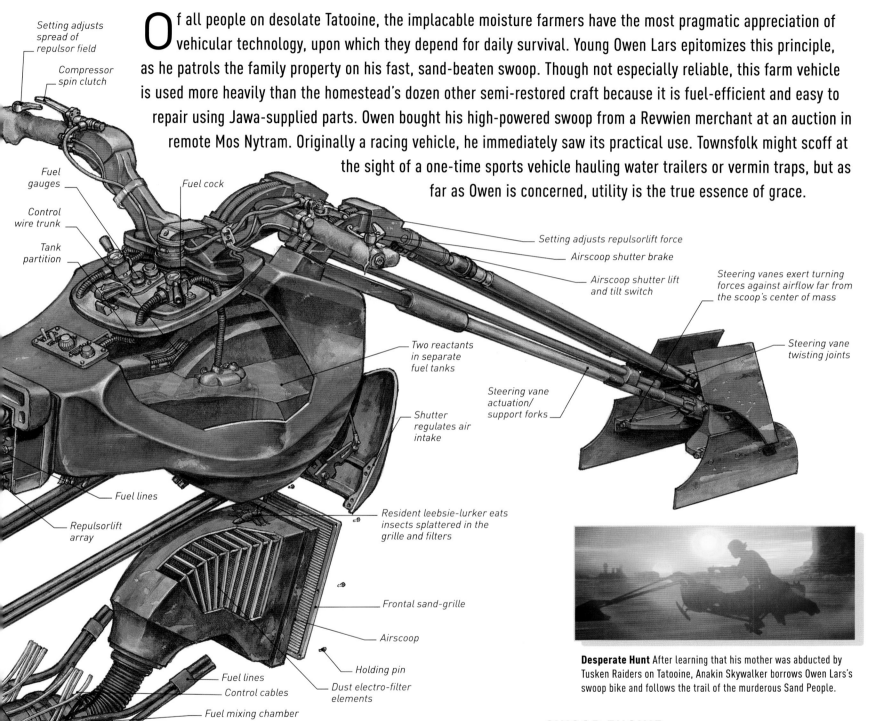

Setting adjusts spread of repulsor field

Compressor spin clutch

Fuel gauges

Fuel cock

Control wire trunk

Tank partition

Setting adjusts repulsorlift force

Airscoop shutter brake

Airscoop shutter lift and tilt switch

Steering vanes exert turning forces against airflow far from the scoop's center of mass

Steering vane twisting joints

Two reactants in separate fuel tanks

Steering vane actuation/ support forks

Shutter regulates air intake

Fuel lines

Repulsorlift array

Resident leebsie-lurker eats insects splattered in the grille and filters

Frontal sand-grille

Airscoop

Fuel lines

Holding pin

Control cables

Dust electro-filter elements

Fuel mixing chamber

Front impeller

Desperate Hunt After learning that his mother was abducted by Tusken Raiders on Tatooine, Anakin Skywalker borrows Owen Lars's swoop bike and follows the trail of the murderous Sand People.

LATEST MODEL

Owen's swoop is regarded as one of the latest styles on the backwater planet of Tatooine, although it slid off an assembly line at least 20 years before his birth. Indeed, this model—and ones like it—had been in common use many years earlier on richer, more central worlds. Down the ages, technological fashions spread incredibly slowly through the galaxy's millions of inhabited systems, even though the actual technology generally fluctuates only in scale and implementation.

SWOOP ENGINE

In its functional simplicity, the swoop is a tube. At the front, an airscoop feeds a turbojet in which fuel is mixed and ignited. At the rear, a tail-piped exhaust stream provides thrust. A repulsor array under the seat keeps the bike aloft, and is sustained by basic power cells and a generator. The only moving parts are the fans and gears of the compressor. These mechanisms are protected from abrasive sand and dust by a coarse grille at the airscoop mouth, followed by multiple electrostatic filters.

PADMÉ'S STARSHIP

This slim yacht from the royal hangars of Naboo is not a spacious diplomatic platform for long-range tours and conferences. It is a relatively fast ship suited to discreet getaways. Its security features include a powerful Naboo-style shield system, electronic countermeasures, and a last-resort passenger escape capsule. Queen Jamillia's royal starships normally sit idle since she prefers to concentrate on Naboo's domestic affairs, entrusting her external powers to Senator Padmé Amidala. The smallest royal yacht is therefore available and ideally suited for Padmé's undercover travels as the galaxy's most threatened political target. The yacht serves Padmé and Anakin well in their dangerous journey from Tatooine to the neighboring Geonosis system.

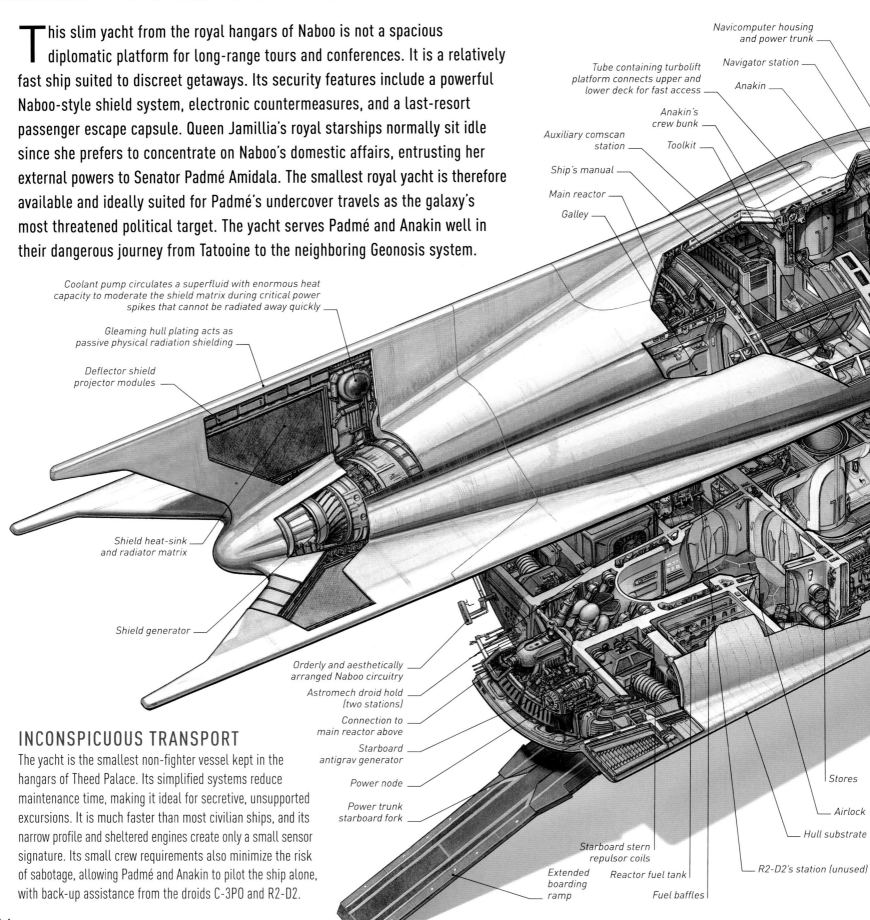

Navicomputer housing and power trunk

Navigator station

Anakin

Tube containing turbolift platform connects upper and lower deck for fast access

Anakin's crew bunk

Auxiliary comscan station

Toolkit

Ship's manual

Main reactor

Galley

Coolant pump circulates a superfluid with enormous heat capacity to moderate the shield matrix during critical power spikes that cannot be radiated away quickly

Gleaming hull plating acts as passive physical radiation shielding

Deflector shield projector modules

Shield heat-sink and radiator matrix

Shield generator

Orderly and aesthetically arranged Naboo circuitry

Astromech droid hold (two stations)

Connection to main reactor above

Starboard antigrav generator

Power node

Power trunk starboard fork

Stores

Airlock

Hull substrate

R2-D2's station (unused)

Starboard stern repulsor coils

Extended boarding ramp

Reactor fuel tank

Fuel baffles

INCONSPICUOUS TRANSPORT

The yacht is the smallest non-fighter vessel kept in the hangars of Theed Palace. Its simplified systems reduce maintenance time, making it ideal for secretive, unsupported excursions. It is much faster than most civilian ships, and its narrow profile and sheltered engines create only a small sensor signature. Its small crew requirements also minimize the risk of sabotage, allowing Padmé and Anakin to pilot the ship alone, with back-up assistance from the droids C-3PO and R2-D2.

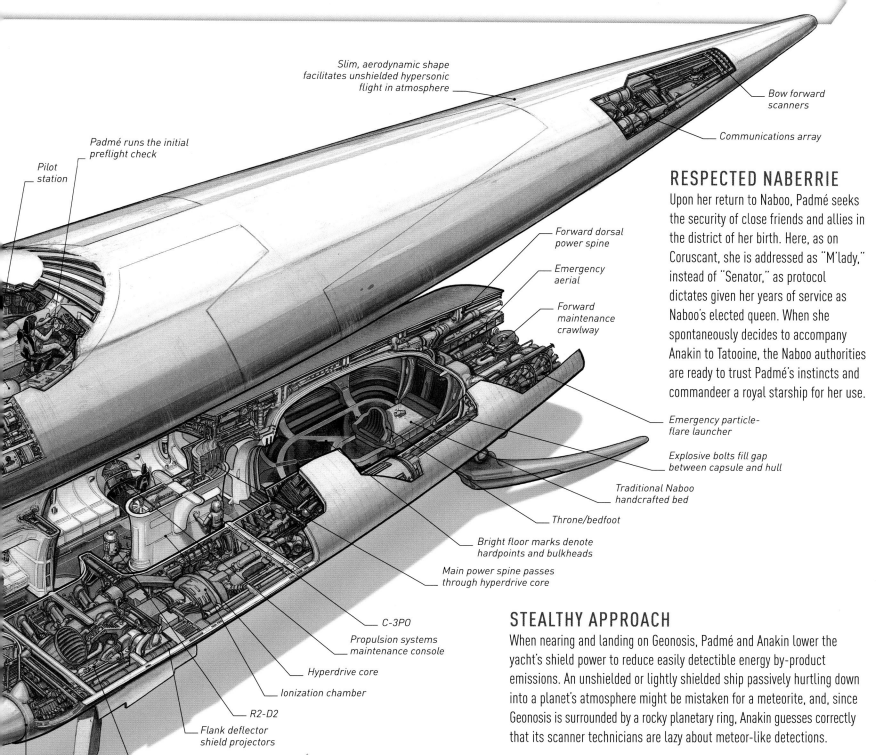

Slim, aerodynamic shape facilitates unshielded hypersonic flight in atmosphere

Bow forward scanners

Communications array

Pilot station

Padmé runs the initial preflight check

Forward dorsal power spine

Emergency aerial

Forward maintenance crawlway

Emergency particle-flare launcher

Explosive bolts fill gap between capsule and hull

Traditional Naboo handcrafted bed

Throne/bedfoot

Bright floor marks denote hardpoints and bulkheads

Main power spine passes through hyperdrive core

C-3PO

Propulsion systems maintenance console

Hyperdrive core

Ionization chamber

R2-D2

Flank deflector shield projectors

Complex magnetic ducts guide ion stream past intruding landing gear housing

Beru Whitesun

Owen Lars

Landing gear

Sublight drive particle exit ring

Starboard inertial compensator

RESPECTED NABERRIE

Upon her return to Naboo, Padmé seeks the security of close friends and allies in the district of her birth. Here, as on Coruscant, she is addressed as "M'lady," instead of "Senator," as protocol dictates given her years of service as Naboo's elected queen. When she spontaneously decides to accompany Anakin to Tatooine, the Naboo authorities are ready to trust Padmé's instincts and commandeer a royal starship for her use.

STEALTHY APPROACH

When nearing and landing on Geonosis, Padmé and Anakin lower the yacht's shield power to reduce easily detectible energy by-product emissions. An unshielded or lightly shielded ship passively hurtling down into a planet's atmosphere might be mistaken for a meteorite, and, since Geonosis is surrounded by a rocky planetary ring, Anakin guesses correctly that its scanner technicians are lazy about meteor-like detections.

SECURITY SENSITIVITY

The Trade Federation occupation significantly changed Naboo defense policy, with increased harmony between Naboo and Gungans resulting in coordinated action plans to withstand any new siege. Gungan shield expertise was combined with Naboo power generation to form a global shield network that activates in minutes to repel any bombardment or hostile landing. The need for such effective, if discreet, homeworld defenses is popularly supported. Captain Panaka's Security Forces have a healthy supply of volunteers, and Theed Palace engineers are designing a steady series of new starships to convey their dignitaries.

Communications Console During their mission to Tatooine, Padmé Amidala and Anakin Skywalker are on the Nubian yacht's bridge when they receive a holographic transmission from Jedi Master Mace Windu on Coruscant.

TRADE FEDERATION CORE SHIP

W ith its fleets of freighter-battleships, the Neimoidian Trade Federation is well-equipped to be one of the powerful merchant factions behind the advent of the Clone Wars. The heart and brain of each battleship is a detachable Core Ship, which comprises a massive central computer and multiple power systems. These huge ships are serviced in special landing pits on planets affiliated to the Trade Federation, while the delicate cargo arms and engine blocks remain in orbit. The Core Ships' ion-drive nozzles provide basic steering and slow acceleration, allowing them to dock in powerful anti-gravity repulsorlift cushions, with eight landing legs for stability. Scores of these ships are grounded on Geonosis, where they are being upgraded for coordination with the newly enhanced Baktoid droid armies. During the battle on Geonosis, the Core Ships are ringed with land and air defenses, allowing a good number to retreat safely to the skies.

VERTICAL ORGANIZATION

The hierarchical arrangement of habitable areas on a Core Ship matches that of Neimoidian hives. The control bridges, executive suites, and treasuries are concentrated in the globe's upper pole and towers, and resemble Neimoidia's luxurious surface palaces. Deeper levels are for junior managers, publicists, brokers, and droid storage. The lowest decks contain engineering areas and conference rooms for meeting outsiders; like the unfavorably dry and hot basements of Neimoidian warrens, frequented by subterranean scavengers and parasites, these decks are shunned by high-ranking officials.

STANDARD PART

Core-Ship design has changed little in the last century. In a typical display of Neimoidian thrift, the spheres can serve a variety of craft: The split-ring freighter-battleships of the Naboo blockade; larger, unarmed container vessels and tankers; and newer warships of the post-Naboo period, including cruisers with improved weapons placement and smaller, faster destroyers that defend the fleets and chase down blockade runners.

Massive Evacuation After the Republic's newly formed army arrives on Geonosis, the Neimoidians flee to their Trade Federation Core Ships. Extremely powerful repulsorlift engines enable the enormous ships to achieve escape velocity.

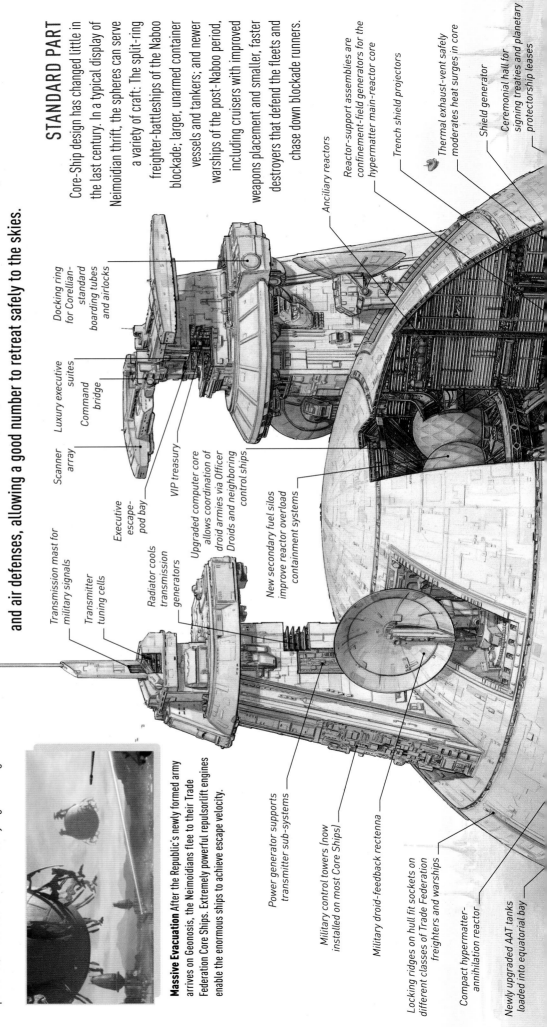

- Docking ring for Corellian-standard boarding tubes and airlocks
- Ancillary reactors
- Reactor-support assemblies are confinement-field generators for the hypermatter main-reactor core
- Trench shield projectors
- Thermal exhaust-vent safely moderates heat surges in core
- Shield generator
- Ceremonial hall for signing treaties and planetary protectorship leases
- Luxury executive suites
- Command bridge
- Scanner array
- VIP treasury
- Executive escape-pod bay
- Upgraded computer core allows coordination of droid armies via Officer Droids and neighboring control ships
- Transmission mast for military signals
- Transmitter tuning cells
- Radiator cools transmission generators
- New secondary fuel silos improve reactor overload containment systems
- Power generator supports transmitter sub-systems
- Military control towers (now installed on most Core Ships)
- Military droid-feedback rectenna
- Locking ridges on hull fit sockets on different classes of Trade Federation freighters and warships
- Compact hypermatter-annihilation reactor
- Newly upgraded AAT tanks loaded into equatorial bay

Lower decks are mostly uninhabited but patrolled by security droids

C-9979 landing ship parts

Droid battalions

Boarding ramp

New storage holds added after full militarization

Heavy cargo lift

Retractable maintenance gantry

Power feeds recharge ship systems

Landing gear retractors

Faster-than-light "hyperwave" transceiver reaches any part of the galaxy directly without use of public HoloNet relays

Hull sections from leg socket cover

Foot-pads

Anti-gravity repulsorlift suspensors

NEW ALLY

After more than a decade of promoting its own trade interests by underhand means, the Trade Federation recognizes the strategic value of Count Dooku. As a persuasive orator with a zealous following on thousands of Separatist worlds, including Geonosis (home to the Federation's favorite dockyards and armorers), he is fostering disunity throughout the galaxy—and, as Nute Gunray knows, weak governments are good for business.

Ventral thruster extends out of a lower hatch

Rings project one-way force-field that confines harmful radiation from the ship's exhaust in the blast shaft

HYPERLANE CONTROL

Core Ships' navicomputers contain precious interstellar data charts. In bygone ages, governments and private agencies shared such information publicly, but now the Trade Federation aggressively protects the coordinates it owns. As changes in astronomical conditions can make routes unsafe, the Trade Federation is gaining a virtual transport monopoly over parts of the galaxy. Now, only the Jedi and the Office of the Supreme Chancellor can afford to maintain more comprehensive charts.

transports

Defensive artillery

Waste fluid vent

Artillery power generator

Observation stations and workshops

Lift shaft

Walls are lined with gravitational reflectors for the ship's repulsors to act against

Particle shields cycle and intensify in trenches

Small, point-defense turrets

Thruster blast and radiation are harmlessly channeled into shaft

GEONOSIAN FIGHTER

During the climactic battle with the Republic, the Geonosian faction launches thousands of standby fighters to break the Republic's orbital cordon blocking Corporate Alliance ground reinforcements. These fightercraft combine high linear acceleration with phenomenal maneuverability as a result of the frictionless rotating mount of their thrusters. Despite their superior agility, few fighters are exported, since Geonosian senses and articulation differ from the galaxy's majority humanoid population. Furthermore, Geonosian policy has become fervently isolationist as the Republic stagnates, and their wary Archduke, Poggle the Lesser, believes that the hoarding of technical advantages is an insurance of power and security.

FLYING BY NOSE

An advanced scent stimulator in the pilot's mask exploits the acute Geonosian sense of smell to convey flight status feedback. The mask also sprays subverbal pheromone signals so that air marshals and flight controllers can remotely modify the pilot's mood and impart collective priorities.

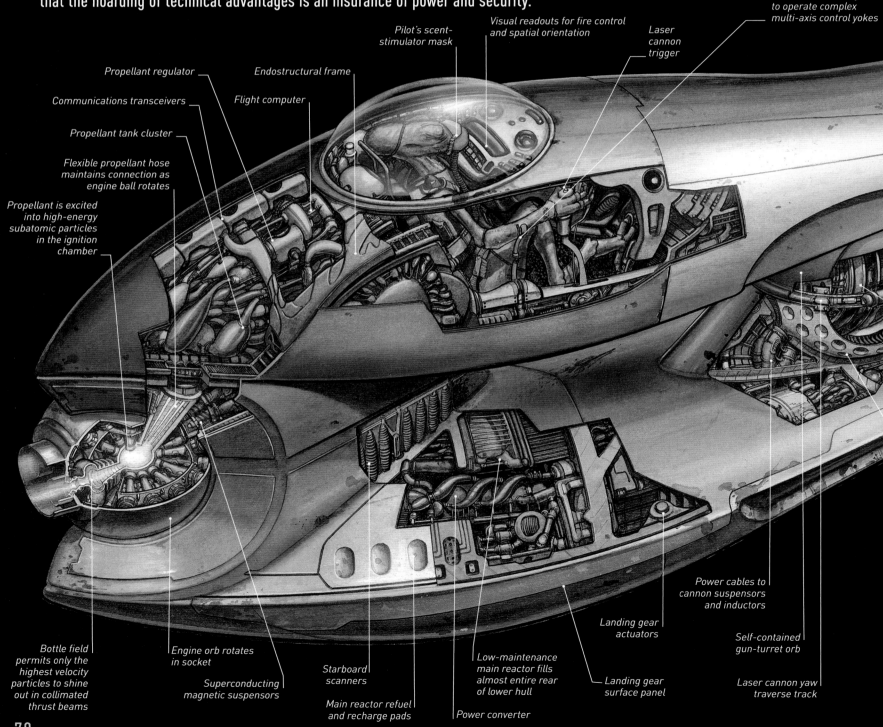

Propellant regulator

Communications transceivers

Propellant tank cluster

Flexible propellant hose maintains connection as engine ball rotates

Propellant is excited into high-energy subatomic particles in the ignition chamber

Endostructural frame

Flight computer

Pilot's scent-stimulator mask

Visual readouts for fire control and spatial orientation

Laser cannon trigger

Geonosian dexterity needed to operate complex multi-axis control yokes

Bottle field permits only the highest velocity particles to shine out in collimated thrust beams

Engine orb rotates in socket

Superconducting magnetic suspensors

Starboard scanners

Main reactor refuel and recharge pads

Low-maintenance main reactor fills almost entire rear of lower hull

Power converter

Landing gear actuators

Landing gear surface panel

Power cables to cannon suspensors and inductors

Self-contained gun-turret orb

Laser cannon yaw traverse track

FLEXIBLE FRAMEWORK

Geonosian starship frames are built from long strings of laminasteel, which can be woven and wrapped at high temperatures, binding together the ship's components. The frame cools to a metallic hardness, yet the bonds can momentarily yield and rebound enough to survive impacts that would break a more rigidly constituted vessel.

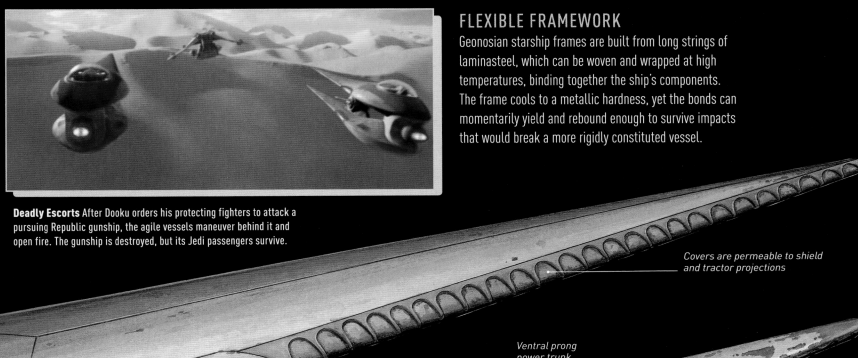

Deadly Escorts After Dooku orders his protecting fighters to attack a pursuing Republic gunship, the agile vessels maneuver behind it and open fire. The gunship is destroyed, but its Jedi passengers survive.

Covers are permeable to shield and tractor projections

Ventral prong power trunk

Forward inertial compensator sub-node

Tractor and shield kickback dampers

Bronze cladding is an austere and inconspicuous hue on the reddish-brown planet Geonosis

Long barrel of laser cannon imparts greater spin to the emergent beam and reduces collateral bolt glow relative to destructive power

Grapple notches for docking clamp

Laser cannon fires along the neutral space in between the prong shields

Recoil brackets cushion cannon during outburst of its own waste gases

MODULAR ORBS

Two of the most distinctive design features of the Geonosian fighter are its gun turret and engine orb. These are magnetically suspended and inductively powered without direct contact with the rest of the ship. The sockets can be fitted with alternative modules such as engine boosters and enhanced scanner suites for surveillance missions.

Green highlights resemble markings on the pygmy porlceetin—a large, venomous, hexapedal creature found on Geonosis

As gun-turret orb rolls, different power-induction spots overlap fixed points on socket wall

Dooku's Speeder Bike On Geonosis, Count Dooku escapes the Republic forces using a Flitknot speeder bike manufactured by Huppla Pasa Tisc, a Geonosian corporation. Dooku's speeder bike has been modified to suit his personal and physical requirements, and a pair of Geonosian fighters serve as Dooku's escorts.

GEONOSIAN TECHNOLOGY

Natives of the Outer Rim planet Geonosis, Geonosians are quasi-insectoids who developed and perfected technology for precision droid manufacturing in bulk. For centuries, they dedicated their hive-based culture to the production of protocol, labor, and combat droids in alliance with the Techno Union's Baktoid Corporation. The Geonosians were responsible for hundreds of thousands of battle droids used during the Battle of Naboo. Their sprawling subterranean complexes contain not only numerous droid factories, but research and development laboratories for exotic vehicles and experimental weapons.

HIVE PILOTS

As well as being masters of battle droid design, the Geonosians raise a caste of living combat pilots in immense cob-shaped air-defence hives. Pilots can potentially spend years poised for action, as their hardy species requires no sleep. In training, each pilot pupa pairs with a fighter's flight computer, and they develop an idiosyncratic, coordination-enhancing rapport.

Geonosis Hangar Not far from the Geonosian Command Center, a hangar holds a waiting shuttle for the Neimoidian dignitaries, two Geonosian fighters, and Count Dooku's speeder bike.

Cockpit hatch opens for technical servicing and cleaning or repairing a pilot

Diagnostics console

Propellant refuelling conjugator

Cockpit hinge

Pilot stairs

Rear hull shield generator

Integrated shield and tractor beam projectors

Dorsal frame spine

Intermediary power cell

Forward dorsal scanner lines

Shoulder for relea docking

Recharge cabling

Dorsal capacitor distributes power throughout upper prong

Blaster coolant gas refiller hose (disengaged)

Docking clamp

Main inertial compensator and internal gravity generator

Laser cannon

Holographic Command Table
In the middle of the Geonosian Command Center, a large circular table displays holograms of the ongoing battle on Geonosis between Republic and Separatist forces.

Death Star Designs
The initial plans for the moon-sized superweapon were secretly passed to the Geonosians, who helped devise the weapon's hypermatter systems.

REPUBLIC ASSAULT FORCES

Mere days after Obi-Wan Kenobi discovers the existence of a clone army allegedly commissioned for the Republic by a since-deceased Jedi, members of the Galactic Senate agree to conscript the army to fight the Separatists. Although the clones have received extensive training on Kamino, none of them has experienced actual combat before arriving on Geonosis. Jedi Masters Yoda and Mace Windu both lead full battle armies, while other veteran Jedi Knights each lead over 36,000 troops.

Command Center Stationed on an air-dropped mobile command center, clone officers and technicians monitor troop positions, enemy movements, communications, and sensor data to assist their comrades and Jedi generals.

SPHA-T Self-Propelled Heavy Artillery-Turbolasers (SPHA-Ts) are deployed in squads of four behind advancing Republic walkers, providing defense for landing assault ships, and destructive direct firepower.

HEAVY ARTILLERY

Just as the Galactic Senate was quick to utilize the clone army without investigating the army's mysterious origin, the Republic readily embraced a ready-made armada of weapons and heavily armed vessels and vehicles. Most of the Galactic Army's arsenal was manufactured by Rothana Heavy Engineering, a subsidiary of Kuat Drive Yards, a corporation that had been opposed to the Separatists for years. The arsenal includes assault ships, transports, bombers, and combat airspeeders. Clone soldiers, all having trained with exotic weapons simulators, have no difficulty operating actual weapons of war.

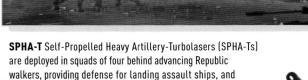

Combined Arms Equipped with laser cannons and missile launchers, assault gunships rain fire on enemy vehicles as they deliver clone troopers to the battlefront.

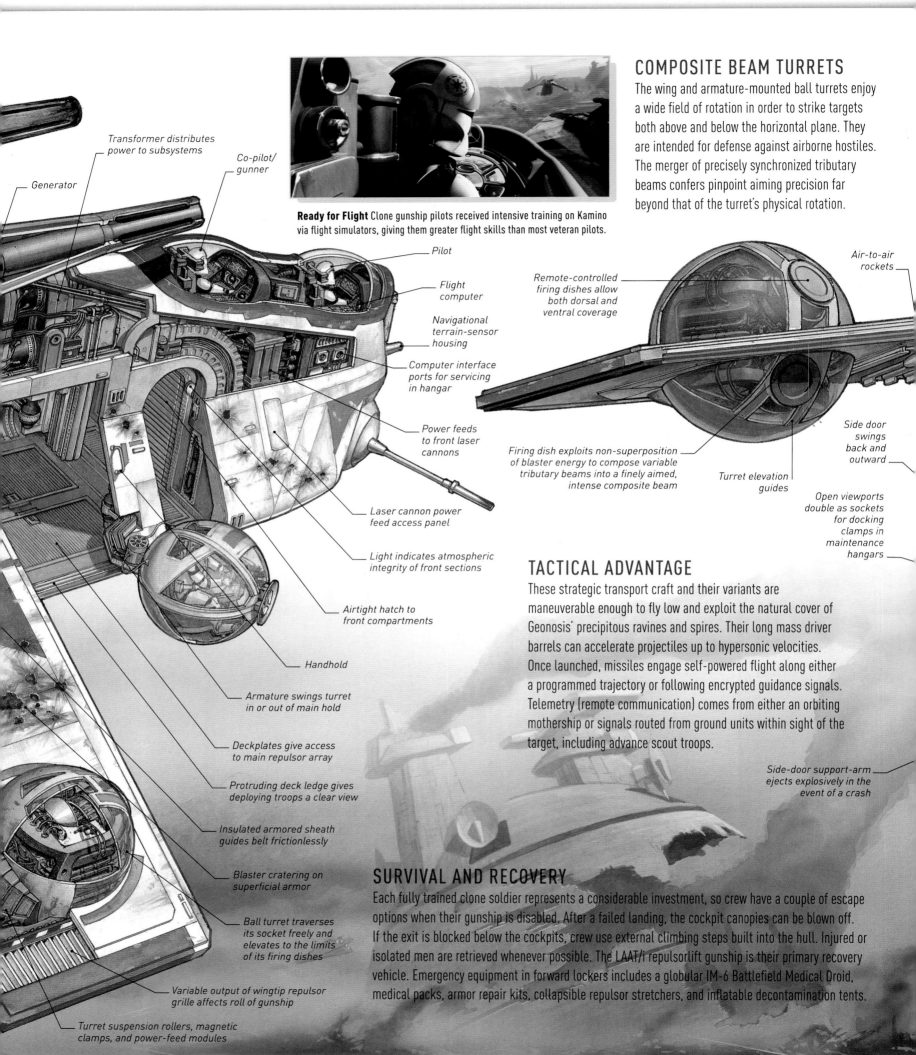

COMPOSITE BEAM TURRETS

The wing and armature-mounted ball turrets enjoy a wide field of rotation in order to strike targets both above and below the horizontal plane. They are intended for defense against airborne hostiles. The merger of precisely synchronized tributary beams confers pinpoint aiming precision far beyond that of the turret's physical rotation.

Ready for Flight Clone gunship pilots received intensive training on Kamino via flight simulators, giving them greater flight skills than most veteran pilots.

Generator

Transformer distributes power to subsystems

Co-pilot/ gunner

Pilot

Flight computer

Navigational terrain-sensor housing

Computer interface ports for servicing in hangar

Power feeds to front laser cannons

Laser cannon power feed access panel

Light indicates atmospheric integrity of front sections

Airtight hatch to front compartments

Handhold

Armature swings turret in or out of main hold

Deckplates give access to main repulsor array

Protruding deck ledge gives deploying troops a clear view

Insulated armored sheath guides belt frictionlessly

Blaster cratering on superficial armor

Ball turret traverses its socket freely and elevates to the limits of its firing dishes

Variable output of wingtip repulsor grille affects roll of gunship

Turret suspension rollers, magnetic clamps, and power-feed modules

Remote-controlled firing dishes allow both dorsal and ventral coverage

Air-to-air rockets

Side door swings back and outward

Turret elevation guides

Open viewports double as sockets for docking clamps in maintenance hangars

Firing dish exploits non-superposition of blaster energy to compose variable tributary beams into a finely aimed, intense composite beam

TACTICAL ADVANTAGE

These strategic transport craft and their variants are maneuverable enough to fly low and exploit the natural cover of Geonosis' precipitous ravines and spires. Their long mass driver barrels can accelerate projectiles up to hypersonic velocities. Once launched, missiles engage self-powered flight along either a programmed trajectory or following encrypted guidance signals. Telemetry (remote communication) comes from either an orbiting mothership or signals routed from ground units within sight of the target, including advance scout troops.

Side-door support-arm ejects explosively in the event of a crash

SURVIVAL AND RECOVERY

Each fully trained clone soldier represents a considerable investment, so crew have a couple of escape options when their gunship is disabled. After a failed landing, the cockpit canopies can be blown off. If the exit is blocked below the cockpits, crew use external climbing steps built into the hull. Injured or isolated men are retrieved whenever possible. The LAAT/i repulsorlift gunship is their primary recovery vehicle. Emergency equipment in forward lockers includes a globular IM-6 Battlefield Medical Droid, medical packs, armor repair kits, collapsible repulsor stretchers, and inflatable decontamination tents.

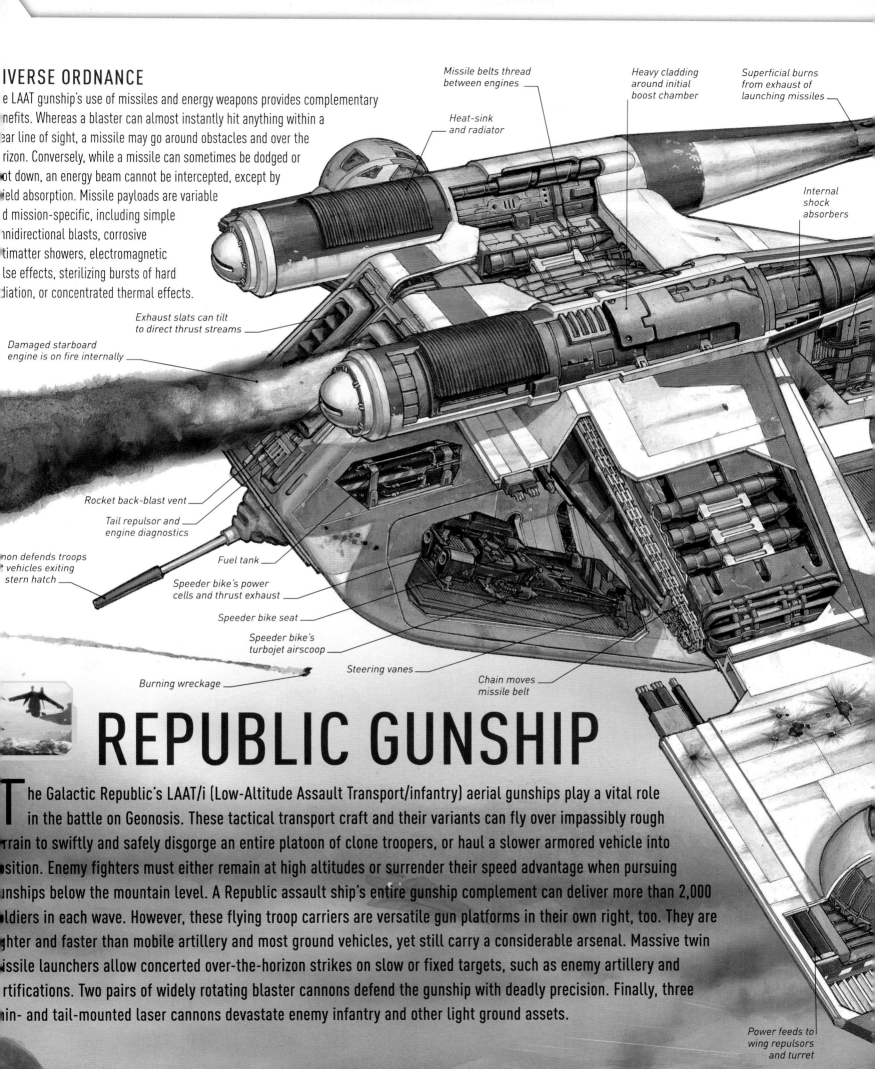

DIVERSE ORDNANCE

[Th]e LAAT gunship's use of missiles and energy weapons provides complementary [be]nefits. Whereas a blaster can almost instantly hit anything within a [cl]ear line of sight, a missile may go around obstacles and over the [ho]rizon. Conversely, while a missile can sometimes be dodged or [sh]ot down, an energy beam cannot be intercepted, except by [sh]ield absorption. Missile payloads are variable [an]d mission-specific, including simple [om]nidirectional blasts, corrosive [an]timatter showers, electromagnetic [pu]lse effects, sterilizing bursts of hard [ra]diation, or concentrated thermal effects.

Missile belts thread between engines

Heat-sink and radiator

Heavy cladding around initial boost chamber

Superficial burns from exhaust of launching missiles

Internal shock absorbers

Exhaust slats can tilt to direct thrust streams

Damaged starboard engine is on fire internally

Rocket back-blast vent

Tail repulsor and engine diagnostics

[Can]non defends troops [and] vehicles exiting [aft] stern hatch

Fuel tank

Speeder bike's power cells and thrust exhaust

Speeder bike seat

Speeder bike's turbojet airscoop

Steering vanes

Burning wreckage

Chain moves missile belt

REPUBLIC GUNSHIP

The Galactic Republic's LAAT/i (Low-Altitude Assault Transport/infantry) aerial gunships play a vital role in the battle on Geonosis. These tactical transport craft and their variants can fly over impassibly rough [ter]rain to swiftly and safely disgorge an entire platoon of clone troopers, or haul a slower armored vehicle into [po]sition. Enemy fighters must either remain at high altitudes or surrender their speed advantage when pursuing [gu]nships below the mountain level. A Republic assault ship's entire gunship complement can deliver more than 2,000 [so]ldiers in each wave. However, these flying troop carriers are versatile gun platforms in their own right, too. They are [lig]hter and faster than mobile artillery and most ground vehicles, yet still carry a considerable arsenal. Massive twin [m]issile launchers allow concerted over-the-horizon strikes on slow or fixed targets, such as enemy artillery and [fo]rtifications. Two pairs of widely rotating blaster cannons defend the gunship with deadly precision. Finally, three [ch]in- and tail-mounted laser cannons devastate enemy infantry and other light ground assets.

Power feeds to wing repulsors and turret

REPUBLIC ASSAULT SHIP

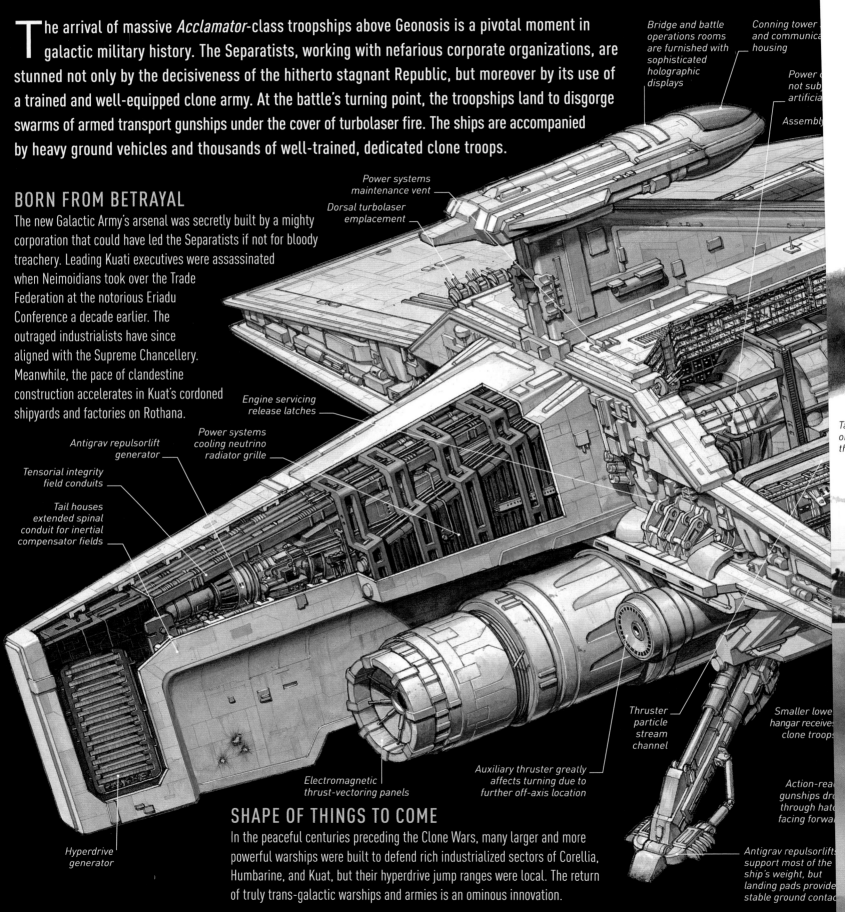

The arrival of massive *Acclamator*-class troopships above Geonosis is a pivotal moment in galactic military history. The Separatists, working with nefarious corporate organizations, are stunned not only by the decisiveness of the hitherto stagnant Republic, but moreover by its use of a trained and well-equipped clone army. At the battle's turning point, the troopships land to disgorge swarms of armed transport gunships under the cover of turbolaser fire. The ships are accompanied by heavy ground vehicles and thousands of well-trained, dedicated clone troops.

BORN FROM BETRAYAL

The new Galactic Army's arsenal was secretly built by a mighty corporation that could have led the Separatists if not for bloody treachery. Leading Kuati executives were assassinated when Neimoidians took over the Trade Federation at the notorious Eriadu Conference a decade earlier. The outraged industrialists have since aligned with the Supreme Chancellery. Meanwhile, the pace of clandestine construction accelerates in Kuat's cordoned shipyards and factories on Rothana.

Bridge and battle operations rooms are furnished with sophisticated holographic displays

Conning tower and communica housing

Power not sub artificia

Assembly

Power systems maintenance vent

Dorsal turbolaser emplacement

Engine servicing release latches

Power systems cooling neutrino radiator grille

Antigrav repulsorlift generator

Tensorial integrity field conduits

Tail houses extended spinal conduit for inertial compensator fields

Tail or s thro

Hyperdrive generator

Electromagnetic thrust-vectoring panels

Thruster particle stream channel

Auxiliary thruster greatly affects turning due to further off-axis location

Smaller lowe hangar receives clone troops

Action-rea gunships dr through hat facing forwa

Antigrav repulsorlifts support most of the ship's weight, but landing pads provide stable ground contac

SHAPE OF THINGS TO COME

In the peaceful centuries preceding the Clone Wars, many larger and more powerful warships were built to defend rich industrialized sectors of Corellia, Humbarine, and Kuat, but their hyperdrive jump ranges were local. The return of truly trans-galactic warships and armies is an ominous innovation.

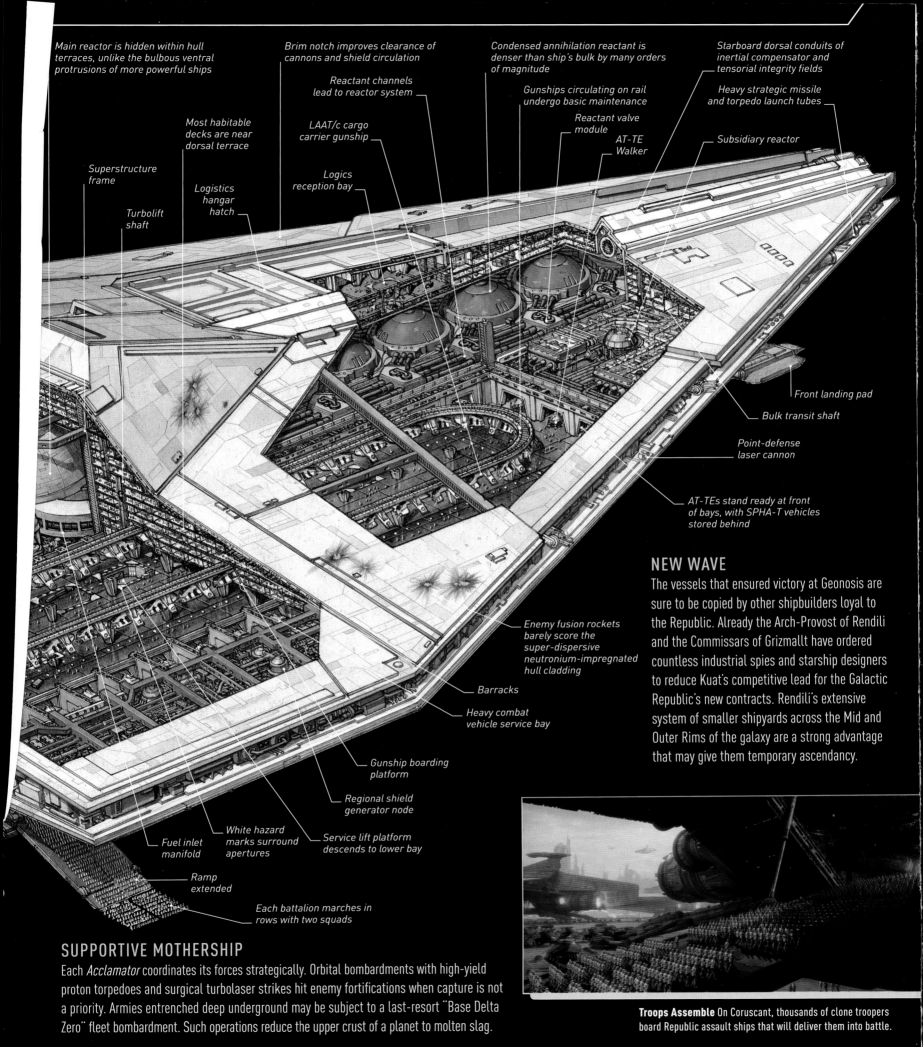

Main reactor is hidden within hull terraces, unlike the bulbous ventral protrusions of more powerful ships

Brim notch improves clearance of cannons and shield circulation

Condensed annihilation reactant is denser than ship's bulk by many orders of magnitude

Starboard dorsal conduits of inertial compensator and tensorial integrity fields

Reactant channels lead to reactor system

Gunships circulating on rail undergo basic maintenance

Heavy strategic missile and torpedo launch tubes

Most habitable decks are near dorsal terrace

LAAT/c cargo carrier gunship

Reactant valve module

Subsidiary reactor

Superstructure frame

Logics reception bay

AT-TE Walker

Turbolift shaft

Logistics hangar hatch

Front landing pad

Bulk transit shaft

Point-defense laser cannon

AT-TEs stand ready at front of bays, with SPHA-T vehicles stored behind

Enemy fusion rockets barely score the super-dispersive neutronium-impregnated hull cladding

Barracks

Heavy combat vehicle service bay

Gunship boarding platform

Regional shield generator node

Service lift platform descends to lower bay

Fuel inlet manifold

White hazard marks surround apertures

Ramp extended

Each battalion marches in rows with two squads

NEW WAVE

The vessels that ensured victory at Geonosis are sure to be copied by other shipbuilders loyal to the Republic. Already the Arch-Provost of Rendili and the Commissars of Grizmallt have ordered countless industrial spies and starship designers to reduce Kuat's competitive lead for the Galactic Republic's new contracts. Rendili's extensive system of smaller shipyards across the Mid and Outer Rims of the galaxy are a strong advantage that may give them temporary ascendancy.

SUPPORTIVE MOTHERSHIP

Each *Acclamator* coordinates its forces strategically. Orbital bombardments with high-yield proton torpedoes and surgical turbolaser strikes hit enemy fortifications when capture is not a priority. Armies entrenched deep underground may be subject to a last-resort "Base Delta Zero" fleet bombardment. Such operations reduce the upper crust of a planet to molten slag.

Troops Assemble On Coruscant, thousands of clone troopers board Republic assault ships that will deliver them into battle.

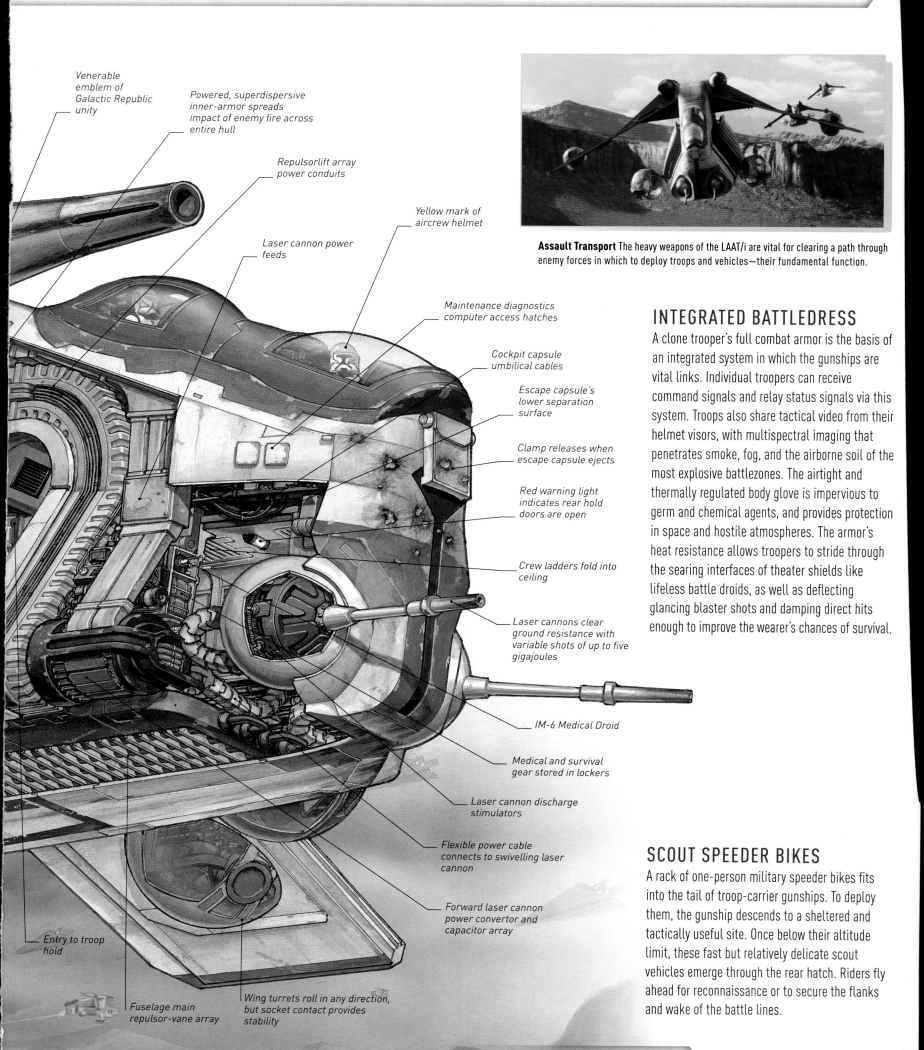

Venerable emblem of Galactic Republic unity

Powered, superdispersive inner-armor spreads impact of enemy fire across entire hull

Repulsorlift array power conduits

Laser cannon power feeds

Yellow mark of aircrew helmet

Maintenance diagnostics computer access hatches

Cockpit capsule umbilical cables

Escape capsule's lower separation surface

Clamp releases when escape capsule ejects

Red warning light indicates rear hold doors are open

Crew ladders fold into ceiling

Laser cannons clear ground resistance with variable shots of up to five gigajoules

IM-6 Medical Droid

Medical and survival gear stored in lockers

Laser cannon discharge stimulators

Flexible power cable connects to swivelling laser cannon

Forward laser cannon power convertor and capacitor array

Entry to troop hold

Fuselage main repulsor-vane array

Wing turrets roll in any direction, but socket contact provides stability

Assault Transport The heavy weapons of the LAAT/i are vital for clearing a path through enemy forces in which to deploy troops and vehicles—their fundamental function.

INTEGRATED BATTLEDRESS

A clone trooper's full combat armor is the basis of an integrated system in which the gunships are vital links. Individual troopers can receive command signals and relay status signals via this system. Troops also share tactical video from their helmet visors, with multispectral imaging that penetrates smoke, fog, and the airborne soil of the most explosive battlezones. The airtight and thermally regulated body glove is impervious to germ and chemical agents, and provides protection in space and hostile atmospheres. The armor's heat resistance allows troopers to stride through the searing interfaces of theater shields like lifeless battle droids, as well as deflecting glancing blaster shots and damping direct hits enough to improve the wearer's chances of survival.

SCOUT SPEEDER BIKES

A rack of one-person military speeder bikes fits into the tail of troop-carrier gunships. To deploy them, the gunship descends to a sheltered and tactically useful site. Once below their altitude limit, these fast but relatively delicate scout vehicles emerge through the rear hatch. Riders fly ahead for reconnaissance or to secure the flanks and wake of the battle lines.

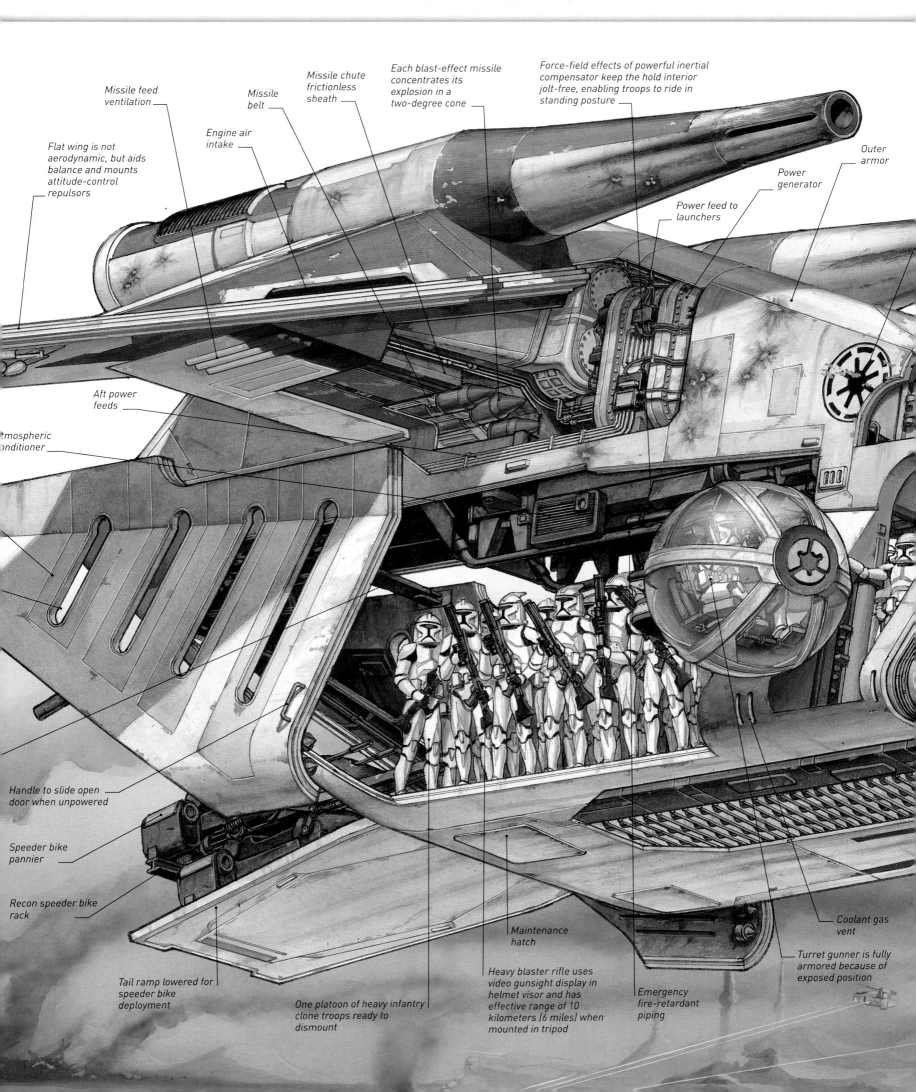

Missile feed
ventilation

Missile
belt

Missile chute
frictionless
sheath

Each blast-effect missile
concentrates its
explosion in a
two-degree cone

Force-field effects of powerful inertial
compensator keep the hold interior
jolt-free, enabling troops to ride in
standing posture

Flat wing is not
aerodynamic, but aids
balance and mounts
attitude-control
repulsors

Engine air
intake

Power
generator

Power feed to
launchers

Outer
armor

Aft power
feeds

tmospheric
onditioner

Handle to slide open
door when unpowered

Speeder bike
pannier

Recon speeder bike
rack

Tail ramp lowered for
speeder bike
deployment

One platoon of heavy infantry
clone troops ready to
dismount

Maintenance
hatch

Heavy blaster rifle uses
video gunsight display in
helmet visor and has
effective range of 10
kilometers (6 miles) when
mounted in tripod

Emergency
fire-retardant
piping

Coolant gas
vent

Turret gunner is fully
armored because of
exposed position

AT-TE

The intimidating All Terrain Tactical Enforcer is an assault vehicle that offers support to the Republic's clone army, obliterating threats to friendly infantry and reinforcing tactical control. Wading through the savage din of battle, the walker's sure-footed, six-legged stance allows it to cross crevices and climb otherwise impassably rugged slopes. Its massive turret-mounted missile-launcher bombards fixed emplacements or smites slow-moving aircraft, while six laser-cannon turrets swivel quickly to devastate faster line-of-sight targets.

LAND CONTROL

Unlike fast-flying aircraft and fighters, each AT-TE exerts a persistently formidable presence on the ground. AT-TEs take possession of territory and equalize the struggle between clone soldiers and the Separatists' war machines. For rapid deployment of troops, AT-TE walkers can ride an LAAT/c cargo gunship to the battlefront. With their passenger cargo unloaded, walkers then hunt down enemies at a more rapid pace.

Vents reduce nozzle pressure effects on emerging projectile

Mass-driver barrel accelerates projectile

Mass-driver coils and waste heat radiator

Top hatch

Exterior gunner with full armor protection

Target screen

Ladder

Elevation axle

Ammunition belt

Canopy opens up at hinge

Periscope and rangefinder

Spotter finds targets and coordinates gunners

Driver

Full armor worn by vehicle crews restricts movement (not enough time before the Battle of Geonosis for crew uniform modifications)

Bar pivots down to give crew a step up into cabin

Laser cannon stimulator forward elements

Laser cannon power feeds

Targeting computer

Notches for holding clamps in hangar

Laser cannon charger/ transformer

Inertial compensator generator under seats

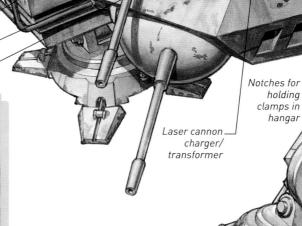

Close Combat In the event of an assault by enemy infantry, an AT-TE can dismount its two squads of troops to enter the fray and secure the immediate surroundings.

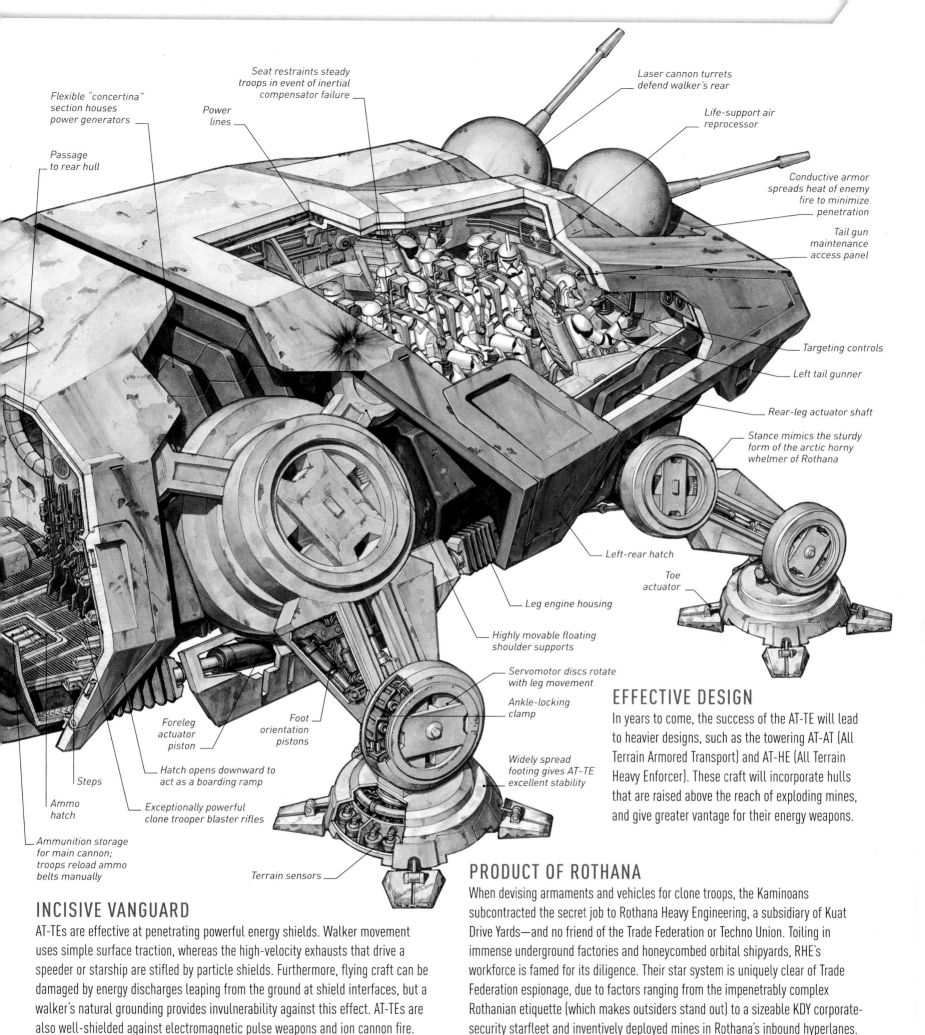

Flexible "concertina" section houses power generators

Seat restraints steady troops in event of inertial compensator failure

Power lines

Laser cannon turrets defend walker's rear

Life-support air reprocessor

Passage to rear hull

Conductive armor spreads heat of enemy fire to minimize penetration

Tail gun maintenance access panel

Targeting controls

Left tail gunner

Rear-leg actuator shaft

Stance mimics the sturdy form of the arctic horny whelmer of Rothana

Left-rear hatch

Toe actuator

Leg engine housing

Highly movable floating shoulder supports

Servomotor discs rotate with leg movement

Ankle-locking clamp

Foreleg actuator piston

Foot orientation pistons

Hatch opens downward to act as a boarding ramp

Widely spread footing gives AT-TE excellent stability

Steps

Ammo hatch

Exceptionally powerful clone trooper blaster rifles

Ammunition storage for main cannon; troops reload ammo belts manually

Terrain sensors

EFFECTIVE DESIGN

In years to come, the success of the AT-TE will lead to heavier designs, such as the towering AT-AT (All Terrain Armored Transport) and AT-HE (All Terrain Heavy Enforcer). These craft will incorporate hulls that are raised above the reach of exploding mines, and give greater vantage for their energy weapons.

INCISIVE VANGUARD

AT-TEs are effective at penetrating powerful energy shields. Walker movement uses simple surface traction, whereas the high-velocity exhausts that drive a speeder or starship are stifled by particle shields. Furthermore, flying craft can be damaged by energy discharges leaping from the ground at shield interfaces, but a walker's natural grounding provides invulnerability against this effect. AT-TEs are also well-shielded against electromagnetic pulse weapons and ion cannon fire.

PRODUCT OF ROTHANA

When devising armaments and vehicles for clone troops, the Kaminoans subcontracted the secret job to Rothana Heavy Engineering, a subsidiary of Kuat Drive Yards—and no friend of the Trade Federation or Techno Union. Toiling in immense underground factories and honeycombed orbital shipyards, RHE's workforce is famed for their diligence. Their star system is uniquely clear of Trade Federation espionage, due to factors ranging from the impenetrably complex Rothanian etiquette (which makes outsiders stand out) to a sizeable KDY corporate-security starfleet and inventively deployed mines in Rothana's inbound hyperlanes.

LAAT/C GUNSHIP

Rothana Heavy Engineering's Low-Altitude Assault Transport/carrier (LAAT/c) is a variant of the LAAT/i gunship, and was initially designed to carry heavy AT-TEs to the front lines. The design was modified to make it more versatile, allowing it to transport a variety of payloads, including forward command centers, portable power generators, and shield generators. The LAAT/c is crewed by a single pilot, and has a rapid cargo-deployment system that features magnetic clamps to hold heavy payloads in place. The clamps can be instantly disengaged, allowing the carrier to lift off without time-consuming offloading operations.

AUTOMATIC ASCENT

The moment an LAAT/c gunship's arms release their hold on an AT-TE, the sudden weight loss causes the LAAT/c to rise rapidly from the drop-off point. Because such sudden ascents would be jarring to most life forms in ordinary repulsorlift ships, the LAAT/c has strong anti-gravity compensators in the cockpit and passenger areas to ensure pilots and crew remain unaffected.

Heavy Hauler LAAT/c cargo gunships have reinforced frames and more powerful repulsorlift engines than standard gunships, enabling them to carry cumbersome AT-TE walkers. Cargo gunships are also used to transport mobile tactical command stations into battle.

Air Support An AT-TE hits the ground walking after an LAAT/c cargo gunship delivers it to a planetary surface. The gunship provides further support by firing at enemy targets that pose the most immediate threat to the AT-TE.

SOLAR SAILERS

Count Dooku, as a man of learning, was long aware of the Geonosians' ancient sailing traditions when they offered to build a new personal craft for him. In early times, these insectoid engineers built cargo kites that flew in the dense air of their low-gravity world. Their first spacecraft were huge, gossamer-thin robotic sheets that sailed on the power of sunshine, followed by more hefty craft pushed from home by intense laser beams. The use of solar sailers declined as the Geonosians discovered modern fusion technologies—although Poggle the Lesser, Archduke of Geonosis, was pleased to draw on ancient technology in order to accommodate an esteemed ally.

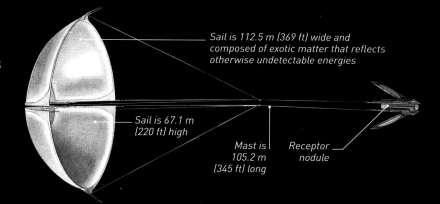

Sail is 112.5 m (369 ft) wide and composed of exotic matter that reflects otherwise undetectable energies

Sail is 67.1 m (220 ft) high

Mast is 105.2 m (345 ft) long

Receptor nodule

SAIL POWER

The delicate reflector-surfaces of most "solar" sails unfurl to moon-like diameters, and are more commonly pushed by tachyon streams and ultraviolet lasers than sunlight. Dooku's unique solar sailer, however, achieves similar performance across the entire galaxy with a much smaller span and no detectable support system.

Geonosis Launch Chute A tubular launch chute built within the wall of an abandoned weapons factory provides an escape route for Count Dooku's Solar Sailer. A combination of exotic tractor-beam technology and small repulsors embedded within the chute's walls enable ships to be ejected at high speed.

Stealth System Dooku's Solar Sailer carries a prototype Sienar Design Systems sensor array, which can deceive the most sophisticated detection systems.

Solar Sail The unexplained mobility of Dooku's Solar Sailer enhances his commanding mystique in Geonosian eyes.

Pilot Droid Instead of relying on an automatic pilot system to operate his Solar Sailer, Count Dooku uses an FA-4 pilot droid that was manufactured by the SoroSuub Corporation.

BOW PRONGS

Geonosian starships typically feature two or more multi-functional bow prongs. Rows of narrow-beam tractor/repulsor emitters along the prongs act as offensive grapples or steering aids when there are surrounding objects to pull and push against. Also, the spread of ray-shield energies around the prongs can be selectively adjusted to give the ship extra maneuverablity.

Yard joint

Collapsed main mast

Power lines to portside dorsal beam elements

Dorsal sail carapace

Dark surface made of heavy metals that are preciously rare on Geonosis

Motorized unfolding sail nexus

Intermediary power cell

Cockpit module can be replaced by a weapons or sensor orb if piloting controls are routed to main hold

FA-4 Pilot Droid

Levers deploy sail

Main console

Prong elements diagnostics hatch

Permeable covers over beamer elements

Shield projectors

MYSTERIOUS ANTIQUE

After leaving the Jedi Order, Dooku developed a taste for rare pre-Republic artifacts. An antiques dealer near the Gree Enclave sold him an ancient sail, with unique and startling properties. The sail is powered by an as-yet undetectable source of supralight emissions, allowing Dooku's custom ship an independence unknown by any other current space-faring vehicle.

Power feed

Dooku's chair rises from longitudinal access shaft

Tractor/repulsor emitter element

Furled ventral sail

Frame

Inertial compensator

Conventional scanner array

Repulsorlift generator

Landing-gear actuators

Last segment is jointed to spread ship's weight

Secret Hangar After landing his Solar Sailer in a hangar in the abandoned LiMerge Power building on Coruscant, Dooku has a clandestine meeting with Darth Sidious.

DOOKU'S SOLAR SAILER

A gift from his Geonosian colleagues, Dooku's ship is a unique melding of a *Punworcca 116*-class sloop with an elegant sail supplied by the Count himself. On Dooku's instructions, Geonosian engineers attached this enigmatic accessory to the ship to provide independent power without the need to carry fuel (apart from guide thrusters). The ship's interior is tailored to Dooku's sense of refinement, with an extensive databook library and ornate decorations.

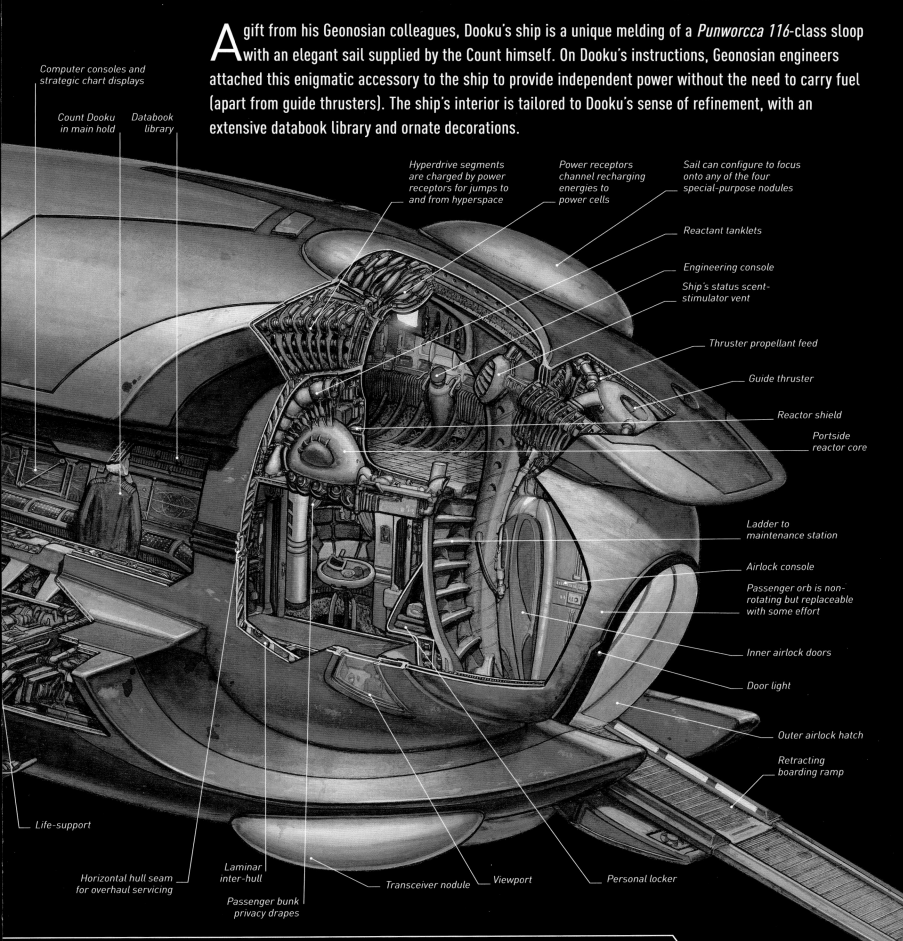

Computer consoles and strategic chart displays

Count Dooku in main hold

Databook library

Hyperdrive segments are charged by power receptors for jumps to and from hyperspace

Power receptors channel recharging energies to power cells

Sail can configure to focus onto any of the four special-purpose nodules

Reactant tanklets

Engineering console

Ship's status scent-stimulator vent

Thruster propellant feed

Guide thruster

Reactor shield

Portside reactor core

Ladder to maintenance station

Airlock console

Passenger orb is non-rotating but replaceable with some effort

Inner airlock doors

Door light

Outer airlock hatch

Retracting boarding ramp

Life-support

Horizontal hull seam for overhaul servicing

Laminar inter-hull

Passenger bunk privacy drapes

Transceiver nodule

Viewport

Personal locker

EPISODE III
REVENGE OF THE SITH

The Clone Wars have escalated into a cataclysmic conflict, with the Republic's Jedi Knights and clone troops engaged in desperate campaigns across the galaxy. The Separatist movement, now known as the Confederacy of Independent Systems, is encircling the crumbling Galactic Republic, advancing ever-nearer to the star systems of the Galactic Core. Neither side is aware that their leaders are secretly in league. The Republic's Supreme Chancellor Palpatine is really the Sith Lord Darth Sidious, and his apprentice is Darth Tyranus, otherwise known as Count Dooku, the leader of the Separatists. Sidious is merely playing for time until he is ready to replace Tyranus with a new, more powerful apprentice, who will help him to achieve his ultimate aim: absolute control of the galaxy under Sith rule and the formation of a merciless new order—the Galactic Empire.

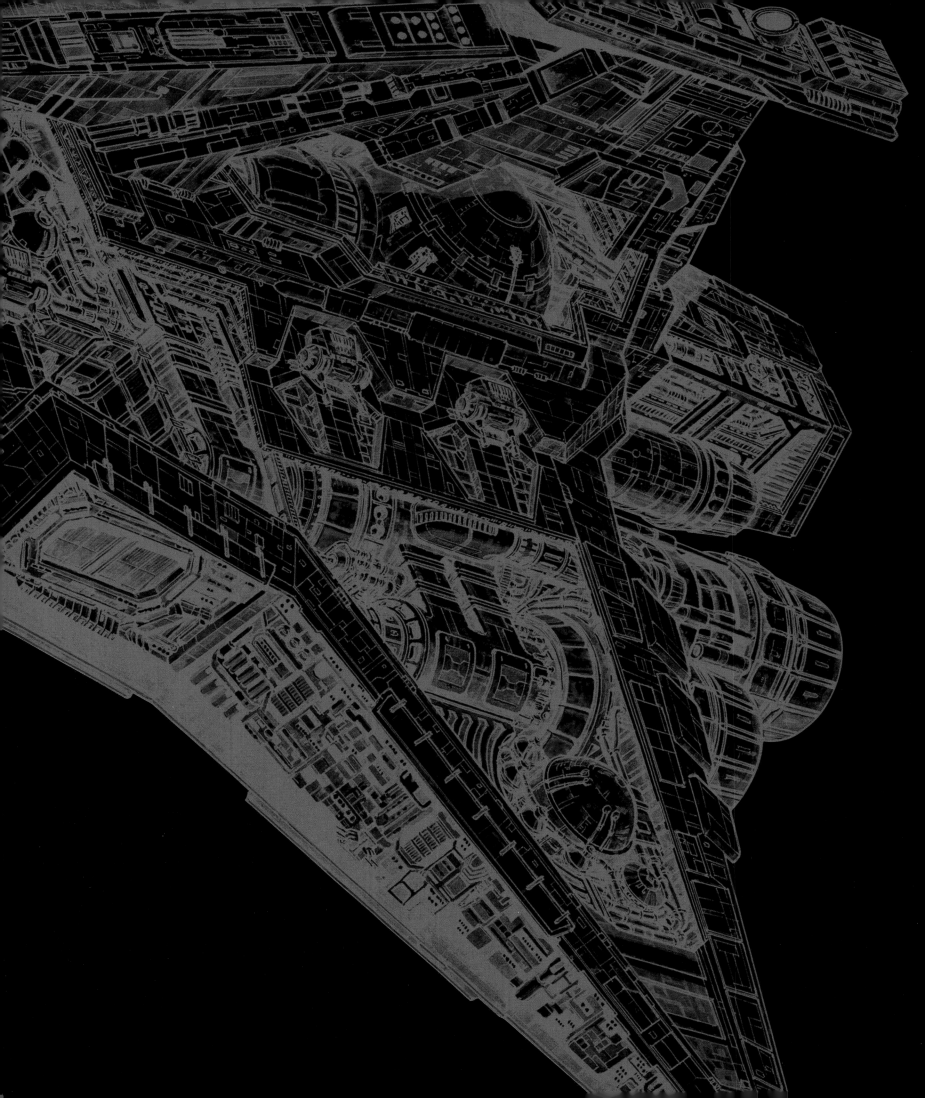

VENATOR-CLASS STAR DESTROYER

The Galactic Republic's new *Venator*-class Star Destroyer is fast enough to chase down blockade runners and big enough to lead independent missions such as the liberation of Utapau. A flotilla of these medium-weight, versatile multi-role warships can blast through the shields of a Trade Federation battleship with ease. The hangars of the *Venator*-class can support hundreds of fightercraft. The ship is also capable of planetary landings as a military transport and can act as an escort in the Republic armada. However, the primary function of the *Venator*-class is its role as a fighting ship and starfighter carrier, making it a firm favorite with Jedi pilots.

Orbital Defender
Venator-class Star Destroyers become a common sight in the skies and orbit of Coruscant during the Clone Wars, and protect the capital planet from numerous Separatist attacks.

Annihilation reactant silo

Markings of Fifth Fleet in Open Circle armada

Heavy turbolaser turret

Hangar door track

Standard complement includes 192 V-wings

Hangar command post

Atmosphere containment shield projectors line door

Open Circle armada's emblem

Flight deck runs parallel to dorsal ridge

Venator typically holds 36 ARC-170 fighters

Eta-2 Actis Interceptor

LAAT/c (Low-Altitude Assault Transport/carrier)

LAAT/i (Low-Altitude Assault Transport/infantry) gunship can deploy when ship is in atmospheric flight

ARC (Aggressive ReCon)-170 fighter on hangar approach

Fighter and vehicle hangars

Local shield generator

Medium dual turbolaser

Ventral docking bay (on the initiative of General Skywalker, some *Venator*-class ships feature additional SPHA-T laser cannons here to increase ventral firepower)

Hull scarring caused by direct impact from a crashing Separatist tri-fighter

Atmosphere ducts

Dorsal doors—powerful deflector shields also protect the ship's interior

Bow tractor beam projector

Tractor beam generator

Crewed areas

AT-TE (All Terrain Tactical Enforcer) walker

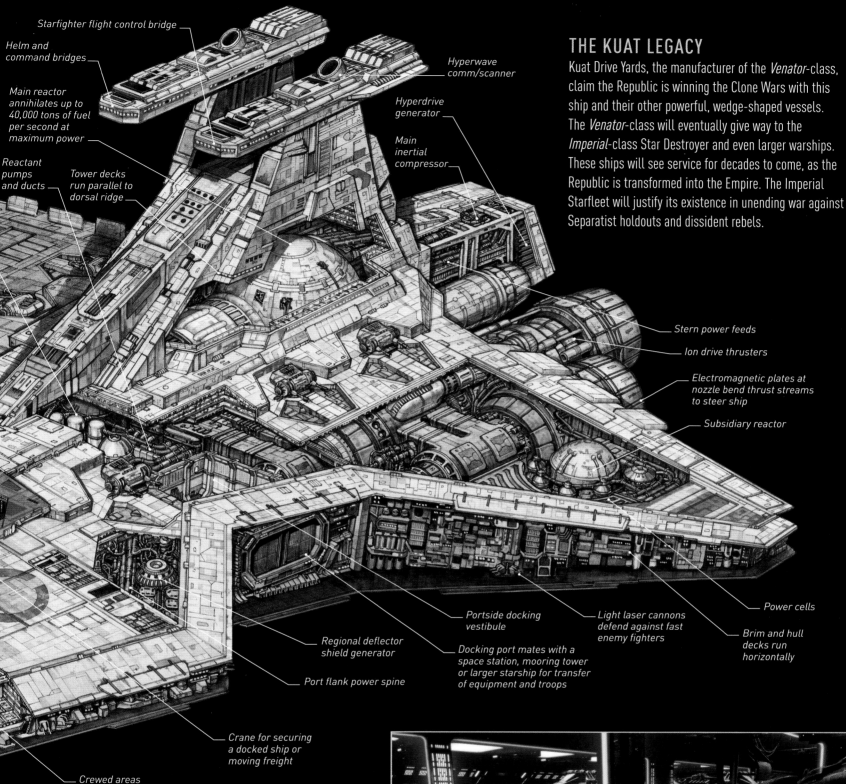

Starfighter flight control bridge

Helm and command bridges

Main reactor annihilates up to 40,000 tons of fuel per second at maximum power

Reactant pumps and ducts

Tower decks run parallel to dorsal ridge

Hyperwave comm/scanner

Hyperdrive generator

Main inertial compressor

Stern power feeds

Ion drive thrusters

Electromagnetic plates at nozzle bend thrust streams to steer ship

Subsidiary reactor

Power cells

Brim and hull decks run horizontally

Light laser cannons defend against fast enemy fighters

Portside docking vestibule

Docking port mates with a space station, mooring tower or larger starship for transfer of equipment and troops

Regional deflector shield generator

Port flank power spine

Crane for securing a docked ship or moving freight

Crewed areas

THE KUAT LEGACY

Kuat Drive Yards, the manufacturer of the *Venator*-class, claim the Republic is winning the Clone Wars with this ship and their other powerful, wedge-shaped vessels. The *Venator*-class will eventually give way to the *Imperial*-class Star Destroyer and even larger warships. These ships will see service for decades to come, as the Republic is transformed into the Empire. The Imperial Starfleet will justify its existence in unending war against Separatist holdouts and dissident rebels.

CARRIER ROLE

The long dorsal flight deck of the *Venator*-class enables hundreds of starfighters to launch rapidly. The slow opening and closing of the deck's armored bow doors, however, can leave the vessel vulnerable. This weakness is compensated for by strong deflector shielding around the deck's entrance, but the design flaw will be eliminated in future Star Destroyers.

Star Destroyer Hangar Inside a hangar on the *Venator*-class Star Destroyer *Vigilance*, Jedi General Obi-Wan Kenobi briefs members of the 212th Attack Battalion, prior to their mission to the Utapau system.

REPUBLIC FIREPOWER

Despite numerous victories over the Confederacy during the Clone Wars, the Republic becomes increasingly aware of the fact that their enemies can produce scores of battle droids much faster than Kaminoan cloners can produce soldiers, who also require training. To compensate for this disparity, Republic-allied engineers ensure Star Destroyers can be operated by a relatively small crew, and weapons designers have created more powerful turbolaser cannons with increased range and accuracy, giving the Republic Navy a strong advantage against Confederate warships.

Star Destroyer Gun Deck Specially trained clone troopers man the laser cannons on *Venator*-class Star Destroyers.

Dangerous Duty Being part of a Star Destroyer gun crew is notoriously hazardous, as they suffer high casualty rates.

HEAVY-DUTY TURBOLASERS

A *Venator*-class Star Destroyer's eight DBY-827 heavy turbolaser turrets are the standard requirement in naval gunnery for intense inter-ship combat and planetary bombardment. The DBY-827's precise, long-range tracking mode enables it to hit a target vessel at distances of over ten light-minutes, while the turret can rotate in three seconds in its close-fighting, fast-tracking mode. Seven different blast intensities provide a choice between crippling shots and outright vaporization of the enemy. The *Venator*-class, as a true warship, can feed almost its entire reactor output to its heavy guns when required.

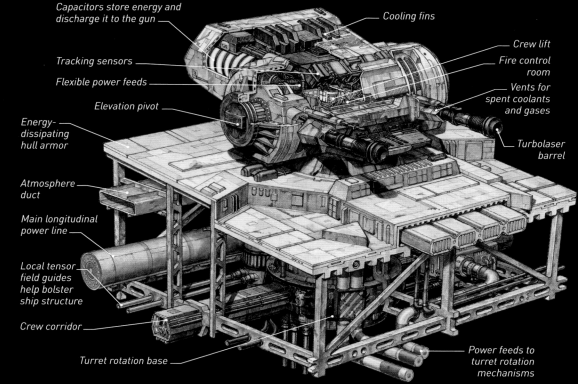

Capacitors store energy and discharge it to the gun

Cooling fins

Crew lift

Fire control room

Tracking sensors

Flexible power feeds

Vents for spent coolants and gases

Elevation pivot

Energy-dissipating hull armor

Turbolaser barrel

Atmosphere duct

Main longitudinal power line

Local tensor field guides help bolster ship structure

Crew corridor

Turret rotation base

Power feeds to turret rotation mechanisms

Broadside Combat The Separatist flagship *Invisible Hand* is pounded into a flaming hulk at point-blank range by the Star Destroyer *Guarlara*.

V-WING

One of the newer and more numerous fightercraft defending the Galactic Republic, V-wings are sharp, compact support ships deployed in epic fleet actions or in defense of fortress worlds. Launched in furious swarms from the Republic's carriers and warships, these fast, agile starfighters are frustratingly elusive targets and their swiveling twin laser cannons make them surprising and deadly opponents. V-wings are piloted by a single clone trooper backed up by an independent Q7-series astromech droid. Like many models mass-produced for Loyalist forces, V-wings are too compact for a hyperdrive, but carry a powerful reactor and use two vertically placed ion drive thrusters for astonishingly fast pitch-turns.

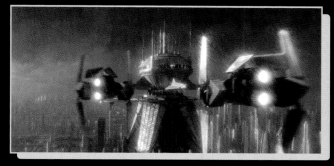

Strength in Numbers Streamlined mass production techniques prompted the V-wing to replace the V-19 Torrent as the preferred compact space superiority fighter.

DOGFIGHTER SPECIAL

Developed by Kuat Systems Engineering, the same company that produced Jedi starfighters, the Alpha-3 Nimbus V-wing utilizes cutting-edge technology for maneuverability, making it far more nimble than an ARC-170, and the best choice for clone pilots to engage in dogfights against speedy vulture droids and tri-fighters. Bracketing the wedge-shaped V-wing are a set of flat wings extending above and below the ship. The wings are on articulated collars that allow them to rotate 90 degrees for landing. Two pairs of laser cannons are mounted on the wing struts, providing the V-wing with rapid-fire capability.

Deflector shield heat sinks

Thruster

Radiator panels aid heat disposal during intense activity

Spherical Q7-series astro-droid copilot aids navigation and in-flight maintenance

Sealed flightsuit equips pilot for possible ejection

Comm/scan processors

Forward sensors

Laser cannons swivel on wing hubs

Repulsorlift vanes

Laser cannon capacitors and power feed

Reactant tank

Shield projector units

Power lines to shield projectors

Wing radiators unfolded in flight position

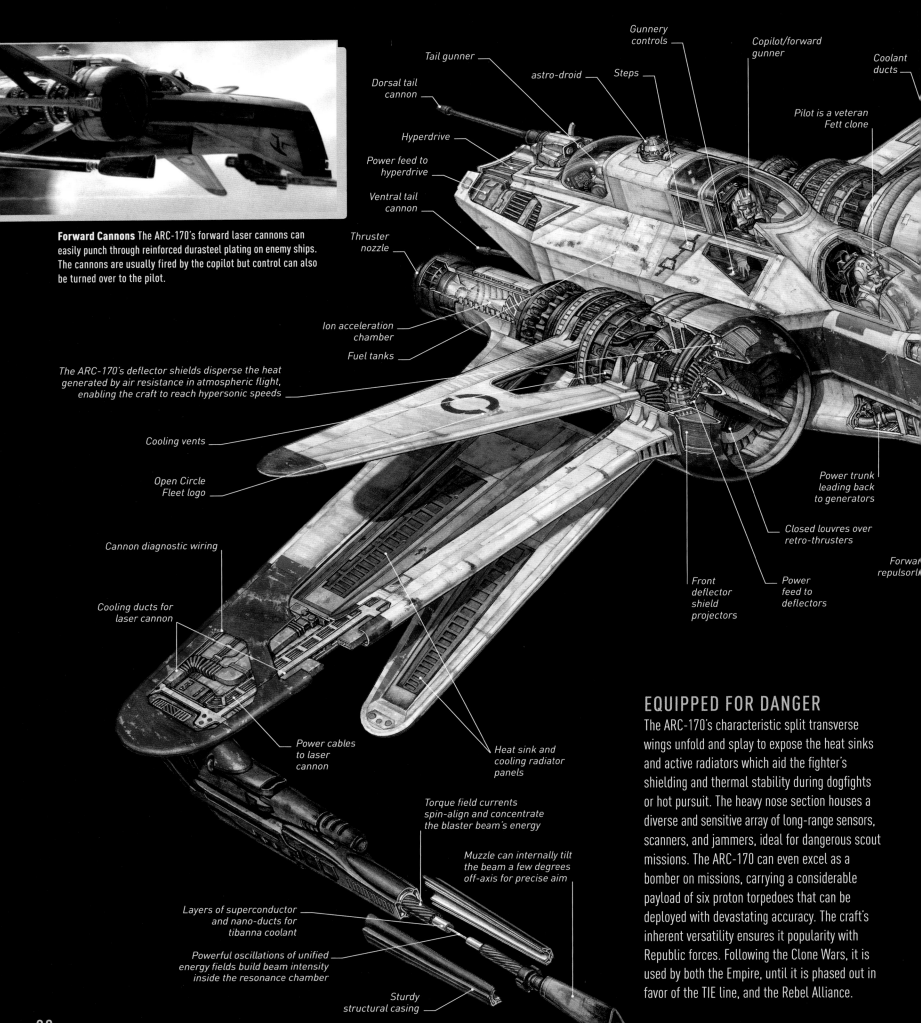

Forward Cannons The ARC-170's forward laser cannons can easily punch through reinforced durasteel plating on enemy ships. The cannons are usually fired by the copilot but control can also be turned over to the pilot.

Gunnery controls

Copilot/forward gunner

Tail gunner

astro-droid

Steps

Coolant ducts

Dorsal tail cannon

Pilot is a veteran Fett clone

Hyperdrive

Power feed to hyperdrive

Ventral tail cannon

Thruster nozzle

The ARC-170's deflector shields disperse the heat generated by air resistance in atmospheric flight, enabling the craft to reach hypersonic speeds

Ion acceleration chamber

Fuel tanks

Cooling vents

Open Circle Fleet logo

Power trunk leading back to generators

Closed louvres over retro-thrusters

Cannon diagnostic wiring

Cooling ducts for laser cannon

Front deflector shield projectors

Power feed to deflectors

Forwar repulsorl

Power cables to laser cannon

Heat sink and cooling radiator panels

Torque field currents spin-align and concentrate the blaster beam's energy

Muzzle can internally tilt the beam a few degrees off-axis for precise aim

Layers of superconductor and nano-ducts for tibanna coolant

Powerful oscillations of unified energy fields build beam intensity inside the resonance chamber

Sturdy structural casing

EQUIPPED FOR DANGER

The ARC-170's characteristic split transverse wings unfold and splay to expose the heat sinks and active radiators which aid the fighter's shielding and thermal stability during dogfights or hot pursuit. The heavy nose section houses a diverse and sensitive array of long-range sensors, scanners, and jammers, ideal for dangerous scout missions. The ARC-170 can even excel as a bomber on missions, carrying a considerable payload of six proton torpedoes that can be deployed with devastating accuracy. The craft's inherent versatility ensures it popularity with Republic forces. Following the Clone Wars, it is used by both the Empire, until it is phased out in favor of the TIE line, and the Rebel Alliance.

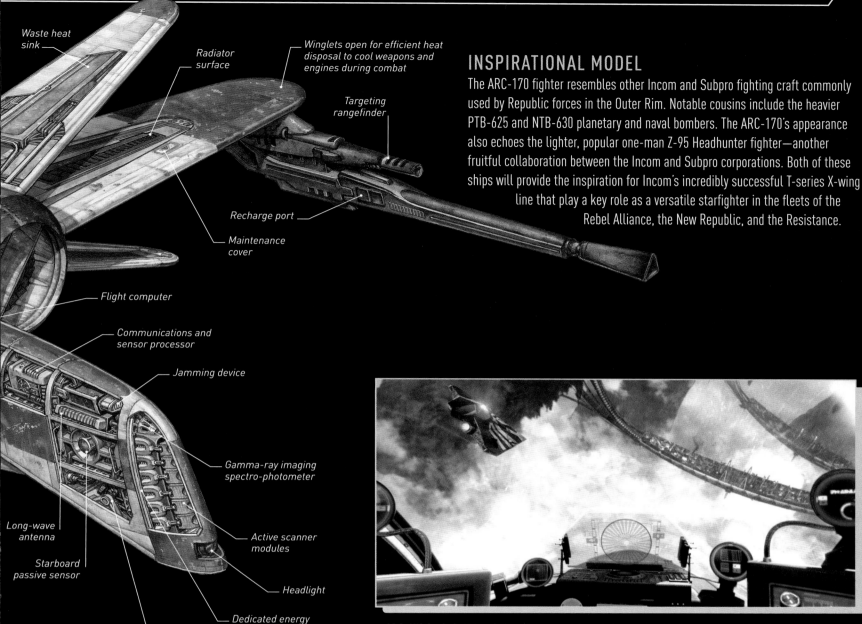

Waste heat sink

Radiator surface

Winglets open for efficient heat disposal to cool weapons and engines during combat

Targeting rangefinder

Recharge port

Maintenance cover

Flight computer

Communications and sensor processor

Jamming device

Gamma-ray imaging spectro-photometer

Long-wave antenna

Active scanner modules

Starboard passive sensor

Headlight

Dedicated energy receptor

Forward landing gear

INSPIRATIONAL MODEL

The ARC-170 fighter resembles other Incom and Subpro fighting craft commonly used by Republic forces in the Outer Rim. Notable cousins include the heavier PTB-625 and NTB-630 planetary and naval bombers. The ARC-170's appearance also echoes the lighter, popular one-man Z-95 Headhunter fighter—another fruitful collaboration between the Incom and Subpro corporations. Both of these ships will provide the inspiration for Incom's incredibly successful T-series X-wing line that play a key role as a versatile starfighter in the fleets of the Rebel Alliance, the New Republic, and the Resistance.

ARC-170 Cockpit Although the widely spaced data displays in the ARC-170 cockpit would baffle most humans, they were designed for clone pilots with superior peripheral vision.

ARC-170 FIGHTER

Rugged, versatile, and durable, the ARC-170 (Aggressive ReConnaissance) fighter embodies the latest developments in starfighter design. With its inbuilt hyperdrive and capacity for a droid navigator, this long-range craft is built to undertake the loneliest, independent, manned patrols or daring raids, as it penetrates deep into hostile sectors. Capable of lasting on its own supplies for five days, it vitally extends the reach of the Republic beyond warships and carrier-dependent fighters. The ARC-170's main laser cannons are uncommonly large and blazingly effective against larger opponents. Robust armor, shields, and tail guns improve the odds of survival when the ship is surrounded by dozens or even hundreds of light, evasive droid fighters. When piloted into battle alongside agile V-wings and Jedi Interceptors, ARC-170 squadrons complete a formidable strike-force mix.

Squad Seven The foremost ARC-170 squadron in the Open Circle Fleet, Squad Seven is led by a clone commander who flies under the call sign "Odd Ball."

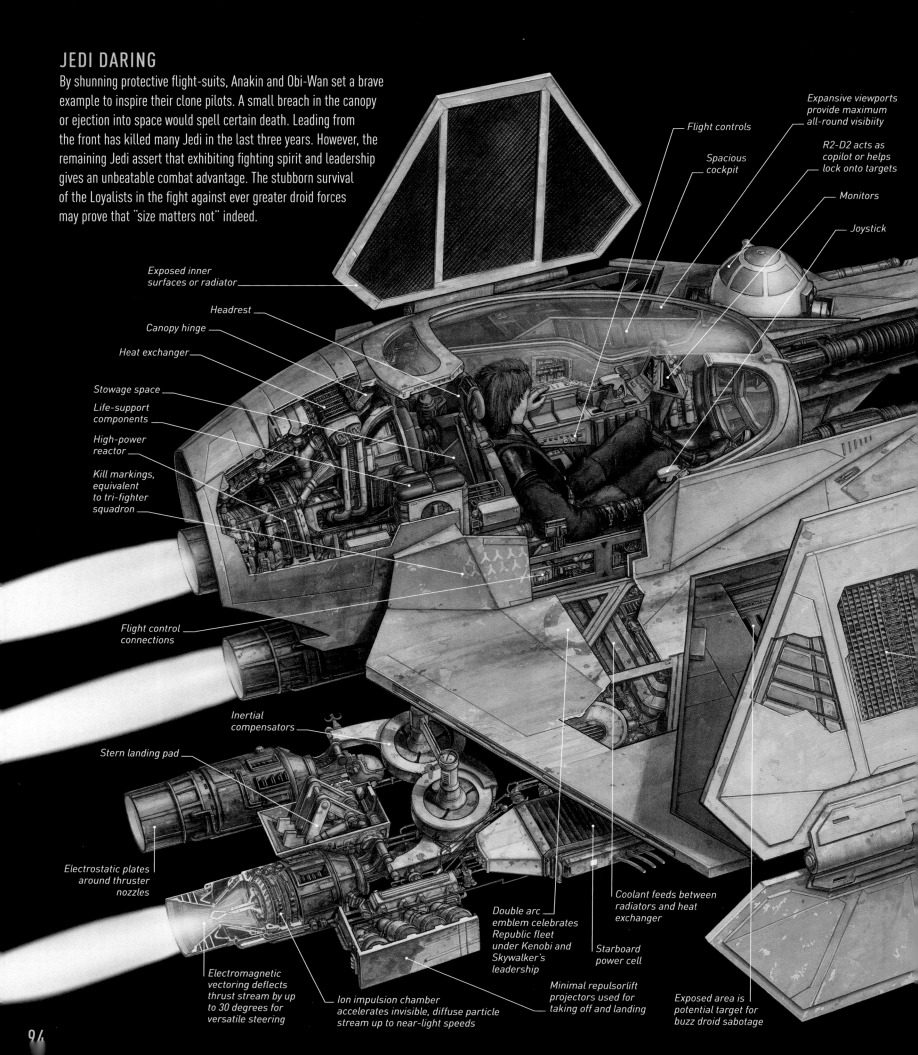

JEDI DARING

By shunning protective flight-suits, Anakin and Obi-Wan set a brave example to inspire their clone pilots. A small breach in the canopy or ejection into space would spell certain death. Leading from the front has killed many Jedi in the last three years. However, the remaining Jedi assert that exhibiting fighting spirit and leadership gives an unbeatable combat advantage. The stubborn survival of the Loyalists in the fight against ever greater droid forces may prove that "size matters not" indeed.

Flight controls

Spacious cockpit

Expansive viewports provide maximum all-round visibiity

R2-D2 acts as copilot or helps lock onto targets

Monitors

Joystick

Exposed inner surfaces or radiator

Headrest

Canopy hinge

Heat exchanger

Stowage space

Life-support components

High-power reactor

Kill markings, equivalent to tri-fighter squadron

Flight control connections

Inertial compensators

Stern landing pad

Electrostatic plates around thruster nozzles

Electromagnetic vectoring deflects thrust stream by up to 30 degrees for versatile steering

Ion impulsion chamber accelerates invisible, diffuse particle stream up to near-light speeds

Double arc emblem celebrates Republic fleet under Kenobi and Skywalker's leadership

Minimal repulsorlift projectors used for taking off and landing

Starboard power cell

Coolant feeds between radiators and heat exchanger

Exposed area is potential target for buzz droid sabotage

JEDI INTERCEPTOR

Racing home from the brutal Outer Rim sieges to rescue the kidnapped Supreme Chancellor Palpatine, Obi-Wan Kenobi and Anakin Skywalker waste no time scrambling to their fighters. Leading the Republic's aerial forces in their Jedi Interceptors, they flit through the battle-zone with astonishing agility. Their spacecraft's compact design is suited to the Force-assisted tactical abilities of Jedi pilots—heavy flight instruments, sensors, and shields are unnecessary. Over the last three years, the distinctive Interceptor profile has become a symbol of authority and hope for the Republic's clone forces, and a frustrating apparition to the Separatists.

Long barrel provides amplified yield and exceptional range

Laser cannons fire glowing, strobing beams of massless energy

Starboard bow landing pad

Lid over pop-up headlight

Hydraulic rams actuate landing gear

Emergency toolkit

Ion cannon fires plasma bursts causing electric disruption to target

Energy capacitors

Hidden outer radiator surface

Radiator wings open during intense dogfight action

Anakin's Eta-2 was painted yellow at his request, allegedly in tribute to his boyhood podracer

Superficial wing armor

AGILE ADVERSARY

In the last battles of the Clone Wars, some Jedi Knights fly one of the lightest, most agile fighters designed in millennia. Hardly larger than the average airspeeder, the Eta-2 *Actis* Interceptor enjoys superior speed and maneuverability compared to the already tiny Delta-7 *Aethersprite*. Compacting a fighter's intense power into a tiny hull made overheating a challenge—which was met by an extensive system of heat sinks, pumps, and radiator wings. The Interceptor's large laser cannons fire intense beams, but its modest capacitors limit continuous fire. This is not usually a handicap for Jedi pilots, who rarely waste a shot.

Customized Controls Each Jedi Interceptor's cockpit controls and data displays are custom fitted for the individual pilot.

Jedi Wingmates Because Obi-Wan Kenobi strongly dislikes piloting, and Anakin has always been a natural behind the controls of vehicles, their relationship as master and apprentice becomes somewhat reversed in space combat.

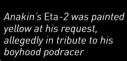

HYPERDRIVE BOOSTERS

Because many Republic starfighters are too small to safely contain a hyperdrive, the fighters must connect to external hyperdrive boosters. Kuat Systems Engineering designed the Delta-7 *Aethersprite* light interceptor, Alpha-3 Nimbus V-wing starfighter, and Eta-2 *Actis* Interceptor with docking clamps for hyperdrive booster rings, and data-feeds that enable the starfighters' astromechs to transmit hyperspace coordinates to the rings' computers. The rings are manufactured by TransGalMeg Industries, Inc. of the Rayter sector, a subcontractor of Kuat.

ORBITAL DEPOTS

The Republic Navy has pools of hyperdrive booster rings stationed in orbit around Coruscant and other worlds, for the use of Jedi starfighters in their fleet. The rings are serviced by technical support droids, which are engineered to operate in zero gravity.

SYLIURE-31 BOOSTER

Powered by twin reactors and ion drives, the Syliure-31 hyperspace docking ring is a class of hyperdrive booster that contains "hypermatter," providing ballast for the attached starfighter during the jump to hyperspace. When traveling at hyperspeed, shields protect the ship and booster against potentially fatal collisions with interstellar gas and dark particles. Stasis fields also act to slow the passage of onboard time, ensuring that the pilot ages only as fast as the rest of the galaxy.

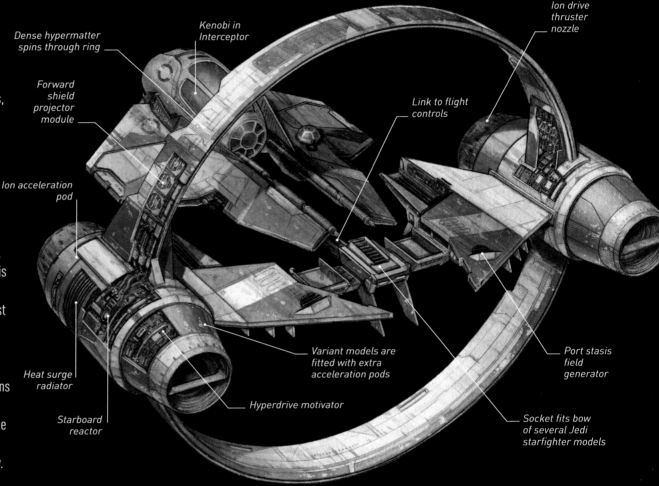

Dense hypermatter spins through ring

Kenobi in Interceptor

Ion drive thruster nozzle

Forward shield projector module

Link to flight controls

Ion acceleration pod

Variant models are fitted with extra acceleration pods

Port stasis field generator

Heat surge radiator

Hyperdrive motivator

Socket fits bow of several Jedi starfighter models

Starboard reactor

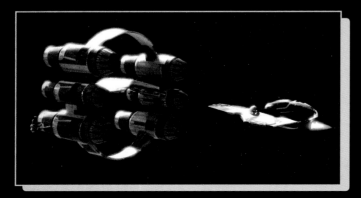

Docking Procedure As the starfighter glides toward the booster ring, the ring's compact tractor beam projectors help guide the fighter directly into the docking socket.

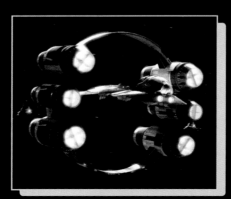

Two orbital tech-support droids monitor the docking procedure, and ensure that the starfighter secures to the ring properly.

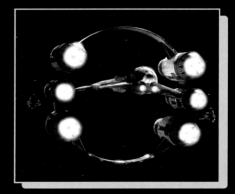

Conceived as an improvement on the Syliure-31 hyperspace docking ring, the Syliure-45 has four additional ion acceleration pods.

CONFEDERACY BUZZ DROID

During the Battle of Coruscant, Confederacy tri-fighters defend General Grievous's stricken flagship by harassing Jedi attackers with special new ordnance. Launched from modified tri-fighters and other vessels, these guided buzz droid missiles are lethal, and able to outturn and outrun nearly any manned starship. But their aim is not a direct kill. Instead of detonating on impact, the missile delivers a swarm of buzz droids: mechanical gremlins expertly programmed in the fine arts of technological sabotage.

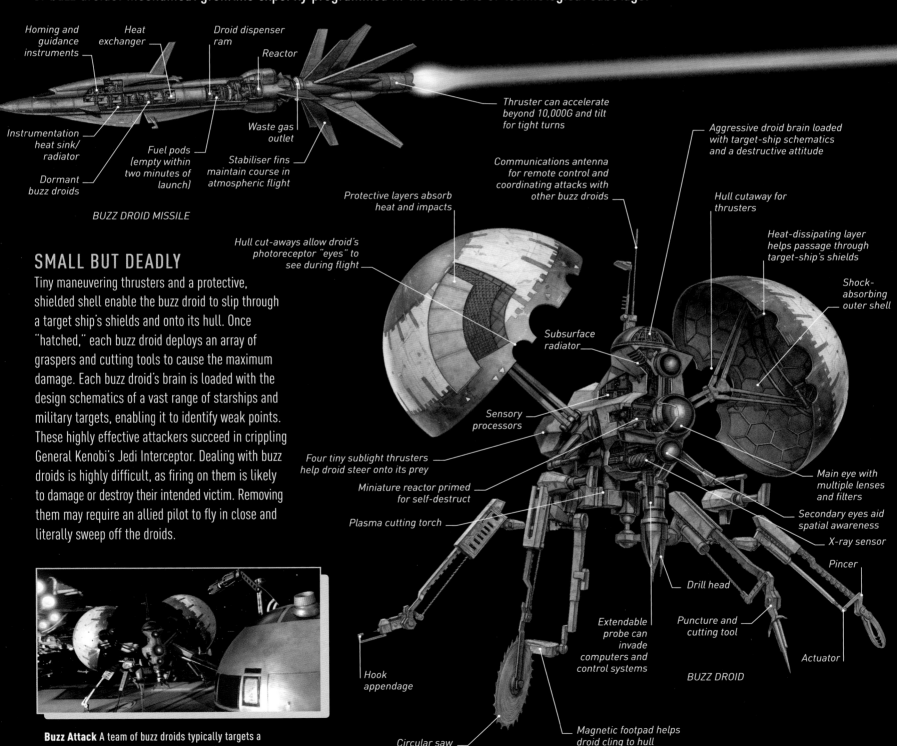

Homing and guidance instruments

Heat exchanger

Droid dispenser ram

Reactor

Instrumentation heat sink/ radiator

Waste gas outlet

Fuel pods (empty within two minutes of launch)

Stabiliser fins maintain course in atmospheric flight

Dormant buzz droids

BUZZ DROID MISSILE

Thruster can accelerate beyond 10,000G and tilt for tight turns

Communications antenna for remote control and coordinating attacks with other buzz droids

Protective layers absorb heat and impacts

Aggressive droid brain loaded with target-ship schematics and a destructive attitude

Hull cutaway for thrusters

Heat-dissipating layer helps passage through target-ship's shields

Shock-absorbing outer shell

Hull cut-aways allow droid's photoreceptor "eyes" to see during flight

Subsurface radiator

Sensory processors

Main eye with multiple lenses and filters

Secondary eyes aid spatial awareness

X-ray sensor

Pincer

Four tiny sublight thrusters help droid steer onto its prey

Miniature reactor primed for self-destruct

Plasma cutting torch

Drill head

Extendable probe can invade computers and control systems

Puncture and cutting tool

Actuator

BUZZ DROID

Hook appendage

Circular saw

Magnetic footpad helps droid cling to hull

SMALL BUT DEADLY

Tiny maneuvering thrusters and a protective, shielded shell enable the buzz droid to slip through a target ship's shields and onto its hull. Once "hatched," each buzz droid deploys an array of graspers and cutting tools to cause the maximum damage. Each buzz droid's brain is loaded with the design schematics of a vast range of starships and military targets, enabling it to identify weak points. These highly effective attackers succeed in crippling General Kenobi's Jedi Interceptor. Dealing with buzz droids is highly difficult, as firing on them is likely to damage or destroy their intended victim. Removing them may require an allied pilot to fly in close and literally sweep off the droids.

Buzz Attack A team of buzz droids typically targets a starfighter's astromech first, and can easily carve up a starfighter's hull in less than a minute.

TRI-FIGHTER

Cunning and eerily determined, droid tri-fighters are frightening new defenders of the Separatist battle fleets. These fast, agile space-superiority fighters are built to excel in dogfighting. Equipped with more advanced droid brains than common Trade Federation Vulture droid fighters, tri-fighters pose a challenge to even the best organic starpilots. They may be outrun by high-speed Jedi Interceptors, but they are bulkier and more heavily armed, which makes them a force to be reckoned with.

Tri-Fighters Over Coruscant Chasing down Republic starfighters during an orbital battle, a tri-fighter aims its cannons and opens fire.

COLICOID DESIGN

The tri-fighter's fearsome appearance and predatory programming is the work of the Colicoids—the creators of the Trade Federation's droideka heavy infantry. The ridged, three-armed design is based on the skull features of a terrifying prehistoric predator native to the planet Colla IV. Three independent thrusters give the craft its agility, and a powerful reactor and control/comms transceiver provide unusual range for a droid fighter.

Six re-arranged triangles from the Confederacy emblem signify the tri-fighter's squadron

Aggressive droid brain surrounding nose cannon's capacitor

COORDINATED ATTACK

Unlike Trade Federation Vulture droid starfighters, which are controlled entirely by signals from a Droid Control Ship computer, tri-fighters have droid brains engineered with basic heuristic processors, which enable them to analyze, anticipate, and mimic enemy tactics. Tri-fighters can enter combat independently or link their intelligence systems to coordinate multi-fighter attacks on a single target.

Droid Onslaught A trio of tri-fighters poses a definite threat to a single starfighter, although Jedi pilots can usually evade or destroy them.

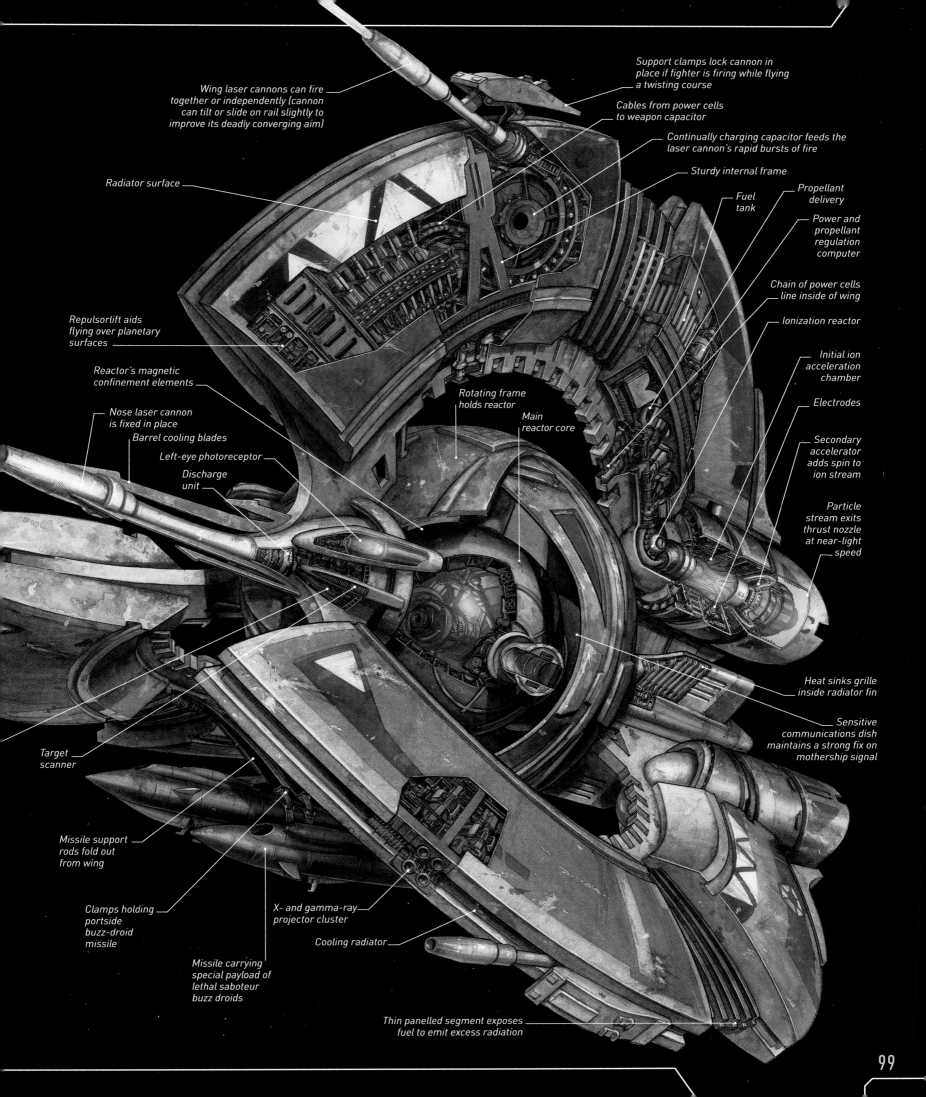

Wing laser cannons can fire together or independently (cannon can tilt or slide on rail slightly to improve its deadly converging aim)

Support clamps lock cannon in place if fighter is firing while flying a twisting course

Cables from power cells to weapon capacitor

Continually charging capacitor feeds the laser cannon's rapid bursts of fire

Radiator surface

Sturdy internal frame

Fuel tank

Propellant delivery

Power and propellant regulation computer

Chain of power cells line inside of wing

Repulsorlift aids flying over planetary surfaces

Ionization reactor

Reactor's magnetic confinement elements

Rotating frame holds reactor

Main reactor core

Initial ion acceleration chamber

Electrodes

Nose laser cannon is fixed in place

Barrel cooling blades

Left-eye photoreceptor

Discharge unit

Secondary accelerator adds spin to ion stream

Particle stream exits thrust nozzle at near-light speed

Heat sinks grille inside radiator fin

Sensitive communications dish maintains a strong fix on mothership signal

Target scanner

Missile support rods fold out from wing

Clamps holding portside buzz-droid missile

X- and gamma-ray projector cluster

Cooling radiator

Missile carrying special payload of lethal saboteur buzz droids

Thin panelled segment exposes fuel to emit excess radiation

99

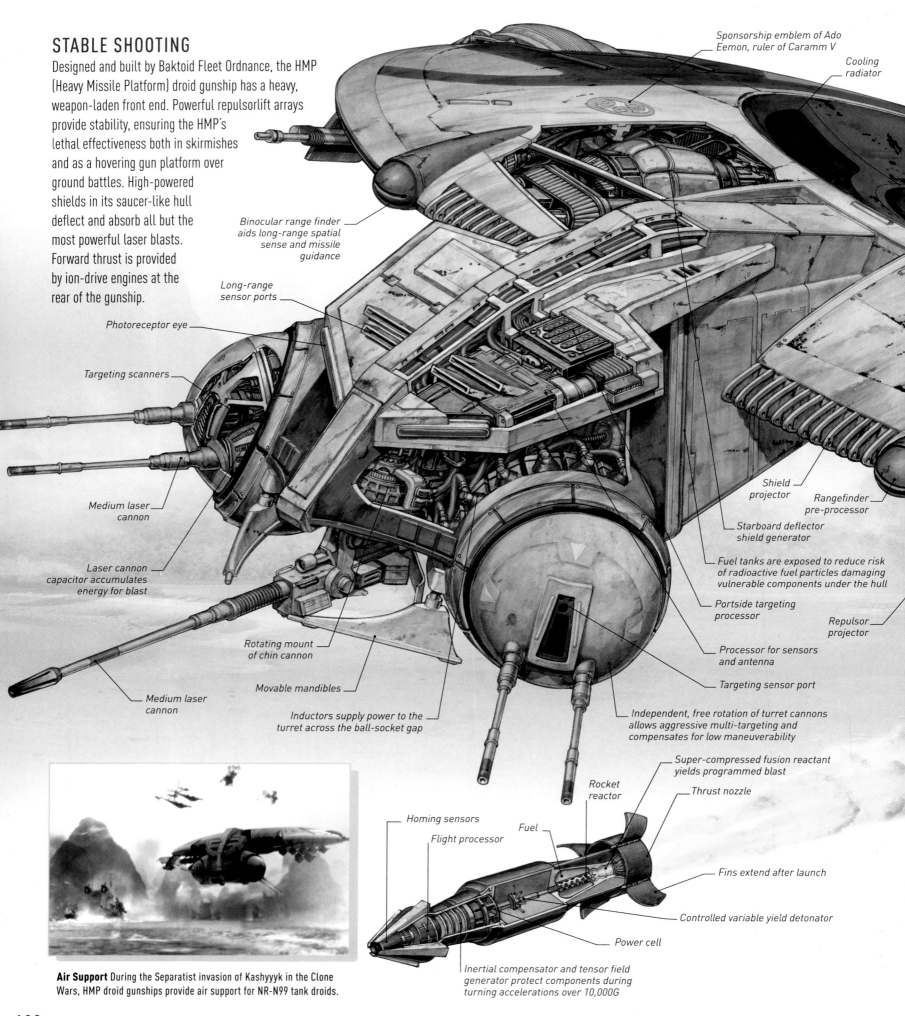

STABLE SHOOTING

Designed and built by Baktoid Fleet Ordnance, the HMP (Heavy Missile Platform) droid gunship has a heavy, weapon-laden front end. Powerful repulsorlift arrays provide stability, ensuring the HMP's lethal effectiveness both in skirmishes and as a hovering gun platform over ground battles. High-powered shields in its saucer-like hull deflect and absorb all but the most powerful laser blasts. Forward thrust is provided by ion-drive engines at the rear of the gunship.

Sponsorship emblem of Ado Eemon, ruler of Caramm V

Cooling radiator

Binocular range finder aids long-range spatial sense and missile guidance

Long-range sensor ports

Photoreceptor eye

Targeting scanners

Medium laser cannon

Laser cannon capacitor accumulates energy for blast

Medium laser cannon

Rotating mount of chin cannon

Movable mandibles

Inductors supply power to the turret across the ball-socket gap

Shield projector

Rangefinder pre-processor

Starboard deflector shield generator

Fuel tanks are exposed to reduce risk of radioactive fuel particles damaging vulnerable components under the hull

Portside targeting processor

Repulsor projector

Processor for sensors and antenna

Targeting sensor port

Independent, free rotation of turret cannons allows aggressive multi-targeting and compensates for low maneuverability

Homing sensors

Flight processor

Fuel

Rocket reactor

Super-compressed fusion reactant yields programmed blast

Thrust nozzle

Fins extend after launch

Controlled variable yield detonator

Power cell

Inertial compensator and tensor field generator protect components during turning accelerations over 10,000G

Air Support During the Separatist invasion of Kashyyyk in the Clone Wars, HMP droid gunships provide air support for NR-N99 tank droids.

100

DROID GUNSHIP

Ominous in appearance and relentless in battle, the droid gunship is a powerful, well-shielded missile platform. Designed for air strikes within planetary atmospheres, it moves at relatively slow speeds and possesses only average maneuverability, but this is compensated for by its awesome firepower. Two laser-cannon turrets can track targets independently, while torpedoes and missiles prove devastating against ground-based installations, attack vehicles, and fast short-range targets. The wing modules can carry extra laser cannons, concussion bombs, and upgraded targeting scanners. The droid gunship is truly a symbol of Separatist military might.

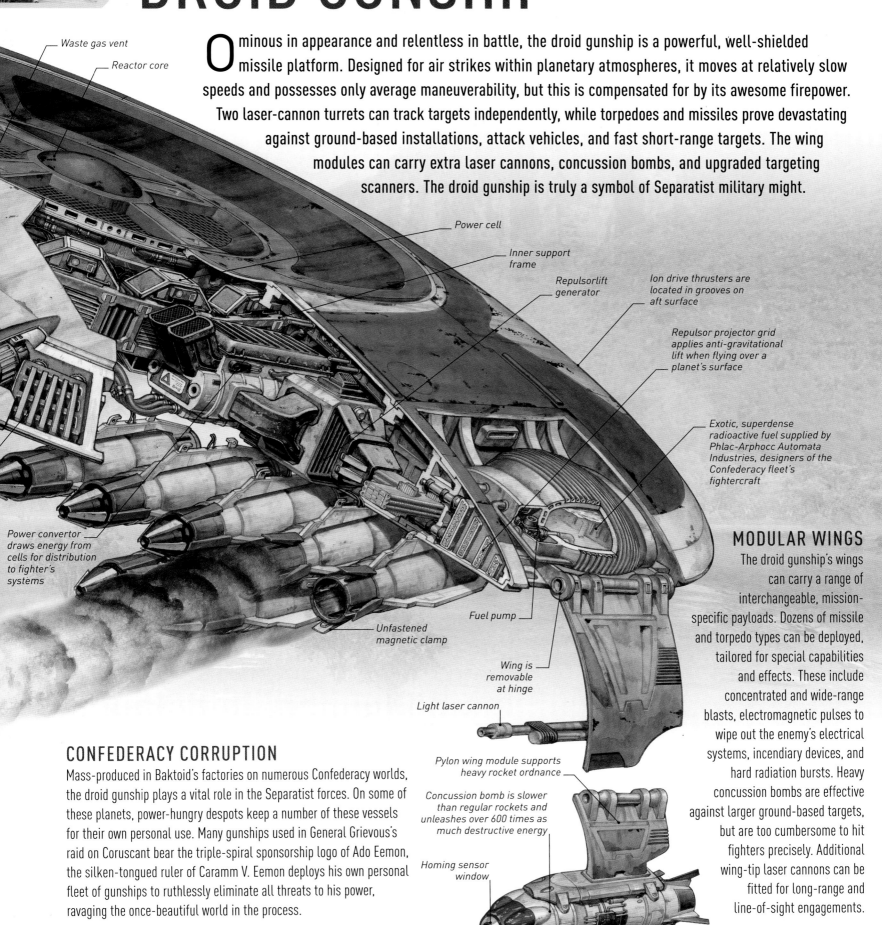

Waste gas vent

Reactor core

Power cell

Inner support frame

Repulsorlift generator

Ion drive thrusters are located in grooves on aft surface

Repulsor projector grid applies anti-gravitational lift when flying over a planet's surface

Exotic, superdense radioactive fuel supplied by Phlac-Arphocc Automata Industries, designers of the Confederacy fleet's fightercraft

Power convertor draws energy from cells for distribution to fighter's systems

Unfastened magnetic clamp

Fuel pump

Wing is removable at hinge

Light laser cannon

Pylon wing module supports heavy rocket ordnance

Concussion bomb is slower than regular rockets and unleashes over 600 times as much destructive energy

Homing sensor window

MODULAR WINGS

The droid gunship's wings can carry a range of interchangeable, mission-specific payloads. Dozens of missile and torpedo types can be deployed, tailored for special capabilities and effects. These include concentrated and wide-range blasts, electromagnetic pulses to wipe out the enemy's electrical systems, incendiary devices, and hard radiation bursts. Heavy concussion bombs are effective against larger ground-based targets, but are too cumbersome to hit fighters precisely. Additional wing-tip laser cannons can be fitted for long-range and line-of-sight engagements.

CONFEDERACY CORRUPTION

Mass-produced in Baktoid's factories on numerous Confederacy worlds, the droid gunship plays a vital role in the Separatist forces. On some of these planets, power-hungry despots keep a number of these vessels for their own personal use. Many gunships used in General Grievous's raid on Coruscant bear the triple-spiral sponsorship logo of Ado Eemon, the silken-tongued ruler of Caramm V. Eemon deploys his own personal fleet of gunships to ruthlessly eliminate all threats to his power, ravaging the once-beautiful world in the process.

JUGGERNAUT

Juggernaut! The very name of these rolling giants calls up memories of crushing defeat for the galaxy's quintillions of battle droids and their Separatist masters. Each of the Galactic Republic's HAVw A6 Juggernauts is a monstrous, ten-wheeled, armored box, built around a powerful reactor core and engine, with blasters and grenade launchers on every side. As well as being a front-line assault vehicle, these hulks provide secure shelter and transport for a company of dedicated clone troopers. Rugged and powerful, Juggernauts are the well-chosen backbone of the clone armies. Under the command of Jedi Master Yoda, they form the most integral part of a dogged campaign to eject battle droid invaders from the strategic Wookiee world of Kashyyyk.

ROLLING WAR-MACHINE

Although wheeled transport may seem like a graceless system from a prehistoric age, the large surface of the Juggernaut's wheels helps to reduce ground pressure, making the vehicle less prone to sinking in soft soil than heavy walkers. Direct ground contact also protects it from electromagnetic attacks and shield discharges, and it can stop and turn in a smaller radius than any repulsorlift craft. Nearly impenetrable armor and an arsenal of beam and missile weapons make the Juggernaut more than a match for most of the Separatists' ground-based war machines.

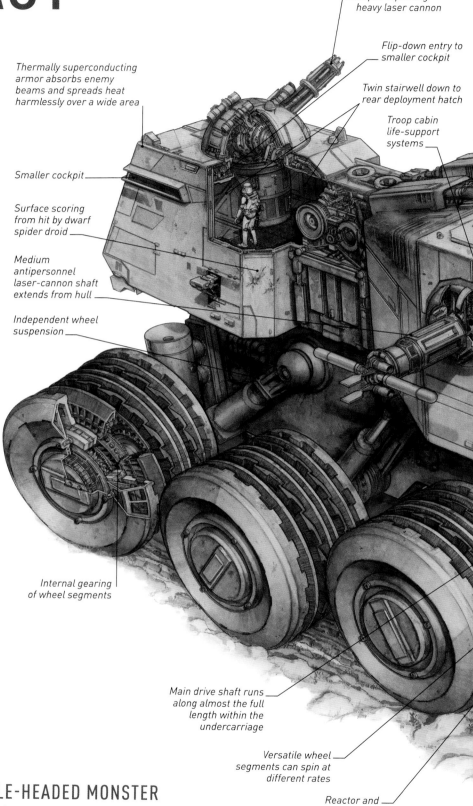

Rapid-repeating heavy laser cannon

Flip-down entry to smaller cockpit

Twin stairwell down to rear deployment hatch

Troop cabin life-support systems

Thermally superconducting armor absorbs enemy beams and spreads heat harmlessly over a wide area

Smaller cockpit

Surface scoring from hit by dwarf spider droid

Medium antipersonnel laser-cannon shaft extends from hull

Independent wheel suspension

Internal gearing of wheel segments

Main drive shaft runs along almost the full length within the undercarriage

Versatile wheel segments can spin at different rates

Reactor and engine systems

Troop Transport Nicknamed the "rolling slab," the Juggernaut's modifiable interior typically carries 50 troops and their gear, but can hold as many as 300.

DOUBLE-HEADED MONSTER

Each of a Juggernaut's wheels consists of three versatile, independently spinning segments, which enable the hulking vehicle to move smoothly across even the most inhospitable terrain. The vehicle can also reverse direction easily, moving equally well in forward and reverse gears. Either cockpit can assume full control, which has led to much debate among Juggernaut clone crews as to which cockpit is the true "front" end.

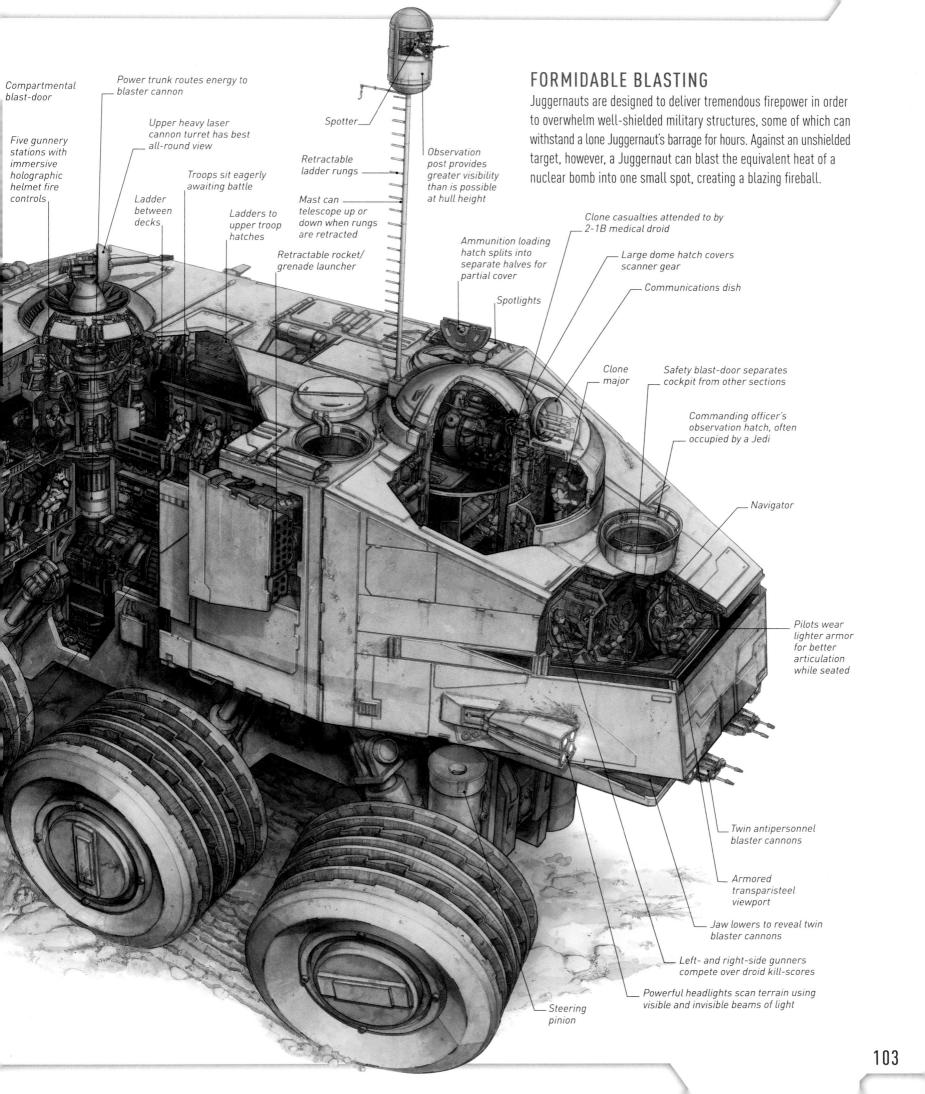

Compartmental blast-door

Power trunk routes energy to blaster cannon

Upper heavy laser cannon turret has best all-round view

Five gunnery stations with immersive holographic helmet fire controls

Ladder between decks

Troops sit eagerly awaiting battle

Ladders to upper troop hatches

Spotter

Retractable ladder rungs

Observation post provides greater visibility than is possible at hull height

Mast can telescope up or down when rungs are retracted

Retractable rocket/grenade launcher

FORMIDABLE BLASTING

Juggernauts are designed to deliver tremendous firepower in order to overwhelm well-shielded military structures, some of which can withstand a lone Juggernaut's barrage for hours. Against an unshielded target, however, a Juggernaut can blast the equivalent heat of a nuclear bomb into one small spot, creating a blazing fireball.

Ammunition loading hatch splits into separate halves for partial cover

Spotlights

Clone casualties attended to by 2-1B medical droid

Large dome hatch covers scanner gear

Communications dish

Clone major

Safety blast-door separates cockpit from other sections

Commanding officer's observation hatch, often occupied by a Jedi

Navigator

Pilots wear lighter armor for better articulation while seated

Twin antipersonnel blaster cannons

Armored transparisteel viewport

Jaw lowers to reveal twin blaster cannons

Left- and right-side gunners compete over droid kill-scores

Powerful headlights scan terrain using visible and invisible beams of light

Steering pinion

AT-RT

The All Terrain Recon Transport (AT-RT) is an armed, mobile platform for a single soldier on a patrol or reconnaissance mission. These walkers support policing actions in dense civilian areas, and are also used in cooling battle zones. A lightweight body makes it faster than the rarer one-man AT-PT (All Terrain Personal Transport). Lacking an enclosed cabin, the driver enjoys a clear view, but is exposed to small-arms fire. The AT-RT's blaster cannon is devastating against infantry, but weak against the armor of tank, spider, and crab droids.

ELEVATED WARRIORS

With the AT-RT's elevated view and nose-mounted repeating laser, a clone pilot is able to spot and attack long-distance targets that might go unseen by allied foot soldiers. Pilots are trained to serve as lone scouts or work in teams, and a squad of four AT-RTs can easily overpower a single Trade Federation Armored Assault Tank (AAT). Hand-held controls, foot-pedals, and a posture-sensitive saddle serve as combined steering mechanisms for the AT-RT, and are designed to operate with intuitive ease. A motion-detection scanner as well as data displays for numerous sensors help the AT-RT pilot sight targets in various environments.

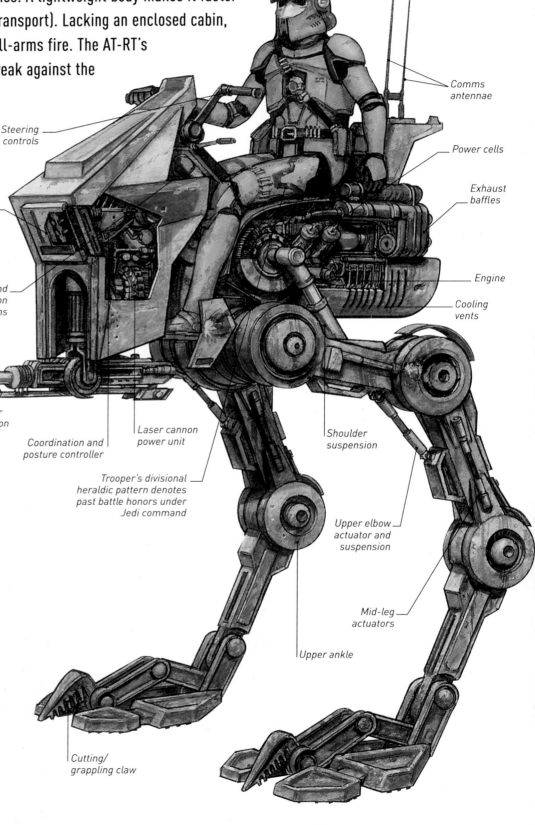

Enhanced
helmet comlink

Comms
antennae

Power cells

Exhaust
baffles

Steering
controls

Engine

Terrain
scanner

Cooling
vents

Control and
navigation
systems

Laser
cannon

Coordination and
posture controller

Laser cannon
power unit

Shoulder
suspension

Trooper's divisional
heraldic pattern denotes
past battle honors under
Jedi command

Upper elbow
actuator and
suspension

Mid-leg
actuators

Upper ankle

Cutting/
grappling claw

Night Patrol AT-RTs are equipped with headlights and floodlights that can be adjusted to cut through dense fog, snow, and dust.

COMMERCE GUILD SUPPORT DESTROYER

Separatist *Recusant*-class light destroyers are mass-produced by zealous workers led by Techno Union foremen, using materials from many Commerce Guild worlds. Since the beginning of the Clone Wars, countless numbers of these support vessels have been built, destroyed in battle, and replaced. Lone *Recusant*-class ships often carry out attacks on Loyalist commercial shipping, but their real effectiveness becomes apparent when deployed in large numbers. Four to six can outgun a Republic *Venator*-class or *Victory*-class Star Destroyer, although it would take 1,000 *Recusant*-class ships to take on Kuat Drive Yard's *Mandator-II* Star Dreadnaught.

Collision Alert Because most Commerce Guild light destroyers are crewed by droids without any sense of self-preservation, they rarely hesitate to deliberately ram Republic Star Destroyers.

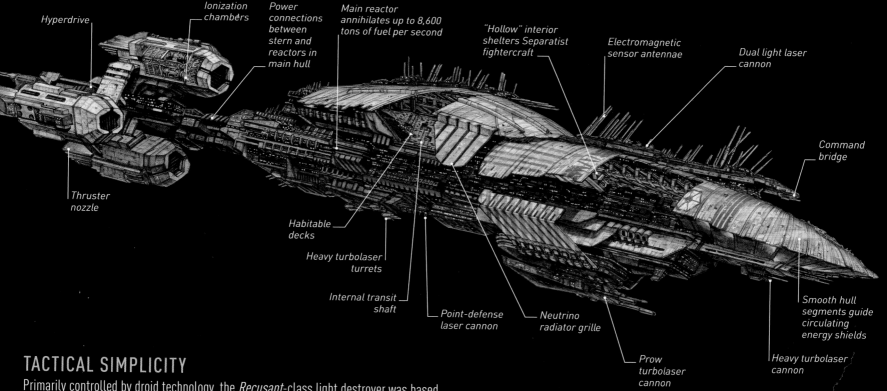

Hyperdrive

Ionization chambers

Power connections between stern and reactors in main hull

Main reactor annihilates up to 8,600 tons of fuel per second

"Hollow" interior shelters Separatist fightercraft

Electromagnetic sensor antennae

Dual light laser cannon

Command bridge

Thruster nozzle

Habitable decks

Heavy turbolaser turrets

Internal transit shaft

Point-defense laser cannon

Neutrino radiator grille

Prow turbolaser cannon

Smooth hull segments guide circulating energy shields

Heavy turbolaser cannon

TACTICAL SIMPLICITY

Primarily controlled by droid technology, the *Recusant*-class light destroyer was based on technical schematics that Quarren Separatists stole from Mon Calamari designers. The destroyer's most significant feature is its strong armament, which includes heavy turbolasers in a fixed mount on the ship's prow. The destroyer's only weakness may be its droid brain's single-mindedness, as it is compelled to stubbornly attack a single target while ignoring all others until the target is destroyed or disabled.

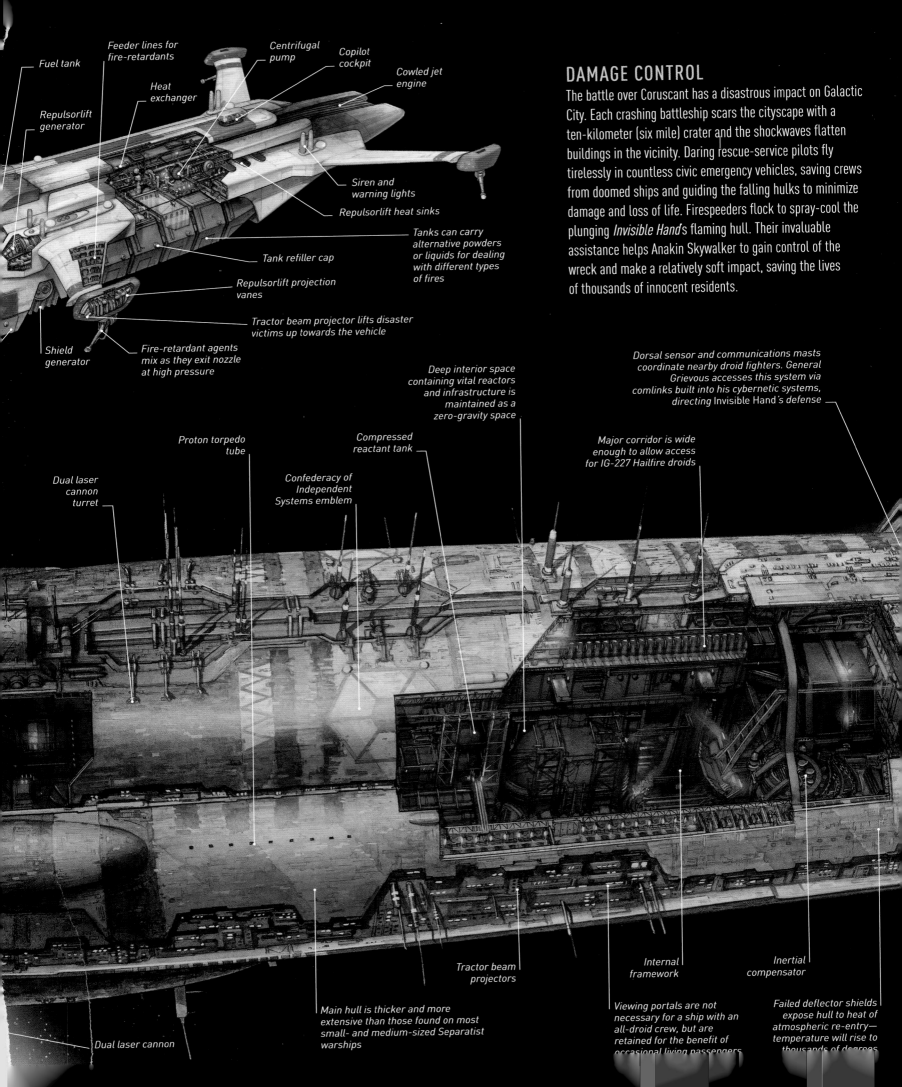

Fuel tank

Feeder lines for fire-retardants

Centrifugal pump

Copilot cockpit

Cowled jet engine

Heat exchanger

Repulsorlift generator

Siren and warning lights

Repulsorlift heat sinks

Tanks can carry alternative powders or liquids for dealing with different types of fires

Tank refiller cap

Repulsorlift projection vanes

Tractor beam projector lifts disaster victims up towards the vehicle

Shield generator

Fire-retardant agents mix as they exit nozzle at high pressure

DAMAGE CONTROL

The battle over Coruscant has a disastrous impact on Galactic City. Each crashing battleship scars the cityscape with a ten-kilometer (six mile) crater and the shockwaves flatten buildings in the vicinity. Daring rescue-service pilots fly tirelessly in countless civic emergency vehicles, saving crews from doomed ships and guiding the falling hulks to minimize damage and loss of life. Firespeeders flock to spray-cool the plunging *Invisible Hand*'s flaming hull. Their invaluable assistance helps Anakin Skywalker to gain control of the wreck and make a relatively soft impact, saving the lives of thousands of innocent residents.

Dorsal sensor and communications masts coordinate nearby droid fighters. General Grievous accesses this system via comlinks built into his cybernetic systems, directing *Invisible Hand*'s defense

Deep interior space containing vital reactors and infrastructure is maintained as a zero-gravity space

Major corridor is wide enough to allow access for IG-227 Hailfire droids

Proton torpedo tube

Compressed reactant tank

Confederacy of Independent Systems emblem

Dual laser cannon turret

Tractor beam projectors

Internal framework

Inertial compensator

Dual laser cannon

Main hull is thicker and more extensive than those found on most small- and medium-sized Separatist warships

Viewing portals are not necessary for a ship with an all-droid crew, but are retained for the benefit of occasional living passengers

Failed deflector shields expose hull to heat of atmospheric re-entry—temperature will rise to thousands of degrees

INVISIBLE HAND

In a bold strike at the galactic capital Coruscant, raiders from the Separatist flagship *Invisible Hand* have abducted Supreme Chancellor Palpatine. The vessel waits in orbit with the Confederacy fleet as the droid kidnappers return with their valuable prize—but before they can flee, thousands of Republic battleships engage the craft, trapping it in an upper atmospheric combat within the planet's defensive shield. *Invisible Hand* is badly damaged by enemy guns, so Jedi rescuers Obi-Wan Kenobi and Anakin Skywalker must find Palpatine in a rapidly decaying spacewreck. Ruptured compartments are flooded with fluidic coolants and propellants laced with invisible, exotic hypermatter fuels. Artificial gravity, tensor fields, and inertial compensators all begin to fail, as the crippled ship threatens to tear itself apart. The battle rages on, until *Invisible Hand* begins its meteoric fall toward the surface of Coruscant.

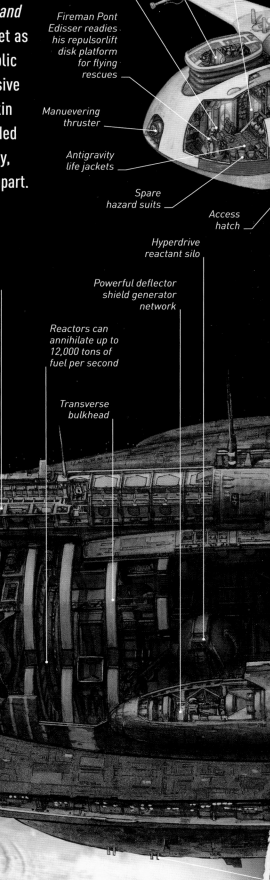

Fireship captain Cott Theefe flies to the aid of the failing Separatist flagship

Medical bay door

Vertical access to upper deck

Fireman Pont Edisser readies his repulsorlift disk platform for flying rescues

Manuevering thruster

Antigravity life jackets

Spare hazard suits

Access hatch

Hyperdrive reactant silo

Powerful deflector shield generator network

Reactors can annihilate up to 12,000 tons of fuel per second

Transverse bulkhead

Chancellor Palpatine and the Jedi prisoners are brought to the bridge to face General Grievous as the ship begins its fiery descent toward Coruscant

Empty escape pod bays, jettisoned by General Grievous to spite his enemies

Invisible Hand is under the overall control of General Grievous, commander of the Confederacy's droid armies

Corridor

Command bridge

Subsidiary reactor

BANKING CLAN FRIGATE

The Banking Clan's *Munificent*-class star frigates are combat-communication ships, which assist with the navigation and coordination of Separatist fleets deep in hostile space. Powerful antennae channel hyperwave supralight transceivers, while jamming devices hinder enemy sensors and targeting systems. Two huge turbolaser cannons can blast-melt an ice-moon measuring 1,000 kilometers (621 miles) in diameter, or pierce the shields of a 10 km-wide (6.2 mile-wide) Grade III battle station. These ships once guarded banker's vaults on Outer Rim worlds and menaced planets heavily in debt to the Banking Clan. Now they escort and coordinate Separatist fleet actions, such as attacks on the interstellar HoloNet relays, which consequently blind and isolate Loyalist forces.

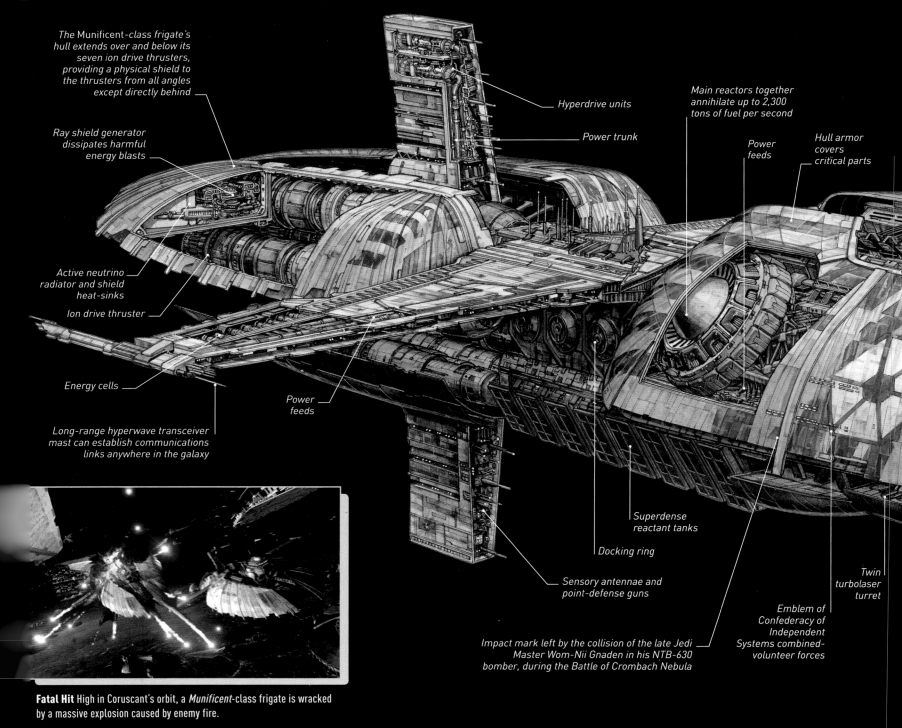

The *Munificent-class* frigate's hull extends over and below its seven ion drive thrusters, providing a physical shield to the thrusters from all angles except directly behind

Ray shield generator dissipates harmful energy blasts

Active neutrino radiator and shield heat-sinks

Ion drive thruster

Energy cells

Long-range hyperwave transceiver mast can establish communications links anywhere in the galaxy

Power feeds

Hyperdrive units

Power trunk

Main reactors together annihilate up to 2,300 tons of fuel per second

Power feeds

Hull armor covers critical parts

Superdense reactant tanks

Docking ring

Sensory antennae and point-defense guns

Twin turbolaser turret

Emblem of Confederacy of Independent Systems combined-volunteer forces

Impact mark left by the collision of the late Jedi Master Wom-Nii Gnaden in his NTB-630 bomber, during the Battle of Crombach Nebula

Fatal Hit High in Coruscant's orbit, a *Munificent*-class frigate is wracked by a massive explosion caused by enemy fire.

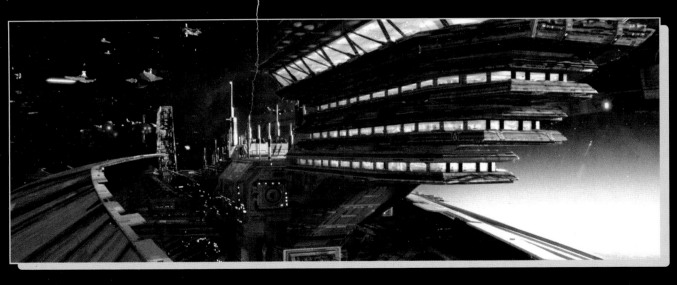

Frigate Bridge Prior to the Clone Wars, the *Munificent*-class frigate's spacious, multi-leveled bridge accommodated a Muun crew, and housed utilitarian cabins as well as suites and observation decks for wealthy Banking Clan administrators and dignitaries. The frigate is now crewed entirely by Separatist droids.

SEPARATIST SHIPS

While vast campaigns detain millions of Separatist warships in the Outer Rim, a few dozen battleships lead thousands of destroyers and frigates in a bold strike on the galactic capital Coruscant. These light warships, bristling with small laser turrets and impressive, oversized cannons, were pledged to Count Dooku by the governments of hundreds of aggressively independent star sectors. As the craft are largely controlled by automated droid-brain technology, little crew space is required. This gives the ships a sinister, skeletal appearance. Destroyers and frigates are not equipped with hangars or ground-attack armies but carry enough security droids for boarding actions. Their hull cavities can also "host" Separatist droid starfighters.

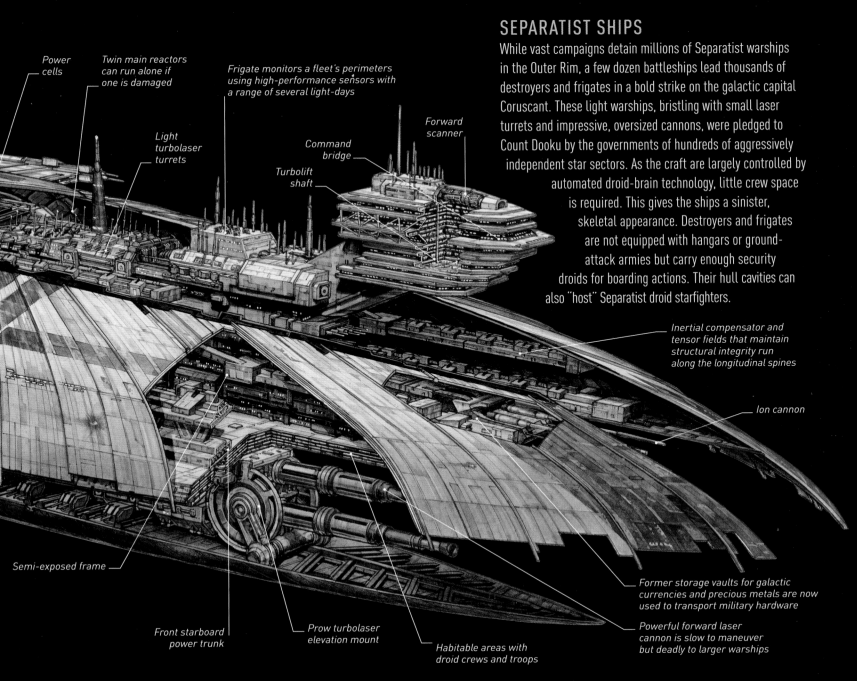

Power cells

Twin main reactors can run alone if one is damaged

Frigate monitors a fleet's perimeters using high-performance sensors with a range of several light-days

Light turbolaser turrets

Command bridge

Turbolift shaft

Forward scanner

Inertial compensator and tensor fields that maintain structural integrity run along the longitudinal spines

Ion cannon

Semi-exposed frame

Front starboard power trunk

Prow turbolaser elevation mount

Habitable areas with droid crews and troops

Former storage vaults for galactic currencies and precious metals are now used to transport military hardware

Powerful forward laser cannon is slow to maneuver but deadly to larger warships

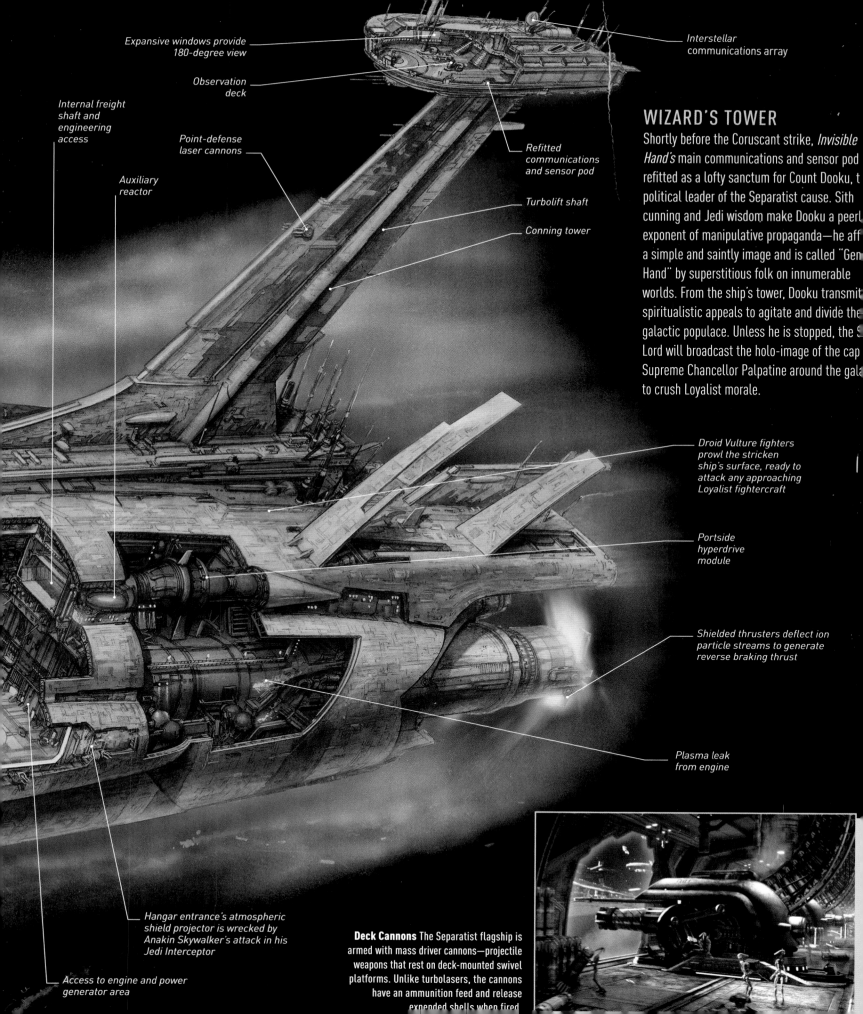

Expansive windows provide
180-degree view

Observation
deck

Internal freight
shaft and
engineering
access

Point-defense
laser cannons

Auxiliary
reactor

Interstellar
communications array

Refitted
communications
and sensor pod

Turbolift shaft

Conning tower

WIZARD'S TOWER

Shortly before the Coruscant strike, *Invisible Hand's* main communications and sensor pod refitted as a lofty sanctum for Count Dooku, t political leader of the Separatist cause. Sith cunning and Jedi wisdom make Dooku a peerl exponent of manipulative propaganda—he aff a simple and saintly image and is called "Gen Hand" by superstitious folk on innumerable worlds. From the ship's tower, Dooku transmit spiritualistic appeals to agitate and divide the galactic populace. Unless he is stopped, the S Lord will broadcast the holo-image of the cap Supreme Chancellor Palpatine around the gala to crush Loyalist morale.

Droid Vulture fighters
prowl the stricken
ship's surface, ready to
attack any approaching
Loyalist fightercraft

Portside
hyperdrive
module

Shielded thrusters deflect ion
particle streams to generate
reverse braking thrust

Plasma leak
from engine

Hangar entrance's atmospheric
shield projector is wrecked by
Anakin Skywalker's attack in his
Jedi Interceptor

Access to engine and power
generator area

Deck Cannons The Separatist flagship is
armed with mass driver cannons—projectile
weapons that rest on deck-mounted swivel
platforms. Unlike turbolasers, the cannons
have an ammunition feed and release
expended shells when fired

A WOUNDED BEAST

Invisible Hand attempts to drift inconspicuously in the concentrated shelter of Separatist battleships, destroyers, and frigates. Large numbers of droid Vulture fighters and tri-fighters cluster protectively around the flagship. When Kenobi and Skywalker approach in their Jedi Interceptors, the ship's deflector shields are already failing—small areas of the hull are open to attack from even the tiniest fighters. Anakin shoots out the atmosphere containment shield protecting the hangar entry, breaching the vessel's defenses.

Command Bridge Captured by Separatist droid soldiers, Obi-Wan Kenobi, Anakin Skywalker, and Supreme Chancellor Palpatine are escorted to *Invisible Hand*'s command bridge.

Droid-crewed maintenance decks

Separatist MTT (Multi-Troop Transport)

Ground forces command section

Anakin Skywalker's Jedi Interceptor

Heavy damage received during encounter with Republic Star Destroyer Guarlara

Thrusters and reactors usually fill the stern of Providence-class ships—Invisible Hand's expansive hangars are a major design modification

Air ducts—minimal atmospheric circulation is required as Invisible Hand carries few living crew or passengers

Ceiling racks typically hold 120 droid tri-fighters and Vulture fighters

Segment of hangar's blast door ready to shut

Heavy lift platform

Claw-like hangar crane

Emergency airbrake panels increase resistance slightly

The stresses of atmospheric entry and loss of internal tensor fields will cause ship to break up near this area

Mass driver deck cannons

Curved panelling is typical of flowing design style of Invisible Hand's Quarren shipbuilders

Quad turbolaser cannon's maximum yield is equivalent to magnitude-10 earthquake

Stored ground vehicles include 160 MTTs (Multi-Troop Transports) plus 280 other vehicles including AATs (Armored Assault Tanks), Hailfire droids, OG-9 spider droids and LM-432 crab droids

ROGUE-CLASS FIGHTER

The spreading hostilities of the Clone Wars see an invigoration of faltering starfighter product lines. The *Rogue*-class fighter is a rarely spotted model along the Mid and Outer Rim of the galaxy, but with the escalation of warfare, local governments and Separatist factions purchase them up in huge numbers. Their use by the formidable MagnaGuard droids bring them into direct combat with Republic forces. On Utapau, *Rogue*-class fighters serve the local resistance forces opposed to the Separatist occupation during the closing days of the Clone Wars.

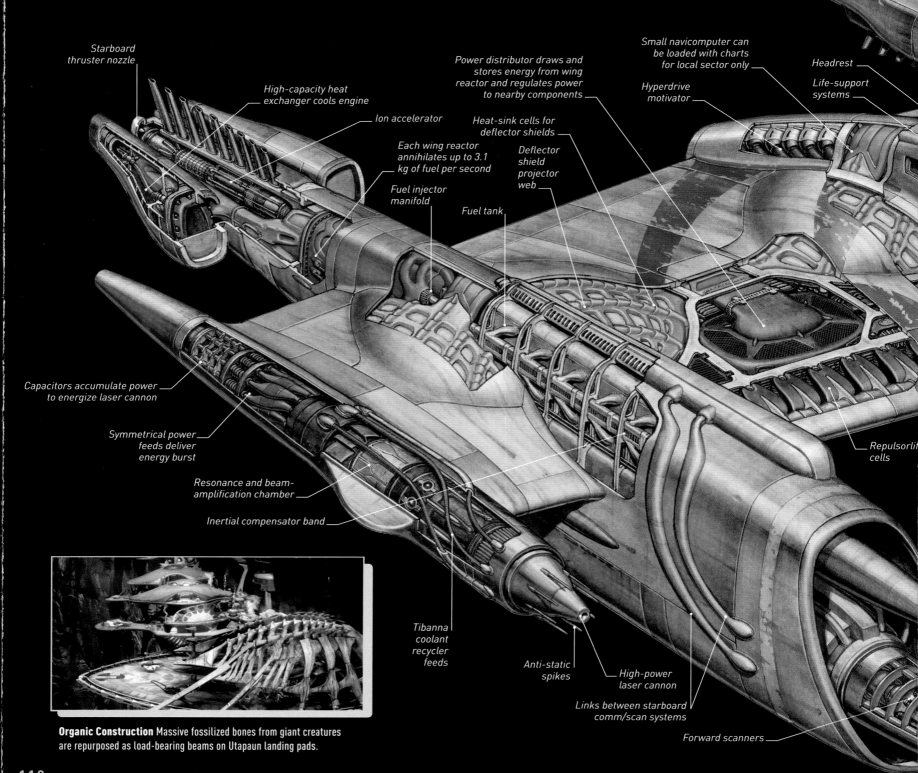

Thruster branch vents direct thrust up or down for pitch maneuvers

Starboard thruster nozzle

High-capacity heat exchanger cools engine

Ion accelerator

Each wing reactor annihilates up to 3.1 kg of fuel per second

Fuel injector manifold

Power distributor draws and stores energy from wing reactor and regulates power to nearby components

Heat-sink cells for deflector shields

Deflector shield projector web

Fuel tank

Small navicomputer can be loaded with charts for local sector only

Hyperdrive motivator

Headrest

Life-support systems

Capacitors accumulate power to energize laser cannon

Symmetrical power feeds deliver energy burst

Resonance and beam-amplification chamber

Inertial compensator band

Repulsorlift cells

Tibanna coolant recycler feeds

Anti-static spikes

High-power laser cannon

Links between starboard comm/scan systems

Forward scanners

Organic Construction Massive fossilized bones from giant creatures are repurposed as load-bearing beams on Utapaun landing pads.

HOME FORCE

The Trade Federation protects its position in remote galactic regions by placing embargoes on arms sales to planetary governments. As a result, Utapauns rely upon downscaled ships—their biggest anti-pirate Rendili Dreadnaught is one-fifth of the size of a Trade Federation battleship. Lacking a heavy navy, Utapauns deploy a rugged and potent starfighter force. Their large *Rogue*-class fighters are capable of independent hyperspace jumps, which enables them to defend the security of Utapau far into the Tarabba sector. The interstellar range of these ships means they can endure longer, more arduous missions than tiny, fleet-based craft such as Separatist droid fighters, Republic V-wings, and Jedi starfighters.

The Utai Since the Separatist invasion, the diminutive Utai workers in Pau city have had to work on their hidden fighters in secret.

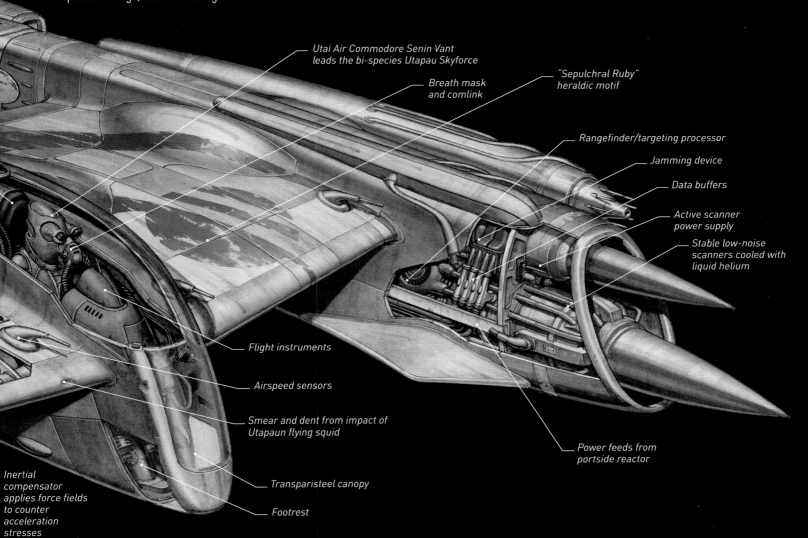

Utai Air Commodore Senin Vant leads the bi-species Utapau Skyforce

Breath mask and comlink

"Sepulchral Ruby" heraldic motif

Rangefinder/targeting processor

Jamming device

Data buffers

Active scanner power supply

Stable low-noise scanners cooled with liquid helium

Flight instruments

Airspeed sensors

Smear and dent from impact of Utapaun flying squid

Power feeds from portside reactor

Inertial compensator applies force fields to counter acceleration stresses

Transparisteel canopy

Footrest

Windswept World The winds in Utapau's atmosphere are so strong that Utapaun pilots often spend more time beneath the surface than in the air.

RECLAIMING UTAPAU

Utapauns live on an eerie world of wind, bones, and caves far from Tarabba Prime, the nearest major shipping and communications hub. The planet is shared by two humanoid species, the Utai and the Pau'ans, known collectively as Utapauns. Utapau's key asset is its obscurity, which General Grievous exploits to keep his new headquarters a secret from Republic forces. When the Utapauns decide to fight back against the Separatist occupation, local knowledge and the *Rogue*-class's advanced scanner systems give them a sharp advantage in high-speed chases through the treacherous canyon terrain. Powerful jammers also prove surprisingly effective at interfering with Separatist droid control signals. Any droids within targeting range are isolated, and must rely on their low-intelligence individual droid-brains.

TECHNO UNION SHIPS

The Techno Union is the galaxy's foremost developer of emerging technologies, including advanced engineering and microelectronics. Strongly devoted to the Separatist agenda, the Techno Union incorporates technology from such cutting-edge corporations as Haor Chall Engineering, Republic Sienar Systems, Kuat Systems Engineering, TaggeCo, and Feethan Ottraw Scalable Assemblies. Feethan Ottraw's contribution to the Techno Union's cause includes the Mankvim-814 light interceptor, Belbullab-23 heavy assault craft, and Belbullab-22 heavy starfighter. Unlike Vulture droids and droid tri-fighters, Belbullab-22s are powerful enough go one-on-one with the Republic's ARC-170 starfighters.

Rapid Retreat When Republic warships arrive on Geonosis, the Techno Union's *Hardcell*-class transports prepare for an emergency evacuation.

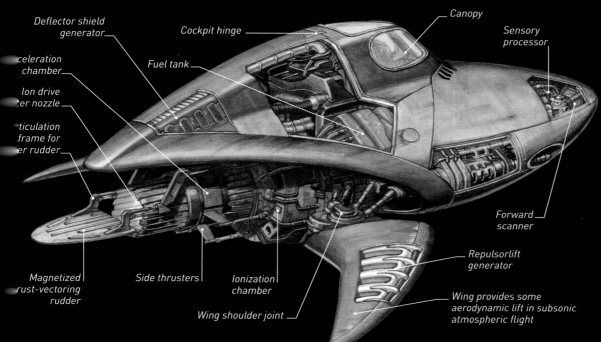

- Deflector shield generator
- Cockpit hinge
- Canopy
- Sensory processor
- Acceleration chamber
- Fuel tank
- Ion drive outer nozzle
- Articulation frame for outer rudder
- Magnetized thrust-vectoring rudder
- Side thrusters
- Ionization chamber
- Wing shoulder joint
- Forward scanner
- Repulsorlift generator
- Wing provides some aerodynamic lift in subsonic atmospheric flight

INTERSTELLAR TRANSPORT

The signature transport for Techno Union officials is the *Hardcell*-class interstellar transport, which features six large, powerful thrusters that wreak havoc on launch sites but enable quick exits from planetary atmospheres. Because the Techno Union was founded and remains largely operated by Skakoans, most *Hardcell*-class transport have pressurized cabins engineered specifically for Skakoan biology, allowing them to forego their bulky pressure suits while traveling. Before the Clone Wars began the Techno Union contributed nearly 300 *Hardcell*-class transports to the Separatist cause. Of those transports, 117 failed to escape the Battle of Geonosis.

MANKVIM-814 LIGHT INTERCEPTOR

Numerous Mankvim-814 interceptors flock to defend the Separatist foothold on Utapau. The Techno Union built these small, short-range starfighters on the planet from local materials, having hastily constructed factories in the ancient Grand Halls with no regard for Utapau's architectural heritage. The Mankvim's simple construction centers on a reactor feeding power and plasma to a high-velocity ion-drive. A magnetized rudder tilts the ion flow for off-axis thrust, while smaller side thrusters aid roll and yaw adjustments. The craft is equipped with twin rapid-fire laser cannons and durable shields for combat. Aerodynamic wings fitted with repulsorlifts also aid overall maneuverability.

Weak Spot Although it can deploy hundreds of battle droids, the *Hardcell*-class transport is only lightly armed, and vulnerable to well-placed shots to the area above the fuel cells, which can destroy the entire transport.

SOULLESS ONE

Although he prefers hand-to-hand combat, General Grievous often flies a battle-worn Belbullab-22 starfighter designed by Feethan Ottraw Scalable Assemblies, specialists in self-constructing armaments factories. Made for a living pilot, the hyperdrive-equipped craft is bulkier and hardier than disposable droid fighters. Two main ion drives enable the Belbullab to keep pace with an *Rogue*-class fighter. A rear-mounted thrust-vectoring fin and auxiliary thrusters built into the wings assist with yaw and roll maneuvers. Rapid-firing triple laser cannons sustain firepower of equivalent destructive force to that of the Republic's V-wing starfighters.

Landing Pad Battle Obi-Wan Kenobi fights to stop the Confederacy's General Grievous from escaping in his Belbullab-22 fighter on Utapau.

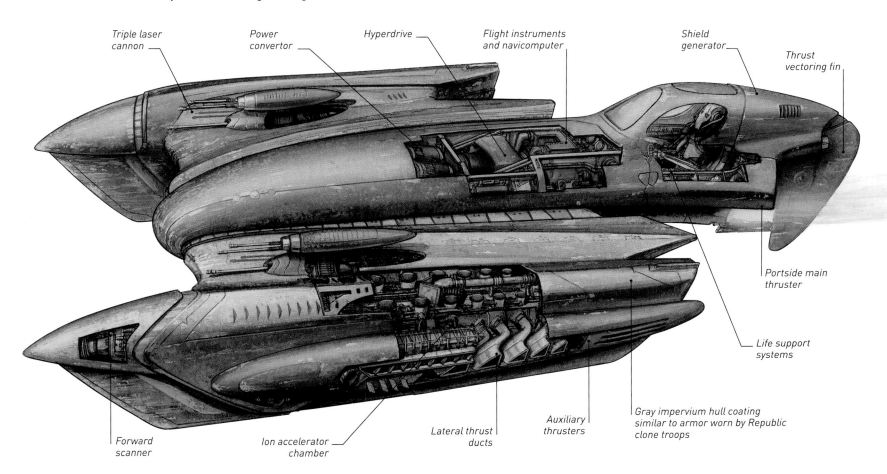

Triple laser cannon

Power convertor

Hyperdrive

Flight instruments and navicomputer

Shield generator

Thrust vectoring fin

Portside main thruster

Life support systems

Gray impervium hull coating similar to armor worn by Republic clone troops

Auxiliary thrusters

Lateral thrust ducts

Ion accelerator chamber

Forward scanner

GETAWAY VEHICLE

To maintain contact with his droid armies, General Grievous's starfighter, *Soulless One*, has a sophisticated compact HoloNet transceiver. The transceiver can also access Republic and pirate networks, allowing Grievous to anticipate enemy activity and avoid confrontations he cannot win. After Republic forces arrive on Utapau, Grievous attempts to escape in his starfighter, which he keeps on a secret landing pad. Unknown to Grievous, his previous use of the starfighter to retreat from battle has prompted some enemies to nickname his fighter *Spineless One*.

Cockpit Layout Like the controls of General Grievous's wheel bike, the Belbullab-22's cockpit features a circular, pressure-sensitive panel for operating the ship. Set within a reinforced yoke, the controls can be operated by most humanoids.

GRIEVOUS'S WHEEL BIKE

General Grievous's fearsome reputation as a merciless military leader is reinforced by a personal fleet of specialized killing machines and vehicles. On cavernous Utapau, the cyborg General drives a wheel bike—a tumbling twin-wheel that surrounds a central motor. Grievous's military vehicle is an offshoot of the Banking Clan's hoop-wheeled Hailfire droids, designed to roll at intimidating speed on hard surfaces. It can also raise itself up on two pairs of legs to walk over the top of battle wrecks and other obstacles. A double laser cannon replaces one side seat, and Grievous can wield either a conveniently placed electrostaff, a blaster, or one of his Jedi lightsaber trophies when he rolls into battle. Flexing claws skirt the wheels to provide a smoother ride, or clutch the ground as climbing teeth.

Knuckle joint of rim claw

Outer drive chain

Side claw

Console graphic display is adjusted to suit the color perception of Grievous's species' eyesight

Claw pivot

Laser cannon's beam-resonance chamber

Cannon elevation motor

Capacitors store charge for laser cannon shots

Anti-static spikes

Double laser cannon

Waste coolant gas discharge vents

Claw actuators

Dense and massive drive chain spins within outer wheel, providing gyro stability

Frictionless magnetic rail

Transformation and accelerator controls

Control Panel The bike's directional controls are housed in an illuminated, touch-sensitive console, reinforced so it won't shatter under the pressure of Grievous's sharp metal fingers.

Control wiring

Magnetic disk brake

NEW HEADQUARTERS

General Grievous's invading forces have constructed command centers and self-replicating Techno Union factories on Utapau. These facilities create new troops, starfighters, wheel bikes, and other vehicles using local materials. If left undisturbed, they will turn Utapau into yet another of the Outer Rim's fortress worlds, riddled with ugly refineries and assembly lines and trembling under the weight of ever-more deadly Separatist war machines.

Teeth of left driver wheel

Driver's footrest

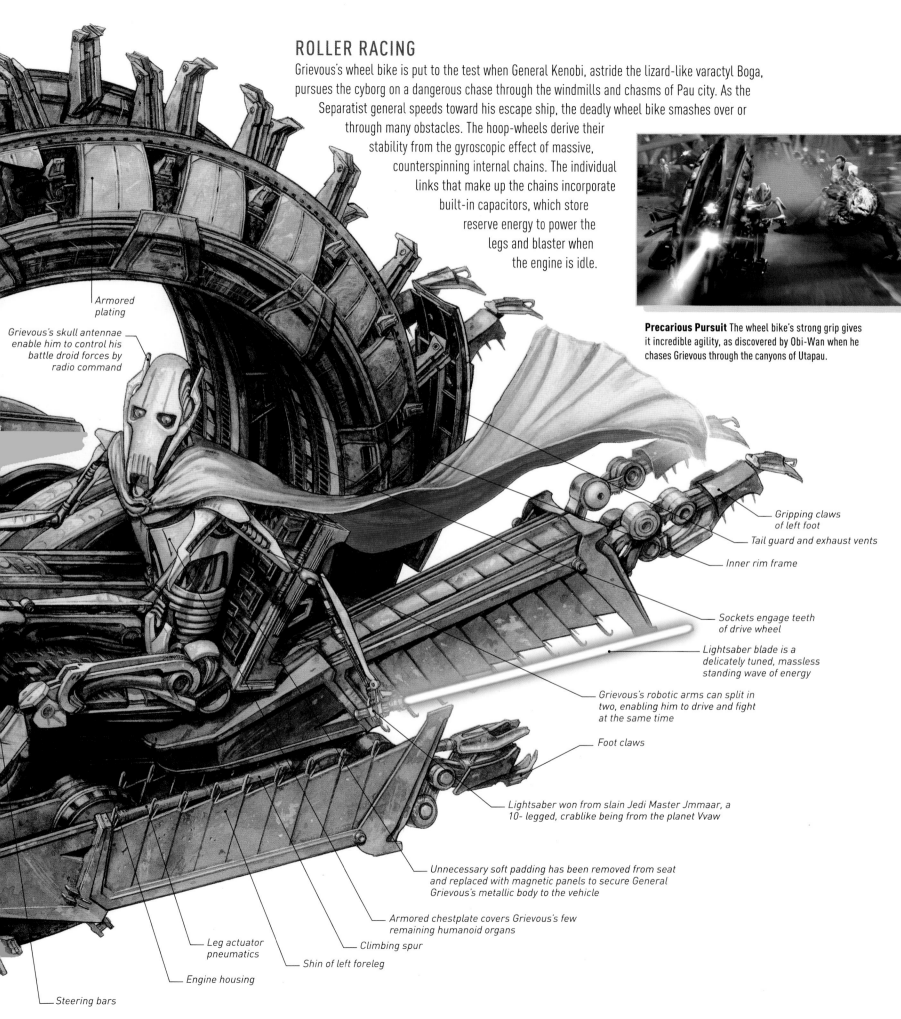

ROLLER RACING

Grievous's wheel bike is put to the test when General Kenobi, astride the lizard-like varactyl Boga, pursues the cyborg on a dangerous chase through the windmills and chasms of Pau city. As the Separatist general speeds toward his escape ship, the deadly wheel bike smashes over or through many obstacles. The hoop-wheels derive their stability from the gyroscopic effect of massive, counterspinning internal chains. The individual links that make up the chains incorporate built-in capacitors, which store reserve energy to power the legs and blaster when the engine is idle.

Precarious Pursuit The wheel bike's strong grip gives it incredible agility, as discovered by Obi-Wan when he chases Grievous through the canyons of Utapau.

Armored plating

Grievous's skull antennae enable him to control his battle droid forces by radio command

Gripping claws of left foot

Tail guard and exhaust vents

Inner rim frame

Sockets engage teeth of drive wheel

Lightsaber blade is a delicately tuned, massless standing wave of energy

Grievous's robotic arms can split in two, enabling him to drive and fight at the same time

Foot claws

Lightsaber won from slain Jedi Master Jmmaar, a 10- legged, crablike being from the planet Vvaw

Unnecessary soft padding has been removed from seat and replaced with magnetic panels to secure General Grievous's metallic body to the vehicle

Armored chestplate covers Grievous's few remaining humanoid organs

Climbing spur

Leg actuator pneumatics

Shin of left foreleg

Engine housing

Steering bars

117

WOOKIEE CATAMARAN

Wookiee *Oevvaor* catamarans are slim, twin-hulled craft that skid over the waters of Kashyyyk at breakneck speeds. They are lifted by a repulsorlift array up to a maximum height of 1,000 meters, propelled by podracer-style jet engines or propeller pods, and steered by knife-like keels and rudders. Wookiee catamarans are normally used as fishing or sports craft, and are not equipped with built-in heavy weapons. But when Kashyyyk is invaded, hundreds of these craft are conscripted to bear Wookiee troops in small-arms attacks, darting through the lines of Separatist vehicles. The catamarans' speed and maneuverability are crucial, as Kashyyyk's defenders know that the enemy must first capture the coasts before attempting incursions into the tangled, dense vegetation of the inland woods.

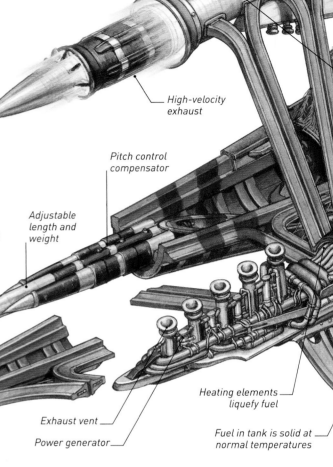

Elderly Attichitcuk has practiced his throw in virtual-reality games played on an addictive Wookiee "mind evaporator" headset

High-velocity exhaust

Pitch control compensator

Adjustable length and weight

Heating elements liquefy fuel

Exhaust vent

Power generator

Fuel in tank is solid at normal temperatures

Rudder actuator

Side rudder

AGILE DEFENDERS

The Wookiee watercraft used in the defence of Kashyyyk are named after the Oevvaor, a predatory marine reptile of the Kashyyyk coasts known for its agility and territorial ferocity. The tough hulls of these aptly named catamarans are handcrafted from wroshyr timber. This light, strong, and durable wood is hewn from Kashyyyk's fabled wroshyr trees, which can grow to hundreds of meters in height.

Lower rudders dip into water when flying at sea level

Air Patrol Soaring over the lagoons and fjords of the Wawaatt Archipelago on Kashyyyk, a Wookiee catamaran angles toward the coastal tree-city of Kachirho.

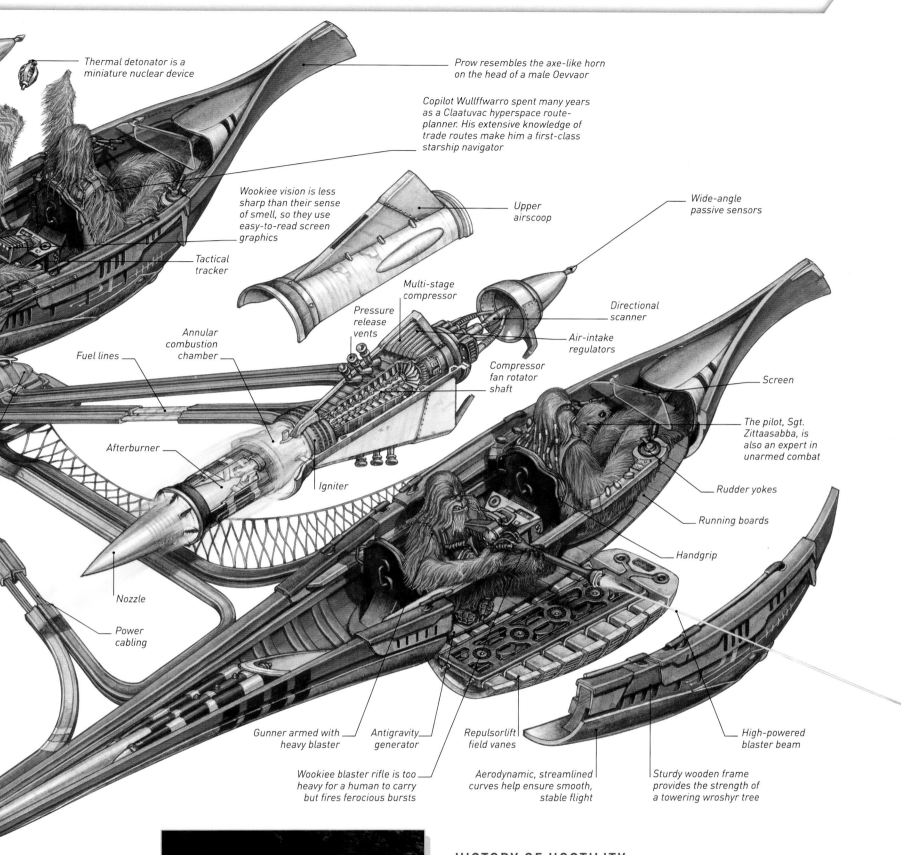

Thermal detonator is a miniature nuclear device

Prow resembles the axe-like horn on the head of a male Oevvaor

Copilot Wullffwarro spent many years as a Claatuvac hyperspace route-planner. His extensive knowledge of trade routes make him a first-class starship navigator

Wookiee vision is less sharp than their sense of smell, so they use easy-to-read screen graphics

Upper airscoop

Wide-angle passive sensors

Tactical tracker

Multi-stage compressor

Directional scanner

Annular combustion chamber

Pressure release vents

Air-intake regulators

Fuel lines

Compressor fan rotator shaft

Screen

Afterburner

The pilot, Sgt. Zittaasabba, is also an expert in unarmed combat

Igniter

Rudder yokes

Running boards

Nozzle

Handgrip

Power cabling

Gunner armed with heavy blaster

Antigravity generator

Repulsorlift field vanes

High-powered blaster beam

Wookiee blaster rifle is too heavy for a human to carry but fires ferocious bursts

Aerodynamic, streamlined curves help ensure smooth, stable flight

Sturdy wooden frame provides the strength of a towering wroshyr tree

Wookiee Ornithopter
Built by the Appazanna Engineering Works, the same manufacturer as the Wookiee catamaran, the *Raddaugh Gnasp* fluttercraft takes its name from large, wasp-like insects native to Kashyyyk's moon Alaris.

HISTORY OF HOSTILITY

For 20 years, the Wookiees of Kashyyyk and its colony worlds have repeatedly repelled encroachments by the greedy Trade Federation. In this new period of unrestrained war, Confederacy invaders now bypass the colonies and attempt a conclusive strike on the Wookiee homeworld. Although the Separatist invasion fleet is driven off by General Yoda's Republic taskforce, a huge army of tank droids, crab droids, and flying gunships occupies the tropical Wawaatt Archipelago. The Wookiees know that they must marshal all their brawn, defensive weaponry, and vehicular power to halt the intruders' advance.

SWAMP SPEEDER

The Grand Army of the Republic bolsters the Wookiees' defensive forces with a wide variety of imported war machines. The light, two-man ISP (Infantry Support Platform) speeder is the clone troops' closest equivalent of the Wookiees' *Oevvaor* catamarans and *Raddadugh Gnasp* fluttercraft. The clone army's antigravity repulsorlift vehicle floats smoothly in the air without touching land or water. It is driven by a powerful turbofan, which can be reversed to fire a braking airblast when needed. Precise, controlled vectoring of the turbofan's thrust makes the ISP a highly maneuverable attack vehicle. The front-mounted pair of twin-blaster cannons are lethal to enemy infantry, but can also prove highly effective against shielded enemy gunships, fighters, and Corporate Alliance NR-N99 tank droids.

UNIQUE TURBOFAN

Developed by Aratech Repulsor Company, and intended as a heavier version of the Republic Army's Biker Advanced Recon Commando (BARC) speeder, the ISP has a a rear-mounted turbofan that can generate a thrust of up to 100 kilometers per hour, and can be reverse vectored in emergencies to provide a sudden stop. The turbofan produces less noise than most ion thrusters.

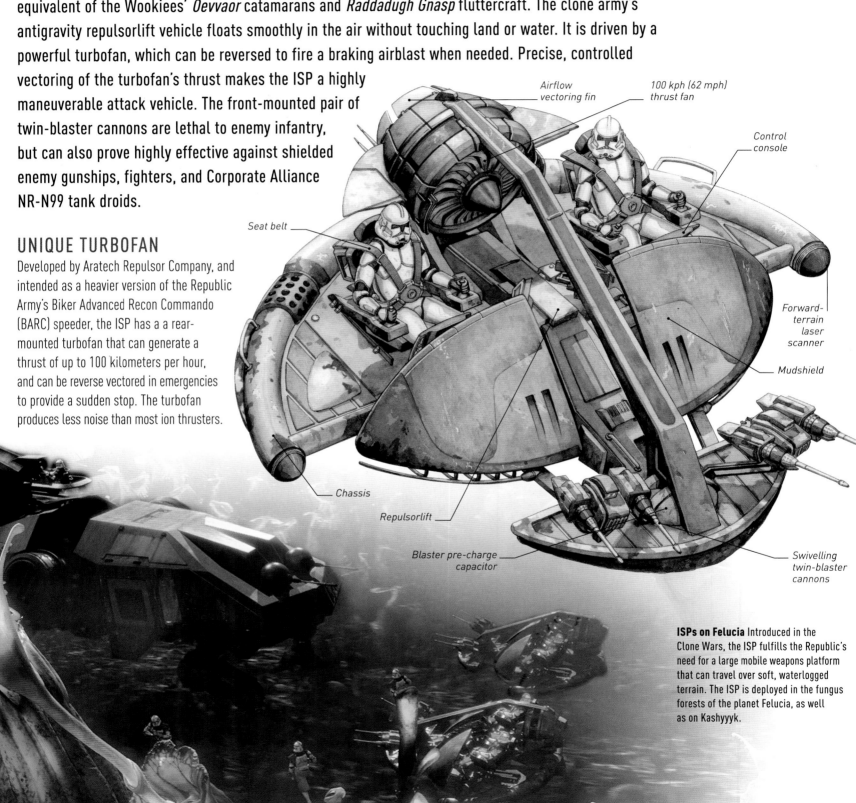

Airflow vectoring fin

100 kph (62 mph) thrust fan

Control console

Seat belt

Forward-terrain laser scanner

Mudshield

Chassis

Repulsorlift

Blaster pre-charge capacitor

Swivelling twin-blaster cannons

ISPs on Felucia Introduced in the Clone Wars, the ISP fulfills the Republic's need for a large mobile weapons platform that can travel over soft, waterlogged terrain. The ISP is deployed in the fungus forests of the planet Felucia, as well as on Kashyyyk.

FIT FOR AN EMPEROR

The Emperor's personal *Theta*-class shuttle serves as a mobile base from which he can further his goal of galactic domination. Separatist leaders, corrupt senators, and other influential figures have been bribed, coerced, or threatened in the ship's secure aft compartment, while Sith truth potions, mind-control enhancers, torture devices, and memory erasers have all assisted Palpatine in his "negotiations."

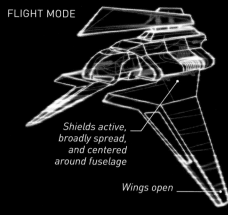

FLIGHT MODE

Shields active, broadly spread, and centered around fuselage

Wings open

LANDING IN SAFETY

When the *Theta*-class shuttle lands, its long wings fold upwards to allow access via the main hatch. The ion drive powers down as antigravity repulsorlifts guide the ship to a gentle touchdown. Scanners linked to the computer-controlled weapons systems survey the landing site as the ship descends, ready to instantly eliminate any threat to the ship or its occupants.

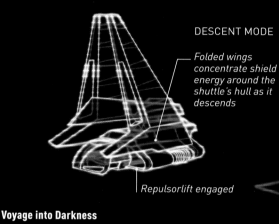

DESCENT MODE

Folded wings concentrate shield energy around the shuttle's hull as it descends

Repulsorlift engaged

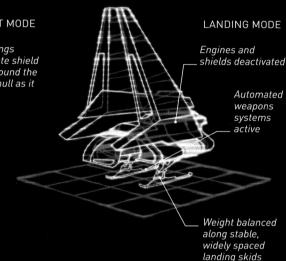

LANDING MODE

Engines and shields deactivated

Automated weapons systems active

Weight balanced along stable, widely spaced landing skids

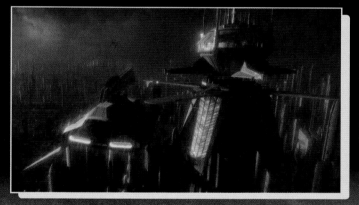

Voyage into Darkness
Mystical Sith equipment capable of channeling the dark side of the Force helps sustain Darth Vader during the trip from Mustafar to a medical center on Coruscant.

PALPATINE'S SHUTTLE

Assassination and abduction have punctuated every stage of the Clone Wars, and a galactic leader such as the newly self-appointed Emperor Palpatine requires a secure personal transport. The new *Theta*-class T-2c shuttle is designed to ferry important officers, senators, and courtiers between planets and ships in safety. Capable of outgunning most starfighters, the ship is fitted with twin forward-mounted quad laser cannons and a single, high-powered tail gun. This destructive arsenal can be computer-controlled or manually operated from a combined communications and gunnery station in the cockpit. The long folding wings are designed to project powerful shielding fields, and they also aid stability during atmospheric flight.

Static discharge devices

Raised boarding ramp

Landing light

Communications transponders

Airlock door

Navicomputer

Prepared for combat, the pilot wears a full flight suit

Gunner/ communications stations

Power feeds inside leading edge are kept apart by heat-sink elements

Repulsorlift generator

High-power portside quad laser cannon

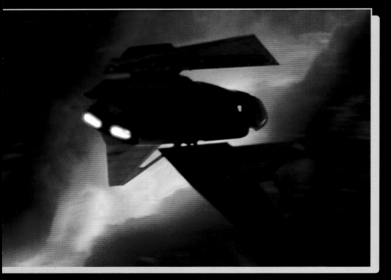

Extreme Shield Power Descending to the volcanic planet Mustafar, Palpatine's shuttle is protected from the intense heat and incendiary ash by energy shields that far exceed military standards.

ELITE TRANSPORT

Emperor Palpatine's shuttle has been upgraded by "Warthan's Wizards," some of the finest starship technicians in the galaxy. To provide instant transgalactic communications, they installed a hyperwave reflector akin to the secret homing devices of the Jedi Order. The shuttle is also lined with sensor masks that make the interior appear empty on conventional scanners. Palpatine's later shuttles will feature a cloaking device—making them invisible to all forms of light, gravity, and other known energies.

IMPERIAL SYMBOL

In the formative years of the Galactic Empire, Cygnus Spaceworks will lose the contract for its shuttle line to Sienar Fleet Systems. Key designers at Cygnus, lured by vast salaries, personal galactic yachts, and a cut of future profits, will defect to Sienar, taking their designs with them. In years to come, the configuration of the *Theta*-class and its descendants will become a symbol of Imperial prestige. Sienar will also produce the Empire's primary space-superiority craft, the TIE (Twin Ion Engine) fighter, as well as downscaled warships built to patrol remote sectors.

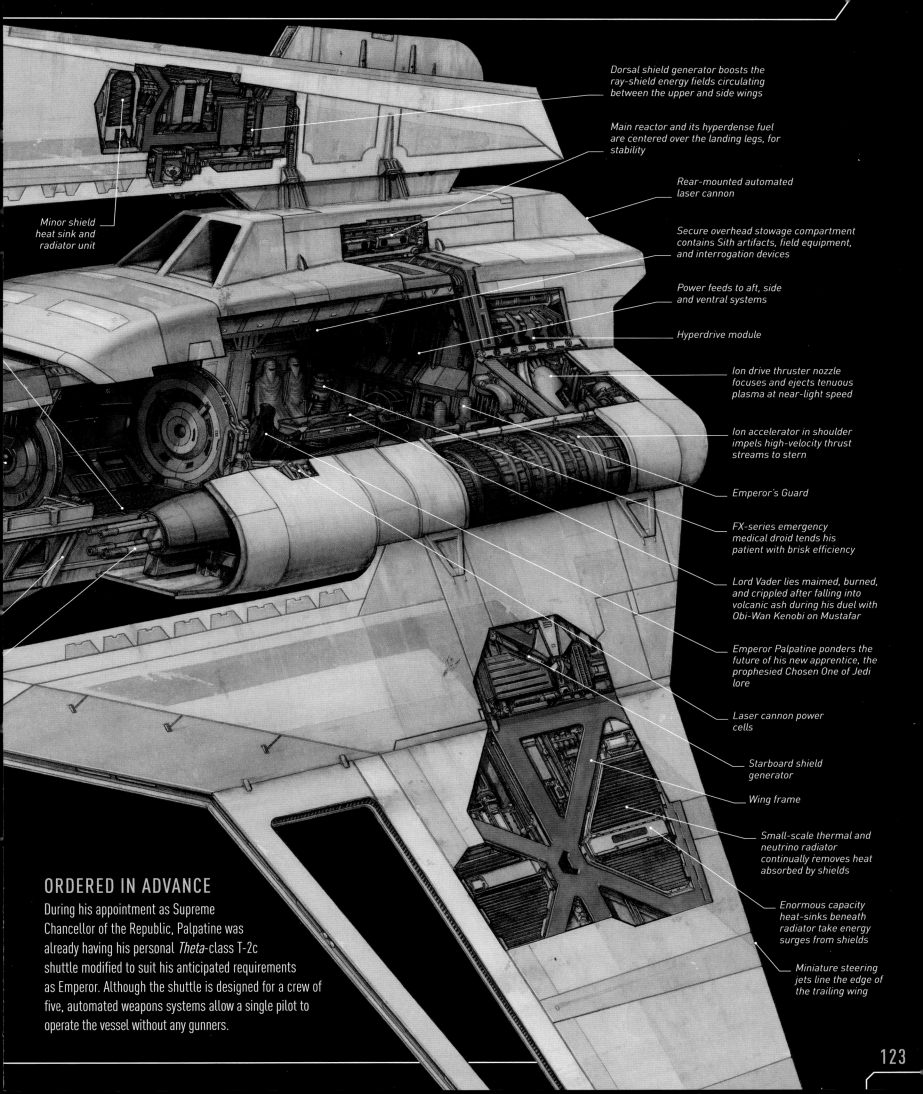

Dorsal shield generator boosts the ray-shield energy fields circulating between the upper and side wings

Main reactor and its hyperdense fuel are centered over the landing legs, for stability

Rear-mounted automated laser cannon

Minor shield heat sink and radiator unit

Secure overhead stowage compartment contains Sith artifacts, field equipment, and interrogation devices

Power feeds to aft, side and ventral systems

Hyperdrive module

Ion drive thruster nozzle focuses and ejects tenuous plasma at near-light speed

Ion accelerator in shoulder impels high-velocity thrust streams to stern

Emperor's Guard

FX-series emergency medical droid tends his patient with brisk efficiency

Lord Vader lies maimed, burned, and crippled after falling into volcanic ash during his duel with Obi-Wan Kenobi on Mustafar

Emperor Palpatine ponders the future of his new apprentice, the prophesied Chosen One of Jedi lore

Laser cannon power cells

Starboard shield generator

Wing frame

Small-scale thermal and neutrino radiator continually removes heat absorbed by shields

Enormous capacity heat-sinks beneath radiator take energy surges from shields

Miniature steering jets line the edge of the trailing wing

ORDERED IN ADVANCE

During his appointment as Supreme Chancellor of the Republic, Palpatine was already having his personal *Theta*-class T-2c shuttle modified to suit his anticipated requirements as Emperor. Although the shuttle is designed for a crew of five, automated weapons systems allow a single pilot to operate the vessel without any gunners.

YODA'S ESCAPE PODS

An escape pod is designed to carry a living being away from danger as quickly as possible. These basic craft roar and shake through the air, propelled by simple ion engines, while the occupant's ride is smoothed by inertial compensators and anti-gravity fields. In his escape from the forces of Emperor Palpatine's newly formed Galactic Empire, Jedi Master Yoda resorts to these devices twice in one week. Yoda's first pod is a simple, Wookiee-made vessel that lifts him away from danger on Kashyyyk. His second craft, which carries him into exile on Dagobah, is a larger, more sophisticated lander from Polis Massa, with advanced guidance systems and landing mechanisms.

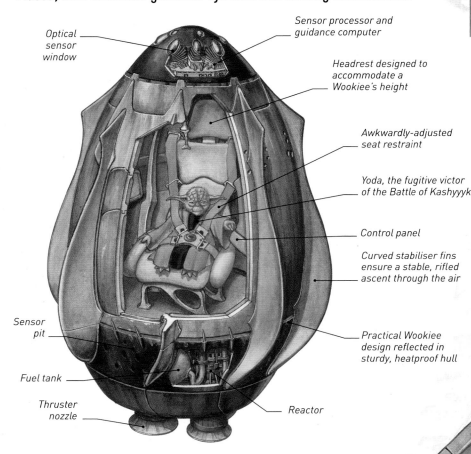

Optical sensor window

Sensor processor and guidance computer

Headrest designed to accommodate a Wookiee's height

Awkwardly-adjusted seat restraint

Yoda, the fugitive victor of the Battle of Kashyyyk

Control panel

Curved stabiliser fins ensure a stable, rifled ascent through the air

Sensor pit

Fuel tank

Thruster nozzle

Reactor

Practical Wookiee design reflected in sturdy, heatproof hull

Adjustable footpad

Reactor/ionization chamber

Fuel tanks are almost empty of reactant and propellant

Leg articulation socket

Fuel lines

Distress beacon, already deactivated by Yoda

Rations and survival gear

Seats designed for average male Massan

ESCAPE FROM KASHYYYK

With Separatist droids invading parts of Kashyyyk, Wookiee defenders prepared thousands of hidden escape pods for last-resort evacuation. General Yoda used the first pod. Its three sublight thrusters—cobbled together from three shipwrecks—contain just enough fuel to bear him safely into interplanetary space. Yoda deactivates its tell-tale distress beacon, relying solely on his Jedi pocket emergency transmitter. Alderaanian agents searching for surviving Jedi intercept Yoda's call, leading Senator Bail Organa to rescue him.

A HIDDEN SANCTUARY

Despite the claims of some within the Jedi Archives, the knowledge contained within the hallowed halls of the Jedi Temple is not complete. Many worlds, including ancient ones strong in the Force, have escaped Jedi attention. Yoda comes to know of one such word, Dagobah, near the end of the Clone Wars, following a vision quest prompted by the disembodied spirit of Qui-Gon Jinn. Wishing to learn some of the deepest secrets of the Force, Yoda voyages to the distant swamp planet. While en route to Corsuscant after escaping Kashyyyk following Order 66, Yoda remembers Dagobah and returns there to hide after the destruction of the Jedi Order.

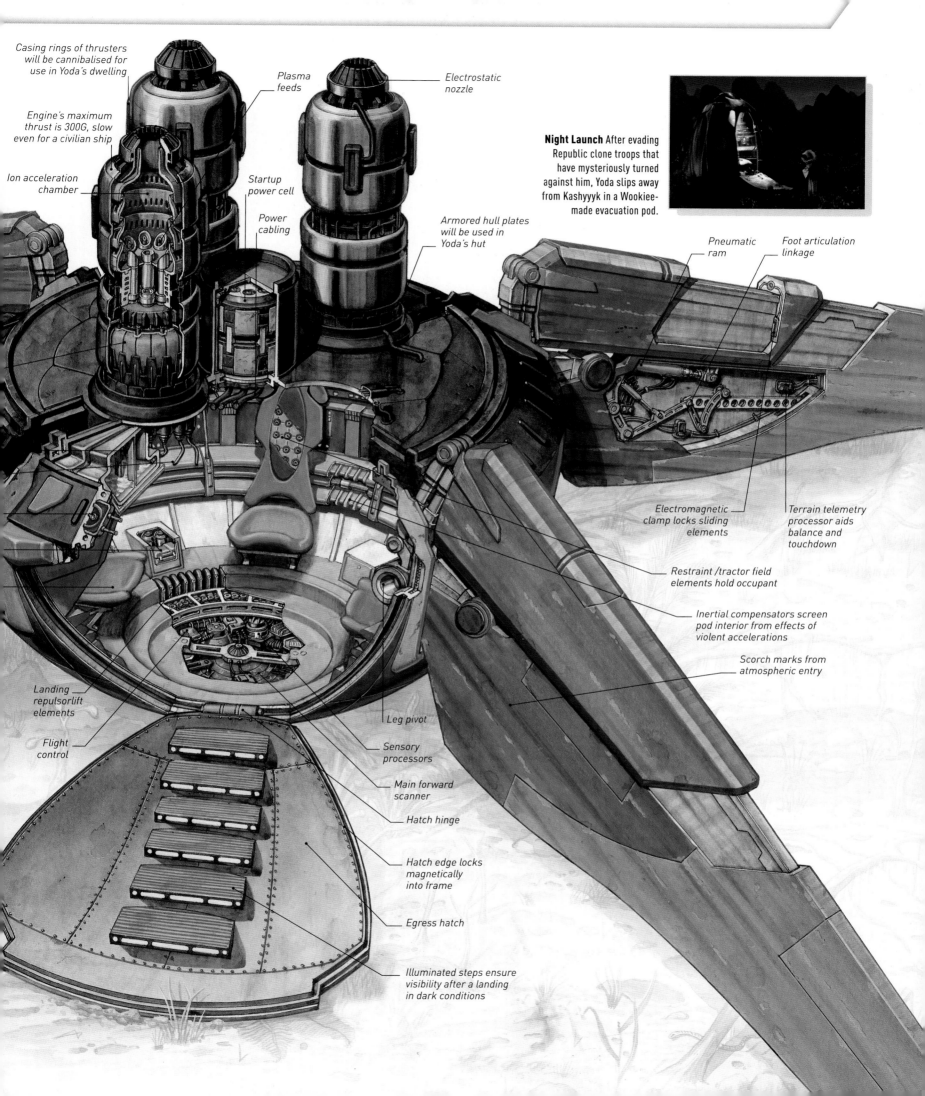

Casing rings of thrusters will be cannibalised for use in Yoda's dwelling

Plasma feeds

Electrostatic nozzle

Engine's maximum thrust is 300G, slow even for a civilian ship

Ion acceleration chamber

Startup power cell

Power cabling

Armored hull plates will be used in Yoda's hut

Night Launch After evading Republic clone troops that have mysteriously turned against him, Yoda slips away from Kashyyyk in a Wookiee-made evacuation pod.

Pneumatic ram

Foot articulation linkage

Electromagnetic clamp locks sliding elements

Terrain telemetry processor aids balance and touchdown

Restraint /tractor field elements hold occupant

Inertial compensators screen pod interior from effects of violent accelerations

Landing repulsorlift elements

Scorch marks from atmospheric entry

Flight control

Leg pivot

Sensory processors

Main forward scanner

Hatch hinge

Hatch edge locks magnetically into frame

Egress hatch

Illuminated steps ensure visibility after a landing in dark conditions

EPISODES IV–VI
ROGUE ONE: A STAR WARS STORY
A NEW HOPE
THE EMPIRE STRIKES BACK
RETURN OF THE JEDI

After two decades of oppressive rule, the Empire's hold on the galaxy is thoroughly entrenched. Anakin Skywalker has become Darth Vader, Emperor Palpatine's Sith Lord apprentice and enforcer. However, a small group of rebels, named the Rebel Alliance, has formed to fight the Empire and restore democracy and peace to the galaxy. When the Rebels learn of an Imperial superweapon the first Death Star, they launch a major offensive and manage to steal the base's schematics in order to find its hidden weakness. Vader fails to reclaim the plans and is determined to crush the rebels. Anakin and Padmé's children, who were separated at birth to protect them from the Emperor, are now thrown together by fate. Unaware of their true parentage, the siblings—Tatooine farm boy Luke Skywalker and Princess Leia Organa of Alderaan—lead the Rebellion to a crucial victory by destroying the first Death Star. While Luke trains to become a Jedi under the ancient Jedi Master Yoda, the Empire retaliates and the Rebellion is severely weakened. But the Alliance regroups and a decisive final battle results in both the destruction of the second Death Star and the redemption of Anakin Skywalker, who ultimately rejects the dark side of the Force and destroys the Emperor.

DELTA-CLASS T-3C SHUTTLE

With its starkly geometric hull shape and folding, batlike wings, an approaching *Delta*-class T-3c shuttle is an ominous sight. The sense of dread it inspires proves warranted when it lands and deploys its deadly passengers. The *Delta*-class did not see much use in the early days of the Empire, being outpaced in popularity by the more versatile *Lambda*-class. But Krennic's eye for bold architecture favored the design and he has kept one in active use for over a decade.

TALL WINGS

Imperial shuttlecraft typically maximize the space requirements of the primary hull by externalizing shield and communications systems into their sizable wing assemblies. The planar surfaces of the foils are ideal transmitters for energies related, but not limited, to hyperspatial signals, subspace radionics, and deflective mantles. The wing structures are also lined with heat dispersal systems. The ship's central computer manages these functions to prevent signal interferences.

TOUCHDOWN MODE

Republic Sienar Systems coaxed the design team from Cygnus Spaceworks to develop their Abecederian line of executive shuttles before the Empire came to power. Their output from their Mid Rim design studios shares many hallmark features—elegant lines, tri-foil symmetry, and articulated wings that fold during landing. The Cygnus design lead, Lamilla Tion, was a sculptor fascinated with paper-folding. She incorporated the variable geometry landing system into her designs at great expense, not only to compress each ship's docked footprint, but also as an artistic acknowledgment of her spiritual beliefs.

Repulsorlift field generator

Transmission quadruplexer processing bank

Radiator grill

Access ladder to troop cabin

Multi-spectrum ranging laser

Taim & Bak KX3 laser cannon

Subspace and hypercomm antenna array

Deflector shield generator

Aft deflector shield generator

SFS-215 ion engine thruster

Formation light

Landing strut (deployed)

Flight deck access door

Deflector shield generator

Service markings

Lateral deflector shield transmission plane

Diagnostics bay and refueling inlet

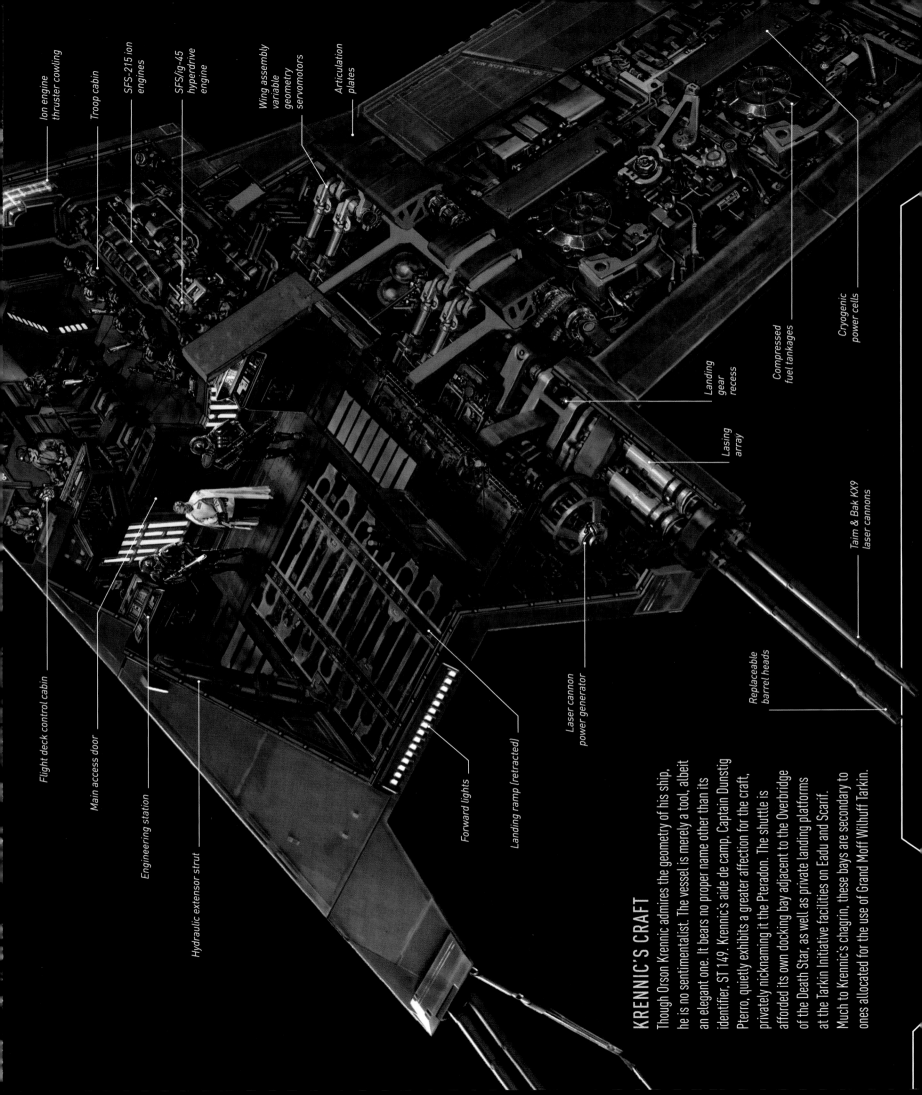

Ion engine thruster cowling

Troop cabin

SFS-215 ion engines

SFS/Ig-45 hyperdrive engine

Wing assembly variable geometry servomotors

Articulation plates

Landing gear recess

Lasing array

Compressed fuel tankages

Cryogenic power cells

Taim & Bak KX9 laser cannons

Replaceable barrel heads

Flight deck control cabin

Main access door

Engineering station

Hydraulic extensor strut

Forward lights

Landing ramp (retracted)

Laser cannon power generator

KRENNIC'S CRAFT

Though Orson Krennic admires the geometry of his ship, he is no sentimentalist. The vessel is merely a tool, albeit an elegant one. It bears no proper name other than its identifier, ST 149. Krennic's aide de camp, Captain Dunstig Pterro, quietly exhibits a greater affection for the craft, privately nicknaming it the Pteradon. The shuttle is afforded its own docking bay adjacent to the Overbridge of the Death Star, as well as private landing platforms at the Tarkin Initiative facilities on Eadu and Scarif. Much to Krennic's chagrin, these bays are secondary to ones allocated for the use of Grand Moff Wilhuff Tarkin.

U-WING

A sturdy troop transport and gunship used by the Rebel Alliance, the U-wing starfighter is a well-armed swing-wing vessel that must penetrate heavy fire zones to deposit soldiers onto battlefields, then fly air support during dangerous missions. Despite its informal "starfighter" moniker, the U-wing fills a support role that starfighters simply cannot. Fighters rely on their speed to keep them out of anti-aircraft range. U-wings, by necessity, must linger in areas filled with flak and enemy fire. The shielding and armor of a U-wing adds to an operational mass on top of a hold full of passengers. In short, a U-wing handles much more like a heavy repulsorcraft than a swift space superiority vessel.

IMPROVISED GUNSHIP

The integrated weapons systems of the U-wing are focused on ship-to-ship combat. With fixed-position laser cannons, the primary weapons use the ship's orientation for targeting, limiting its application in ground support. The Rebel Alliance has not opted to refit the U-wing with side-firing modifications, but instead employs improvised weapon mounts to transform one or both of the loading doors into gunports. This is essential for covering landings and extractions. Any infantry-based heavy weapon could thus become part of the U-wing's loadout.

LIMITED RUN

One of the last designs to emerge from the Incom Corporation before it was entirely nationalized by the Empire, the UT-60D never enjoyed a full production run. The careful manipulation of Senate records by Bail Organa led to a rare shipment of U-wings being "lost" in transit to be found by the Rebellion. The U-wing's nearest cousin, the BT-45D civilian version of the craft—stripped of all its military offensive and defensive applications as well as its hyperdrive—can still be found on a few scattered worlds in the Mid Rim.

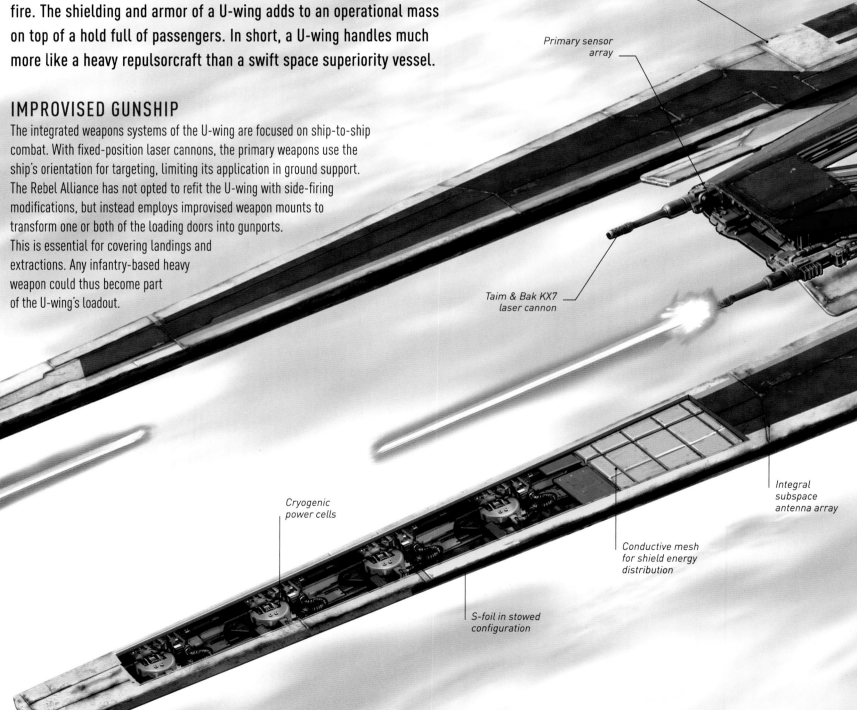

Deflector shield radiating plane

Primary sensor array

Taim & Bak KX7 laser cannon

Cryogenic power cells

Integral subspace antenna array

Conductive mesh for shield energy distribution

S-foil in stowed configuration

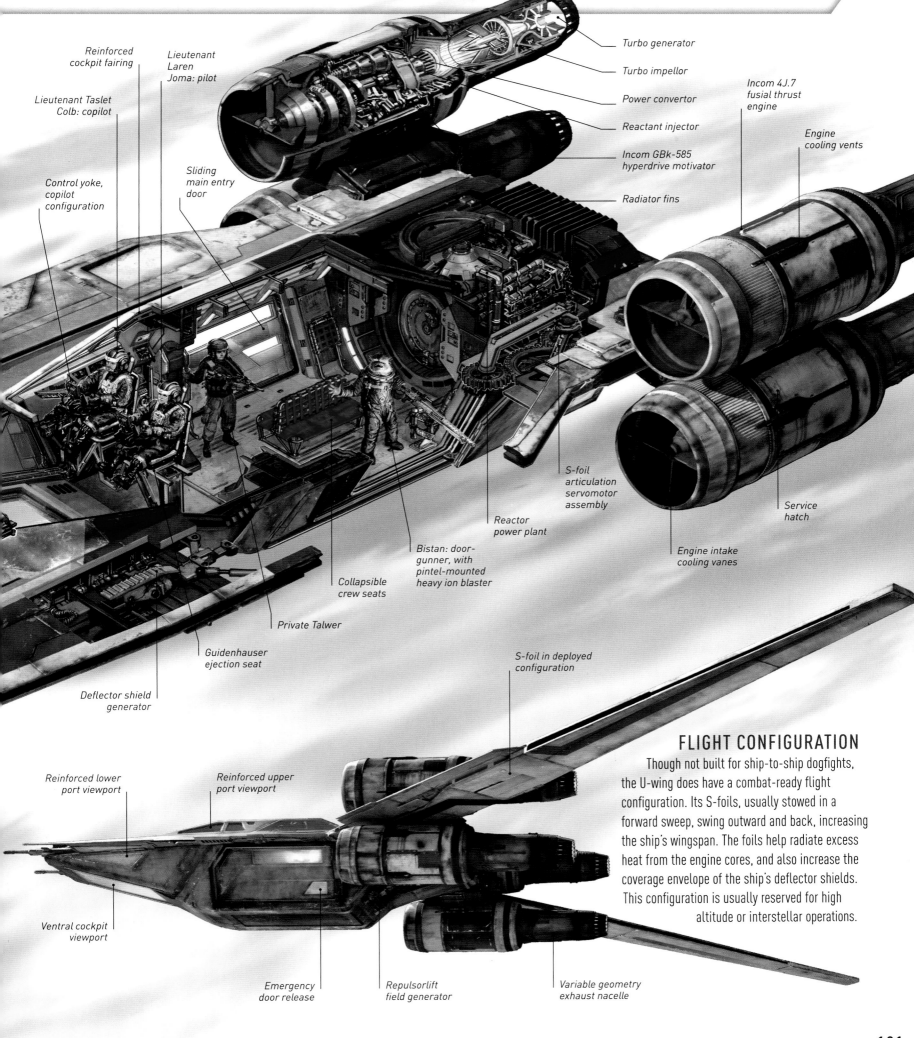

Reinforced cockpit fairing

Lieutenant Laren Joma: pilot

Lieutenant Taslet Colb: copilot

Turbo generator

Turbo impellor

Power convertor

Incom 4J.7 fusial thrust engine

Reactant injector

Engine cooling vents

Control yoke, copilot configuration

Sliding main entry door

Incom GBk-585 hyperdrive motivator

Radiator fins

S-foil articulation servomotor assembly

Reactor power plant

Service hatch

Collapsible crew seats

Bistan: door-gunner, with pintel-mounted heavy ion blaster

Engine intake cooling vanes

Private Talwer

Guidenhauser ejection seat

Deflector shield generator

S-foil in deployed configuration

FLIGHT CONFIGURATION

Though not built for ship-to-ship dogfights, the U-wing does have a combat-ready flight configuration. Its S-foils, usually stowed in a forward sweep, swing outward and back, increasing the ship's wingspan. The foils help radiate excess heat from the engine cores, and also increase the coverage envelope of the ship's deflector shields. This configuration is usually reserved for high altitude or interstellar operations.

Reinforced lower port viewport

Reinforced upper port viewport

Ventral cockpit viewport

Emergency door release

Repulsorlift field generator

Variable geometry exhaust nacelle

ZETA-CLASS SHUTTLES

The Telgorn Corporation and Sienar Fleet Systems pooled resources to create the *Zeta*-class shuttle, one of the most versatile transport craft employed by the Empire. Pressed into both military and civilian government service, the Zeta is built around a modular pod that can accommodate varied cargo needs. Zeta shuttles are in constant use as the Death Star operation nears completion, and components from scattered hidden laboratories need to be ferried to the battle station.

Outbound shuttle SW-4415 with deflector shield matrix circuitry

Self-diagnostic sensor node

Laser cannon positioning servo cap

Bodhi Rook and Corporal Tonc sit in the cockpit

Replaceable laser cannon barrel tip

Tech station

Forward viewpoint

Avionics bay and control interfaces

Primary active sensor bay

MODULAR CARGO

The *Zeta*-class shuttle's ventral cargo pod uses standardized umbilicals and docking sleeves for firm purchase into the spaceframe. These pods draw power from the Zeta's reactor plant, providing energy for specific cargo needs such as refrigeration or life support. Seasoned pilots can drop off and pick up without having to commit to a full landing, should expediency require it. Larger *Eta*-class supply barges can hold multiple pods aloft on a dorsal cargo bed.

Cassian Andor (disguised as Lieutenant Colin Hakelia)

Jyn Erso (disguised as Technician Kent Deezling)

Hydraulic ramp actuator

K-2SO

Deployed entry ramp

Auxiliary communications terminal and patch bay

Heavy repulsorlift generator
(linked set of 20)

Inbound shuttle SW-1721 with
turbolaser barrel sleeves

Heavy power trunking in
ion-shielded conduits

Deflector shield
projection duct

SCARIF INSERTION

During the Battle of Scarif, Rogue One land on a landing
pad on the planet and incapacitate an inspection team,
so Cassian Andor, Jyn Erso, and K-2SO can enter the
Scarif complex in disguise. The other commandos
use the cover afforded by blasts of coolant from
the shuttle's purge vents, which spew at steady
intervals as per standard landing procedure,
to sneak out of a belly hatch in the cargo pod.

Heat sink
radiator ports

Heavy servomotor
rotation gear

Tensor field
actuator
access panel

Wing articulation
servo hub

Chirrut
Îmwe

Baze
Malbus

Lieutenant Taidu Sefla
holds open hatch door

Loadlifter
interface handle

Incapacitated stormtroopers
crammed in floor space

Empty kyber crystal
shipment modules

Rebel commandos crawl
beneath belly of craft

Heavy load-bearing
landing strut

ALDERAAN CRUISER

Princess Leia Organa of Alderaan travels far and wide aboard her consular starship *Tantive IV*, negotiating peace settlements and bringing aid to imperiled populations. Commanded by the daring and loyal Captain Antilles, Leia's *Tantive IV* is a Corellian Corvette: an older, hand-crafted ship of a make seen throughout the galaxy. Owned by the Royal House of Alderaan, this versatile craft has served two generations of Alderaanian Senators since it was first acquired by Leia's father, Bail Organa, as one of his personal transports. Under the cover of diplomatic immunity, the *Tantive IV* has carried out a range of missions for the Rebel Alliance, making its added armor plate as vital as its formal state conference chamber. This sturdy ship has brought the Organas through many harrowing adventures, and it is only under the pursuit of Darth Vader that the *Tantive IV* is finally overtaken and captured.

"If this is a consular ship, where is the Ambassador?"
Darth Vader

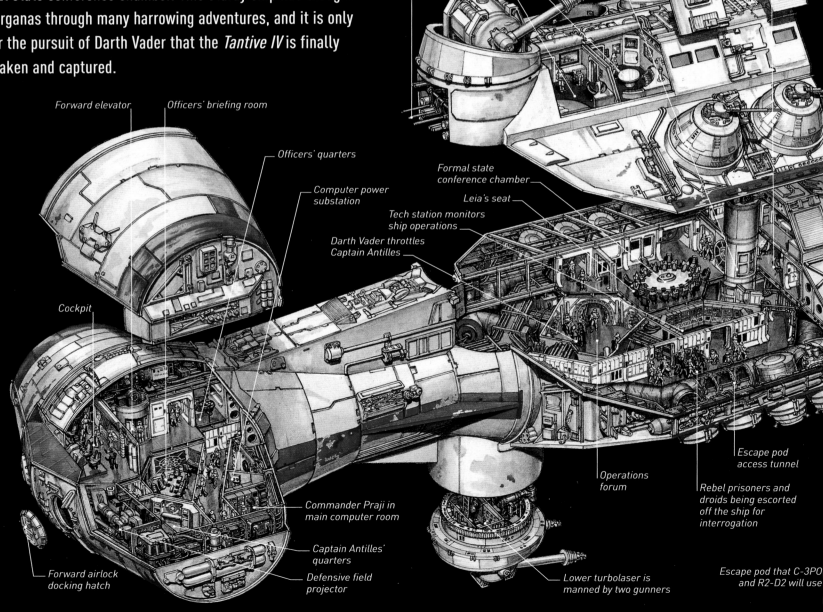

High-capacity pod is boarded via central access ladder

Armed high-capacity escape pod doubles as long-range laser turret

Leia's stateroom suite

Added armor plate permanently covers stateroom windows

Formal dining room

Control and power linkages

Mid-ship elevator

Forward elevator

Officers' briefing room

Officers' quarters

Computer power substation

Formal state conference chamber

Leia's seat

Tech station monitors ship operations

Darth Vader throttles Captain Antilles

Cockpit

Commander Praji in main computer room

Captain Antilles' quarters

Defensive field projector

Operations forum

Escape pod access tunnel

Rebel prisoners and droids being escorted off the ship for interrogation

Forward airlock docking hatch

Lower turbolaser is manned by two gunners

Escape pod that C-3PO and R2-D2 will use

ESCAPE PODS

Spacecraft escape pods range from coffin-like capsules to large lifeboats that are small ships in their own right. The Alderaan Cruiser carries eight small escape pods rated for up to three people, and four laser-armed pods that seat 12. More sophisticated than the smaller pods, these lifeboats nonetheless have a very limited range. None of the *Tantive IV*'s escape systems could save its crew from the *Devastator*'s guns.

No Escape The heavily damaged *Tantive IV* is pulled into the main hangar of the Imperial Star Destroyer *Devastator*.

SHIPBOARD SYMBOLS

The components of functional systems within the Corvette are coded with symbols such as these for identification and maintenance purposes.

Atmosphere substation
Power substation
Hyperdrive
Deflector system

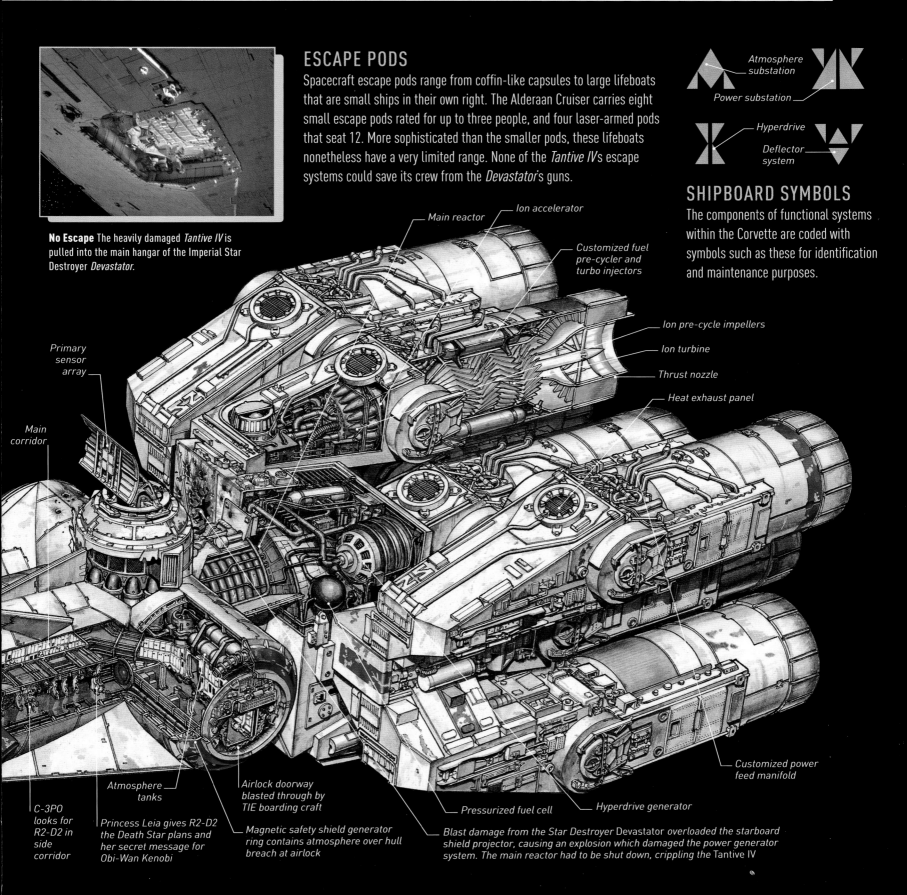

Main reactor
Ion accelerator
Customized fuel pre-cycler and turbo injectors
Ion pre-cycle impellers
Ion turbine
Thrust nozzle
Heat exhaust panel

Primary sensor array

Main corridor

Customized power feed manifold

C-3PO looks for R2-D2 in side corridor

Atmosphere tanks

Princess Leia gives R2-D2 the Death Star plans and her secret message for Obi-Wan Kenobi

Airlock doorway blasted through by TIE boarding craft

Magnetic safety shield generator ring contains atmosphere over hull breach at airlock

Pressurized fuel cell

Hyperdrive generator

Blast damage from the Star Destroyer *Devastator* overloaded the starboard shield projector, causing an explosion which damaged the power generator system. The main reactor had to be shut down, crippling the *Tantive IV*

THE CAPABLE CORVETTE

Sporting twin turbolaser turrets and a massive drive block of eleven ion turbine engines for speed, the Corellian Corvette balances defensive capabilities with a high power-to-mass ratio, meaning that what it can't shoot down it can generally outrun. The *Tantive IV* has been extensively refitted to suit Princess Leia's requirements.

REBEL SPIRIT

The *Tantive IV*'s crew have served under Princess Leia on many missions in the years leading up to the Battle of Scarif. During her trials to become the Crown Princess of Alderaan, Leia's first trial is to travel to Wobani aboard the *Tantive IV* and provide humanitarian relief to its people. While Leia cannot save everyone, she circumnavigates Imperial laws by enlisting 100 Wobani as crew, who escape Imperial opression and find sanctuary on Alderaan.

ESCAPE POD

The small pod used by R2-D2 and C-3PO carries a minimum of equipment: simple rocket engines propel the pod away from danger as it ejects, using basic technology unaffected by magnetic or electrical interference. A gravity ring beneath the seat helps keep passengers secure above and cushions the shock of landing by projecting an antigravity field below. Only a single viewport is built in: a small slot window that is used for checking the landing environment before emerging. Fore and aft cameras feed a monitor inside to help it escape peril and find a suitable landing site.

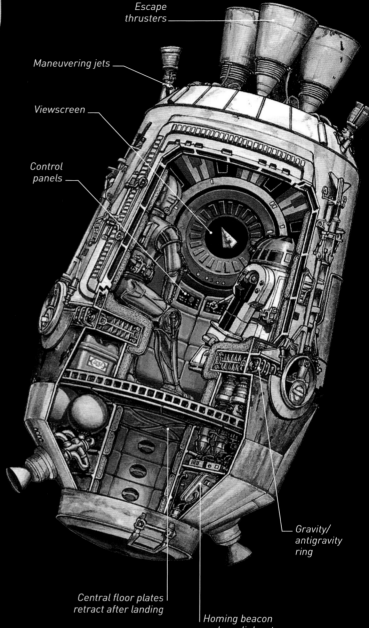

Escape thrusters

Maneuvering jets

Viewscreen

Control panels

Gravity/antigravity ring

Central floor plates retract after landing

Homing beacon and comlink set

Landing Systems Most pods are equipped with parachutes, repulsorlifts, and flotation devices to allow safe landings in a variety of environments.

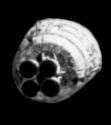

NO-FRILLS DESIGN

Devoid of ornamentation or unnecessary features, the Corellian Corvette escape pod was designed so only the retro-rocket propulsion thrusters and attitude-control thrusters protrude from the cylindrical body, allowing the pod to neatly deploy from a starship's ejection tube. Instead of a single button or switch to open the hatch that leads directly to the open escape pod, the hatch is equipped with a cluster of pressure-sensitive tabs, designed for ease of use by various dexterous life forms. Although escape pods are generally off limits to droids, an astromech can extend a control arm to press the tabs.

Automatic Pilot Although most escape pods are equipped with a simple piloting station, the shipboard systems are heavily automated, enabling the pod to find and travel to the nearest habitable planet without a pilot at the controls.

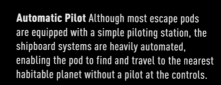

IMPERIAL NAVY

After the Clone Wars, the Republic Navy of the Galactic Republic was reformed into the Imperial Navy, its purpose to enforce the Emperor's rule. Despite this transition, the Navy's mission remains largely the same: to eliminate hazards to profitable commerce in Imperial systems, assure the safety of member worlds from enemy forces, and to bolster planetary governments in times of crisis. The heart of the Imperial Navy are its enormous capital ships—the Star Destroyers.

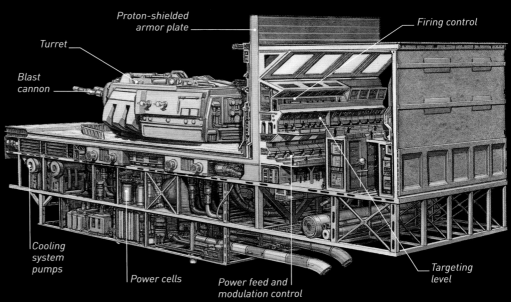

Proton-shielded armor plate

Firing control

Turret

Blast cannon

Cooling system pumps

Power cells

Power feed and modulation control

Targeting level

HEAVY BLASTER STATION

The heaviest weapons on board an *Imperial I*-class Star Destroyer are the six turbolaser turrets positioned with the two heavy ion cannon turrets along the flanks of the upper deck structure. Fifty meters in diameter, these turbolasers can overload deflector shields and punch holes in the most heavily armored spacecraft. While smaller, fast-moving ships are difficult to target with the turret guns, even a glancing hit from these cannons will destroy them.

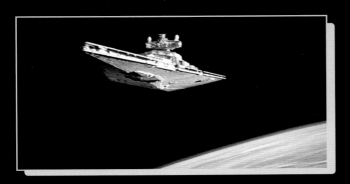

Orbital Blockades Although it is impossible to garrison every inhabited world in Imperial space, the Navy can deploy its Star Destroyers to even remote planets in a short period of time. The very idea of an orbital blockade or bombardment encourages most worlds to comply with Imperial laws.

Super Star Destroyers Impressive though *Imperial*-class Star Destroyers are, they are by no means the largest vessels in the fleet. Super Star Destroyers, such as Darth Vader's *Executor*, are many times larger and vastly more powerful, with crews numbering in the hundreds of thousands.

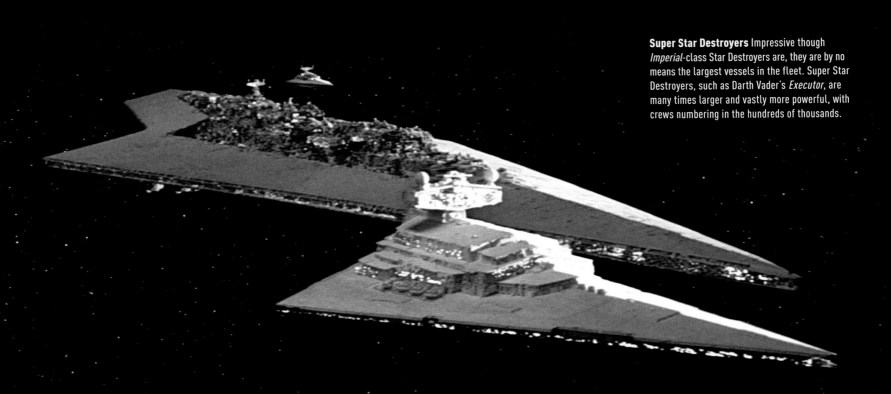

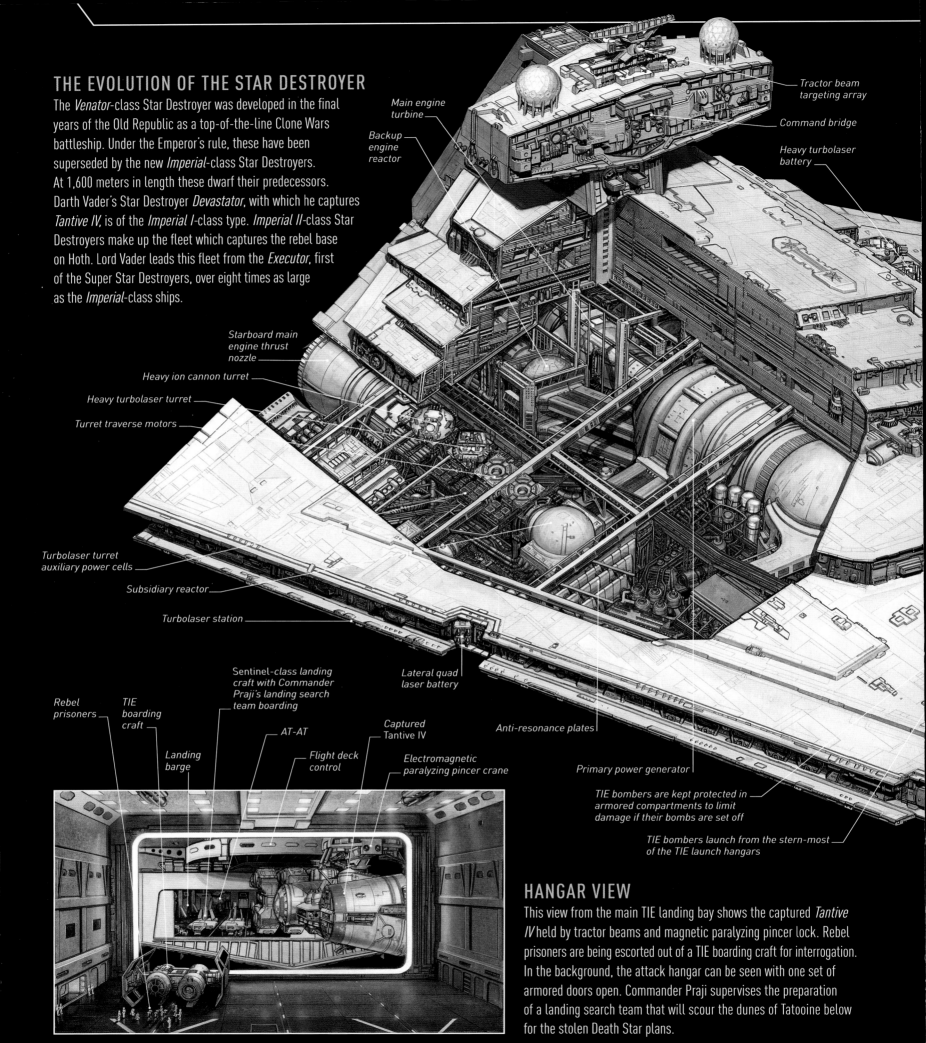

THE EVOLUTION OF THE STAR DESTROYER

The *Venator*-class Star Destroyer was developed in the final years of the Old Republic as a top-of-the-line Clone Wars battleship. Under the Emperor's rule, these have been superseded by the new *Imperial*-class Star Destroyers. At 1,600 meters in length these dwarf their predecessors. Darth Vader's Star Destroyer *Devastator*, with which he captures *Tantive IV*, is of the *Imperial I*-class type. *Imperial II*-class Star Destroyers make up the fleet which captures the rebel base on Hoth. Lord Vader leads this fleet from the *Executor*, first of the Super Star Destroyers, over eight times as large as the *Imperial*-class ships.

Main engine turbine

Backup engine reactor

Tractor beam targeting array

Command bridge

Heavy turbolaser battery

Starboard main engine thrust nozzle

Heavy ion cannon turret

Heavy turbolaser turret

Turret traverse motors

Turbolaser turret auxiliary power cells

Subsidiary reactor

Turbolaser station

Rebel prisoners

TIE boarding craft

Landing barge

Sentinel-class landing craft with Commander Praji's landing search team boarding

AT-AT

Flight deck control

Captured Tantive IV

Electromagnetic paralyzing pincer crane

Lateral quad laser battery

Anti-resonance plates

Primary power generator

TIE bombers are kept protected in armored compartments to limit damage if their bombs are set off

TIE bombers launch from the stern-most of the TIE launch hangars

HANGAR VIEW

This view from the main TIE landing bay shows the captured *Tantive IV* held by tractor beams and magnetic paralyzing pincer lock. Rebel prisoners are being escorted out of a TIE boarding craft for interrogation. In the background, the attack hangar can be seen with one set of armored doors open. Commander Praji supervises the preparation of a landing search team that will scour the dunes of Tatooine below for the stolen Death Star plans.

STAR DESTROYER

The Star Destroyer is a symbol of the Empire's military might, carrying devastating firepower and assault forces anywhere in the galaxy to subjugate opposition. A Star Destroyer can easily overtake most fleeing craft, blasting them into submission or drawing them into its main hangar with tractor beams. *Imperial*-class Star Destroyers are 1,600 meters long, bristling with turbolasers and ion cannons, and equipped with eight giant turret gun stations. Star Destroyers carry 9,700 stormtroopers and a full wing of 72 TIE ships (typically including 48 TIE/In fighters, 12 TIE bombers, and 12 TIE boarding craft) as well as a range of attack and landing craft. A single Star Destroyer can overwhelm an entire rebellious planet. Major industrialized worlds are usually assaulted with a fleet of six Star Destroyers operating with support cruisers and supply craft. Such a force can obliterate any defenses, occupying or completely destroying cities or settlements.

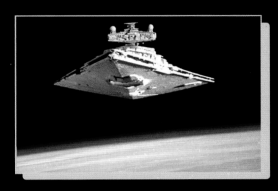

The *Devastator* An *Imperial I*-class Star Destroyer, the *Devastator* serves as Darth Vader's flagship when he pursues the *Tantive IV* to Tatooine, and is part of his fleet, Death Squadron.

Axial defense turret

Flight deck control

Armored doors of attack hangar, where landing craft are launched and landed

Tantive IV, held in main hangar

Command Bridge Only high-ranking officers have the privilege to gaze through the large windows that line a Star Destroyer's bridge. The remaining crew perform their duties in sunken pits without any window views to distract them from their sensor scopes.

Main TIE landing bay

Auxiliary reactor

Tractor beam power cells

Pursuit tractor beams

TIE fighter service and fueling bays

Raw materials

TIE fighters and bombers land in the main TIE landing bay and are transferred to these TIE launch hangars in transfer carriers

Liquid stores

Shuttle craft for high-ranking officials are deployed through the small forward hangar, which also serves as back-up to the main hangar

SANDCRAWLER

A leftover titan from a forgotten mining era long ago, the Jawa sandcrawler patrols the desert wastelands of Tatooine in search of metal salvage and minerals. Serving as home to an entire clan of Jawas, the sandcrawler migrates across a wide territory over the course of a year, hunting for the wrecks that dot Tatooine's surface from spaceship crashes through centuries past. Jawas also round up stray droids, junked vehicles, and unwanted metal of any kind from settlements and moisture farmers. Pitted and scoured by numberless sandstorms, the sandcrawler serves the Jawas as transport, workshop, traveling store, and safe protection from the untold dangers of the desert.

JAWA REPAIRS

Jawas are experts at making use of available components to repair machinery and can put together a working droid from the most surprising variety of scrap parts. However, they are notorious for peddling shoddy workmanship that will last just long enough for the sandcrawler to disappear over the horizon.

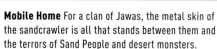

Mobile Home For a clan of Jawas, the metal skin of the sandcrawler is all that stands between them and the terrors of Sand People and desert monsters.

Case-hardened smashers crush minerals or compact metal for storage

Conveyor at top of elevator

Ore crusher

Drill grinders

Laser pre-processor

Power generators

Reactor powers entire sandcrawler

Engineering station

Maintenance passage

Reactor melts processed ore and metal into a superheated cascade

Power cell

Ingots are extruded from purified underlevels of slag pool

Primary drive

Rear treads non-steerable, for drive only

Electrostatic repellers keep sand from interior components

Steam-heating array

Extensible starboard boarding gantry

Repulsorlift tube energizer

Extensible repulsorlift tube

DANGEROUS PRIZES

The furious winds of Tatooine's storm season can scour ancient spacewrecks from the deep sands of the Dune Sea. Jawa sandcrawlers venture into remote territories after the storms, searching for newly exposed prizes. Larger finds may cause them to call in other sandcrawlers to share in the processing. Field smelting factories and awnings are quickly erected as the Jawa work to beat the arrival of the next storm.

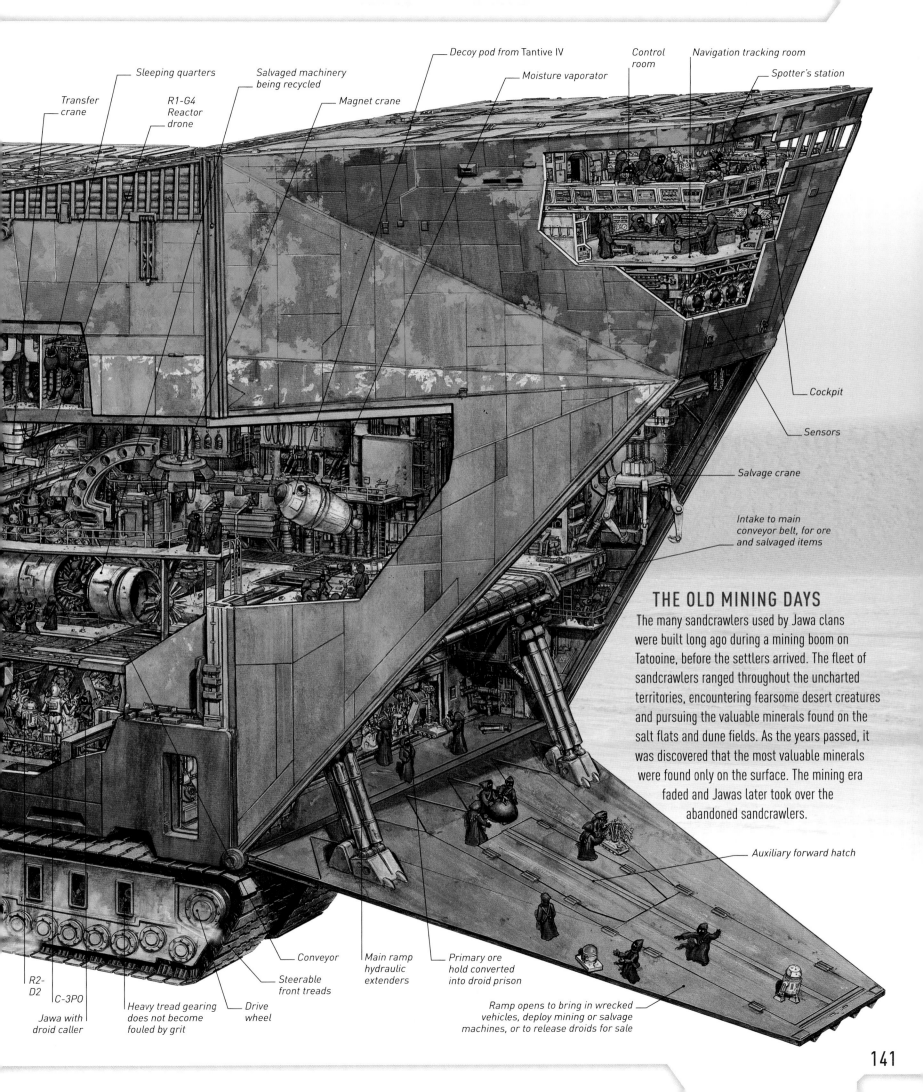

Transfer crane

Sleeping quarters

R1-G4 Reactor drone

Salvaged machinery being recycled

Magnet crane

Decoy pod from Tantive IV

Moisture vaporator

Control room

Navigation tracking room

Spotter's station

Cockpit

Sensors

Salvage crane

Intake to main conveyor belt, for ore and salvaged items

THE OLD MINING DAYS

The many sandcrawlers used by Jawa clans were built long ago during a mining boom on Tatooine, before the settlers arrived. The fleet of sandcrawlers ranged throughout the uncharted territories, encountering fearsome desert creatures and pursuing the valuable minerals found on the salt flats and dune fields. As the years passed, it was discovered that the most valuable minerals were found only on the surface. The mining era faded and Jawas later took over the abandoned sandcrawlers.

Auxiliary forward hatch

R2-D2

C-3PO

Jawa with droid caller

Heavy tread gearing does not become fouled by grit

Drive wheel

Conveyor

Steerable front treads

Main ramp hydraulic extenders

Primary ore hold converted into droid prison

Ramp opens to bring in wrecked vehicles, deploy mining or salvage machines, or to release droids for sale

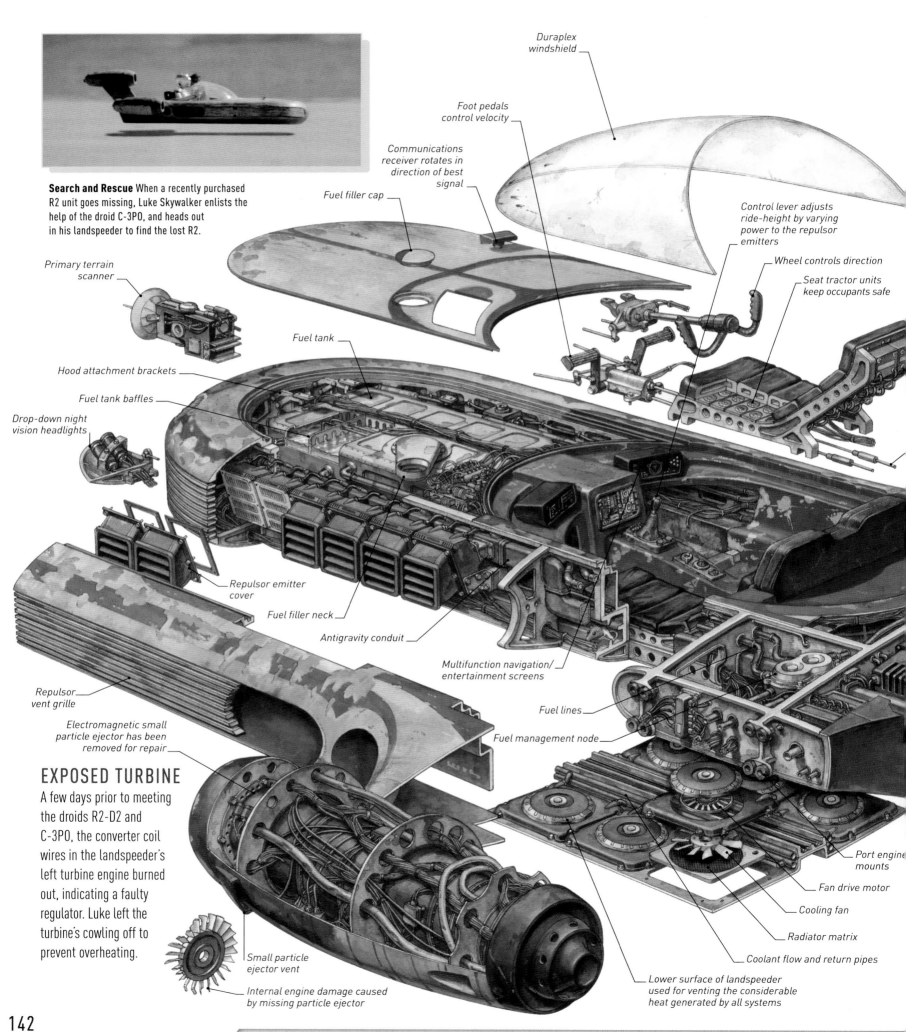

Search and Rescue When a recently purchased R2 unit goes missing, Luke Skywalker enlists the help of the droid C-3PO, and heads out in his landspeeder to find the lost R2.

Duraplex windshield

Foot pedals control velocity

Communications receiver rotates in direction of best signal

Fuel filler cap

Control lever adjusts ride-height by varying power to the repulsor emitters

Wheel controls direction

Seat tractor units keep occupants safe

Primary terrain scanner

Hood attachment brackets

Fuel tank

Fuel tank baffles

Drop-down night vision headlights

Repulsor emitter cover

Fuel filler neck

Antigravity conduit

Multifunction navigation/entertainment screens

Repulsor vent grille

Fuel lines

Fuel management node

Electromagnetic small particle ejector has been removed for repair

EXPOSED TURBINE

A few days prior to meeting the droids R2-D2 and C-3PO, the converter coil wires in the landspeeder's left turbine engine burned out, indicating a faulty regulator. Luke left the turbine's cowling off to prevent overheating.

Small particle ejector vent

Internal engine damage caused by missing particle ejector

Port engine mounts

Fan drive motor

Cooling fan

Radiator matrix

Coolant flow and return pipes

Lower surface of landspeeder used for venting the considerable heat generated by all systems

LUKE'S LANDSPEEDER

Luke Skywalker's late-model SoroSuub X-34 landspeeder is one of his few sources of excitement. Having been raised by his Uncle Owen Lars and Aunt Beru on their Tatooine moisture farm, Luke obtained the landspeeder after Owen asked him to take responsibility for more moisture vaporators across their vast property. Luke argued that the most efficient way to inspect and maintain the vaporators would be to have his own landspeeder, and Owen grudgingly allowed Luke to purchase the poor-condition SoroSuub X-34 for 2,400 credits. The open cockpit seats a driver and a passenger, and built-in magnetic clamps behind the seats can secure droids or small cargo modules. The windshield is designed to close to a sealed bubble, but Luke keeps the cockpit open because he has yet to fix the shield's back half. Luke has put considerable time into restoring the vehicle, and uses the best parts he can afford to upgrade the repulsorlifts and turbine engines.

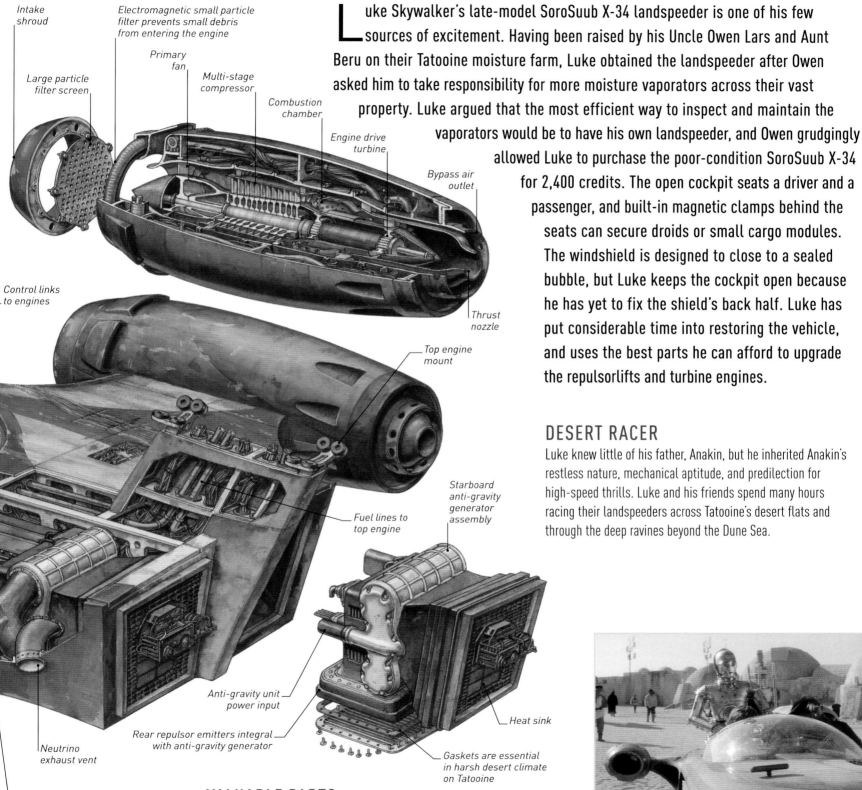

Intake shroud

Electromagnetic small particle filter prevents small debris from entering the engine

Primary fan

Large particle filter screen

Multi-stage compressor

Combustion chamber

Engine drive turbine

Bypass air outlet

Control links to engines

Thrust nozzle

Top engine mount

Starboard anti-gravity generator assembly

Fuel lines to top engine

Anti-gravity unit power input

Rear repulsor emitters integral with anti-gravity generator

Heat sink

Gaskets are essential in harsh desert climate on Tatooine

Neutrino exhaust vent

Power generator: All major systems are duplicated and have sufficient capacity to keep craft airborne in the event of component failure

DESERT RACER

Luke knew little of his father, Anakin, but he inherited Anakin's restless nature, mechanical aptitude, and predilection for high-speed thrills. Luke and his friends spend many hours racing their landspeeders across Tatooine's desert flats and through the deep ravines beyond the Dune Sea.

VALUABLE PARTS

Because Tatooine has few factories or significant manufacturing facilities, the planet depends heavily on imported technology and recycled materials. Left unattended, a landspeeder makes a tempting target for Tusken Raiders, who by tradition transform scavenged metal into lethal weapons.

Mid-Air Parking Like most landspeeders, Luke's vehicle continues to hover above the ground after he has brought it to a complete stop.

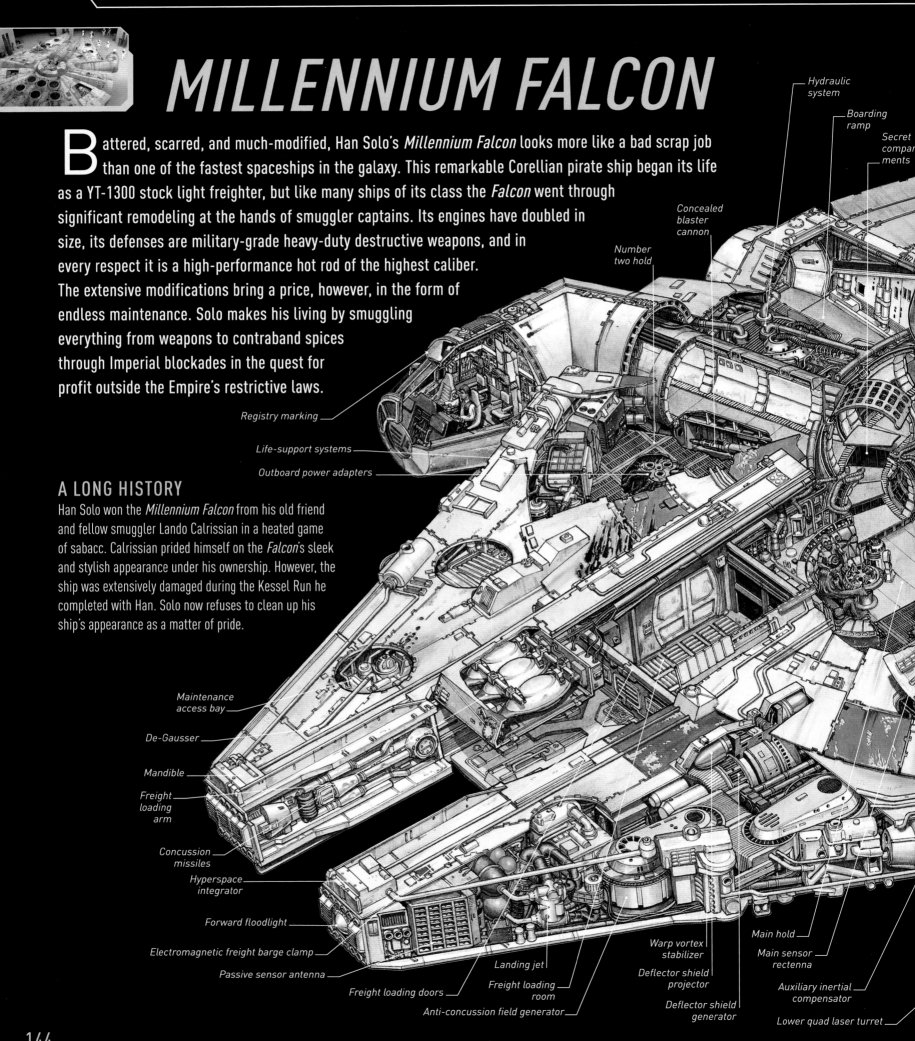

MILLENNIUM FALCON

Battered, scarred, and much-modified, Han Solo's *Millennium Falcon* looks more like a bad scrap job than one of the fastest spaceships in the galaxy. This remarkable Corellian pirate ship began its life as a YT-1300 stock light freighter, but like many ships of its class the *Falcon* went through significant remodeling at the hands of smuggler captains. Its engines have doubled in size, its defenses are military-grade heavy-duty destructive weapons, and in every respect it is a high-performance hot rod of the highest caliber. The extensive modifications bring a price, however, in the form of endless maintenance. Solo makes his living by smuggling everything from weapons to contraband spices through Imperial blockades in the quest for profit outside the Empire's restrictive laws.

A LONG HISTORY

Han Solo won the *Millennium Falcon* from his old friend and fellow smuggler Lando Calrissian in a heated game of sabacc. Calrissian prided himself on the *Falcon's* sleek and stylish appearance under his ownership. However, the ship was extensively damaged during the Kessel Run he completed with Han. Solo now refuses to clean up his ship's appearance as a matter of pride.

Hydraulic system

Boarding ramp

Secret compartments

Concealed blaster cannon

Number two hold

Registry marking

Life-support systems

Outboard power adapters

Maintenance access bay

De-Gausser

Mandible

Freight loading arm

Concussion missiles

Hyperspace integrator

Forward floodlight

Electromagnetic freight barge clamp

Passive sensor antenna

Freight loading doors

Anti-concussion field generator

Landing jet

Freight loading room

Warp vortex stabilizer

Deflector shield projector

Deflector shield generator

Main hold

Main sensor rectenna

Auxiliary inertial compensator

Lower quad laser turret

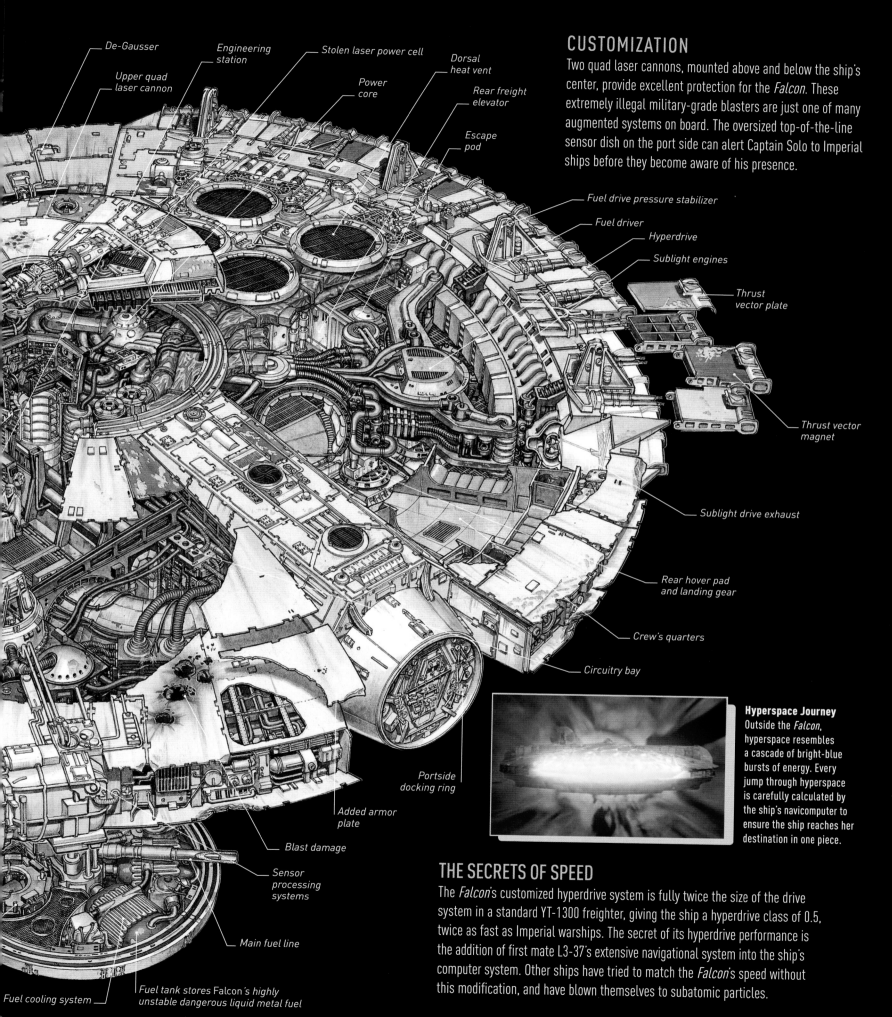

De-Gausser

Upper quad
laser cannon

Engineering
station

Stolen laser power cell

Power
core

Dorsal
heat vent

Rear freight
elevator

Escape
pod

CUSTOMIZATION

Two quad laser cannons, mounted above and below the ship's center, provide excellent protection for the *Falcon*. These extremely illegal military-grade blasters are just one of many augmented systems on board. The oversized top-of-the-line sensor dish on the port side can alert Captain Solo to Imperial ships before they become aware of his presence.

Fuel drive pressure stabilizer

Fuel driver

Hyperdrive

Sublight engines

Thrust
vector plate

Thrust vector
magnet

Sublight drive exhaust

Rear hover pad
and landing gear

Crew's quarters

Circuitry bay

Hyperspace Journey
Outside the *Falcon*, hyperspace resembles a cascade of bright-blue bursts of energy. Every jump through hyperspace is carefully calculated by the ship's navicomputer to ensure the ship reaches her destination in one piece.

Portside
docking ring

Added armor
plate

Blast damage

Sensor
processing
systems

Main fuel line

Fuel cooling system

Fuel tank stores Falcon's highly
unstable dangerous liquid metal fuel

THE SECRETS OF SPEED

The *Falcon's* customized hyperdrive system is fully twice the size of the drive system in a standard YT-1300 freighter, giving the ship a hyperdrive class of 0.5, twice as fast as Imperial warships. The secret of its hyperdrive performance is the addition of first mate L3-37's extensive navigational system into the ship's computer system. Other ships have tried to match the *Falcon's* speed without this modification, and have blown themselves to subatomic particles.

"WHAT A PIECE OF JUNK!"

Like most people, Luke Skywalker has difficulty finding any obvious qualities in the *Millennium Falcon* when he first views the ship, but he soon discovers that the *Falcon*'s ramshackle appearance belies the fact that she is one of the fastest ships in the galaxy. Thanks to the *Falcon* crew's innovations with sensor-jamming technology, even the sophisticated scanners used by authorities in Imperial space and the Corporate Sector fail to detect the *Falcon*'s unique capabilities.

Docking Bay 94 Typical of the landing bays scattered throughout Mos Eisley Spaceport, Docking Bay 94 is simply a large, open-roof pit with reinforced walls.

GALACTIC ADVENTURES

After capturing the *Millennium Falcon* near the remains of the planet Alderaan, Imperial boarding parties find nothing remarkable about the *Falcon*'s grimy interior, and their scanners fail to detect any lifeforms on board. Unknown to them, Captain Han Solo has concealed compartments for smuggling, and the below-deck chambers also prove useful for hiding crew and passengers. The ship's occupants escape, rescue the captive Princess Leia, and assist in the destruction of the first Death Star, striking a crucial blow against the Empire.

Dejarik Gameboard
The *Falcon* was equipped with a holographic dejarik table. This table projects a range of hologames on a surface of checkered circles. Dejarik chess is shown here.

M'onnok

Ng'ok

Grimtaash the Molator

Kintan Strider

Mantellian Savrip

K'lor'slug

Ghhhk

Houjix

Quick Getaway Docking Bay 94's old walls were designed to withstand the backblast of ion sublight engines. When attacked by Imperial stormtroopers, the *Falcon*'s repulsorlift engines allow for a hasty exit through the bay's open roof.

Blind Spot The *Millenium Falcon* escapes the pursuing Star Destroyer *Avenger* by hiding in a senso blind spot on the rear of its bridge conning tower

Reunion on Cloud City
Han Solo lands the damaged *Falcon* in Cloud City, where he seeks help from Lando Calrissian, the *Falcon*'s previous owner.

The Battle of Endor
At the controls of the *Falcon*, Lando Calrissian leads the rebel fleet into battle against the second Death Star.

SHIP OF DESTINY

The *Millennium Falcon* is one of many ships forced to flee from the secret rebel base on Hoth, in the face of an Imperial assault. Han Solo guides the *Falcon* into the Hoth system's asteroid belt to escape the pursuing Imperial warships, despite the probability of successfully navigating an asteroid field being approximately 3,720 to 1. In need of repairs to the *Falcon*'s hyperdrive, Han then reluctantly travels to Cloud City in the Bespin system, and seeks help from the *Falcon*'s former owner, Lando Calrissian. However, in the process he is captured by the infamous bounty hunter Boba Fett. Once again under the command of Lando Calrissian, the *Falcon* subsequently plays a pivotal role in the climactic Battle of Endor, leading the assault on the second Death Star, and successfully destroying the giant battle station.

Tight Squeeze Lando pilots the *Falcon* through the second Death Star's skeletal superstructure to destroy the battle station's reactor core. The *Falcon* proves more nimble on sharp turns than the pursuing Imperial TIE fighters.

DETENTION BLOCK AA-23

A desperate plan takes Luke, Han, and Chewbacca into the heart of peril as they try to rescue Princess Leia. Disguised as stormtroopers, Luke and Han escort Chewbacca, their "prisoner," into Leia's detention block. The supervisor suspects trouble, and only immediate action will save the rebels.

TRASH COMPACTOR 32-6-3827

Escaping Leia's cell block, the rebels dive into a garbage chute and land in a trash compactor, where refuse of every kind is collected before being processed and dumped into space.

AIR SHAFT

Throughout the Death Star are vast air shafts. Extendable bridges connect passages across the shafts, but can be disabled. When Luke and Leia find themselves trapped at one of the air shafts, quick thinking and bravery provide the only way across.

TRACTOR BEAM REACTOR COUPLING

The Death Star tractor beam is coupled to the main reactor in seven locations. These power terminals stand atop generator towers 35 kilometers tall. The air is taut with high-voltage electricity throughout the shaft surrounding the tower. It is in this setting that Ben Kenobi secretly deactivates one of the power beams to allow the *Millennium Falcon* to escape.

CHALLENGE AND SACRIFICE

Darth Vader senses the presence of his old Jedi master Obi-Wan Kenobi aboard the Death Star, and confronts him alone in a deadly lightsaber duel. Kenobi sacrifices himself to help his young friends escape, yielding to Vader in an empty victory in which, mysteriously, Obi-Wan becomes one with the Force.

Tractor beam power coupling deactivated by Ben Kenobi

Secondary power converters

Power processing networks

Atmosphere processing unit

Ion drive reactor

Atmosphere processing substation

Equatorial docking bay

Ion sublight engines

DEATH STAR

The Empire's gigantic battle station code-named Death Star is 160 kilometers in diameter, large enough to be mistaken for a small moon. This colossal superweapon is designed to enforce the Emperor's rule through terror, presenting both the symbol and reality of ultimate destructive power. Making use of the Empire's most advanced discoveries in super-engineering, the Death Star is built around a hypermatter reactor that can generate enough power to destroy an entire planet. Partially designed in secret on Geonosis, and then built in orbit around the planet, its construction was promoted by Wilhuff Tarkin and supervised by Orson Krennic. The Death Star's vast structure houses over a million individuals and thousands of armed spacecraft, making it capable of occupying whole star systems by force. Elite gunners and troopers man the station's advanced weapons. The Death Star, once fully operational, represents a chilling specter of totalitarian domination and threatens to extinguish all hope for freedom in the galaxy.

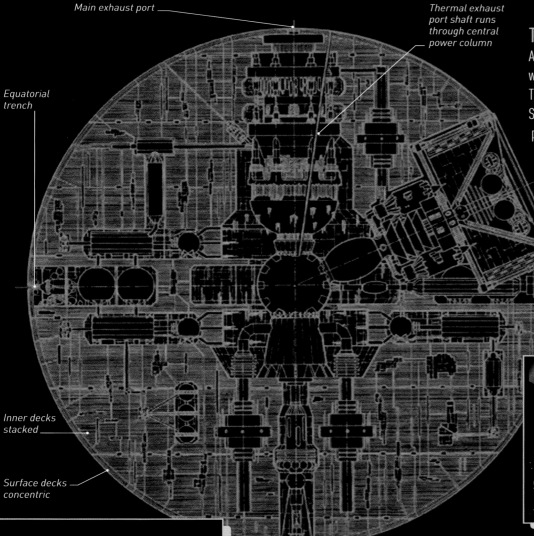

Main exhaust port

Thermal exhaust port shaft runs through central power column

Equatorial trench

Inner decks stacked

Surface decks concentric

THE STOLEN PLANS

A complete technical readout of the battle station (left) was stolen by rebel troops during the Battle of Scarif. These plans reveal the overwhelming might of the Death Star, detailing its myriad weapons systems and immense power structures. Ion engines, hyperdrives, and hangar bays ring the station's equatorial trench, while power cells over 15 kilometers wide distribute energy throughout the thousands of internal decks of the station. Air shafts and void spaces honeycomb the interior. Occupying the polar axis of the Death Star is its central power column, with the hypermatter reactor at its core. However, rebellious scientist Galen Erso included one fatal flaw in the Death Star's defenses—a small thermal exhaust port that lead from the surface to the heart of the main reactor.

ALDERAAN DESTROYED

Following the superlaser's use to partially destroy Jedha and Scarif, Grand Moff Tarkin orders the complete destruction of the peaceful planet Alderaan. As the superlaser lances out at the blue-green planet, this horrific act wipes out billions of people.

SUPERLASER TRIBUTARY BEAM SHAFT

Powered by kyber crystals, eight tributary beams unite to form the superlaser's primary beam. These tributary beams are arranged around the invisible central focusing field, firing in alternate sequence to build the power necessary to destroy a planet. The titanic energy of these beams must be monitored to prevent imbalance explosions.

TIE FIGHTER

TIE fighters are the most visible image of the Empire's wide-reaching power, and the TIE engine is the most precisely manufactured propulsion system in the galaxy. Solar arrays collect light energy, channeling it through a reactor to fire emissions from a high-pressure radioactive gas. The engine has no moving parts, reducing its maintenance requirements. These lightweight ships are built without defensive shields or hyperdrives, so they gain speed and maneuverability at the price of fragility, and reliance on nearby Imperial bases or vessels for support.

ALL THE SAME

TIE pilots may never use the same ship twice, and develop no sentimental attachment to their craft as rebels often do. TIE pilots know that every reconditioned fighter is identical to a factory-fresh ship; one is the same as many thousands—another reinforcement of Imperial philosophy of absolute conformity.

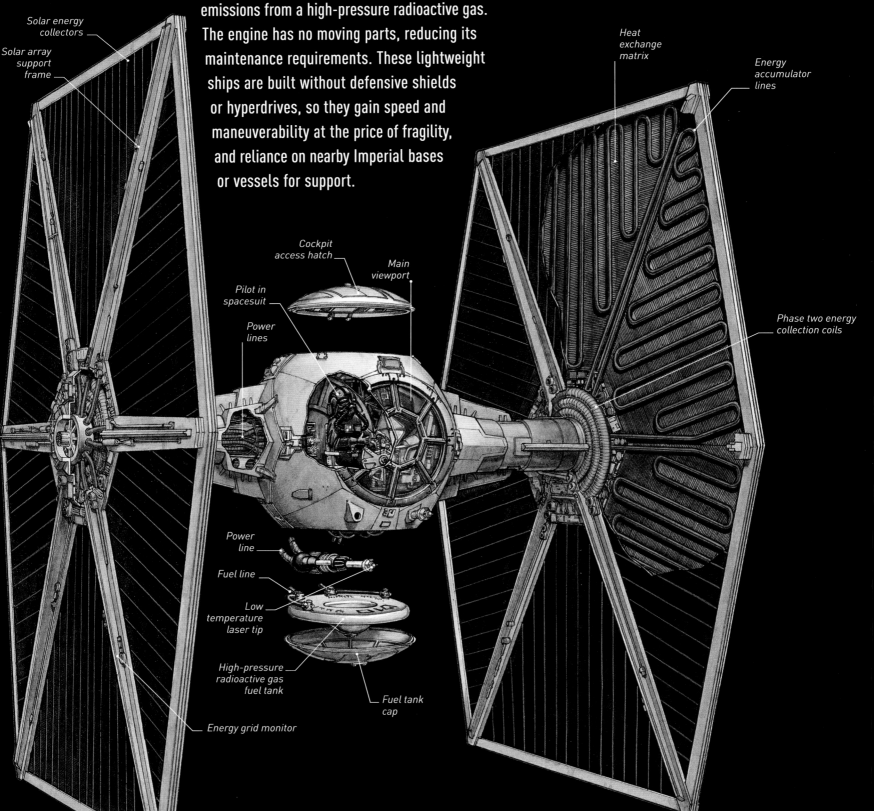

Solar energy collectors

Solar array support frame

Heat exchange matrix

Energy accumulator lines

Cockpit access hatch

Main viewport

Pilot in spacesuit

Power lines

Phase two energy collection coils

Power line

Fuel line

Low temperature laser tip

High-pressure radioactive gas fuel tank

Fuel tank cap

Energy grid monitor

TIE MISSION PROFILES

TIE fighters are deployed for a variety of mission profiles. Their primary role is as space superiority fighters, engaging rebel craft and defending Imperial bases and capital ships. Scout TIEs may travel alone to cover wide areas of space. Such individual scouts patrol the huge asteroid field left by the explosion of the planet Alderaan. Ships are assigned to escort duty in pairs, such as the twin TIEs that escort all flights of the Emperor's shuttle. Regular sentry groups of four TIE fighters patrol the space around Imperial bases, stations, and capital starships. A typical TIE fighter attack squadron consists of 12 ships, and a full attack wing consists of six squadrons, or 72 TIE fighters.

Upgraded Lasers
Originally, TIE laser cannons drew power from the ion engines. Because this reduced maneuverability in heavy combat when the lasers were used frequently, a separate power generator has been installed to increase the lasers' range and lethality.

Retaining claw

TIE in launch position

Pilots' boarding gantry

Transfer tunnel

Pilot boarding ship

Hangar control room

Launching TIE fighter

Elevator well

Service gantry

TIE arriving from landing hangar

Service droid

TIE HANGAR

TIEs are launched from cycling racks of up to 72 ships. Pilots board the TIEs from overhead gantries and the ships are released into space as they disengage from the front position in the rack system. Returning ships land in separate hangars, where they are guided into receiver-carriers by small tractor beams. The receivers carry the TIE to a debarkation station where the pilot exits. From there the TIE may be serviced and refueled in a separate bay on its way through transfer tunnels to a launch hangar. In the launch hangar the TIE is cycled into the launch rack, ready for its next mission.

PILOT PSYCHOLOGY

Aspiring TIE pilots are rigorously trained in Imperial academies to fly the full range of TIEs. They are taught that they are the best pilots in the galaxy and only a small number graduate with commissions, so they all tend to be very arrogant and proud. They are completely focused on completing the mission, even if it results in their deaths.

Overbridge

Beam emitter
kyber crystal

Primary beam
focusing magnet

Targeting field
generator

Static discharge
tower

Star Destroyer

Docking Bay 327

Magnetic
shielding

Hyperdrive

Tributary superlaser
beam shaft

Induction hyperphase
generator

Firing field
amplifier

Main power
generator

Carrier beam
crystal

Primary power
amplifier

Insulator plating

Hypermätter reactor

DOCKING BAY 327

Drawn in by a tractor beam, the *Millennium Falcon* comes to rest in a pressurized hangar within the Death Star's equatorial trench. Magnetic shields over the entrance retain the atmosphere. Outboard power-feeds hook up to landed craft so that the ship reactors can be shut down while in the hangar.

ASSAULT ON THE POLAR TRENCH

The exhaust port target of the rebel assault is protected in a trench, which is in turn protected by a hail of fire from deadly turbolaser towers on the Death Star surface. To bomb the exhaust port, the rebel fighters must maneuver down the trench beneath the fire zone, but they find themselves pursued closely by Imperial TIE fighters and Darth Vader himself. The defense is lethal: all but three of the rebel fighters are destroyed.

OVERBRIDGE

The primary control room of the Death Star is the overbridge, situated at the top edge of the superlaser dish. From this nerve center Grand Moff Tarkin commands the gigantic battle station. The staff feeds critical information to the main viewscreen.

EXHAUST PORT

The rebels target this two-meter-wide thermal exhaust port as their one chance of destroying the Death Star. Red Leader's shot at the small port is only a near miss.

Target exhaust shaft

Concentric surface structure

Power cell

Tractor beam generator tower

T-65 X-WING

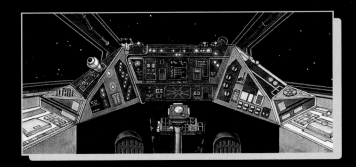

The X-wing starfighter finds its origins in the Clone Wars, with predecessors like the Z-95 Headhunter and ARC-170 fighter serving the Republic Navy well. With the transition of the Republic to the Empire, naval operations emphasized the might of capital ships, and investment in starfighter superiority withered. But, in the hands of the Rebellion, the Incom T-65 X-wing rose to prominence. Carrying heavy firepower, hyperdrive, and defensive shields, the X-wing is nonetheless maneuverable enough for close combat with the Empire's lethally agile TIE fighters. Although a formidable space superiority fighter, the X-wing's complex systems and rare alloys have delayed full-scale production of the craft for years.

The on-board R2 astromech droid carries out hyperspace calculations and handles in-flight operational adjustments and damage control

Cockpit canopy

INSIDE THE COCKPIT

The X-wing's highly responsive maneuverability can make it a dangerous craft for new pilots to handle. In addition to the fairly straightforward flight control systems, comprehensive cockpit displays allow the pilot to monitor and control energy distribution throughout the ship's systems during combat.

Pitch and roll control pedals

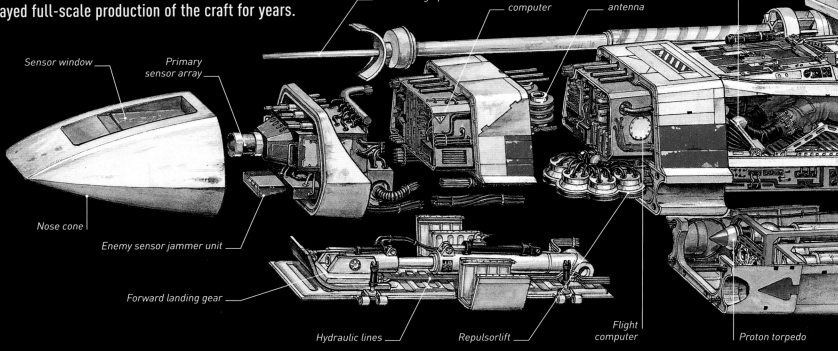

Laser firing tip
Sensor computer
Communications antenna
Sensor window
Primary sensor array
Nose cone
Enemy sensor jammer unit
Forward landing gear
Hydraulic lines
Repulsorlift
Flight computer
Proton torpedo

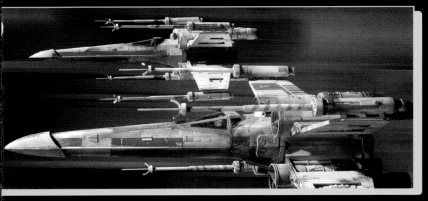

Farmboy to Fighter Pilot
Luke Skywalker had never piloted an Incom Corporation X-wing prior to the Battle of Yavin. However, his experience flying an Incom T-16 Skyhopper through the twisting canyons on Tatooine proves invaluable when he enters the Death Star's polar trench.

INDEPENDENT OPERATION

Thanks to its hyperdrive and its ability to launch and land without special support enable the X-wing to operate independently. The X-wing is equipped with life support sufficient for one week in space: air, water, food, and life-process support equipment are packed into the area behind the pilot's seat. When the ship lands, the air supply can be renewed, and the water and life support systems partially recharged. A cargo bay carries survival gear for pilots who land in hostile environments.

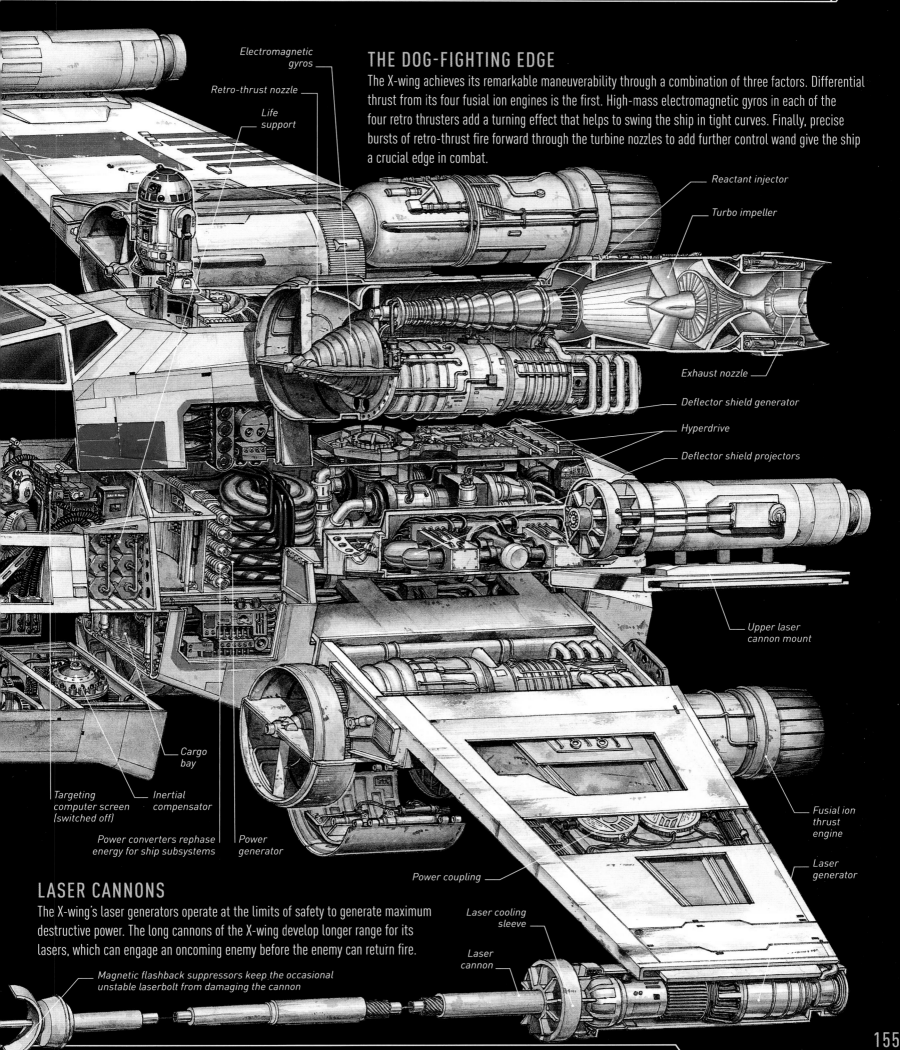

Electromagnetic
gyros

Retro-thrust nozzle

Life
support

THE DOG-FIGHTING EDGE

The X-wing achieves its remarkable maneuverability through a combination of three factors. Differential thrust from its four fusial ion engines is the first. High-mass electromagnetic gyros in each of the four retro thrusters add a turning effect that helps to swing the ship in tight curves. Finally, precise bursts of retro-thrust fire forward through the turbine nozzles to add further control wand give the ship a crucial edge in combat.

Reactant injector

Turbo impeller

Exhaust nozzle

Deflector shield generator

Hyperdrive

Deflector shield projectors

Upper laser
cannon mount

Cargo
bay

Targeting
computer screen
(switched off)

Inertial
compensator

Power converters rephase
energy for ship subsystems

Power
generator

Power coupling

Fusial ion
thrust
engine

Laser
generator

LASER CANNONS

The X-wing's laser generators operate at the limits of safety to generate maximum destructive power. The long cannons of the X-wing develop longer range for its lasers, which can engage an oncoming enemy before the enemy can return fire.

Laser cooling
sleeve

Laser
cannon

Magnetic flashback suppressors keep the occasional
unstable laserbolt from damaging the cannon

THE BATTLE OF YAVIN

After Luke Skywalker and the crew of the *Millennium Falcon* rescue Princess Leia from the Death Star, they flee across space with an unwelcome passenger: an Imperial homing beacon. This allows Imperial forces to trace the *Falcon* to her destination, the rebels' secret base on the moon Yavin 4. As the ponderous Death Star crawls across hyperspace to the Yavin system, the rebels discover a crucial flaw in the battle station's design, and race to form a plan of attack before Grand Moff Tarkin makes Yavin 4 his next target for annihilation.

Improvised Hangar The ancient Great Temple on Yavin 4 serves as the headquarters for the Rebel Alliance. Rebel engineers transformed the temple's ground floor and underground levels into hangars for starfighters and transports.

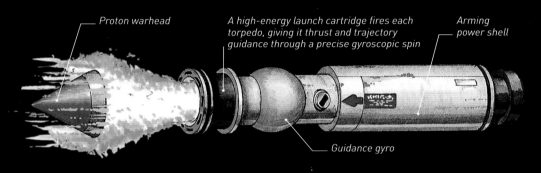

Proton warhead

A high-energy launch cartridge fires each torpedo, giving it thrust and trajectory guidance through a precise gyroscopic spin

Arming power shell

Guidance gyro

DESTROYER OF THE DEATH STAR

Proton torpedoes such as the MG7-As carried by the X-wing and Y-wing are extremely dangerous focused nuclear explosives. They are used for critical target destruction or to punch through ray shielding that will deflect laser weapons. Proton torpedoes are very expensive and available to Alliance forces only in limited numbers. Luke Skywalker carries only a single pair for his critical shots that destroy the Death Star.

Rebel Squadrons Skirting the orbit of the gas giant Yavin, X-wing and Y-wing starfighters fly toward the Death Star. The groups include Red Squadron, which consists of X-wings, and Gold Squadron with Y-wings.

Attack Formation Innovative twin-split "S-foil" wings give the X-wing improved performance in atmospheric flight. In combat, the wings deploy in an "X" shape, increasing weapons coverage.

Y-WING: REBEL WORKHORSE

O riginally produced by Koensayr Manufacturing for the Republic fleet during the Clone Wars, the BTL Y-wing is a combination starfighter and light bomber, and is the most prevalent fighter in the Rebel Alliance. Koensayr produced several different models, adapted for different missions, including one-man and two-man versions, but most of the Alliance's Y-wings are so stripped down that they only skeletally resemble the stock models. The Y-wing's solid construction weathers combat damage that would destroy similar-sized fighters, and has earned its reputation as the workhorse of the rebel fighting forces.

Tunnel Vision The Y-wing's cockpit offers limited visibility when compared with later Alliance fighter designs such as the T-65 X-wing or RZ-1 A-wing.

ORIGINAL SPLENDOR

Originally all versions of the the Y-wing were entirely sheathed in body shells (right). Because the aged ships in the rebel fleet require constant repairs, aggravated rebel technicians, tired of removing body hull panels to access inner machinery, opted to remove the panels permanently. The Alliance's Y-wings have been so heavily repaired and modified that no two of them are identical.

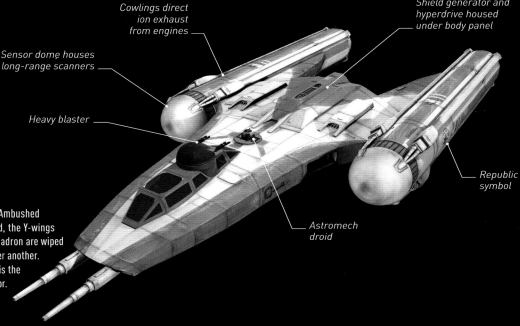

Cowlings direct ion exhaust from engines

Shield generator and hyperdrive housed under body panel

Sensor dome houses long-range scanners

Heavy blaster

Republic symbol

Astromech droid

Fiery End Ambushed from behind, the Y-wings of Gold Squadron are wiped out one after another. Gold Three is the only survivor.

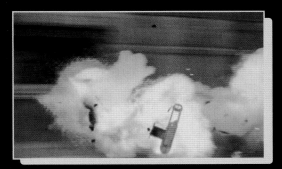

Trench Tactics Speeding through the Death Star trench to reach their target, the pilots of Gold Squadron switch all power to their Y-wings' front deflector screens to defend themselves against a barrage of enemy fire.

BTL-A4 Y-WING

Built to last and made to last even longer by dedicated Rebel Alliance mechanics, most of the Y-wings in the rebel fleet are over two decades old. The Y-wings have been retrofitted for Taim & Bak laser cannons, ArMek light ion cannons, and Arakyd flex tube proton torpedo launchers. Like most rebel starfighters, the Y-wing is equipped with a hyperdrive but requires an astromech unit to fully calculate the necessary course vectors and power settings for any hyperspace jump. Although it is not as fast, maneuverable, or heavily armed as other starfighters, the Y-wing remains a potent craft for its ability to endure and deliver tremendous punishment.

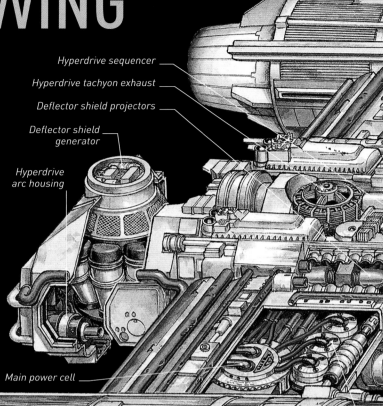

Hyperdrive sequencer

Hyperdrive tachyon exhaust

Deflector shield projectors

Deflector shield generator

Hyperdrive arc housing

Main power cell

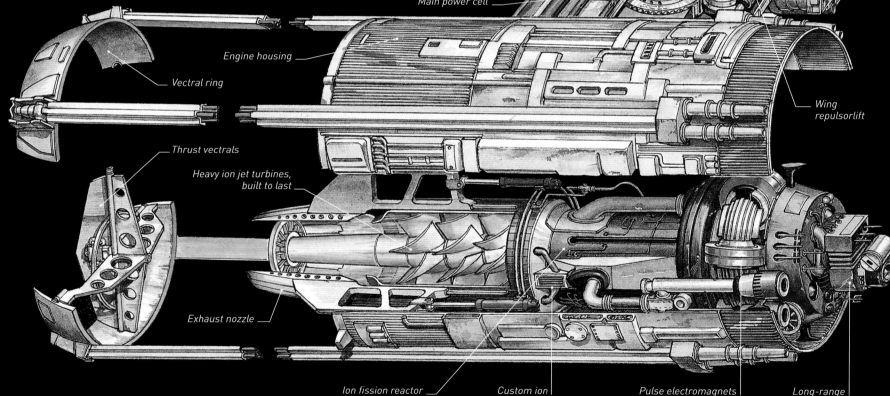

Engine housing

Vectral ring

Wing repulsorlift

Thrust vectrals

Heavy ion jet turbines, built to last

Exhaust nozzle

Ion fission reactor

Custom ion turbo injector

Pulse electromagnets accelerate ionized fuel for injection into turbines

Long-range targeting sensor array

ION CANNONS

Ion cannons fire an electrical charge to disrupt the control circuits of an enemy craft without destroying it. The Y-wing features twin ion cannons, but they are notoriously delicate instruments. Their crystal matrices invariably get vibrated out of alignment in flight and combat, and rebel mechanics hate them for the time they cost in maintenance. For the attack on the Death Star, only two Y-wings in the entire rebel force had functioning ion cannons. These proved critically useful, and one of these craft was the only Y-wing to survive the battle.

COOLING SYSTEM

The Y-wing runs very hot for a ship of its size, and employs a complicated cooling system that runs throughout the ship. Parts of this system need maintenance after every flight. Coolant tubes are often jerry-rigged by rebel mechanics when leaks render inaccessible sections frustratingly inoperative.

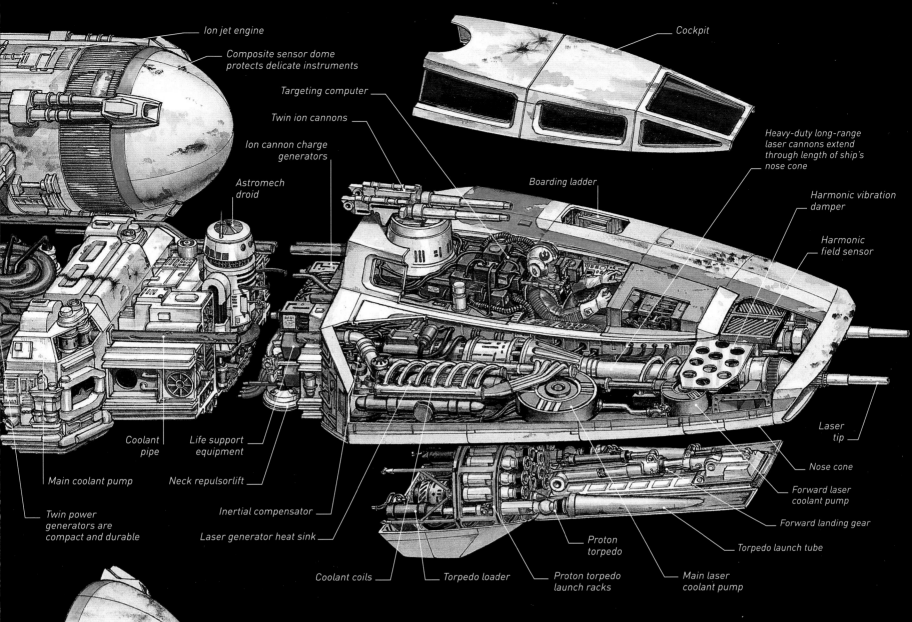

Ion jet engine

Composite sensor dome
protects delicate instruments

Targeting computer

Twin ion cannons

Ion cannon charge
generators

Astromech
droid

Cockpit

Heavy-duty long-range
laser cannons extend
through length of ship's
nose cone

Harmonic vibration
damper

Harmonic
field sensor

Boarding ladder

Coolant
pipe

Life support
equipment

Main coolant pump

Neck repulsorlift

Inertial compensator

Twin power
generators are
compact and durable

Laser generator heat sink

Coolant coils

Torpedo loader

Proton torpedo
launch racks

Proton
torpedo

Main laser
coolant pump

Laser
tip

Nose cone

Forward laser
coolant pump

Forward landing gear

Torpedo launch tube

TWIN SENSOR SYSTEMS

The Y-wing's secondary role as a bomber craft requires a tandem long-range
sensor set to provide binocular range-finding. When both sets are working,
the Y-wing offers slightly better targeting precision than the X-wing—one
reason why Y-wings were the primary attack craft in the Death Star trench.

Rebel Retrofit Prior to the attack
on the Death Star, Rebel Alliance
technicians make sure all late-model
Y-wings are equipped with two Arakyd
proton torpedo launchers, each of
which holds four MG7-A torpedoes.

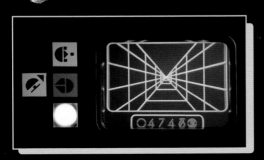

Targeting Computer Like the X-wing, the Y-wing utilizes
the IN-344-B "Sightline" holographic imaging system.

TIE ADVANCED X1

Darth Vader's personal spacecraft is a TIE Advanced x1 prototype, which he uses to devastating effect against the rebel fleet. It is the successor to the TIE Advanced v1 model used by the Imperial Inquisitors. The TIE Advanced x1 prototype is a more capable ship than the standard TIE/ln fighters, with a more sophisticated target tracking system and an augmented engine assembly fed by high-conversion solar cells on its bent wings, giving deadly speed and maneuverability. Unlike standard TIEs, it has both protective shields and hyperdrive capability. The hyperdrive saved Vader after the Death Star was destroyed, enabling him to reach an Imperial outpost and return to power.

High-performance solar cells

Power carrier pulse generator

Auxiliary fuel capsule

Exhaust nozzle

Deflector shield generator

Hyperdrive capacitor

Hyperdrive thermal radiator ports

Hyperdrive power module

Hyperdrive

Energizer

Power cell

Secondary power distributor

Rear deflector shield projector

Stabilizing field projector bar

Solar power collector line

Solar power phase one converter

Main support strut

EXPERIMENTAL SHIELDS

While the standard TIE fighter carries no shields, the x1 is strengthened and protected by an experimental deflector shield system. A stabilizing field is projected by a supermagnet at the rear of the ship, while deflector energies are deployed from forward and lateral pairs of projector bars. These experimental deflector bars sometimes require last-minute tuning for best performance, and x1s have gone into combat more than once with the deflector bar maintenance access panels removed.

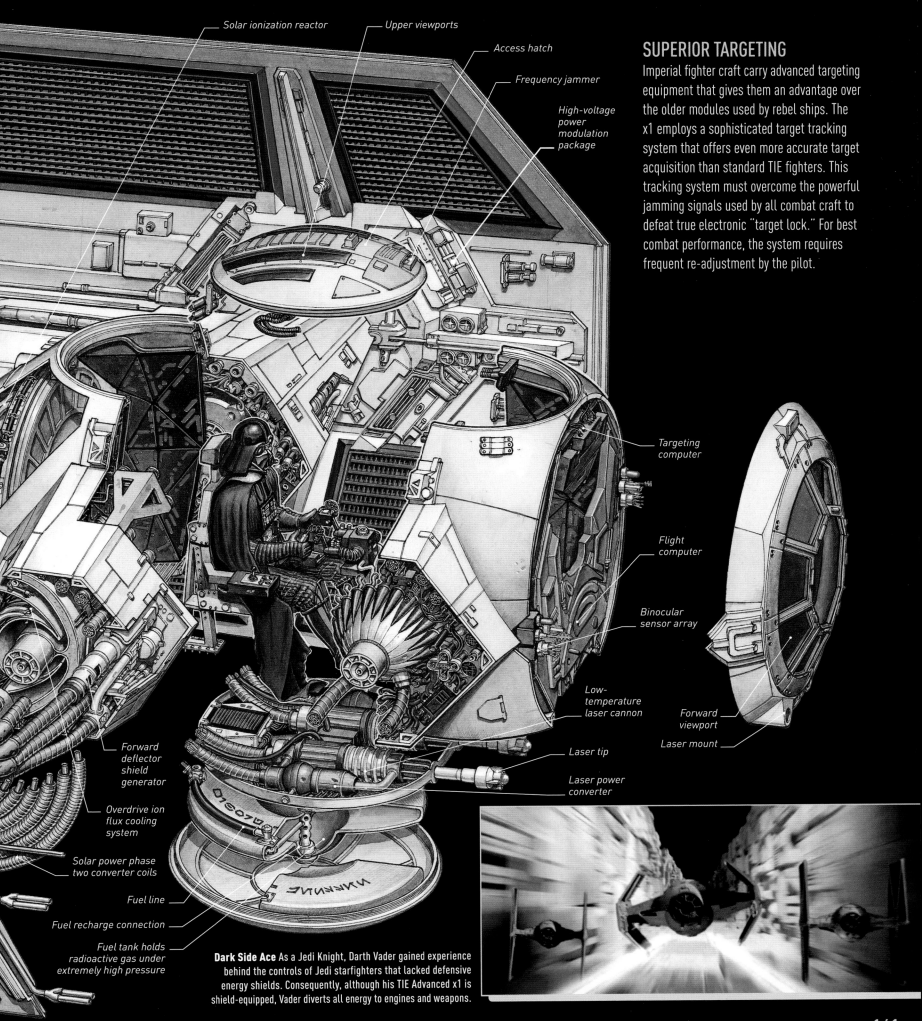

Solar ionization reactor

Upper viewports

Access hatch

Frequency jammer

High-voltage power modulation package

SUPERIOR TARGETING

Imperial fighter craft carry advanced targeting equipment that gives them an advantage over the older modules used by rebel ships. The x1 employs a sophisticated target tracking system that offers even more accurate target acquisition than standard TIE fighters. This tracking system must overcome the powerful jamming signals used by all combat craft to defeat true electronic "target lock." For best combat performance, the system requires frequent re-adjustment by the pilot.

Targeting computer

Flight computer

Binocular sensor array

Forward viewport

Laser mount

Low-temperature laser cannon

Laser tip

Laser power converter

Forward deflector shield generator

Overdrive ion flux cooling system

Solar power phase two converter coils

Fuel line

Fuel recharge connection

Fuel tank holds radioactive gas under extremely high pressure

Dark Side Ace As a Jedi Knight, Darth Vader gained experience behind the controls of Jedi starfighters that lacked defensive energy shields. Consequently, although his TIE Advanced x1 is shield-equipped, Vader diverts all energy to engines and weapons.

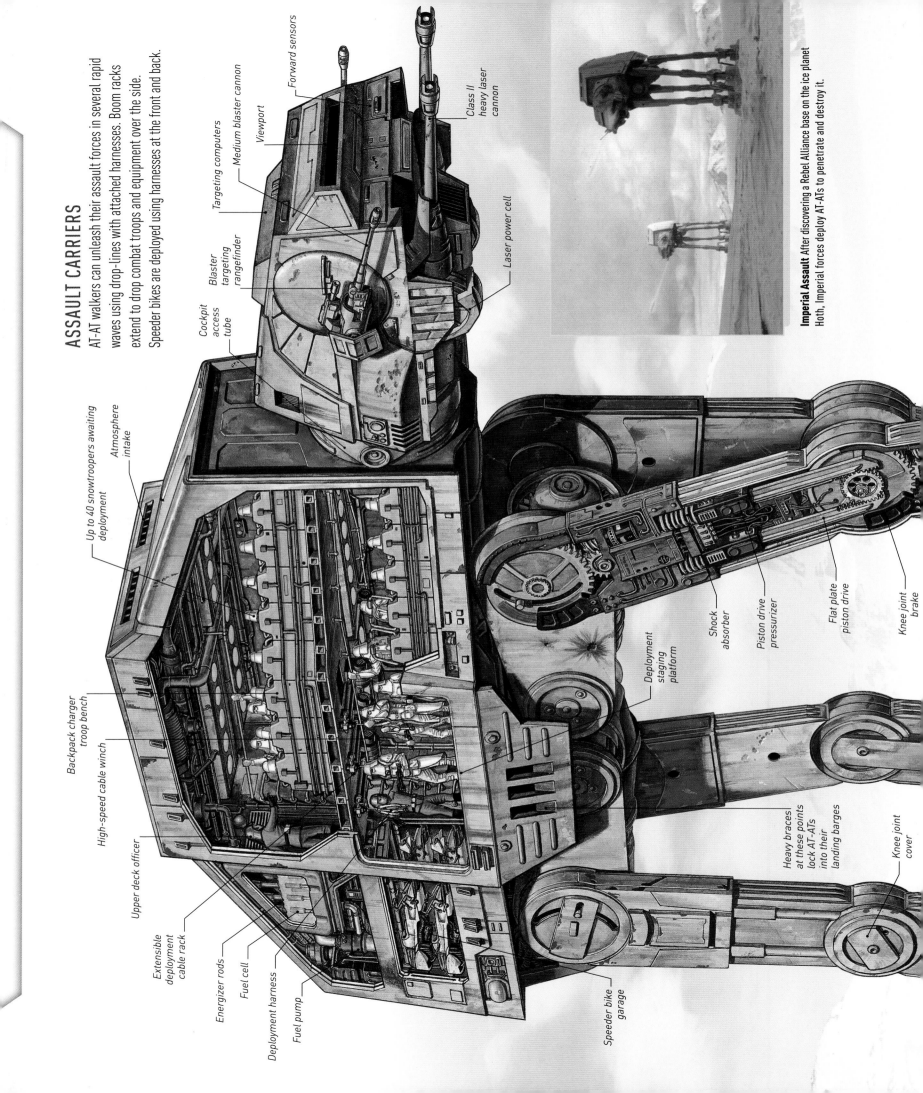

ASSAULT CARRIERS

AT-AT walkers can unleash their assault forces in several rapid waves using drop-lines with attached harnesses. Boom racks extend to drop combat troops and equipment over the side. Speeder bikes are deployed using harnesses at the front and back.

Forward sensors

Class II heavy laser cannon

Targeting computers

Medium blaster cannon

Viewport

Blaster targeting rangefinder

Laser power cell

Cockpit access tube

Atmosphere intake

Up to 40 snowtroopers awaiting deployment

Backpack charger troop bench

High-speed cable winch

Upper deck officer

Extensible deployment cable rack

Energizer rods

Fuel cell

Deployment harness

Fuel pump

Speeder bike garage

Heavy braces at these points lock AT-ATs into their landing barges

Knee joint cover

Flat plate piston drive

Knee joint brake

Piston drive pressurizer

Shock absorber

Deployment staging platform

Imperial Assault After discovering a Rebel Alliance base on the ice planet Hoth, Imperial forces deploy AT-ATs to penetrate and destroy it.

ALL-TERRAIN ABILITIES

The thick armor plating of the Imperial walker makes it too heavy for effective repulsorlifts, hence its huge legs for striding over obstacles and rugged terrain. While steep hillsides or deep swamps can thwart the progress of the walker, AT-AT pilots can guide walkers across surprisingly rugged ground.

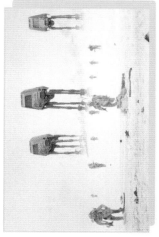

Battle of Hoth Although rebels manage to down a few AT-ATs, they are soon overwhelmed by the lumbering vehicles' heavy firepower.

Ankle pitch brake

Energizer and drive control systems

Footpad yaw strut

Toe flap

Terrain sensor computer

Impulse terrain sensor

Terrain scanners

Toe flap piston

Reinforced heavy armor

Service access cover

Footpad

AT-AT

D eployed as weapons of terror, the gigantic Imperial All Terrain Armored Transport (AT-AT) walkers advance inexorably on the battlefield like unstoppable giants. These behemoth monsters are shielded with heavy armor cladding, making them invulnerable to all but the heaviest turbolaser weaponry. Blaster bolts from ordinary turrets and cannons merely glance off the walker's armor or are harmlessly absorbed and dissipated. A powerful reactor produces the raw energy needed to move this weighty battle machine. Cannons in the movable cockpit spit death at helpless foes below, cutting a swath of destruction which the mighty footpads then crash through. Breaking enemy lines with its blaster fire and lumbering mass, the walker also functions as a troop carrier, holding in its body platoons of crack assault soldiers, ground weaponry, and speeder bike antipersonnel/reconnaissance vehicles. When this cargo of terror is released into the chaos and destruction a walker has created, another Imperial victory is nearly complete.

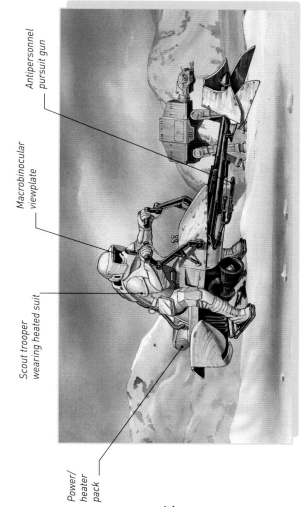

Antipersonnel pursuit gun

Macrobinocular viewplate

Scout trooper wearing heated suit

Power/ heater pack

SPEEDER BIKES

AT-AT walkers usually carry a set of high-velocity repulsorlift speeder bikes for scouting or survivor-hunting missions. The speed and agility of these bikes complement the plodding might of the walkers, making the combined assault capability thorough and overwhelming. The colossal size and nightmarish animal resemblance of the AT-AT combine with its combat strengths to give it tremendous psychological power. Until the Battle of Hoth, no army had ever fought resolutely against an onslaught of walkers, so frightening and devastating is their presence.

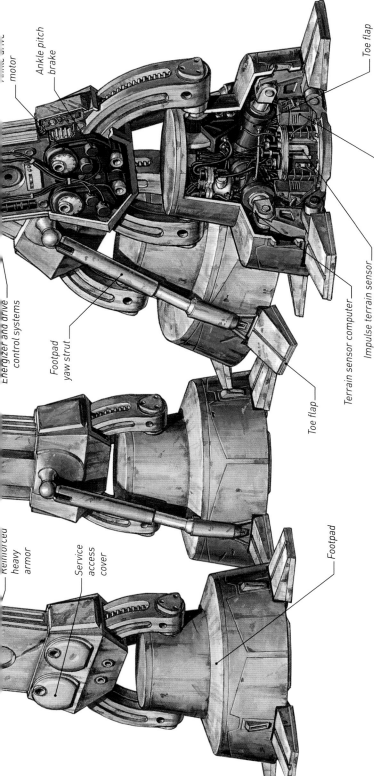

AT-AT COCKPIT

The AT-AT's heavily armored head serves as a cockpit for the two pilots and the vehicle commander. On its exterior are mounted the vehicle's weapons systems. While both pilots are fully qualified to perform all control functions, in normal practice one serves as driver while the other acts as gunner. Firing controls can at any time be yielded to the vehicle commander, who uses a periscope display capable of tactical and photographic readouts. The two pilots are guided by terrain sensors under the cockpit and ground sensors built into the feet of the vehicle. Scans read the nature and shape of the terrain ahead, ensuring infallible footing.

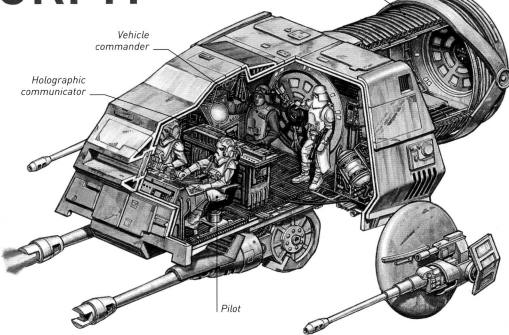

Ringed electromagnet systems enable the neck to flex

Vehicle commander

Holographic communicator

Pilot

ASSAULT ARMOR DIVISION
Handpicked by Darth Vader to lead the Imperial Army's Assault Armor Division against the rebel forces on Hoth, General Maximilian Veers commands both the Thundering Herd AT-AT squadron and the elite Imperial snowtrooper unit Blizzard Force.

Elevated Advantage AT-ATs are highly conspicuous on open terrain, however AT-AT armor is nearly impervious to blaster fire, and the crew in the elevated command cockpit have a clear view of obstacles and targets over vast distances.

Periscope Display The AT-AT commander uses a periscope display mounted into the cockpit's ceiling, which provides enhanced views of targets, sensor readouts, and tactical data.

Heavy Cannons The AT-AT's two Taim & Bak MS-1 heavy laser cannons can be fired alternately in quick succession, or simultaneously for a single, powerful blast.

AT-ST

The scout walker, or All Terrain Scout Transport (AT-ST) walks easily through rugged terrain to carry out its missions. Reconnaissance, battle line support, and anti-personnel hunting make excellent use of the craft's armaments and capabilities. Faster than a full-size AT-AT, the scout walker is also able to step through denser terrain with greater ease, traveling through small canyons or forest that would stop an AT-AT. While AT-ATs crush main rebel defensive emplacements, AT-STs ferret out small pockets of resistance. Since the scout walker is almost impossible to flee on foot, the sight of patrolling AT-STs strikes fear into isolated ground troops.

The Cockpit View Viewscreens and holo-projectors allow AT-ST crew to see ahead and behind simultaneously. While the computer can guide the scout walker over even ground, an expert human pilot must balance the wide variety of data input and control the craft's walking in difficult terrain.

Scout Transport With a top speed of 90 kph (55.6 mph), the All Terrain Scout Transport (AT-ST) is faster and more maneuverable than an AT-AT, but less heavily armed and armored.

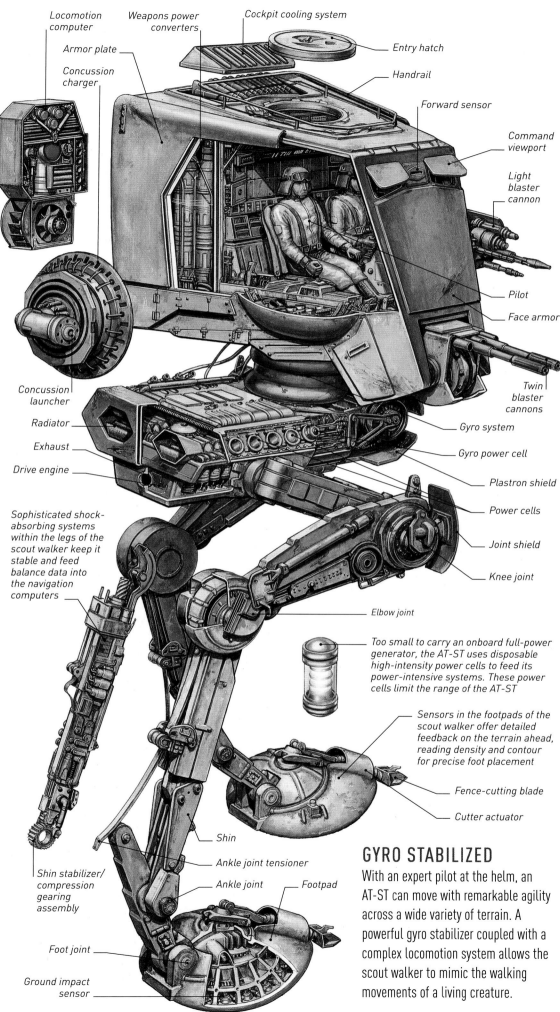

Locomotion computer

Armor plate

Concussion charger

Weapons power converters

Cockpit cooling system

Entry hatch

Handrail

Forward sensor

Command viewport

Light blaster cannon

Pilot

Face armor

Twin blaster cannons

Concussion launcher

Radiator

Exhaust

Drive engine

Gyro system

Gyro power cell

Plastron shield

Power cells

Joint shield

Knee joint

Sophisticated shock-absorbing systems within the legs of the scout walker keep it stable and feed balance data into the navigation computers

Elbow joint

Too small to carry an onboard full-power generator, the AT-ST uses disposable high-intensity power cells to feed its power-intensive systems. These power cells limit the range of the AT-ST

Sensors in the footpads of the scout walker offer detailed feedback on the terrain ahead, reading density and contour for precise foot placement

Fence-cutting blade

Cutter actuator

Shin

Ankle joint tensioner

Shin stabilizer/ compression gearing assembly

Ankle joint

Footpad

GYRO STABILIZED

With an expert pilot at the helm, an AT-ST can move with remarkable agility across a wide variety of terrain. A powerful gyro stabilizer coupled with a complex locomotion system allows the scout walker to mimic the walking movements of a living creature.

Foot joint

Ground impact sensor

T-47 AIRSPEEDER

Soon after establishing their new secret base on the ice planet Hoth, the rebels acquired a small squadron of Incom T-47 airspeeders, also know as snowspeeders, to serve as defensive units. These airspeeders had been equipped with power converters and military-grade laser cannons. Highly maneuverable and fast, these airspeeders seemed ideal for the defense of Echo Base. The intense cold of Hoth initially proved too severe for the T-47s, until rebel technicians modified them to suit their new environment.

> "Use your harpoons and tow cables. Go for the legs."
> Luke Skywalker

Polarized view screen

Pilot

Gunner

Targeting sensors

Collimating tip

FROM CIVILIAN TO MILITARY USE

To convert the T-47 civilian airspeeder into a military craft, laser cannon assemblies were bolted to the wings. External power converters and a laser generator system tapped the extra energy of the T-47's powerful generators, and added armor plate strengthened the craft's hull. The result is a short-range attack craft of exceptionally high maneuverability. The rebel snowspeeder's civilian origins and small size explain its lack of defensive shields. In battle, the craft relies on its speed and agility to evade laser blasts.

Homing sensors

Armor plate

Laser barrel

Speeding to Battle Incom T-47 airspeeders are designed to fly in middle and upper atmospheres, but skilled pilots have little difficulty skimming planetary surfaces at high speed. The T-47's aerodynamic design allows turning without reducing speed, making it nearly impossible to track with flight-predictor sensors.

Final stage energizer

Laser generator

Power coupling

Laser activator

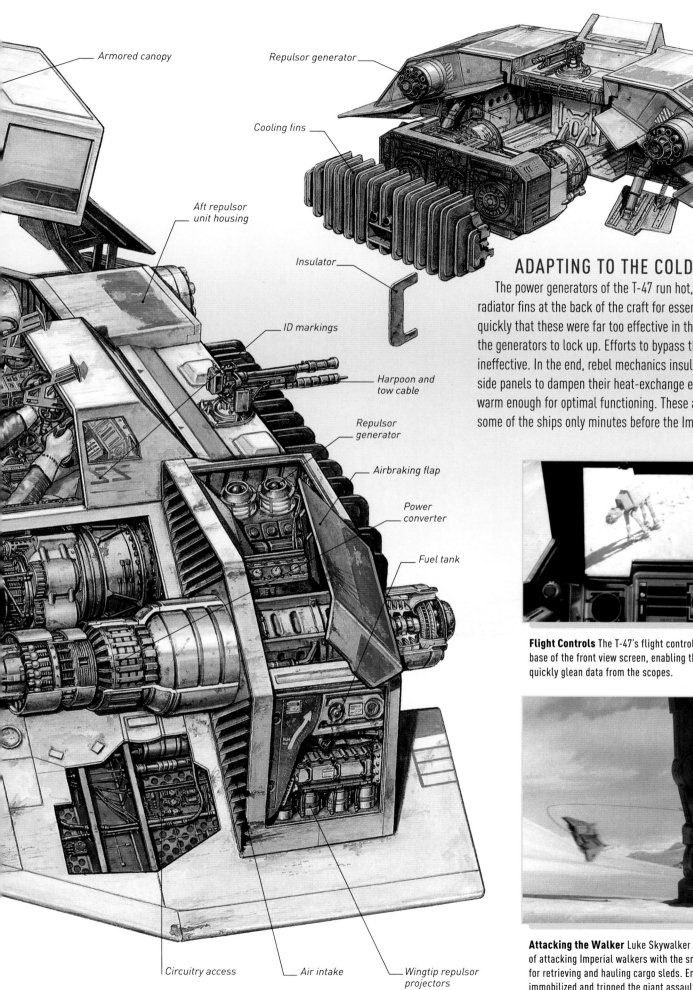

Armored canopy

Repulsor generator

Power generator

Cooling fins

Air brakes

Aft repulsor
unit housing

Insulator

ADAPTING TO THE COLD

The power generators of the T-47 run hot, requiring a large bank of heat radiator fins at the back of the craft for essential cooling. The rebels learned quickly that these were far too effective in the icy cold of Hoth, which caused the generators to lock up. Efforts to bypass the radiator system proved ineffective. In the end, rebel mechanics insulated each of the radiator fins with side panels to dampen their heat-exchange effect and keep the engine systems warm enough for optimal functioning. These adaptations were completed on some of the ships only minutes before the Imperial attack on Echo Base began.

ID markings

Harpoon and
tow cable

Repulsor
generator

Airbraking flap

Power
converter

Fuel tank

Flight Controls The T-47's flight control scopes jut upward slightly across the base of the front view screen, enabling the pilot to rely on peripheral vision to quickly glean data from the scopes.

Circuitry access

Air intake

Wingtip repulsor
projectors

Attacking the Walker Luke Skywalker devised the unorthodox strategy of attacking Imperial walkers with the snowspeeder's tow cable, designed for retrieving and hauling cargo sleds. Entangling the legs of the walker immobilized and tripped the giant assault vehicle, a victory for determination and bravery over raw strength.

TIE BOMBER

Derived from the TIE/gt variant of the TIE starfighter family, the TIE bomber was developed to take over the task of orbital bombardment from the Empire's capital ships. With its massive ordnance capacity, this formidable assault ship can be deployed against ground- and space-based targets, delivering its lethal load with pinpoint accuracy. The craft's precision targeting is an important capability—where capital ship bombardment often results in extensive collateral damage, the TIE bomber's ability to make "surgical strikes" enables specific targets to be taken out, while leaving surrounding facilities intact.

Precision Targeting Traveling over a large asteroid, two TIE bombers drop proton bombs into craters in an effort to flush out an elusive rebel ship.

THE TIE COMPANY

The TIE family of Imperial warcraft is probably the most recognizable product of Sienar Fleet Systems, one of the Empire's major military starship manufacturers. During the Republic's final days, Raith Sienar—a friend of Wilhuff Tarkin—is in charge of the company, originally called Republic Sienar Systems. He allegedly constructs a range of top-secret vessels, including the *Scimitar*, for Darth Sidious himself. During the time of the Empire, the company renames itself Sienar Fleet Systems (SFS), and the company's Imperial connections help it secure lucrative military contracts. Sienar's loyalty to the Empire enables his company to manufacture a large range of TIE-line craft as well as the *Lambda*-class shuttle, and the *Interdictor* Cruiser. Following the Empire's fall, the company splits into two entities, Sienar-Jaemus Fleet Systems and Sienar-Jaemus Army Systems. These companies mainly build vehicles, including new and advanced TIE models, for the First Order.

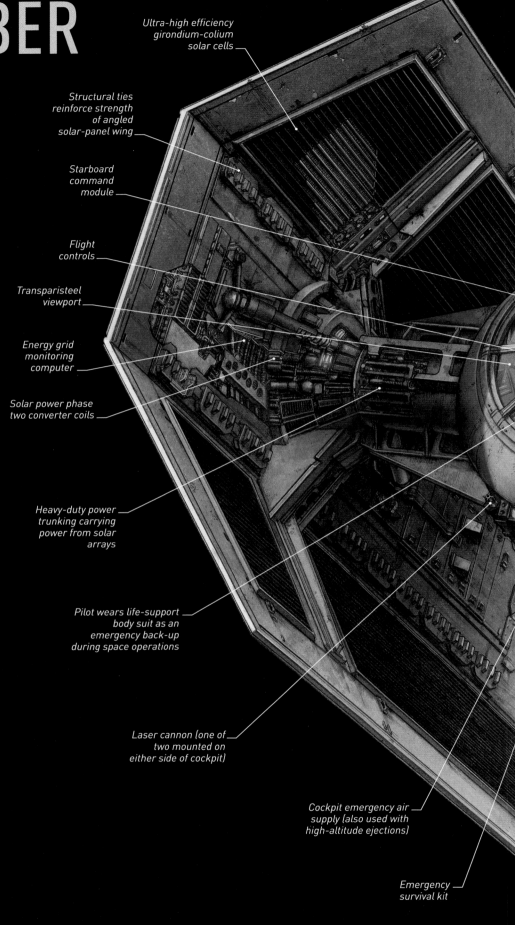

Ultra-high efficiency girondium-colium solar cells

Structural ties reinforce strength of angled solar-panel wing

Starboard command module

Flight controls

Transparisteel viewport

Energy grid monitoring computer

Solar power phase two converter coils

Heavy-duty power trunking carrying power from solar arrays

Pilot wears life-support body suit as an emergency back-up during space operations

Laser cannon (one of two mounted on either side of cockpit)

Cockpit emergency air supply (also used with high-altitude ejections)

Emergency survival kit

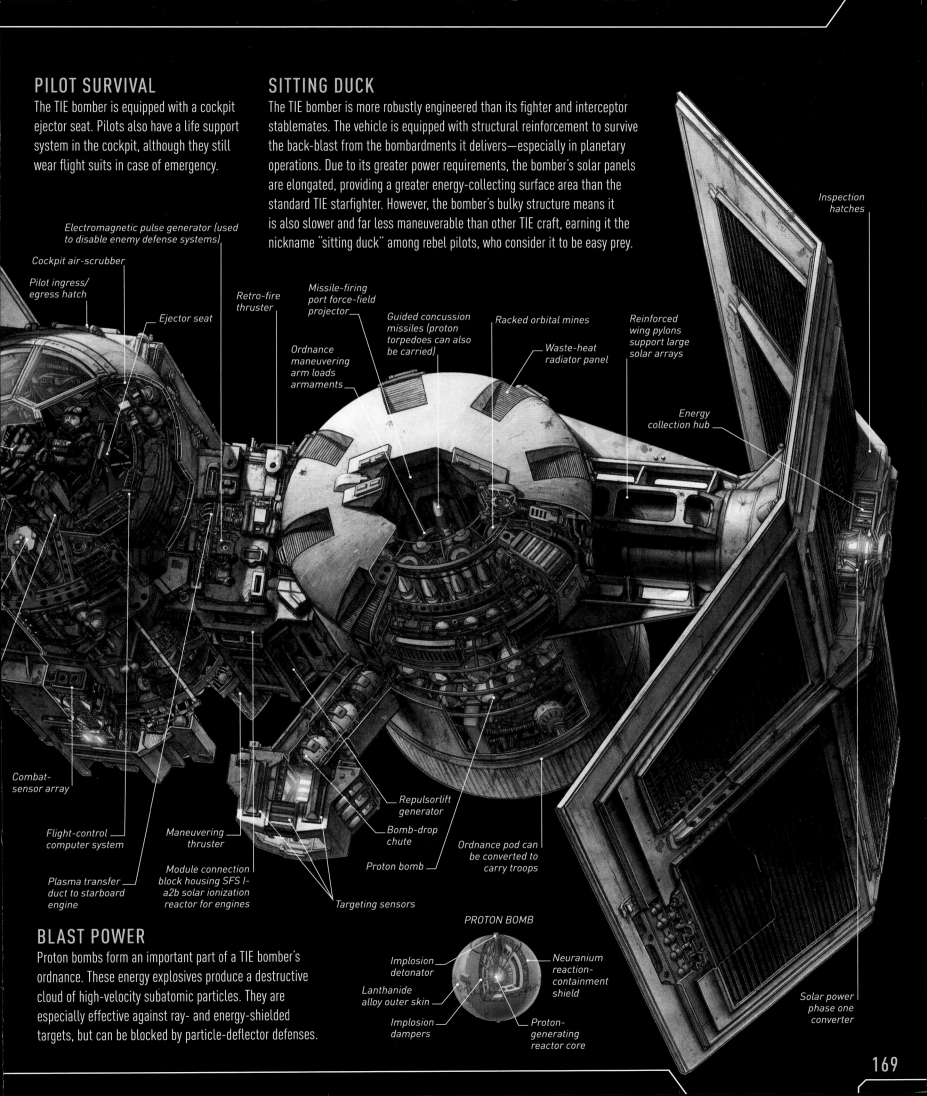

PILOT SURVIVAL

The TIE bomber is equipped with a cockpit ejector seat. Pilots also have a life support system in the cockpit, although they still wear flight suits in case of emergency.

SITTING DUCK

The TIE bomber is more robustly engineered than its fighter and interceptor stablemates. The vehicle is equipped with structural reinforcement to survive the back-blast from the bombardments it delivers—especially in planetary operations. Due to its greater power requirements, the bomber's solar panels are elongated, providing a greater energy-collecting surface area than the standard TIE starfighter. However, the bomber's bulky structure means it is also slower and far less maneuverable than other TIE craft, earning it the nickname "sitting duck" among rebel pilots, who consider it to be easy prey.

Electromagnetic pulse generator (used to disable enemy defense systems)

Cockpit air-scrubber

Pilot ingress/ egress hatch

Ejector seat

Retro-fire thruster

Missile-firing port force-field projector

Ordnance maneuvering arm loads armaments

Guided concussion missiles (proton torpedoes can also be carried)

Racked orbital mines

Waste-heat radiator panel

Reinforced wing pylons support large solar arrays

Inspection hatches

Energy collection hub

Combat-sensor array

Flight-control computer system

Maneuvering thruster

Plasma transfer duct to starboard engine

Module connection block housing SFS I-a2b solar ionization reactor for engines

Targeting sensors

Repulsorlift generator

Bomb-drop chute

Proton bomb

Ordnance pod can be converted to carry troops

Solar power phase one converter

BLAST POWER

Proton bombs form an important part of a TIE bomber's ordnance. These energy explosives produce a destructive cloud of high-velocity subatomic particles. They are especially effective against ray- and energy-shielded targets, but can be blocked by particle-deflector defenses.

PROTON BOMB

Implosion detonator

Lanthanide alloy outer skin

Implosion dampers

Neuranium reaction-containment shield

Proton-generating reactor core

169

TIE INTERCEPTOR

Fortunately for the rebels, Darth Vader's TIE Advanced x1 prototype proved too expensive for full-scale production. However, its high-performance solar cells and bent-wing configuration have survived in the form of the TIE interceptor—one of the most advanced starfighters produced for the Imperial Navy. Equipped with upgraded ion engines and four blaster cannons, the TIE interceptor is faster, more maneuverable, and better armed than most of its predecessors; it is only surpassed by the prototype TIE Defender that never entered mass-production. To achieve its increased performance, the craft sacrifices armor, deflector shields, hyperdrive systems, and life-support: pilots must rely on their skills and superior numbers to survive.

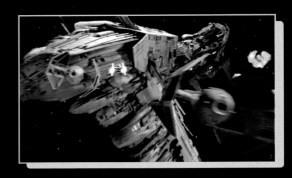

Lethal Adversary
Veteran rebel pilots know not to underestimate the deadly speed and maneuverability of the TIE interceptor.

INNOVATIVE DESIGN

To maximize speed for the TIE interceptor, Imperial designers increased the size of the standard twin ion engines and provided the necessary additional power input by increasing the size of the solar panels. Designers also utilized the "bent-wing" configuration of Darth Vader's prototype TIE fighter, but reshaped the side panels to create dagger-shaped wings that give the pilot a wider field of view from the cockpit.

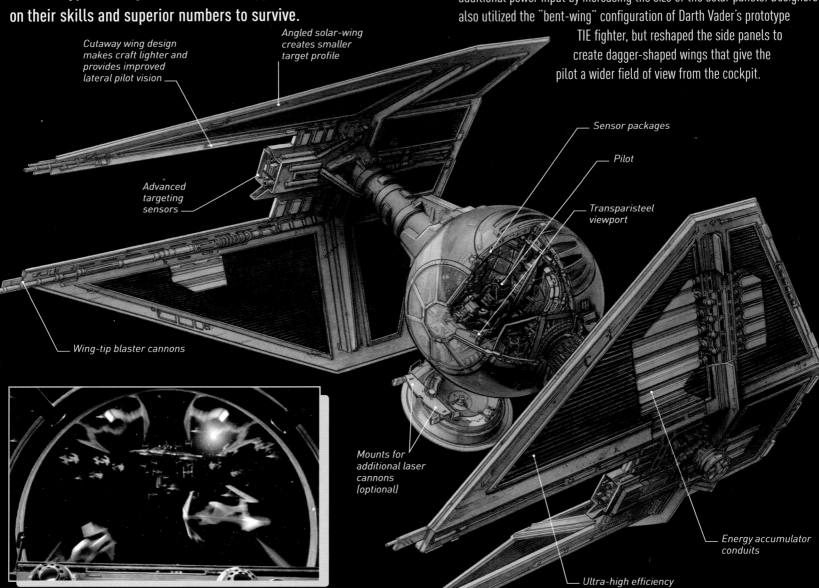

Cutaway wing design makes craft lighter and provides improved lateral pilot vision

Angled solar-wing creates smaller target profile

Advanced targeting sensors

Wing-tip blaster cannons

Sensor packages

Pilot

Transparisteel viewport

Mounts for additional laser cannons (optional)

Energy accumulator conduits

Ultra-high efficiency girondium-colium solar cells

Increased Firepower Unlike the twin chin-mounted lasers found on the TIE fighter, the interceptor has four cannons on the tips of its solar arrays.

LEGACY OF A BOUNTY HUNTER

After the bounty hunter Jango Fett died at the Battle of Geonosis, his son Boba fled in his father's ship, *Slave I*, and almost immediately began plotting his revenge. He also began working as a bounty hunter, and used his profits to maintain and refurbish *Slave I*. Despite his youth and limited experience, he became the leader of a group of hunters, most of whom were more than twice his age. By the end of the Clone Wars, he had gained a professional reputation in his own right.

"Put Captain Solo in the cargo hold."

Boba Fett

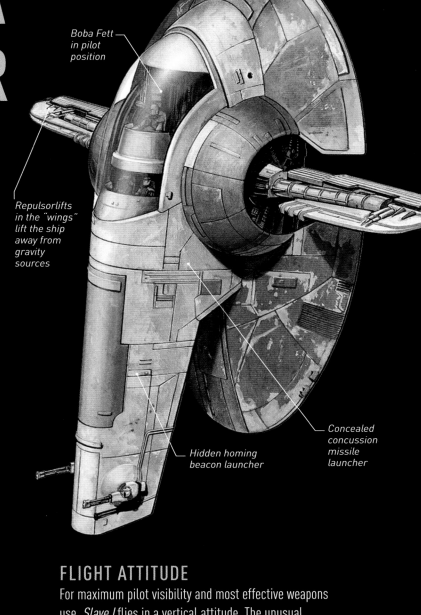

Boba Fett in pilot position

Repulsorlifts in the "wings" lift the ship away from gravity sources

Hidden homing beacon launcher

Concealed concussion missile launcher

FLIGHT ATTITUDE

For maximum pilot visibility and most effective weapons use, *Slave I* flies in a vertical attitude. The unusual configuration requires unorthodox piloting skills, which Boba Fett learned at an early age by watching his father, Jango. *Slave I* is built more for stealth, defense, and attack than for speed, but with maximum power diverted to the main drives the ship can match the space velocities of a Y-wing starfighter.

Illegal Technology *Slave I*'s sensor jamming and masking system originated as a highly classified experimental project for the Imperial Navy, and enables Fett to closely pursue other ships across space while remaining invisible on their sensors.

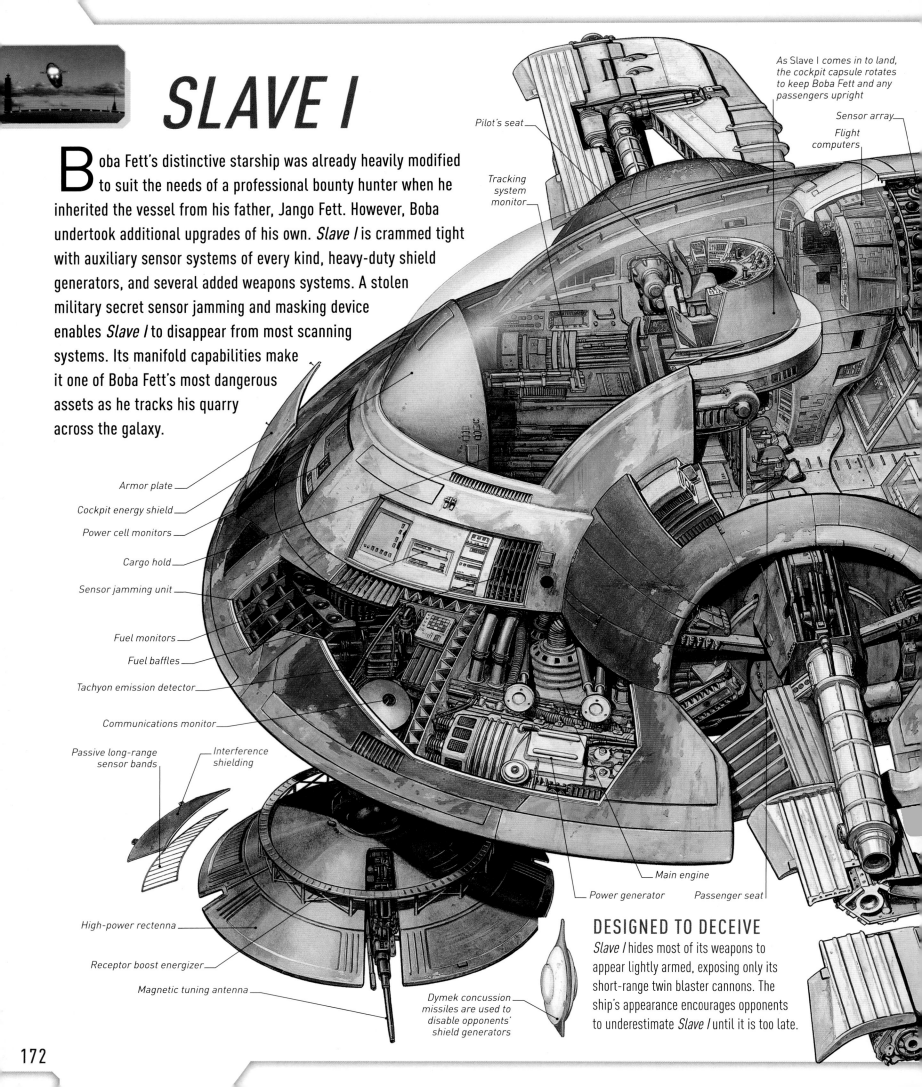

SLAVE I

Boba Fett's distinctive starship was already heavily modified to suit the needs of a professional bounty hunter when he inherited the vessel from his father, Jango Fett. However, Boba undertook additional upgrades of his own. *Slave I* is crammed tight with auxiliary sensor systems of every kind, heavy-duty shield generators, and several added weapons systems. A stolen military secret sensor jamming and masking device enables *Slave I* to disappear from most scanning systems. Its manifold capabilities make it one of Boba Fett's most dangerous assets as he tracks his quarry across the galaxy.

As Slave I comes in to land, the cockpit capsule rotates to keep Boba Fett and any passengers upright

Sensor array

Flight computers

Pilot's seat

Tracking system monitor

Armor plate

Cockpit energy shield

Power cell monitors

Cargo hold

Sensor jamming unit

Fuel monitors

Fuel baffles

Tachyon emission detector

Communications monitor

Passive long-range sensor bands

Interference shielding

High-power rectenna

Receptor boost energizer

Magnetic tuning antenna

Main engine

Power generator

Passenger seat

Dymek concussion missiles are used to disable opponents' shield generators

DESIGNED TO DECEIVE

Slave I hides most of its weapons to appear lightly armed, exposing only its short-range twin blaster cannons. The ship's appearance encourages opponents to underestimate *Slave I* until it is too late.

172

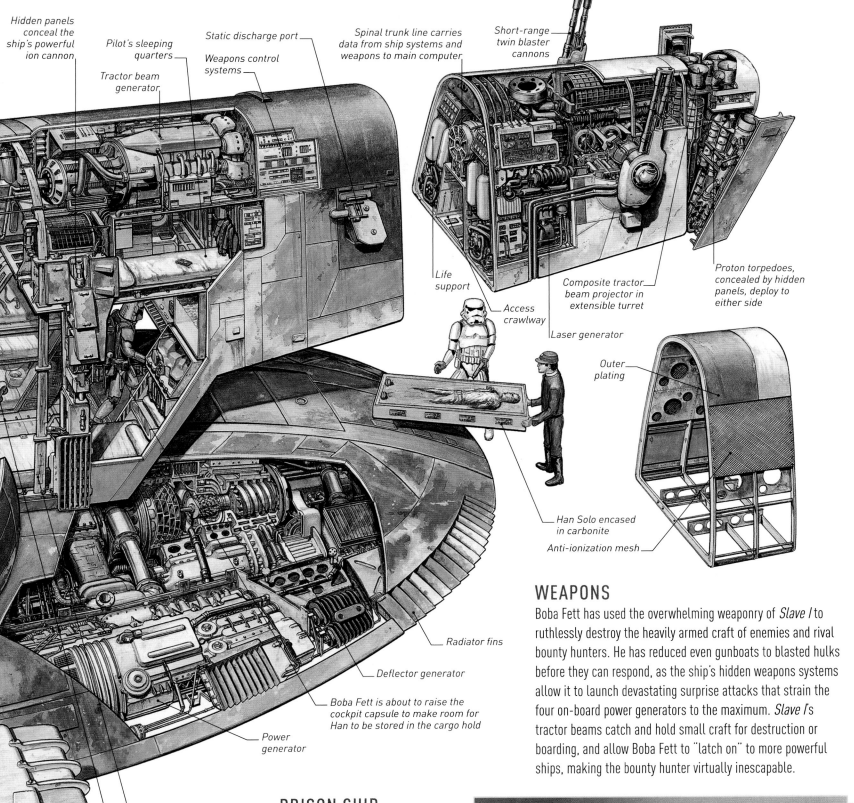

Hidden panels conceal the ship's powerful ion cannon

Pilot's sleeping quarters

Tractor beam generator

Weapons control systems

Static discharge port

Spinal trunk line carries data from ship systems and weapons to main computer

Short-range twin blaster cannons

Life support

Access crawlway

Composite tractor beam projector in extensible turret

Laser generator

Proton torpedoes, concealed by hidden panels, deploy to either side

Outer plating

Han Solo encased in carbonite

Anti-ionization mesh

Radiator fins

Deflector generator

Boba Fett is about to raise the cockpit capsule to make room for Han to be stored in the cargo hold

Power generator

Stabilizing field projector

Prisoner cages

Wing extension struts

Repulsorlifts rotate to maintain support for ship as it comes in to land on its back

WEAPONS

Boba Fett has used the overwhelming weaponry of *Slave I* to ruthlessly destroy the heavily armed craft of enemies and rival bounty hunters. He has reduced even gunboats to blasted hulks before they can respond, as the ship's hidden weapons systems allow it to launch devastating surprise attacks that strain the four on-board power generators to the maximum. *Slave I*'s tractor beams catch and hold small craft for destruction or boarding, and allow Boba Fett to "latch on" to more powerful ships, making the bounty hunter virtually inescapable.

PRISON SHIP

While Boba Fett is notorious for disintegrating those whom he has been hired to kill, some bounties require that the quarry be brought back alive. Accordingly, *Slave I* is equipped with prisoner cages, with six immobilizing bunks.

Valuable Cargo Frozen in carbonite, Han Solo is transferred to *Slave I*'s cargo hold for transport to Jabba the Hutt, who will reward Fett with a bounty of 250,000 credits.

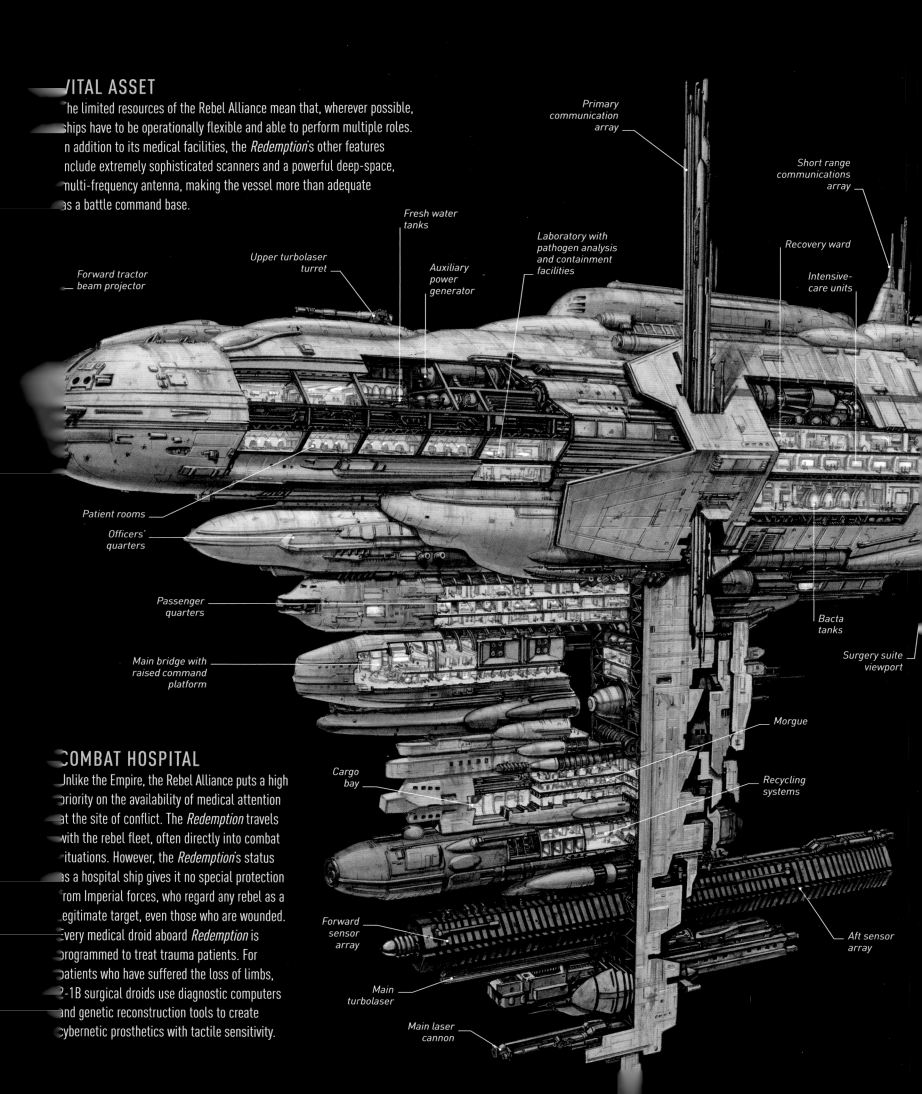

VITAL ASSET

The limited resources of the Rebel Alliance mean that, wherever possible, ships have to be operationally flexible and able to perform multiple roles. In addition to its medical facilities, the *Redemption's* other features include extremely sophisticated scanners and a powerful deep-space, multi-frequency antenna, making the vessel more than adequate as a battle command base.

COMBAT HOSPITAL

Unlike the Empire, the Rebel Alliance puts a high priority on the availability of medical attention at the site of conflict. The *Redemption* travels with the rebel fleet, often directly into combat situations. However, the *Redemption's* status as a hospital ship gives it no special protection from Imperial forces, who regard any rebel as a legitimate target, even those who are wounded. Every medical droid aboard *Redemption* is programmed to treat trauma patients. For patients who have suffered the loss of limbs, 2-1B surgical droids use diagnostic computers and genetic reconstruction tools to create cybernetic prosthetics with tactile sensitivity.

Forward tractor beam projector

Upper turbolaser turret

Fresh water tanks

Auxiliary power generator

Laboratory with pathogen analysis and containment facilities

Primary communication array

Short range communications array

Recovery ward

Intensive-care units

Patient rooms

Officers' quarters

Passenger quarters

Main bridge with raised command platform

Bacta tanks

Surgery suite viewport

Morgue

Recycling systems

Cargo bay

Forward sensor array

Aft sensor array

Main turbolaser

Main laser cannon

REDEMPTION

The Alliance owns a number of EF76 Nebulon-B escort frigate and has adapted them for a range of uses, including reconnaissance missions and search-and-rescue operations. The *Redemption* is a hospital ship, and it has had most of its weapons and replaced them with back-up systems for power generators and shield projectors. The frigate's standard starfighter launch bay configuration is now a hospital facility that can treat more than 700 patients simultaneously. Equipped with intensive-care units, operating theaters, recovery wards, numerous medical droids, and 16 bacta tanks, the ship's patient-survival rate is nearly 98 percent.

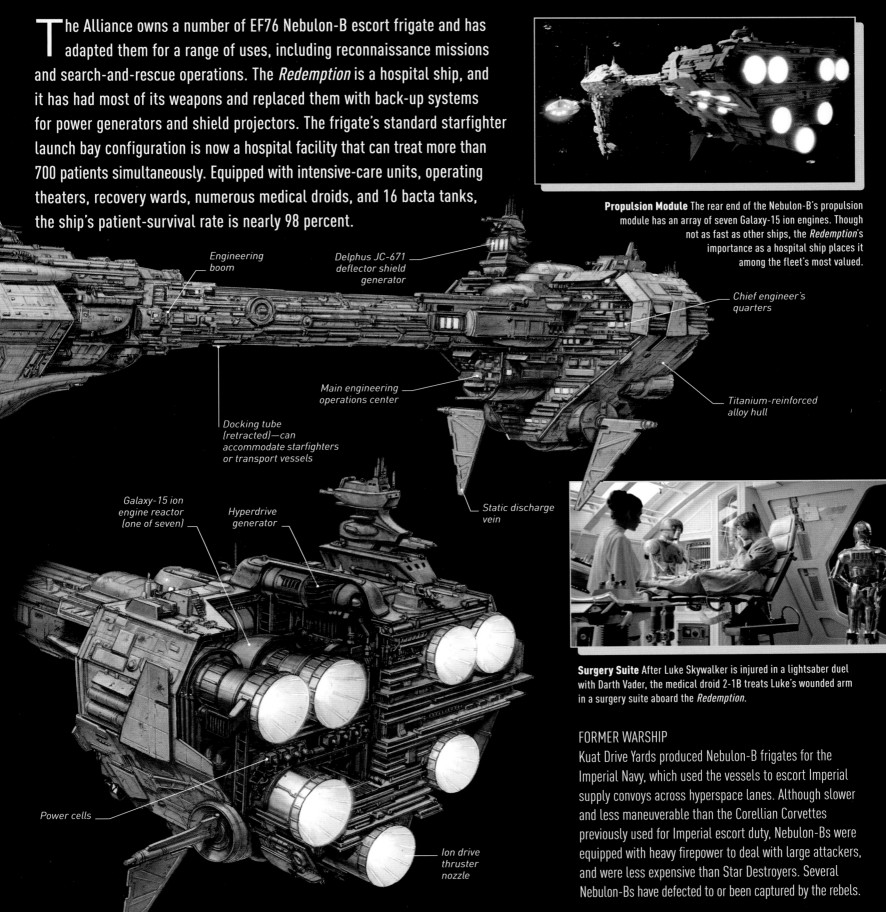

Propulsion Module The rear end of the Nebulon-B's propulsion module has an array of seven Galaxy-15 ion engines. Though not as fast as other ships, the *Redemption*'s importance as a hospital ship places it among the fleet's most valued.

Engineering boom

Delphus JC-671 deflector shield generator

Chief engineer's quarters

Main engineering operations center

Titanium-reinforced alloy hull

Docking tube (retracted)—can accommodate starfighters or transport vessels

Galaxy-15 ion engine reactor (one of seven)

Hyperdrive generator

Static discharge vein

Power cells

Ion drive thruster nozzle

Surgery Suite After Luke Skywalker is injured in a lightsaber duel with Darth Vader, the medical droid 2-1B treats Luke's wounded arm in a surgery suite aboard the *Redemption*.

FORMER WARSHIP

Kuat Drive Yards produced Nebulon-B frigates for the Imperial Navy, which used the vessels to escort Imperial supply convoys across hyperspace lanes. Although slower and less maneuverable than the Corellian Corvettes previously used for Imperial escort duty, Nebulon-Bs were equipped with heavy firepower to deal with large attackers, and were less expensive than Star Destroyers. Several Nebulon-Bs have defected to or been captured by the rebels.

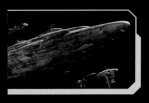

HOME ONE

Originally a deep-space exploration ship constructed on Mon Cala, the MC80 Star Cruiser *Home One* has been extensively modified for war against the Empire. Thousands of viewports that once virtually covered the ship's exterior have been covered with heavy armor plating. Hangars for small shuttles were expanded to carry squadrons of starfighters. Standard defensive weaponry for eliminating asteroid obstacles were replaced with turbolaser batteries, ion cannon batteries, and tractor beam emitters capable of snaring enemy starfighters. *Home One* famously served as Admiral Ackbar's command vessel for the attack on the second Death Star at the Battle of Endor.

Command Center On the bridge of *Home One*, Admiral Ackbar gives instructions to his Mon Calamari crew as he leads them into battle.

Main shuttle integrates with ship and transports personnel to and from planets

Main bridge and briefing area

Cargo modules

Docking clamp

Umbilicals link shuttle to ship's primary systems

Main reactor

Reactor/ hyperdrive interface

Hyperdrive generator

Hyperdrive field emitter

Ion injection manifold

Escape pods

Starboard thrusters

Starboard main sublight ion engines

DISTINCTIVE CONTROLS

Various species from across the galaxy make up the rebel personnel on *Home One*, but due to the design of the ship's controls, the command crew is exclusively made up of Mon Calamari. Holo-displays and battle graphics are designed specifically for the Mon Calamari, who do not see in the same spectrum as humans. So long as Admiral Ackbar and his crew are at the controls, however, the Alliance trusts their fleet is in good hands.

REBEL RETROFIT

Like most Mon Calamari cruisers, *Home One* was originally designed with numerous water-filled passage tubes that snaked throughout the ship's interior, allowing the Mon Calamari crew to swim to different areas of the ship. To accommodate non-amphibious rebel crewmembers, various tubes were drained and retrofitted with flooring, stairs, and ventilation.

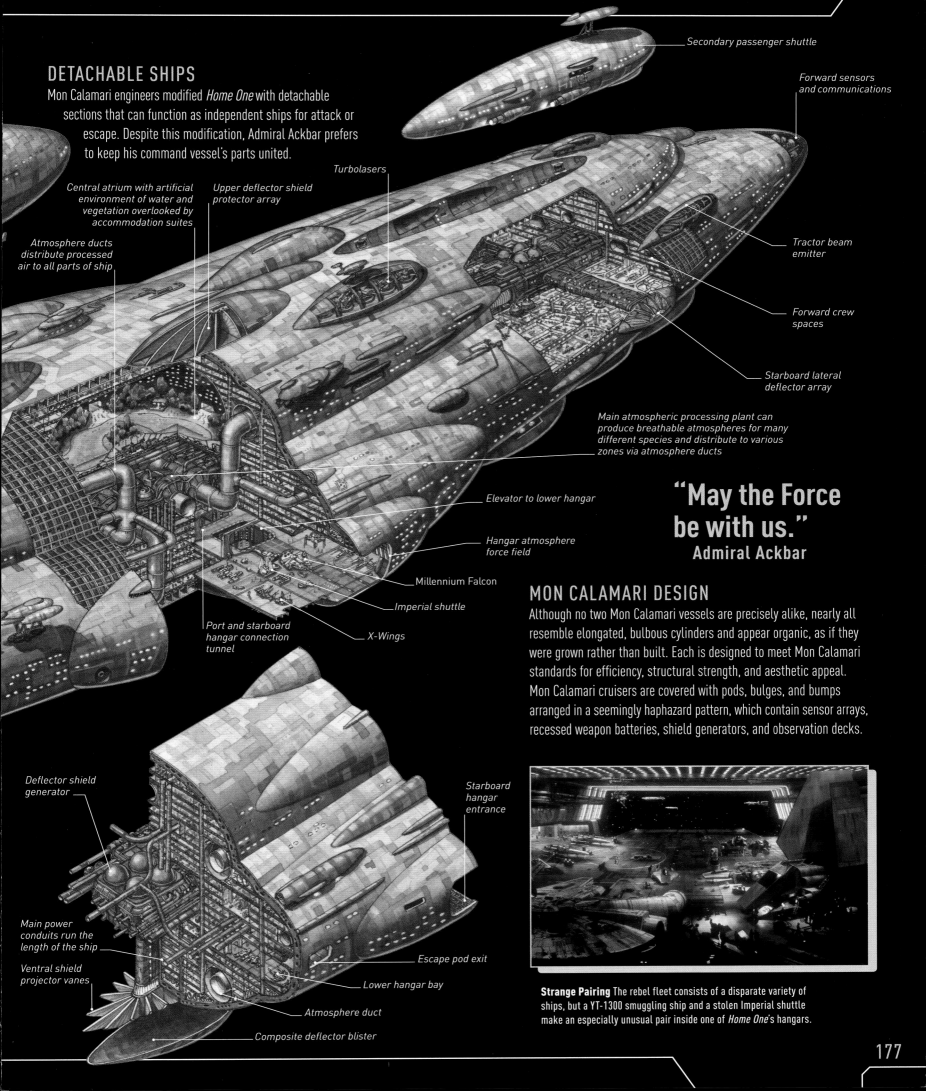

DETACHABLE SHIPS

Mon Calamari engineers modified *Home One* with detachable sections that can function as independent ships for attack or escape. Despite this modification, Admiral Ackbar prefers to keep his command vessel's parts united.

Secondary passenger shuttle

Forward sensors and communications

Central atrium with artificial environment of water and vegetation overlooked by accommodation suites

Upper deflector shield protector array

Turbolasers

Tractor beam emitter

Atmosphere ducts distribute processed air to all parts of ship

Forward crew spaces

Starboard lateral deflector array

Main atmospheric processing plant can produce breathable atmospheres for many different species and distribute to various zones via atmosphere ducts

Elevator to lower hangar

Hangar atmosphere force field

Millennium Falcon

Imperial shuttle

Port and starboard hangar connection tunnel

X-Wings

"May the Force be with us."
Admiral Ackbar

MON CALAMARI DESIGN

Although no two Mon Calamari vessels are precisely alike, nearly all resemble elongated, bulbous cylinders and appear organic, as if they were grown rather than built. Each is designed to meet Mon Calamari standards for efficiency, structural strength, and aesthetic appeal. Mon Calamari cruisers are covered with pods, bulges, and bumps arranged in a seemingly haphazard pattern, which contain sensor arrays, recessed weapon batteries, shield generators, and observation decks.

Deflector shield generator

Starboard hangar entrance

Main power conduits run the length of the ship

Ventral shield projector vanes

Escape pod exit

Lower hangar bay

Atmosphere duct

Composite deflector blister

Strange Pairing The rebel fleet consists of a disparate variety of ships, but a YT-1300 smuggling ship and a stolen Imperial shuttle make an especially unusual pair inside one of *Home One*'s hangars.

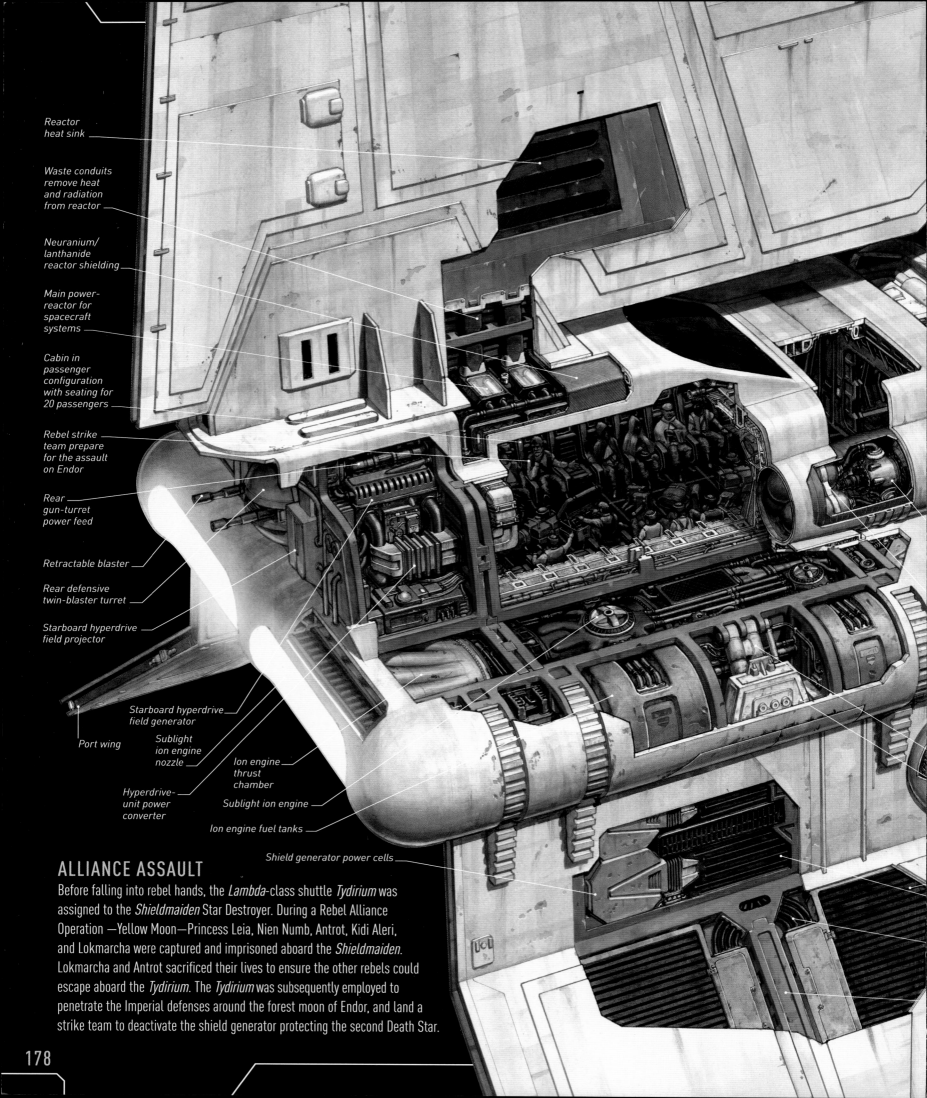

Reactor
heat sink

Waste conduits
remove heat
and radiation
from reactor

Neuranium/
lanthanide
reactor shielding

Main power-
reactor for
spacecraft
systems

Cabin in
passenger
configuration
with seating for
20 passengers

Rebel strike
team prepare
for the assault
on Endor

Rear
gun-turret
power feed

Retractable blaster

Rear defensive
twin-blaster turret

Starboard hyperdrive
field projector

Starboard hyperdrive
field generator

Port wing

Sublight
ion engine
nozzle

Ion engine
thrust
chamber

Hyperdrive-
unit power
converter

Sublight ion engine

Ion engine fuel tanks

Shield generator power cells

ALLIANCE ASSAULT

Before falling into rebel hands, the *Lambda*-class shuttle *Tydirium* was
assigned to the *Shieldmaiden* Star Destroyer. During a Rebel Alliance
Operation —Yellow Moon—Princess Leia, Nien Numb, Antrot, Kidi Aleri,
and Lokmarcha were captured and imprisoned aboard the *Shieldmaiden*.
Lokmarcha and Antrot sacrificed their lives to ensure the other rebels could
escape aboard the *Tydirium*. The *Tydirium* was subsequently employed to
penetrate the Imperial defenses around the forest moon of Endor, and land a
strike team to deactivate the shield generator protecting the second Death Star.

IMPERIAL SHUTTLE

Renowned for its reliability, the *Lambda*-class T-4a shuttle is one of the most widely used vessels in the Imperial fleet. Its primary function is to transfer personnel and cargo between the Empire's capital ships, but it is also used for planetary landings and ship-to-ship transfers between smaller Imperial vessels. A versatile craft, the shuttle is capable of being configured in several versions—as a cargo carrier, troop ship, courier vessel, or diplomatic transport. Many Imperial officials use the T-4a shuttle as a personal transport, as its armaments, heavily reinforced hull, and shielding enable it to travel in safety, even without a military escort—the Emperor himself uses a highly modified *Lambda*-class vessel. The shuttle's distinctive tri-wing design enables it to function in both space and planetary atmospheres. On landing, the heavily shielded lower wings fold upward to protect the ship's occupants.

Reinforced blast-door to seal bulkhead in the event cockpit is used as an escape craft

C-3PO

Han Solo

Chewbacca

Gunner's station

Leia Organa

Forward scanner array

R2-D2

Luke Skywalker

Flight engineer's station

Fixed-position offensive laser cannons

Twin rotating long-range blasters

Starboard retro-thrust engine

Retro-thrust engine fuel cells

Blaster power-feed

Blaster rotation mechanism

Landing-gear extension jacks

Starboard landing gear

Deflector shield generator heat-sink

Starboard-wing deflector shield projector

Starboard-wing deflector shield generator

Power feeds for deflector shield projectors

Main wing structural support beam

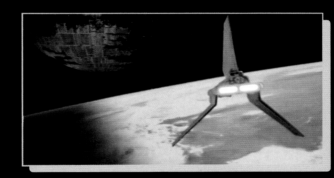

Covert Mission
Piloted by Han Solo and Chewbacca, and carrying a rebel strike force, the Lambda-class shuttle *Tydirium* arrives in the Imperial-occupied Endor system.

MULTIPLE MANUFACTURERS

Designed by Sienar Fleet Systems, the standard version of the T-4a shuttle is one of the manufacturer's most popular lines. In addition to Imperial contracts for the T-4a, the shuttle is also in great demand by many planetary governments and some of the galaxy's wealthiest individuals. To fulfill orders for a heavily armed, military version of the shuttle, technological genius Raith Sienar subcontracted production of the variant to Cygnus Spaceworks. However, this rival manufacturer has since tried to compete with Sienar by producing a non-military model that is almost identical to the standard T-4a design.

EMERGENCY LIFEBOAT

In the event that the *Lambda*-class T-4a is disabled, the cockpit can be jettisoned from the main body of the vehicle and used to travel a short distance at sublight speed. The cockpit, however, is not large enough to carry the shuttle's full complement of 20 passengers—on Imperial craft, priority for a place on the lifeboat is given to the most senior personnel on board.

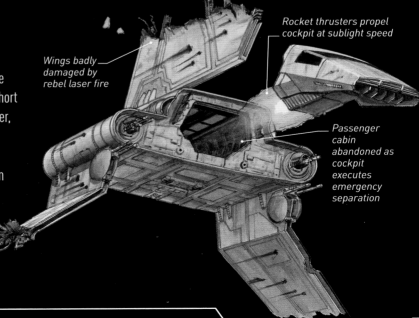

Wings badly damaged by rebel laser fire

Rocket thrusters propel cockpit at sublight speed

Passenger cabin abandoned as cockpit executes emergency separation

JABBA'S SAIL BARGE

Jabba the Hutt's sail barge *Khetanna* represents a strange combination of opulence and crude minimalism, befitting the tastes of its vile owner. The giant pleasure craft floats on repulsorlifts, carrying the crime lord from his palace in the Tatooine wastes to his Mos Eisley estate and back again. Jabba is also known to take the *Khetanna* sailing far across the Dune Sea to conduct dark negotiations, or to attend distant high-stakes races that contribute to his gambling empire. Its most nefarious purposes have involved conveying the Hutt to scenes of execution, or to violent and deadly gladiatorial combats staged for his entertainment in remote desert valleys. Wherever it is seen, the barge brings the ominous shadow of its master's presence.

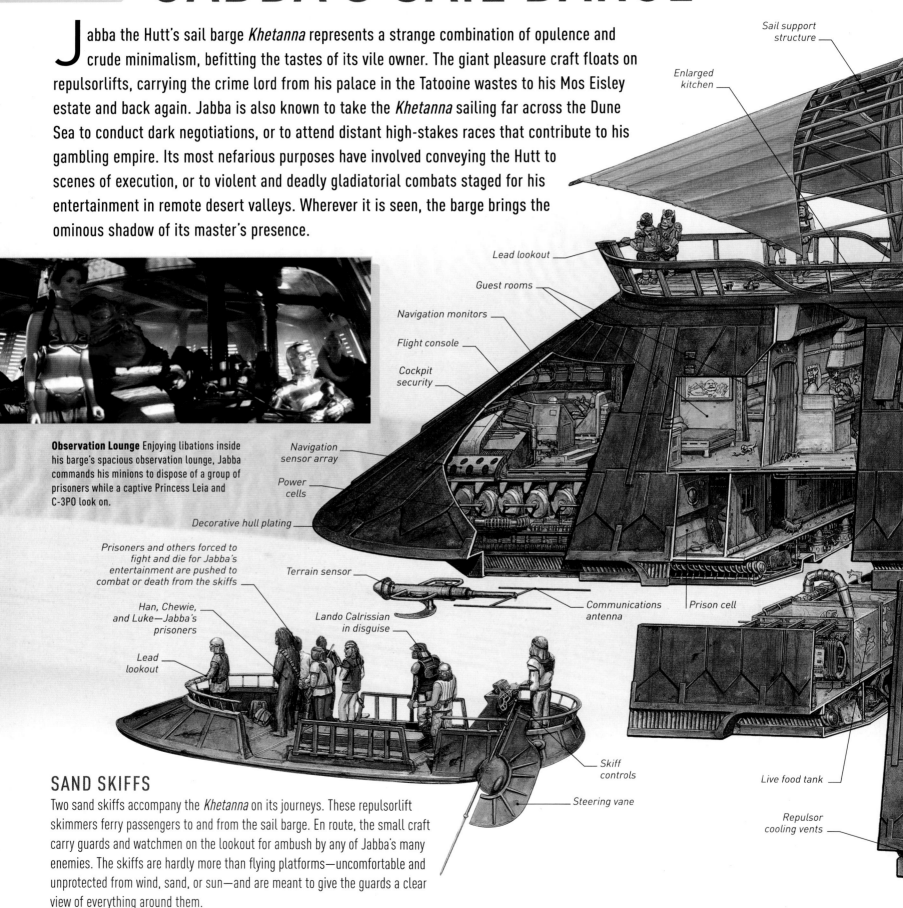

Observation Lounge Enjoying libations inside his barge's spacious observation lounge, Jabba commands his minions to dispose of a group of prisoners while a captive Princess Leia and C-3PO look on.

Sail support structure

Enlarged kitchen

Lead lookout

Guest rooms

Navigation monitors

Flight console

Cockpit security

Navigation sensor array

Power cells

Decorative hull plating

Prisoners and others forced to fight and die for Jabba's entertainment are pushed to combat or death from the skiffs

Terrain sensor

Communications antenna

Prison cell

Han, Chewie, and Luke—Jabba's prisoners

Lando Calrissian in disguise

Lead lookout

Skiff controls

Live food tank

Steering vane

Repulsor cooling vents

SAND SKIFFS

Two sand skiffs accompany the *Khetanna* on its journeys. These repulsorlift skimmers ferry passengers to and from the sail barge. En route, the small craft carry guards and watchmen on the lookout for ambush by any of Jabba's many enemies. The skiffs are hardly more than flying platforms—uncomfortable and unprotected from wind, sand, or sun—and are meant to give the guards a clear view of everything around them.

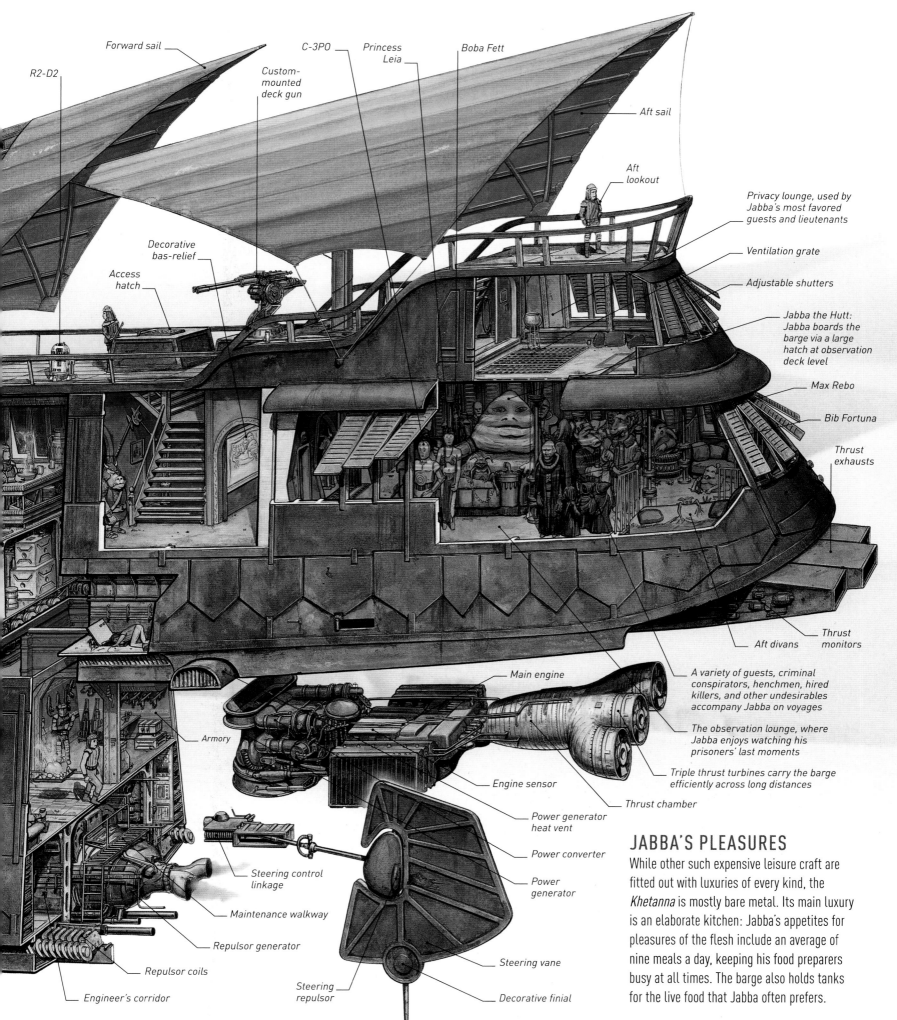

R2-D2

Forward sail

C-3PO

Princess Leia

Boba Fett

Custom-mounted deck gun

Aft sail

Aft lookout

Privacy lounge, used by Jabba's most favored guests and lieutenants

Decorative bas-relief

Access hatch

Ventilation grate

Adjustable shutters

Jabba the Hutt: Jabba boards the barge via a large hatch at observation deck level

Max Rebo

Bib Fortuna

Thrust exhausts

Thrust monitors

Aft divans

A variety of guests, criminal conspirators, henchmen, hired killers, and other undesirables accompany Jabba on voyages

Armory

Main engine

The observation lounge, where Jabba enjoys watching his prisoners' last moments

Triple thrust turbines carry the barge efficiently across long distances

Engine sensor

Thrust chamber

Power generator heat vent

Power converter

Steering control linkage

Power generator

Maintenance walkway

JABBA'S PLEASURES

While other such expensive leisure craft are fitted out with luxuries of every kind, the *Khetanna* is mostly bare metal. Its main luxury is an elaborate kitchen: Jabba's appetites for pleasures of the flesh include an average of nine meals a day, keeping his food preparers busy at all times. The barge also holds tanks for the live food that Jabba often prefers.

Repulsor generator

Steering vane

Repulsor coils

Steering repulsor

Decorative finial

Engineer's corridor

SAILING THE DUNE SEA

Archaeological evidence suggests Tatooine's Dune Sea was once an actual sea, but the punishing heat of the planet's twin suns evaporated the waters long ago. Now, the terrain consists of rolling dunes and trackless wastes, dotted with the occasional remains of dead creatures and crashed starships. Yet to some brave and foolhardy inhabitants of Tatooine, the Dune Sea is not a place to be avoided, but actually an opportunity for travel, utilizing sail barges like Jabba the Hutt's *Khetanna*. These look rather like primitive wind-driven craft, but in fact the decorative sails are most important as awnings, shading those on deck from the glare of Tatooine's twin suns. The sails can and do propel barges in moderate winds, but primary propulsion is provided by conventional thrust systems.

Double Duty Traveling alongside Jabba's sail barge, the skiff's crew serves not only as guards for Jabba's prisoners, but as lookouts for Tusken snipers who may be hiding in the surrounding dunes.

Deck Gun Put in place to protect Jabba, the sail barge's deck gun ultimately becomes its destroyer, when Princess Leia fires it through the top deck.

ARMED LUXURY

The *Khetanna* was designed long ago as a pleasure vehicle, and was never meant to be armed. Jabba's activities have brought him under attack more than once, however, and the Dune Sea is a dangerous place, so armament modifications were made to the barge at his palace workshops. The handrails were drilled to provide fittings for portable heavy blasters, and a powerful deck gun was installed to disable attacking vehicles. This gun has also been used to destroy the dwellings of those on Tatooine who oppose or displease Jabba.

Sail Barge Wreck Following its destruction at the hands of Luke Skywalker and his companions, the wreck of Jabba's sail barge joins the countless others dotting the Dune Sea.

FAST AND DANGEROUS

After Imperial forces decided to build a massive shield generator on Endor's forest moon to protect the second Death Star, they initially utilized AT-STs and AT-ATs for reconnaissance of the cleared areas surrounding the generator. However, because the moon's thick underbrush and dense woodland terrain made most Imperial vehicles impractical, the bulk of the vehicular patrol duty was handled by Imperial scout troopers riding explosively fast Aratech 74-Z speeder bikes.

Modified Guidance Systems
Speeder bikes on Endor were equipped with an extra sensor plate added on to the front control vanes.

Forest Patrol Although the tall Endor trees presented a definite hazard to speeder bikes, the forest was crisscrossed by numerous trails that scout troopers could traverse safely.

Blaster Cannon The 74-Z speeder bike is armed with a rotating blaster cannon located under the chassis. The cannon's controls are on the bike's handlebars.

Rapid Deceleration Although modified guidance systems gave troopers a much clearer idea of the terrain and obstacles beyond the trees immediately ahead of them, in combat, mistakes were easily made.

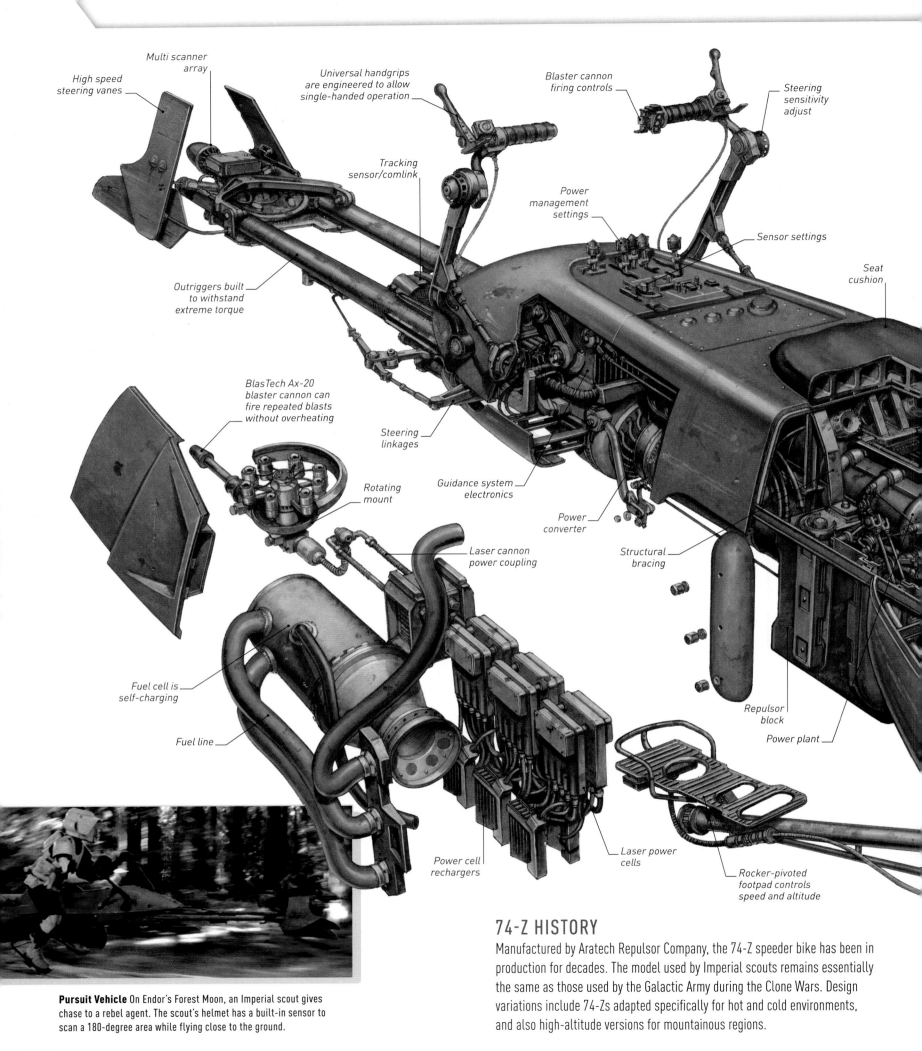

High speed
steering vanes

Multi scanner
array

Universal handgrips
are engineered to allow
single-handed operation

Blaster cannon
firing controls

Steering
sensitivity
adjust

Power
management
settings

Tracking
sensor/comlink

Sensor settings

Seat
cushion

Outriggers built
to withstand
extreme torque

BlasTech Ax-20
blaster cannon can
fire repeated blasts
without overheating

Steering
linkages

Rotating
mount

Guidance system
electronics

Laser cannon
power coupling

Power
converter

Structural
bracing

Fuel cell is
self-charging

Repulsor
block

Power plant

Fuel line

Power cell
rechargers

Laser power
cells

Rocker-pivoted
footpad controls
speed and altitude

Pursuit Vehicle On Endor's Forest Moon, an Imperial scout gives
chase to a rebel agent. The scout's helmet has a built-in sensor to
scan a 180-degree area while flying close to the ground.

74-Z HISTORY

Manufactured by Aratech Repulsor Company, the 74-Z speeder bike has been in
production for decades. The model used by Imperial scouts remains essentially
the same as those used by the Galactic Army during the Clone Wars. Design
variations include 74-Zs adapted specifically for hot and cold environments,
and also high-altitude versions for mountainous regions.

SCOUT SPEEDER BIKE

The Aratech 74-Z speeder bike is a small, one-man repulsorlift vehicle, and is the core equipment of an Imperial scout troop. Used to perform reconnaissance, perimeter defense, patrol missions in cooperation with AT-ST walkers, and surgical strikes against small enemy forces, the explosively quick vehicle is far more maneuverable than landspeeders or airspeeders. In addition, it allows the Imperial military to establish and maintain a tangible presence across vast areas of occupied worlds. The 74-Z has a self-charging energy source that allows a scout to explore and patrol far from base without worrying about fuel capacity. Speeder bikes are armed with small blaster cannons and are lightly armored for added protection.

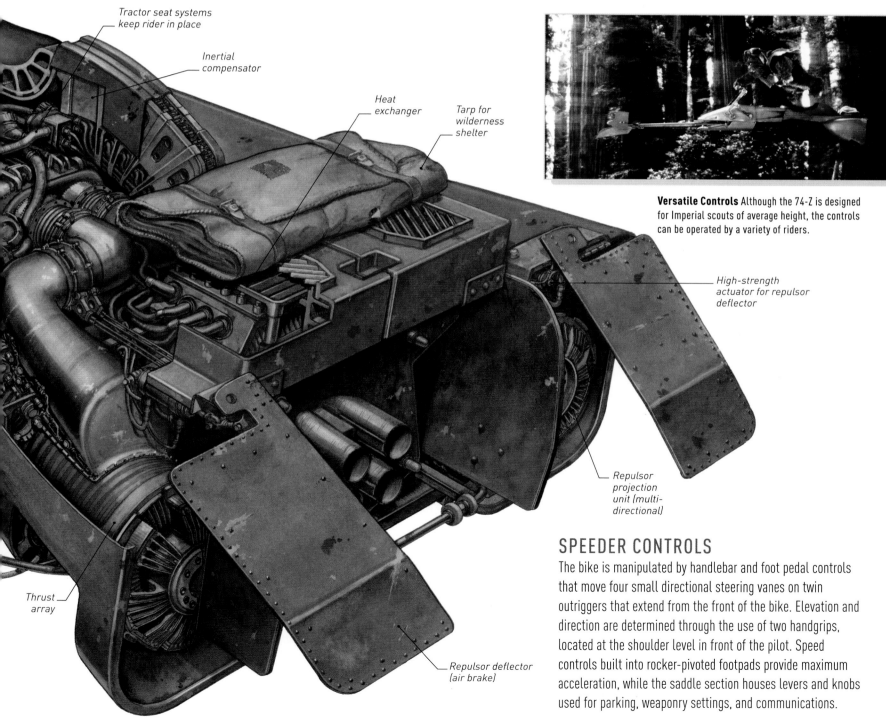

Tractor seat systems keep rider in place

Inertial compensator

Heat exchanger

Tarp for wilderness shelter

High-strength actuator for repulsor deflector

Repulsor projection unit (multi-directional)

Thrust array

Repulsor deflector (air brake)

Versatile Controls Although the 74-Z is designed for Imperial scouts of average height, the controls can be operated by a variety of riders.

SPEEDER CONTROLS

The bike is manipulated by handlebar and foot pedal controls that move four small directional steering vanes on twin outriggers that extend from the front of the bike. Elevation and direction are determined through the use of two handgrips, located at the shoulder level in front of the pilot. Speed controls built into rocker-pivoted footpads provide maximum acceleration, while the saddle section houses levers and knobs used for parking, weaponry settings, and communications.

RZ-1 A-WING

The small, wedge-shaped RZ-1 A-wing was designed to be the fastest starfighter in the galaxy. The sleek ship sacrifices shields, heavy weapons, and hull armor for speed and lightning-fast acceleration. Manufactured by Kuat Systems Engineering, the A-wing draws inspiration from Republic starfighter designs. A favorite of the Rebel Alliance, this craft has been a mainstay of local rebel cells since the early days of the Imperial era. The famous Phoenix Squadron is predominantly comprised of A-wings and even faces Darth Vader during the Siege of Lothal. The A-wing is ideally suited to hit-and-run missions, surgical strikes on capital ships, long-range patrols, and reconnaissance and intelligence-gathering missions. Its twin stabilizers and control surfaces also enable it to operate effectively as an atmospheric fighter.

INTELLIGENCE GATHERER

The hyperdrive capability, speed, and maneuverability of the A-wing make it ideal for intelligence-gathering and reconnaissance missions. An experienced A-wing pilot can drop out of hyperspace close to an Imperial fleet or space-installation, and make a blistering run around it (or even through a fleet, if the flier is daring enough). Using concealed multi-spectral imagers and other sensors, the pilot is able to gather information and escape back into hyperspace before TIE fighters can be scrambled. The A-wing's intelligence-gathering and strike capabilities are enhanced by its powerful sensor-jamming system, which can disrupt the detection and targeting systems of TIE fighters and other small vessels. However, this equipment is not so effective against capital ships as their sensors are more complex. The A-wing's jamming system can also endanger the craft when directed at a larger vessel, as its powerful broadcasts can be detected to reveal the starfighter's exact position to the enemy.

Green Leader
Rebel pilot Arvel Crynyd flew under the call sign "Green Leader" at the Battle of Endor, where he led the pilots who made up Green Squadron, and helped destroy Darth Vader's flagship, the *Executor*.

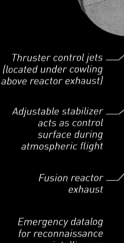

Corrugated carbo-plas provides structural strength with light weight

Concealed multi-spectral holographic imager for reconnaissance missions

Deflector shield generator

Deflector shield projector

Thruster control jets (located under cowling above reactor exhaust)

Adjustable stabilizer acts as control surface during atmospheric flight

Fusion reactor exhaust

Emergency datalog for reconnaissance intelligence information (can be ejected if craft is in danger of capture or destruction)

Thrust vector control

LAST RESORT

The A-wing typically relies on its exceptional speed to evade attack or pursuit, but, in the event that a pilot cannot escape, the craft provides one last-resort option. The wedge-shaped prow is fitted with a reinforced heat shield for atmospheric entry, which can also act as an effective "battering ram" at close range in atmospheric flight. In space battles, an A-wing pilot with no hope of escape or survival might choose to ram an enemy vessel, relying on the nose wedge to breach the ship's hull and destroy it.

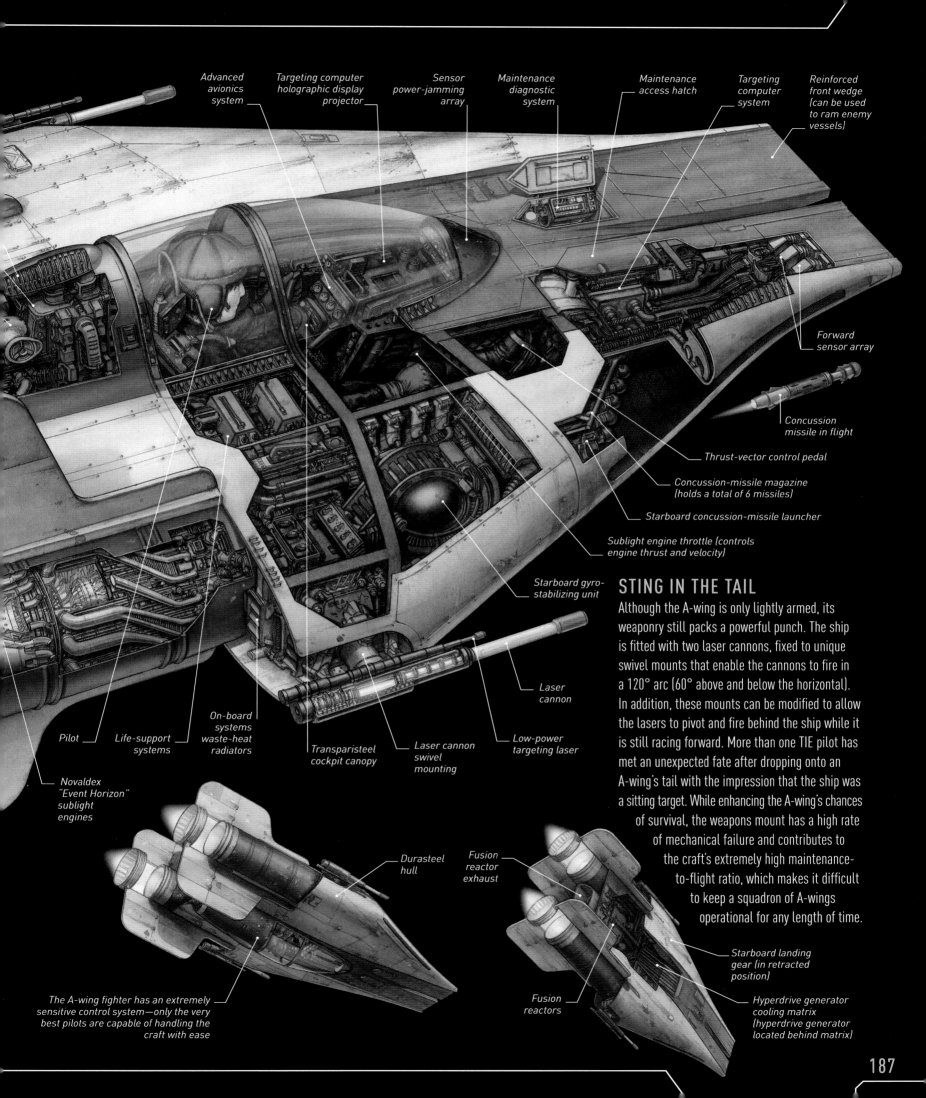

Advanced avionics system

Targeting computer holographic display projector

Sensor power-jamming array

Maintenance diagnostic system

Maintenance access hatch

Targeting computer system

Reinforced front wedge (can be used to ram enemy vessels)

Forward sensor array

Concussion missile in flight

Thrust-vector control pedal

Concussion-missile magazine (holds a total of 6 missiles)

Starboard concussion-missile launcher

Sublight engine throttle (controls engine thrust and velocity)

Starboard gyro-stabilizing unit

Laser cannon

Low-power targeting laser

Laser cannon swivel mounting

Transparisteel cockpit canopy

On-board systems waste-heat radiators

Life-support systems

Pilot

Novaldex "Event Horizon" sublight engines

STING IN THE TAIL

Although the A-wing is only lightly armed, its weaponry still packs a powerful punch. The ship is fitted with two laser cannons, fixed to unique swivel mounts that enable the cannons to fire in a 120° arc (60° above and below the horizontal). In addition, these mounts can be modified to allow the lasers to pivot and fire behind the ship while it is still racing forward. More than one TIE pilot has met an unexpected fate after dropping onto an A-wing's tail with the impression that the ship was a sitting target. While enhancing the A-wing's chances of survival, the weapons mount has a high rate of mechanical failure and contributes to the craft's extremely high maintenance-to-flight ratio, which makes it difficult to keep a squadron of A-wings operational for any length of time.

Durasteel hull

Fusion reactor exhaust

The A-wing fighter has an extremely sensitive control system—only the very best pilots are capable of handling the craft with ease

Fusion reactors

Starboard landing gear (in retracted position)

Hyperdrive generator cooling matrix (hyperdrive generator located behind matrix)

SWIVEL-WING STARFIGHTER

The B-wing has a unique design in which the cockpit remains fixed in regard to the plane of travel, while the gyroscopically mounted main wing can pivot around it, swiveling through 360°. This enables the entire wing assembly to swing from side to side horizontally and vertically, providing a wider arc of weapons' fire. This motion also changes the sensor-reflection configuration of the vessel, making it a much harder target to hit. While the B-wing's design and capabilities enhance the ship's tactical value, they also make it a difficult craft to fly, both in space combat and in atmospheric operations. Only the most skilled pilots can handle the B-wing—these fighter aces tend to become attached to their ships and supervise every repair and modification.

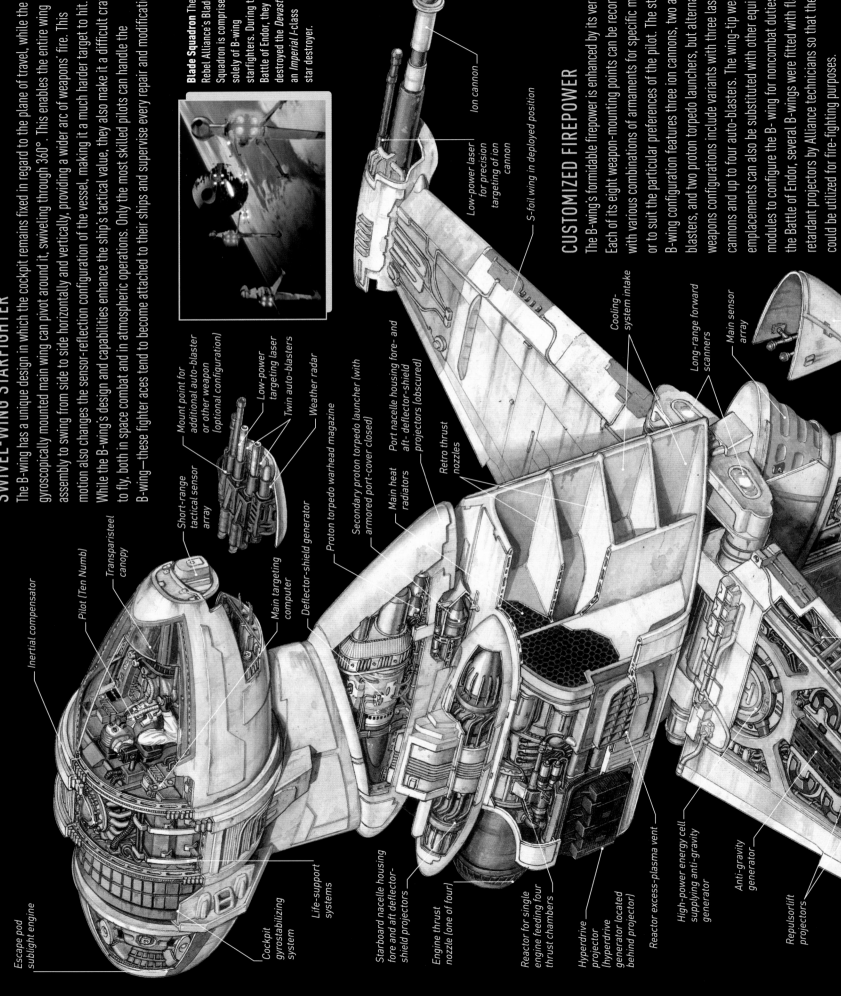

Blade Squadron The Rebel Alliance's Blade Squadron is comprised solely of B-wing starfighters. During the Battle of Endor, they destroyed the *Devastator* an *Imperial I*-class star destroyer.

CUSTOMIZED FIREPOWER

The B-wing's formidable firepower is enhanced by its versatility. Each of its eight weapon-mounting points can be reconfigured with various combinations of armaments for specific missions, or to suit the particular preferences of the pilot. The standard B-wing configuration features three ion cannons, two auto-blasters, and two proton torpedo launchers, but alternate weapons configurations include variants with three laser cannons and up to four auto-blasters. The wing-tip weapon emplacements can also be substituted with other equipment modules to configure the B- wing for noncombat duties. After the Battle of Endor, several B-wings were fitted with flame-retardant projectors by Alliance technicians so that the craft could be utilized for fire-fighting purposes.

Ion cannon

Low-power laser for precision targeting of ion cannon

S-foil wing in deployed position

Cooling-system intake

Long-range forward scanners

Main sensor array

Retro thrust nozzles

Port nacelle housing fore- and aft- deflector-shield projectors (obscured)

Main heat radiators

Secondary proton torpedo launcher (with armored port-cover closed)

Proton torpedo warhead magazine

Deflector-shield generator

Main targeting computer

Short-range tactical sensor array

Mount point for additional auto-blaster or other weapon (optional configuration)

Low-power targeting laser

Twin auto-blasters

Weather radar

Inertial compensator

Pilot (Ten Numb)

Transparisteel canopy

Escape pod sublight engine

Cockpit gyrostabilizing system

Life-support systems

Starboard nacelle housing fore and aft deflector-shield projectors

Engine thrust nozzle (one of four)

Reactor for single engine feeding four thrust chambers

Hyperdrive projector (hyperdrive generator located behind projector)

Reactor excess-plasma vent

High-power energy cell supplying anti-gravity generator

Anti-gravity generator

Repulsorlift projectors

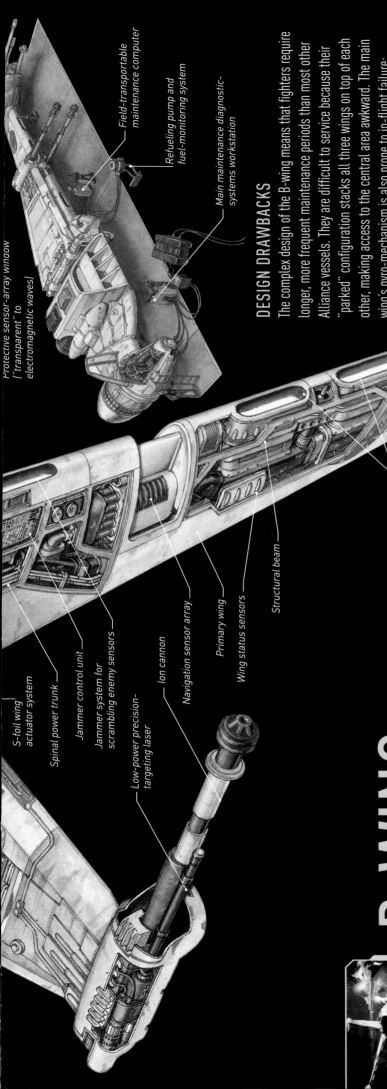
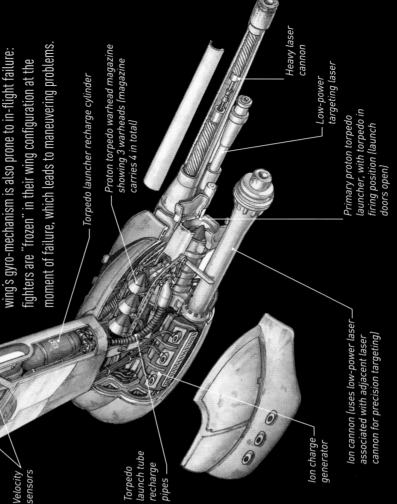

B-WING

The A/SF-01 B-wing starfighter—or blade wing—is one of the Rebellion's most well-armed crafts. An ingenious Mon Calamari engineer named Quarrie constructs the first B-wing prototype on Shantipole. He is convinced by rebel Captain Hera Syndulla's expert piloting skills to hand over his unique craft to the rebels and oversee the mass production of his design. The B-wing packs firepower equal to an Imperial Corvette—though at a much lower construction price. The ship's primary role is as an attack vessel targeting the Empire's capital ships. It also escorts X- and Y-wing fighter squadrons and Alliance convoys, and can be deployed for assaults on space-based or planetary-surface Imperial facilities. The starfighter is essentially a long wing with a pair of folding S-foils, and it boasts a formidable array of weapons, including ion cannons and proton torpedo launchers. These armaments are linked to the ship's advanced targeting computer for coordinated precision strikes, with the assistance of low-power targeting lasers. The B-wing's arsenal can be computer-controlled for coordinated fire, or independently targeted by the pilot. The craft also has a unique cockpit design—the pilot remains stationary while the rest of the ship rotates during flight.

DESIGN DRAWBACKS

The complex design of the B-wing means that fighters require longer, more frequent maintenance periods than most other Alliance vessels. They are difficult to service because their "parked" configuration stacks all three wings on top of each other, making access to the central area awkward. The main wing's gyro-mechanism is also prone to in-flight failure: fighters are "frozen" in their wing configuration at the moment of failure, which leads to maneuvering problems.

Field-transportable maintenance computer

Refueling pump and fuel-monitoring system

Main maintenance diagnostic-systems workstation

Protective sensor-array window ("transparent" to electromagnetic waves)

S-foil wing actuator system

Spinal power trunk

Jammer control unit

Jammer system for scrambling enemy sensors

Ion cannon

Navigation sensor array

Primary wing

Wing status sensors

Structural beam

Velocity sensors

Low-power precision-targeting laser

Torpedo launch tube recharge pipes

Torpedo launcher recharge cylinder

Proton torpedo warhead magazine showing 3 warheads (magazine carries 4 in total)

Heavy laser cannon

Low-power targeting laser

Primary proton torpedo launcher, with torpedo in firing position (launch doors open)

Ion charge generator

Ion cannon (uses low-power laser associated with adjacent laser cannon for precision targeting)

VEHICLE TECHNICAL DATA

REPUBLIC CRUISER

Manufacturer: Corellian Engineering Corporation
Make: Space Cruiser
Length: 115 m (380 ft)
Sublight engines: 3 Dyne 577 radial atomizers

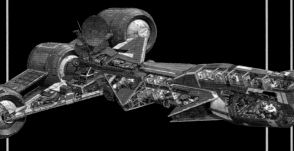

Hyperdrive: Longe Voltrans tri-arc CD-3.2
Crew: 8 (captain, 2 co-pilots, 2 communications officers, 3 engineers)
Passenger capacity: 16
Armament: None (unarmed diplomatic vessel)
Escape pods: two 8-person pods plus salon pod

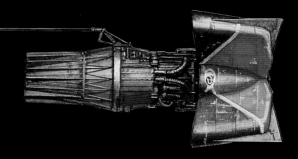

SEBULBA'S PODRACER

Engine manufacturer/type: Collor Pondrat Plug-F Mammoth racing engines, fitted with Split-X ram air/radiator intakes
Engine length: 7.47 m (24 ft 6 in)
Max. speed: 829 kph (515 mph)
Max. repulsorlift altitude: 85 m (275 ft)
Fuel: Tradium power fluid pressurized with quold runium, activated with ionized injectrine

ANAKIN'S PODRACER

Engine manufacturer/type: Radon-Ulzer 620C racing engines, modified heavily by Anakin Skywalker
Engine length: 7 m (23 ft)
Max. speed: estimated 947 kph (588 mph)
Max. repulsorlift altitude: 105 m (350 ft)
Fuel: straight Tradium power fluid activated with injectrine, no additives

LANDING SHIP

Design and manufacture: Haor Chall Engineering
Wingspan: 370 m (1,213 ft 11 in)
Hyperdrive: none
Max. atmospheric speed: 587 kph (365 mph)
Troop carrier capacity: 7 per wing; total 28
AAT (Armored Assault Tank) capacity: 24 per fore wing, 33 per aft wing; total 114
MTT (Multi-Troop Transport) capacity: 3 per fore wing, 3 in stage area, 2 in landing pedestal; total 11
Crew: 88 (droids only)
Armament: 2 pairs of wing-tip laser cannons, 4 turret-mounted cannons

MTT

Design and manufacture: Baktoid Armor Workshop
Troop capacity: 112 battle droids carrying standard blaster rifles
Armament: four 17 kv anti-personnel blasters twin-mounted in ball turrets
Length: 31 m (101 ft 8 in)
Height: 13 m (43 ft)
Max. ground speed: 35 kph (22 mph)
Max. lift altitude: 4 m (13 ft)
Deployment method: carried to planet surface in C-9979 landing ship

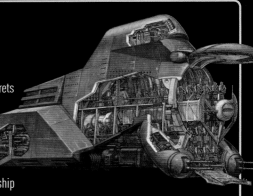

GUNGAN SUB

Design and manufacture: Otoh Gunga Bongameken Cooperative
Make: tribubble bongo sub
Length: 15 m (49 ft 3 in)
Cargo capacity: 800 kg (1800 lb) in each of 2 cargo bubbles
Crew: 1 (with 2 passengers)
Special features: the forward cockpit can eject as an escape pod in emergencies, but can sustain its hydrostatic field only briefly, so it must race for the surface before its power runs out

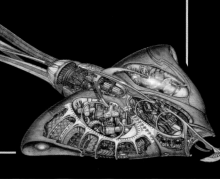

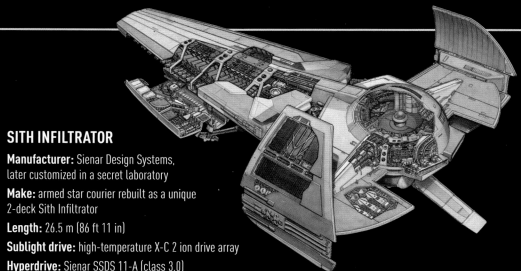

SITH INFILTRATOR

Manufacturer: Sienar Design Systems, later customized in a secret laboratory

Make: armed star courier rebuilt as a unique 2-deck Sith Infiltrator

Length: 26.5 m (86 ft 11 in)

Sublight drive: high-temperature X-C 2 ion drive array

Hyperdrive: Sienar SSDS 11-A (class 3.0)

Crew: 1, with capacity for 6 passengers

Primary armament: 6 low-profile laser cannons (4 original, 2 added)

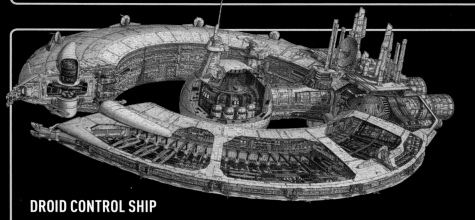

DROID CONTROL SHIP

Design and manufacture: Hoersch-Kessel Drive, Inc. (primary contractor)

Diameter: 3,170 m (10,400 ft 3 in)

Sublight engines: Rendili stardrive proton 2 (primary)/ proton 12 (secondary)

Droid control signal max. safe broadcast range: 16,500 km (10,300 miles)

Droid starfighter max. capacity: 1,500 fighters

C-9979 landing ship max. load: 25 per cargo arm; total 50

MTT (Multi-Troop Transport) max. load: 550

AAT (Armored Assault Tank) max. load: 6,250

Troop carrier max. load: 1,500

Armament: 42 quad laser emplacements

AAT

Design and manufacture: Baktoid Armor Workshop

Make: AAT (Armored Assault Tank)

Length: 9.75 m (32 ft)

Max. speed: 55 kph (35 mph)

Crew: 4 battle droids (commander, pilot, 2 gunners)

Armament: primary turret laser cannon; twin lateral range-finding lasers; twin lateral antipersonnel lasers; 6 energy shell projectile launchers

DROID STARFIGHTER

Design and manufacture: Xi Char cathedral factories, Charros IV

Length: 3.5 m (11 ft 6 in) wing tip to wing tip

Crew: permanent automated droid brain controlled by remote signal

Armament: 4 blaster cannons, 2 energy torpedo launchers

Flight time before refueling: 35 minutes

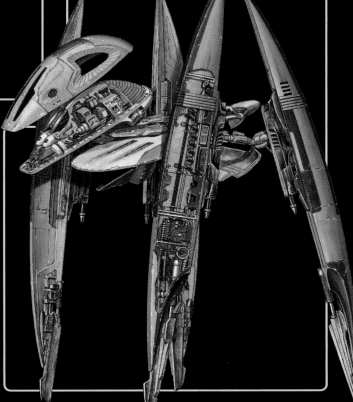

NABOO N-1 STARFIGHTER

Design and manufacture: Spaceframe by Theed Palace Space Vessel Engineering Corps

Configuration: J-type (twin radial sublight engines)

Length: 11 m (36 ft)

Sublight engines: Nubian 221, modified

Hyperdrive: Nubian Monarc C-4

Crew: 1 pilot, assisted by 1 mandatory astromech droid

Armament: twin laser cannons; proton torpedo magazine with capacity of 10 torpedoes

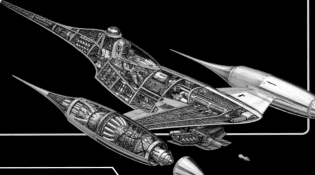

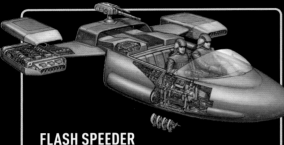

FLASH SPEEDER

Length: 4.5 m (14 ft 9 in)
Crew: 1
Passengers: 1
Armament: 1 laser blaster

GIAN SPEEDER

Length: 5.7 m (18 ft 8 in)
Crew: 1 pilot, 1 gunner
Passengers: 2
Armament: 3 laser blasters

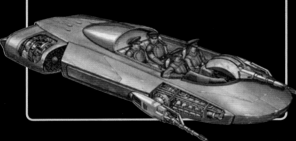

CORUSCANT TAXI

Length: 8 m (26 ft 3 in)
Top speed: 191 kph (115 mph)
Max. altitude: 3.4 km (2.1 miles)
Normal max. trip range: 210 km (131 miles)
Crew: 1
Passengers: depends on species
Armament: none

NABOO CRUISER

Manufacturer: Theed Palace Space Vessel Engineering Corps
Make: J-type custom-built diplomatic barge
Dimensions: length 39 m (127 ft 11 in); width 91 m (298 ft 7 in); depth 6.8 m (22 ft 4 in)
Max. speed (in standard atmosphere): 2,000 kph (1,240 mph)
Max. acceleration (in space): 2,500G
Hyperdrive: Nubian 288 cores; S-6 generators (class 0.7; range 80,000 light years fully fuelled)
Crew: 1 pilot; 1 co-pilot; 3 others optional (navigator/comscan/ shield operator); 5 astromech droids
Passengers: 4 prestige passengers; 6 guards
Armament: none

ZAM'S AIRSPEEDER

Manufacturer: Desler Gizh Outworld Mobility Corp.
Make: *Koro-2* all-environment exodrive airspeeder
Dimensions: 6.6 m (21 ft 8 in); width 2.1 m (6 ft 11 in); depth 0.9 m (3 ft)
Max. speed: 800 kph (496 mph)

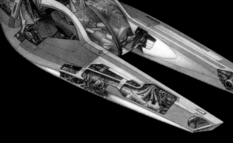

Cargo Capacity: 80 kg (176 lbs) or 0.04 m³ (1.4 ft³) in cabin and storage bins
Consumables: approx. five years' gas for irradiation system; two weeks' cabin air supply
Hyperdrive: Nubian 288 cores; S-6 generators (class 0.7; range 80,000 light years fully fuelled)
Passengers: 1 (excluding pilot)
Armament: none

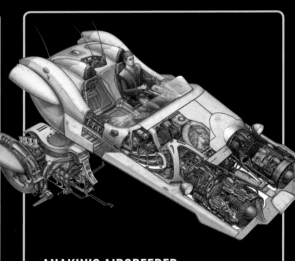

ANAKIN'S AIRSPEEDER

Manufacturer: mechanics at Senator Greyshade's private vehicle workshop
Make: unique, custom-built luxury airspeeder hotrod
Dimensions: length 6.23 m (20 ft 5 in); width 2.66 m (8 ft 9 in); depth (excluding antennas) 1.4 m (4 ft 7 in)
Mass: 1,600 kg (3,520 lbs)
Engine power: 30 megawatts
Max. airspeed: 720 kph (450 mph)
Max. acceleration: 70G (approx. engine limit)
Passengers: 1 (excluding pilot)
Armament: none

JEDI STARFIGHTER

Manufacturer: Kuat Systems Engineering, subsidiary of Kuat Drive Yards

Make: Delta-7 *Aethersprite* light interceptor

Dimensions: length 8 m (26 ft 3 in); width 3.92 m (12 ft 10 in); depth 1.44 m (4 ft 9 in)

Max. speed (in standard atmosphere): 12,000 kph (7,400 mph)

Max. acceleration (linear, in open space): 5,000G

Cargo capacity (in cockpit): 60 kg (132 lbs) or 0.03 m³ (1.06 ft³)

Consumables: five hours' fuel and air in normal sublight operation (air supply prolonged if pilot uses Jedi hibernation trance)

Crew: 1 pilot and 1 modified, integrated astromech droid

Armament: 2 dual laser cannons

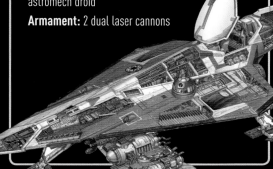

JANGO FETT'S *SLAVE I*

Manufacturer: Kuat Systems Engineering

Make: *Firespray*-class patrol and attack ship

Dimensions: length 21.5 m (70 ft 6 in); wingspan 21.3 m (69 ft 11 in); depth (excluding guns) 7.8 m (25 ft 7 in)

Max. speed (in standard atmosphere): 1,000 kph (620 mph)

Max. acceleration (linear, in open space): 2,500G

Hyperdrive: class 1.0

Crew: 1 pilot; up to 2 co-pilots/navigator/gunners

Passengers: 2 seated (immobilized captives are stored in lockers)

Armament: 2 blaster cannons; 2 laser cannons; missile-launcher; minelayer; other unknown weapons

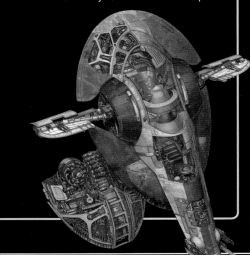

OWEN LARS'S SWOOP BIKE

Manufacturer: Mobquet

Make: Zephyr-G

Dimensions: length 3.68 m (12 ft); width 0.66 m (2 ft 2 in); depth 0.72 m (2 ft 4 in)

Max. airspeed: 350 kph (217 mph)

Max. acceleration: 2G (no inertial compensator; limited only by rider's grip and stamina)

Cargo capacity: 50 kg (110 lbs) per pannier; 200 kg (440 lbs) lifting capacity including rider

Consumables: approx. 3,000 km (1,860 miles) worth of fuel

Crew: 1 (and 1 passenger, in discomfort)

Armament: none

PADMÉ'S STARSHIP

Manufacturer: Theed Palace Space Vessel Engineering Corps

Make: Customised H-type Nubian yacht

Propulsion: 2 Nubian Sossen-3 ion drives

Dimensions: length 47.9 m (157 ft); width 8.1 m (26 ft 7 in); depth 7.1 m (23 ft 4 in)

Max. acceleration (linear, in open space): 2,800G

Max. speed (in standard atmosphere): 2,000 kph

Hyperdrive: Nubian 150 core and S-5 generator (class 0.9)

Crew: 1 pilot; 1 co-pilot; 2 optional (navigator/comscan plus shield operator); 2 astromech droids

Passengers: 1 prestige cabin

Armament: none

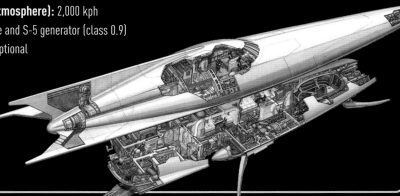

TRADE FEDERATION CORE SHIP

Manufacturer: Hoersch-Kessel Drive Inc. (basic Core Ship); Baktoid Combat Automata (droid-army control core)

Model: Lucrehulk-class modular control core (LH-1740)

Dimensions: diameter 696 m (2283 ft 6 in); depth (when landed, minus transmission mast) 914 m (2,998 ft 8 in)

Max. acceleration (linear, in open space): 300G

Cargo capacity: approx. 66 million m³ (2.3 billion ft³)

Consumables: 3 years' supplies

Crew: 60 Trade Federation supervisors; 3,000 Droid Crew; 200,000 Maintenance Droids

Passengers: stateroom capacity for 60,000 trade representatives

Armament: 280 point-defense light laser cannons

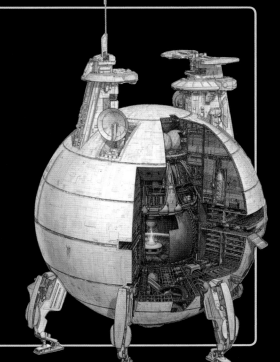

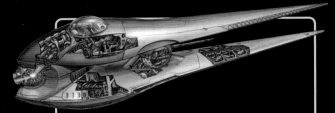

GEONOSIAN FIGHTER

Manufacturer: Huppla Pasa Tisc Shipwrights Collective

Make: *Nantex*-class territorial defense starfighter

Dimensions (excluding cockpit bubble): length 9.8 m (32 ft 2 in); width 1.9 m (6 ft 3 in); depth 2.2 m (7 ft 3 in)

Max. speed (in standard atmosphere): 20,000 kph (12,400 mph)

Max. acceleration (linear, in open space): 4,500G

Hyperdrive: none

Crew: 1 pilot (bonded to specific fighter)

Armament: 1 laser cannon turret; 100 independently aiming narrow-beam tractor/repulsor projectors

AT-TE

Manufacturer: Rothana Heavy Engineering (local subsidiary of Kuat Drive Yards)

Make: AT-TE (All Terrain Tactical Enforcer) assault walker

Dimensions: (hull only) length 13.2 m (43 ft 4 in); width 5.7 m (18.7 ft); (hull and legs) height 5.7 m (18.7 ft)

Max. landspeed: 60 kph (37.2 mph)

Consumables: fuel for 500 km (310 miles) walking; three standard weeks' air and rations

Crew: 1 pilot; 1 spotter; 4 gunner/support crew; 1 turret gunner outside

Passengers: 20 clone troopers; 1 IM-6 Battlefield Medical Droid (stowed in emergency locker)

Armament: 6 anti-personnel laser cannon turrets (4 front; 2 back); 1 heavy projectile cannon (variable yield)

REPUBLIC ASSAULT SHIP

Manufacturer: Rothana Heavy Engineering (subsidiary of KDY)

Make: *Acclamator*-class trans-galactic military transport ship

Dimensions: length 752 m (2,467 ft 2 in); width 460 m (1,509 ft 2 in); depth (with landing gear); 200 m (656 ft 2 in); depth (in flight) 183 m (600 ft 5 in)

Max. acceleration (linear, in open space): 3,500G

Hyperdrive: class 0.6

Cargo capacity: 320 speeder bikes; 80 infantry and cargo gunships; 48 armored walkers; 36 heavy self-propelled artillery pieces; 200,000 m³ (7,060,000 ft³) cargo space in addition to hangar space and consumables

Crew: 700

Passengers: 16,000 clone troops and support personnel

Armament: 12 quad turbolaser turrets; 24 laser cannons; 4 missile/torpedo launch tubes

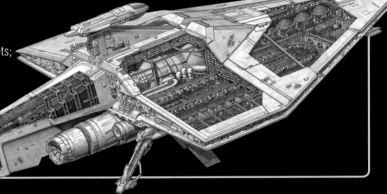

REPUBLIC GUNSHIP

Manufacturer: Rothana Heavy Engineering (local subsidiary of KDY)

Make: LAAT/i (Low-Altitude Assault Transport/infantry) repulsorlift gunship

Dimensions: length (clearance with guns) 17.4 m (57 ft); wingspan 17 m (55 ft 9 in); depth 6.1 m (20 ft)

Max. airspeed: 620 kph (384 mph)

Cargo capacity: 4 military speeder bikes; approx. 17 m³ (600 ft³) in main hold (if troops absent)

Consumables: 8 hours' flying fuel (approx.)

Crew: 1 pilot; 1 co-pilot/gunner; 2 auxiliary turret gunners

Passengers: 30 clone troopers approx.; 1 IM-6 Battlefield Medical Droid (stowed in emergency locker)

Armament: 3 anti-personnel turrets (2 front; 1 back); 2 mass-driver missile launchers (variable payload); 4 composite-beam, pinpoint laser turrets (2 manned; 2 remote); 8 light air-to-air rockets

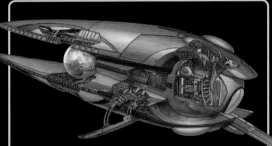

DOOKU'S SOLAR SAILER

Manufacturer: Huppla Pasa Tisc Shipwrights Collective

Make: *Punworcca 116*-class interstellar sloop

Dimensions: (with sail undeployed) length 16.8 m (55 ft); width 4.6 m (15 ft); depth 4.8 m (15 ft 9 in)

Max. acceleration: sail approx. 1,000G; thrusters 30G

Max. airspeed: 1,600 kph (992 mph)

Crew: 1 droid pilot; optional living co-pilot

Passengers: 1 in cabin; standing room for 10

Hyperdrive : class 1.5

Armament: 84 narrow tractor/repulsor beams

STAR DESTROYER – VENATOR CLASS

Manufacturer: Kuat Drive Yards

Make: *Venator*-class Star Destroyer

Dimensions: length 1,137 m (3,730 ft 4 in); wingspan 548 m (1,797 ft 11 in); height (in flight) 268 m (938 ft 4 in)

Max. acceleration (linear, in open space): 3,000G

Hyperdrive: class 1.0

Crew: 7,400

Armament: 8 heavy turbolaser turrets; 2 medium dual turbolaser cannons; 52 point-defense laser cannons; 4 proton torpedo tubes; 6 tractor beam projectors

Complement: 192 V-wing fighters; 192 Eta-2 *Actis* Interceptors; 36 ARC-170 fighters; 24 military walkers; 40 LAAT/i (Low Altitude Assault Transport/infantry) gunships; miscellaneous shuttles

ARC-170 STARFIGHTER

Manufacturer: Incom/Subpro

Make: ARC-170 (Aggressive ReConnaissance starfighter)

Dimensions: length 14.5 m (47 ft 7 in); wingspan 22.6 m (74 ft 2 in); height 4.78 m (15 ft 8 in)

Max. acceleration (linear, in open space): 2,600G

Max. airspeed (in standard atmosphere): 44,000 kph (27,341 mph)

Hyperdrive: class 1.5

Consumables: 5 days' air

Crew: 3 (pilot/copilot/gunner); 1 astromech droid

Armament: 2 medium laser cannons; 2 aft laser cannons; 6 proton torpedoes

V-WING STARFIGHTER

Manufacturer: Kuat Systems Engineering

Make: Alpha-3 Nimbus "V-wing" starfighter

Dimensions: length 7.9 m (25 ft 11 in); width 3.8 m (12 ft 6 in); height with open wings 5.84 m (19 ft 2 in)

Max. acceleration (linear, in open space): 4,800G

Max. airspeed (in standard atmosphere): 52,000 kph (32,312 mph)

Hyperdrive: none

Consumables: 15 hours' air

Crew: 1 pilot and 1 astromech droid

Armament: 2 twin laser cannons

JEDI INTERCEPTOR

Manufacturer: Kuat Systems Engineering, subsidiary of Kuat Drive Yards (fighter); TransGalMeg Industries Inc. (hyperdrive ring)

Make: Eta-2 *Actis* Interceptor; Syliure-45 hyperdrive module

Dimensions: length 5.47 m (17 ft 11 in); width 4.3 m (14 ft 1 in); height with open wings 2.5 m (8 ft 2 in)

Max. acceleration (linear, in open space): 5,200G

Max. speed (in standard atmosphere): 15,000 kph (9,321 mph)

Crew: 1 pilot and 1 astromech droid

Shields: none

Armament: 2 dual laser cannons; 2 secondary ion cannons

TRI-FIGHTER

Manufacturer: Colla Designs and Phlac-Arphocc Automata Industries

Make: space superiority starfighter

Dimensions: length 5.4 m (17 ft 9 in); wing diameter 1.96 m (6 ft 5 in); width 3.45 m (11 ft 4 in)

Max. acceleration (linear, in open space): 3,600G

Max. airspeed (in standard atmosphere): 37,000 kph (22,990 mph)

Hyperdrive: none

Crew: integrated droid brain

Armament: 1 medium laser cannon; 3 light laser cannons; 2–6 buzz-droid missiles

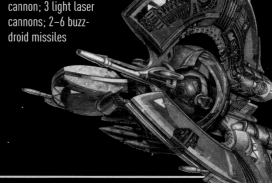

DROID GUNSHIP

Manufacturer: Baktoid Fleet Ordnance

Make: HMP (Heavy Missile Platform) droid gunship

Function: Ground assault fighter

Dimensions (excluding guns): length 12.3 m (40 ft 4 in); width 11 m (36 ft 1 in); height 3.1 m (10 ft 2 in)

Max. acceleration (linear, in open space): 100G

Max. airspeed (in standard atmosphere): 14,200 kph (8,824 mph)

Crew: Integrated droid brain

Armament (standard configuration): 2 laser cannon turrets; 1 medium laser cannon; 2 light laser cannons; 14 missiles

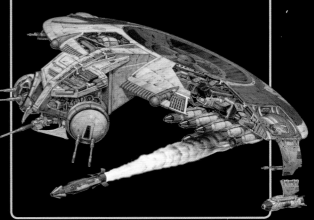

DATA FILES CONTINUED

JUGGERNAUT

Manufacturer: Kuat Drive Yards

Make: HAVw A6 Juggernaut

Dimensions: length 49.4 m (162 ft); width 19.6 m (64 ft 4 in); height 30.4 m (99 ft 9 in)

Max. landspeed: 160 kph (99 mph)

Crew: 12 (excluding gunners)

Passengers: 50–300 depending on internal configuration

Consumables: 20 days' provisions; fuel for 30,000 km (18,641 miles)

Armament: 1 heavy laser cannon turret; 1 rapid repeating laser cannon; 2 medium antipersonnel laser cannons; 2 twin blaster cannons; 2 rocket/grenade launchers—variable yield, 30 km (19.6 miles) range

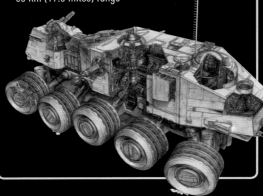

INVISIBLE HAND

Manufacturer: Free Dac Volunteers, Pammant Docks

Make: Modified Providence-class carrier/destroyer

Dimensions: length 1,088 m (3,569 ft 7 in); width 198 m (649 ft 7 in); height 347 m (1,138 ft 5 in)

Propulsion: 4 Nubian Creveld-4 radial ion drives

Max. acceleration (linear, in open space): 2,500G

Max. speed (in standard atmosphere): 2,000 kph (1,240 mph)

Hyperdrive: class 1.5

Crew: 600; up to 1.5 million deactivated battle droids

Armament: 14 quad turbolaser turrets; 34 dual laser cannons; 2 ion cannons; 12 point-defense ion cannons; 102 proton torpedo tubes

Complement: 120 droid tri-fighters; 120 droid Vulture fighters; 160 MTTs (Multi-Troop Transport); 280 assorted droid armored vehicles

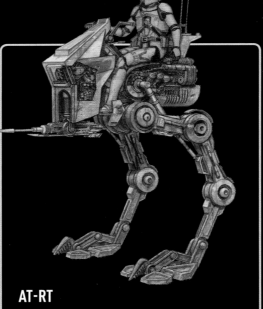

AT-RT

Manufacturer: Kuat Drive Yards

Product line: All Terrain Series

Height: 3.2 m (10 ft 6 in)

Crew: 1 pilot

Max. speed: 75 kph (46.6 mph)

Armament: 1 laser cannon

Cargo capacity: 20kg

Consumables: 1 day

BANKING CLAN FRIGATE

Manufacturer: Hoersch-Kessel Drive Inc. and Gwori Revolutionary Industries

Make: *Munificent*-class star frigate

Dimensions: length 825 m (2,706 ft 8 in); width 426 m (1,397 ft 8 in); height 243 m (797 ft 3 in)

Max. acceleration (linear, in open space): 2,300G

Hyperdrive: class 1.0

Crew: 200; up to 150,000 deactivated battle droids

Weapons: 2 heavy turbolaser cannons; 2 long-range ion cannons; 26 twin turbolaser cannons; 20 light turbolaser turrets; 38 point-defense laser cannons

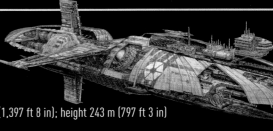

COMMERCE GUILD DESTROYER

Manufacturer: Hoersch-Kessel Drive Inc. and Free Dac Volunteers Engineering Corps

Make: *Recusant*-class light destroyer

Dimensions: length 1,187 m (3,894 ft 4 in); width 157 m (515 ft 1 in); height 163 m (534 ft 9 in)

Max. acceleration (linear, in open space): 2,800G

Hyperdrive: class 2.0

Crew: 300; up to 40,000 deactivated battle droids

Armament: 1 prow heavy turbolaser cannon; 4 heavy turbolaser cannons; 6 heavy turbolaser turrets; 5 turbolaser cannons; 30 dual laser cannons; 12 dual light laser cannons 60 point-defense laser cannons

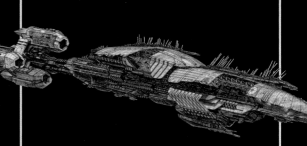

ROGUE-CLASS STARFIGHTER

Manufacturer: Buuper Torsckil Abbey Devices

Make: *Rogue*-class Porax-38 (P-38) starfighter

Dimensions: length 12.7 m (41 ft 8 in); width 12.88 m (42 ft 3 in); height 2.71 m (8 ft 11 in)

Max. acceleration (linear, in open space): 3,300G

Max. airspeed (in standard atmosphere): 61,000 kph (37, 905 mph)

Hyperdrive: class 2

Consumables: 20 days' air, fuel, and food

Crew: 1

Armament: 2 laser cannons

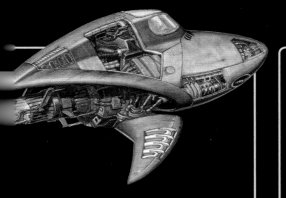

MANKVIM-814 LIGHT INTERCEPTOR

Manufacturer: Feethan Ottraw Scalable Assemblies

Make: Mankvim-814 light interceptor

Dimensions: length 10.7 m (35 ft 1 in); width 6.46 m (21 ft 2 in); height 3.45 m (11 ft 4 in)

Max. acceleration (linear, in open space): 3,400G

Max. airspeed (in standard atmosphere): 62,000 kph (37,905 mph)

Hyperdrive: none

Consumables: 2 hours' fuel

Crew: 1

Armament: 2 laser cannons

GRIEVOUS'S WHEEL BIKE

Manufacturer: Z-Gomot Ternbuell Guppat Corp., Lug system

Make: Tsmeu-6 personal wheel bike

Dimensions: wheel diameter 2.5 m (8 ft 2 in); length (including double laser cannon, excluding legs) 3.5 m (11 ft 6 in); height (including legs) 3.9 m 12 ft 10 in)

Crew: 1

Max. landspeed: 330 kph (205 mph) rolling; 10 kph 6 mph) on legs

Consumables: fuel for 500 km (311 miles) travel

Armament: 1 double laser cannon

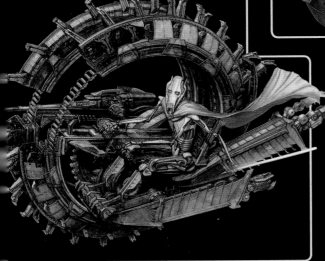

WOOKIEE CATAMARAN

Manufacturer: Appazanna Engineering Works

Make: *Oevvaor* jet catamaran

Dimensions: length 15.1 m (49 ft 6 in); width 10.2 m (33 ft 6 in); height 4.3 m (14 ft 1 in)

Max. waterspeed: 370 kph (230 mph)

Crew: 2

Passengers: 2

Consumables: 2 days' rations

Armament: none

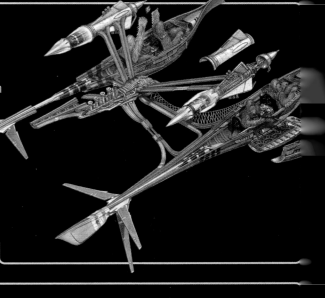

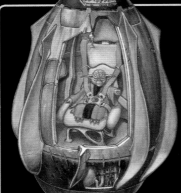

PALPATINE'S SHUTTLE

Manufacturer: Cygnus Spaceworks

Make: *Theta*-class T-2c Personnel Transport

Dimensions: length (excluding guns) 18.5 m (60 ft 8 in); width 29.3 m (96 ft 2 in); height 18.5 m (60 ft 8 in)

Max. acceleration (linear, in open space): 1,800G

Max. airspeed (in standard atmosphere): 2,000 kph (1,240 mph)

Hyperdrive: class 1; 8,000 light-year range

Consumables: 60 days fuel and air

Crew: 1–5

Armament: 2 quad laser cannons; 1 aft laser cannon

KASHYYYK POD

Manufacturer: Uurbahhahvoovv Joiners & Artisans

Make: homemade evacuation pod

Dimensions: diameter 2.3 m (7 ft 7 in); height 3.4 m (11 ft 2 in)

Max. acceleration (linear, in open space): 140G

Max. airspeed (during descent): over 70,000 kph (43,497 mph)

Hyperdrive: none

Passengers: 1

Consumables: 1 week's food and air

DAGOBAH POD

Manufacturer: His Grace the Duke Gadal-Herm's Safety Inspectorate

Dimensions: diameter 3.5 m (11 ft 6 in); length (legs retracted) 4 m (13 ft 1 in)

Make: E3-standard starship lifeboat

Max. acceleration (linear, in open space): 300G

Max. airspeed (during descent): over 40,000 kph (24,856 mph)

Hyperdrive: none

Passengers: 3

Consumables: 4 weeks' food and air

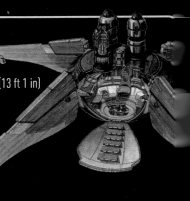

DELTA-CLASS T-3C SHUTTLE

Manufacturer: Sienar Fleet Systems

Model: *Delta*-class T-3c shuttle

Height: 25.1m (82ft 4in) with wings upright

Length: 14.39m (47ft 2in)

Crew: 2, plus 15 passengers

Atmospheric speed: 970kph (603mph)

Weapons: 2 twin laser cannons; 3 wingtip laser cannons

U-WING

Manufacturer: Incom Corporation

Model: UT-60D U-wing starfighter / support craft

Height: 3.35m (11ft)

Length: 24.98m (82ft) with S-foils forward

Crew 2: plus 8 passengers

Atmospheric speed: 950kph (590mph)

Weapons: 2 laser cannons

ZETA-CLASS SHUTTLE

Manufacturer: Telgorn Corporation

Model: *Zeta*-class cargo shuttle

Height: 28.74m (94ft 4in) with wings upright

Length: 35.50m (116ft 5in)

Crew : 2 passenger load variable— depending on cargo requirements

Atmospheric Speed: 700kph (435mph)

Weapons: 2 wing-mounted paired heavy laser cannons, 3 hull-mounted paired laser cannons

STAR DESTROYER

Manufacturer: Kuat Drive Yards

Make: *Imperial-I* Star Destroyer

Length: 1,137 m (3,730 ft 3 in)

Crew: (standard complement): 9,235 officers, 27,850 enlisted, 9,700 stormtroopers

Engines: SFS I-a2b solar ionization reactor powering Cygnus Spaceworks Gemon-4 ion engines

Hyperdrive: class 2

Complement: 48 TIE/In fighters, 12 TIE bombers, 12 TIE boarding craft, 12 landing craft, 20 AT-AT walkers, 30 AT-ST walkers, 8 *Lambda*-class Imperial shuttles, 15 stormtrooper transports, 5 assault gunboats

Armament: 60 Taim & Bak XX-9 heavy turbolaser batteries, 60 Borstel NK- 7 ion cannons, 10 Phylon Q7 tractor beam projectors

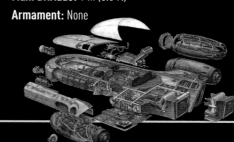

SANDCRAWLER

Manufacturer: Corellia Mining Corporation

Make: Corellia Mining Corporation digger/crawler

Length: 36.8 m (120 ft 9 in)

Height: 20 m (65 ft 7 in)

Crew: approximately 50 (members of single Jawa clan)

Engines: Girodyne Ka/La steampowered nuclear fusion engine

Max. speed: 30 kph (18.6 mph)

Cargo capacity: approximately 50 metric tons (110,231 lbs), in addition to storage for 1,500 droids

Consumables: 2 months' fuel and food

Armament: None

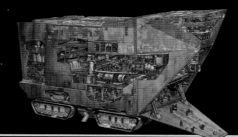

TANTIVE IV

Manufacturer: Corellian Engineering Corporation

Make: CR90 Corellian Corvette ("Blockade Runner")

Length: original; 150 m (492 ft 2 in) after refit; 125 m (410 ft 1 in)

Crew: 85 (46 crew, 39 diplomatic/consular staff)

Engines: 11 Girodyne Ter58 ion turbine engines

Hyperdrive: class 2

Armament: 6 Taim & Bak H9 turbolasers (2 dual, 4 single)

LUKE'S LANDSPEEDER

Manufacturer: SoroSuub Corporation

Length: 3.4 m (11 ft 2 in)

Crew: 1 pilot

Passengers: 1

Max. speed: 250 kph (155.3 mph)

Max. altitude: 1 m (3.3 ft)

Armament: None

MILLENNIUM FALCON

Manufacturer: Corellian Engineering Corporation

Make: Corellian YT-1300 transport (modified)

Length: 34.36 m (112 ft 9 in)

Crew: 2 (minimum)

Passengers: 6

Cargo: 100 metric tons (220,462 lbs)

Engines: Quadex power core, powering Isu-Sim SSP05 hyperdrive generator (heavily modified); 2 Girodyne SRB42 sublight engines (heavily modified)

Hyperdrive: class 0.5

Armament: 2 CEC AG-2G quad laser cannons, 2 Arakyd ST2 concussionmissile tubes, 1 BlasTech Ax-108 Ground Buzzer" blaster cannon

DEATH STAR

Manufacturer: Imperial Department of Military Research/Sienar Fleet Systems (construction overseen by Wilhuff Tarkin)

Make: Mk.1 deep-space mobile battle station

Dimensions: 160 km (99.4 miles) diameter; interior comprising 84 levels, each 1,428 m (4,685 ft) in height, each level divided into 357 sublevels, 4 m (13 ft 1 in) in height

Crew: 342,953 (285,675 operational staff, 57,278 gunners)

Passengers: 843,342

Hyperdrive: class 4

Engines: SFS-CR27200 hypermatter reactor powering 123 Isu-Sim SSP06 hyperdrive generators; 2 Sepma 30-5 sublight engines

Armament: 1 superlaser—range 47,060,000 km (29,241,719 miles), 5,000 Taim & Bak D6 turbolaser batteries, 5,000 Taim & Bak XX-9 heavy turbolasers, 2,500 SFS L-s 4.9 laser cannons, 2,500 Borstel MS-1 ion cannons, 768 Phylon tractorbeam emplacements, 11,000 combat vehicles

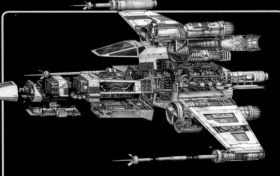

T-65 X-WING

Manufacturer: Incom Corporation

Make: Incom T-65C-A2 X-wing starfighter

Length: 13.4 m (43 ft 11 in)

Crew: 1 pilot and 1 astromech droid

Engines: Incom GBk-585 hyperdrive; 4 Incom 4L4 fusial thrust engines

Hyperdrive: class 1

Armament: 4 Taim & Bak KX9 laser cannons, 2 Krupx MG7 proton torpedo launchers

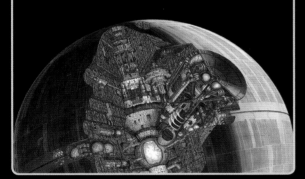

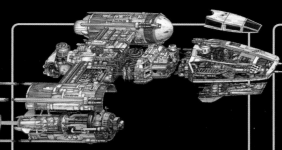

BTL A-4 Y-WING

Manufacturer: Koensayr

Make: BTL-A4 Y-wing starfighter

Length: 16 m (52 ft 6 in)

Crew: 1 or 2, and 1 astromech droid

Engines: Koensayr R300-H hyperdrive; 2 Koensayr R200 ion fission engines

Hyperdrive: class 1

Armament: 2 Taim & Bak KX5 laser cannons, 2 Arakyd Flex Tube proton torpedo launchers (4 torpedoes per launcher), 2 ArMek SW-4 light ion cannons

AT-AT

Manufacturer: Kuat Drive Yards

Designer: Imperial Department of Military Research

Make: Imperial All Terrain Armored Transport

Length: 25.9 m (84 ft 11 in)

Height: 22.2 (72 ft 10 in)

Crew: 3

Passengers: 40

Cargo: 5 speeder bikes

Engines: 2 KDYFW62 compact fusion drive systems

Max. speed: 60 kph (37.3 mph)

Armament: 2 Taim & Bak MS-1 heavy laser cannons, 2 Taim & Bak FF-4 medium repeating blasters

T-47 AIRSPEEDER

Manufacturer: Incom Corporation

Make: Incom T-47 airspeeder (modified)

Length: 5.3 m (17 ft 5 in)

Crew: 2

Engines: 2 Karydee KD49 repulsorlift drive units; 2 Incom 5i.2 high-powered ion drive afterburners

Max. speed: 1,100 kph (683.5 mph)

Flight ceiling: 175 km (108.7 miles)

Armament: 1 CEC Ap/11 double laser cannon, Ubrikkian Mo/Dk power harpoon and tow cable

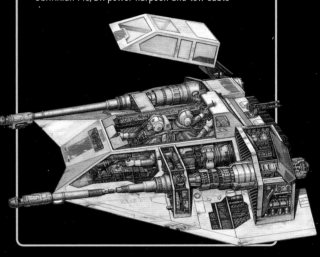

AT-ST

Manufacturer: Kuat Drive Yards

Designer: Imperial Department of Military Research

Make: Imperial All Terrain Scout Transport

Height: 8.6 m (28 ft 3 in)

Crew: 2

Cargo: 200 kg (440.9 lbs)

Engines: PowaTek AH-50 disposable high-intensity power cells

Max. speed: 90 kph (55.6 mph)

Armament: 1 Taim & Bak MS-4 twin blaster cannon, 1 E-web twin light blaster cannon, Dymek DW-3 concussion grenade launcher

TIE ADVANCED X1

Make: TIE Advanced x1 starfighter
Length: 11.45 m (37 ft 7 in)
Crew: 1 pilot
Engines: SFS I-S3a solar ionization reactor powering SFS P-s5.6 twin ion engines
Hyperdrive: class 4
Consumables: 5 days' air and food
Armament: 2 Sienar Fleet Systems L-s9.3 TIE laser cannons

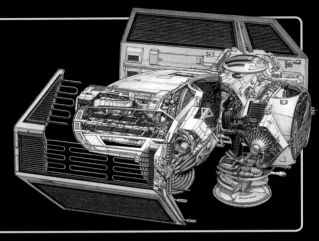

TIE FIGHTER

Manufacturer: Sienar Fleet Systems (for all TIE variants)
Make: TIE/ln space superiority fighter
Length: 7.2 m (23 ft 7 in)
Crew: 1 pilot
Engines: SFS I-a2b solar ionization reactor powering SFS P-s4 twin ion engines
Hyperdrive: none
Consumables: 2 days' air and food
Armament: 2 Sienar Fleet Systems L-s1 laser cannons

TIE INTERCEPTOR

Make: TIE interceptor
Length: 7.9 m (25 ft 11 in)
Crew: 1 pilot
Engines: SFS I-a3a solar ionization reactor powering SFS P-s5.6 twin ion engines
Hyperdrive: none
Consumables: 2 days' air and food
Armament: 4 Sienar Fleet Systems L-s9.3 laser cannons

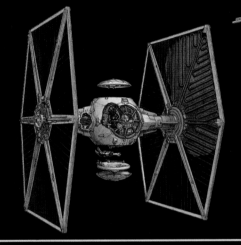

SLAVE I

Manufacturer: Kuat Systems Engineering
Make: *Firespray*-class patrol craft
Length: 21.5 m (70 ft 6 in)
Crew: 1
Passengers: 6 (prisoners)
Engines: 4 Kuat X-F-16 generators powering Kuat Engineering Systems F-31 ion engines
Hyperdrive: class 1
Armament: Borstel GN-40 twin rotating blaster cannons, 2 Dymek HM-8 concussion missile tube launchers, Brugiss C/ln ion cannon, Phylon F1 tractor beam projector, 2 Arakyd AA/SL proton torpedo launchers (3 torpedoes per launcher)

TIE BOMBER

Make: TIE bomber
Length: 11.05 m (36 ft 3 in)
Crew: 1 pilot
Engines: SFS I-a2b solar ionization reactor powering SFS P-s4 twin ion engines
Hyperdrive: none
Consumables: 2 days' air and food
Armament: 2 SFS L-s1 laser cannons, SFS-M-s3 concussion missiles; ArmaTek SJ-62/68 orbital mines, ArmaTek VL-61/79 proton bombs

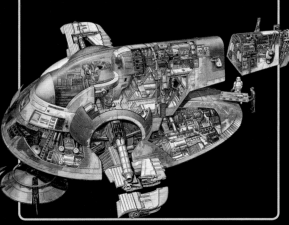

NEBULON-B FRIGATE (MEDICAL CONVERSION)

Manufacturer: Kuat Drive Yards
Length: 300 m (984 ft 3 in)
Crew: 850 (77 officers, 773 enlisted)
Passengers: 80 (medical personnel), and up to 745 patients
Engines: Kuat Galaxy-15 ion engines
Hyperdrive: Triple Taim, class 2
Armament: 6 Taim & Bak XI 7 turbolasers, 8 Borstel RH8 laser cannons, 2 Phylon-Q7 tractor beam projectors

HOME ONE

Manufacturer: Mon Calamari Shipyards

Length: 1,300 m (4265 ft 1 in)

Crew: 5,500

Passengers: 1,200 troops

Engines: M8.0-StarDrive engines

Hyperdrive: TriLuna 400MGS

Complement: 120 starfighters (mixture of A-wings, B-wings, X-wings, and Y-wings)

Armament: 36 heavy turbolasers, 36 heavy ion cannons

JABBA'S SAIL BARGE

Manufacturer: Ubrikkian Custom Vehicle Division

Make: Ubrikkian luxury sail barge *Khetanna*

Length: 30 m (98 ft 5 in)

Crew: 26

Passengers: 500

Engines: 3 Karydee KD57 3-chamber repulsorlift engines

Max. speed: 100 kph (62.1 mph)

Armament: 1 CEC Me/7double laser cannon; 20 CEC Gi/9 antipersonnel laser cannons

RZ-1 A-WING

Manufacturer: Various Alliance-linked organizations

Make: RZ-1 A-Wing starfighter

Length: 9.6 m (31 ft 6 in)

Crew: 1 pilot

Engines: 2 Novaldex J-77 "Event Horizon" engines

Hyperdrive: class 1

Armament: 2 Borstel RG9 laser cannons, 2 Dymek HM-6 concussion missile launchers (6 missiles per launcher)

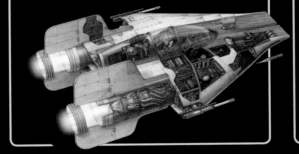

B-WING STARFIGHTER

Manufacturer: Slayn & Korpil

Designer: Quarrie

Make: B-wing heavy assault starfighter

Length: 16.9 m (55 ft 5 in)

Crew: 1 pilot

Engines: 1 Quadex Kyromaster engine with 4 thrust nozzles (or alternatively 4 Slayn & Korpil JZ-5 fusial thrust engines)

Hyperdrive: class 2

Armament (standard configuration) : 3 ArMek SW-7a ion cannons; 1 Gyrhil R-9X heavy laser cannon; Gyrhil 72 twin auto-blasters; 2 Krupx MG9 proton torpedo launchers

IMPERIAL SHUTTLE

Manufacturer: Sienar Fleet Systems

Make: *Lambda*-class Shuttle

Length: 20 m (65 ft 7 in)

Crew: 2–6

Passengers: 10–20 (or 80 metric tons [176,370 lbs] of cargo)

Engines: SFS S/ig-37 hyperdrive engine; 2 SFS-204 sublight ion engines

Hyperdrive: class 1

Armament (shuttle *Tydirium* configuration): 2 Taim & Bak KX5 double blaster cannons (forward-mounted), 1 ArMek R-Z0 retractable double blaster cannon (rear-mounted), 2 Taim & Bak GA-60s double laser cannons

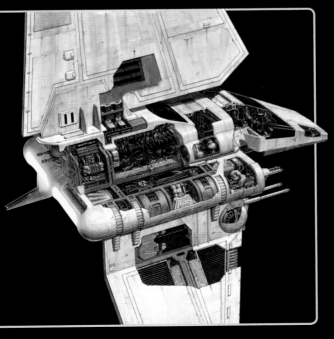

SCOUT SPEEDER BIKE

Manufacturer: Aratech Repulsor Company

Make: 74-Z speeder bike

Length: 3 m (9 ft 11 in)

Crew: 1 pilot

Max. airspeed: 500 kph (310.6 mph)

Armament: 1 light blaster cannon

Cargo capacity: 3 kilograms

Consumables: 1 day

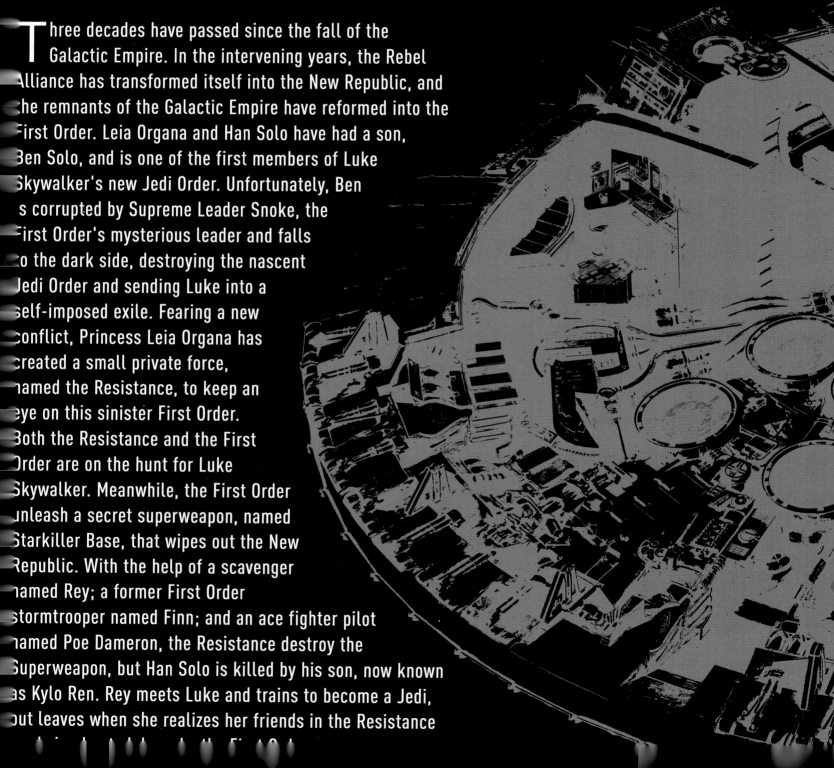

EPISODES VII–VIII

THE FORCE AWAKENS
THE LAST JEDI

Three decades have passed since the fall of the Galactic Empire. In the intervening years, the Rebel Alliance has transformed itself into the New Republic, and the remnants of the Galactic Empire have reformed into the First Order. Leia Organa and Han Solo have had a son, Ben Solo, and is one of the first members of Luke Skywalker's new Jedi Order. Unfortunately, Ben is corrupted by Supreme Leader Snoke, the First Order's mysterious leader and falls to the dark side, destroying the nascent Jedi Order and sending Luke into a self-imposed exile. Fearing a new conflict, Princess Leia Organa has created a small private force, named the Resistance, to keep an eye on this sinister First Order. Both the Resistance and the First Order are on the hunt for Luke Skywalker. Meanwhile, the First Order unleash a secret superweapon, named Starkiller Base, that wipes out the New Republic. With the help of a scavenger named Rey; a former First Order stormtrooper named Finn; and an ace fighter pilot named Poe Dameron, the Resistance destroy the superweapon, but Han Solo is killed by his son, now known as Kylo Ren. Rey meets Luke and trains to become a Jedi, but leaves when she realizes her friends in the Resistance

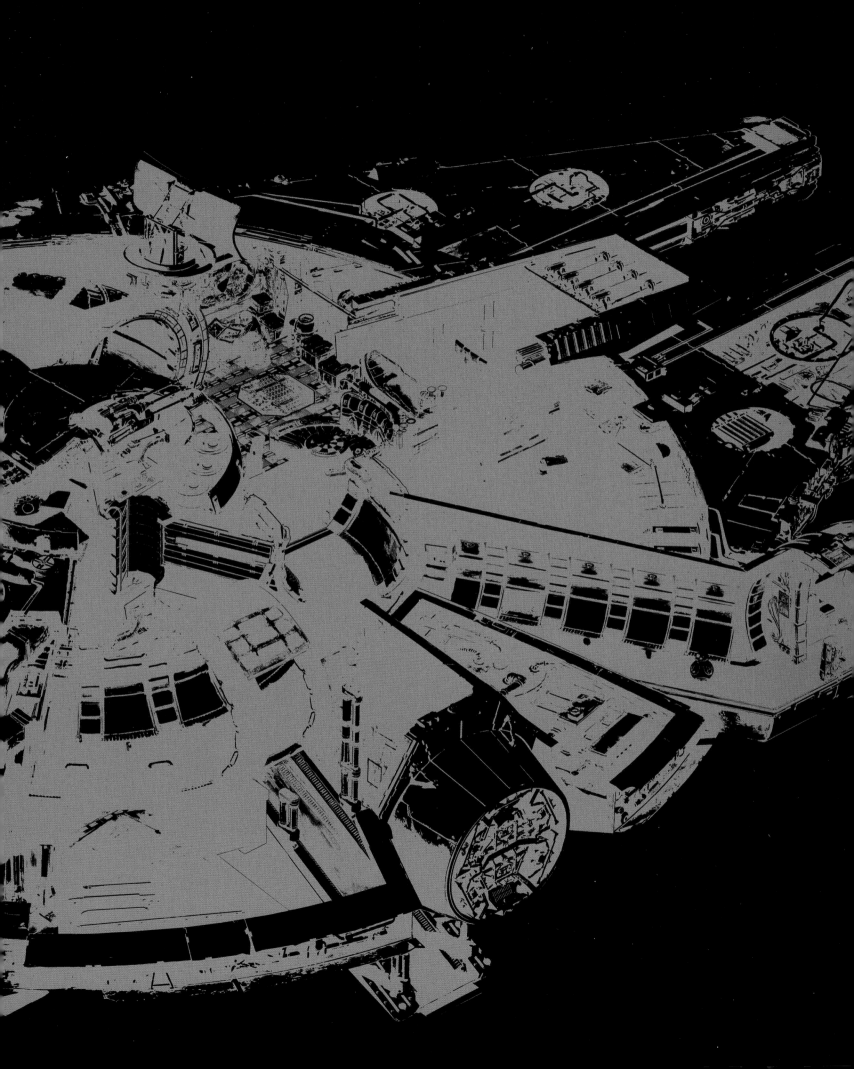

STORMTROOPER TRANSPORT

The First Order's stormtroopers know no family except their fellow soldiers, and have trained from childhood with a variety of weapons, practicing combat tactics until they can execute any military maneuver with unthinking precision. The First Order's assault landers can deliver two full squads of troopers to the battlefield for ground operations. These no-frills vehicles ferry troops from orbit and forward bases to drop zones, then return when combat is complete to pick up the survivors. For defense, assault landers rely on their shields, tough armor, and a single gunner occupying a dorsal turret.

BATTLEFIELD VIEW

A pilot guides the assault lander to its drop zone from a cockpit elevated for maximum visibility. As veterans of duty in TIE fighters, assault lander pilots are not troubled by this exposed vantage point, though they do complain that the landers are far less maneuverable than starfighters. If the pilot's control connections are severed, the assault lander can also be flown from a console inside the craft, but this backup system offers far less precision than the primary controls.

Main forward deflector projector

Minimal lighting to preserve trooper night vision

Troop compartment emergency hatch

Voids contain inert gas to dampen blaster impacts

F-11D blaster rifle

Forward deflector augmenter and sensor array

Searchlight (dazzles enemy)

FWMB-10 repeating blaster provides covering fire

Flametrooper

Exit ramp

Troopers disembark in standard two-abreast formation

Ramp actuator

QUICK DEPLOYMENT

First Order stormtroopers deploy the instant their craft's boarding ramp is lowered, with skirmishers rushing out to establish a perimeter as the rest of the troops emerge. Two squads can clear their vehicle and begin combat operations in as little as 30 seconds, allowing their lander to evacuate the drop zone.

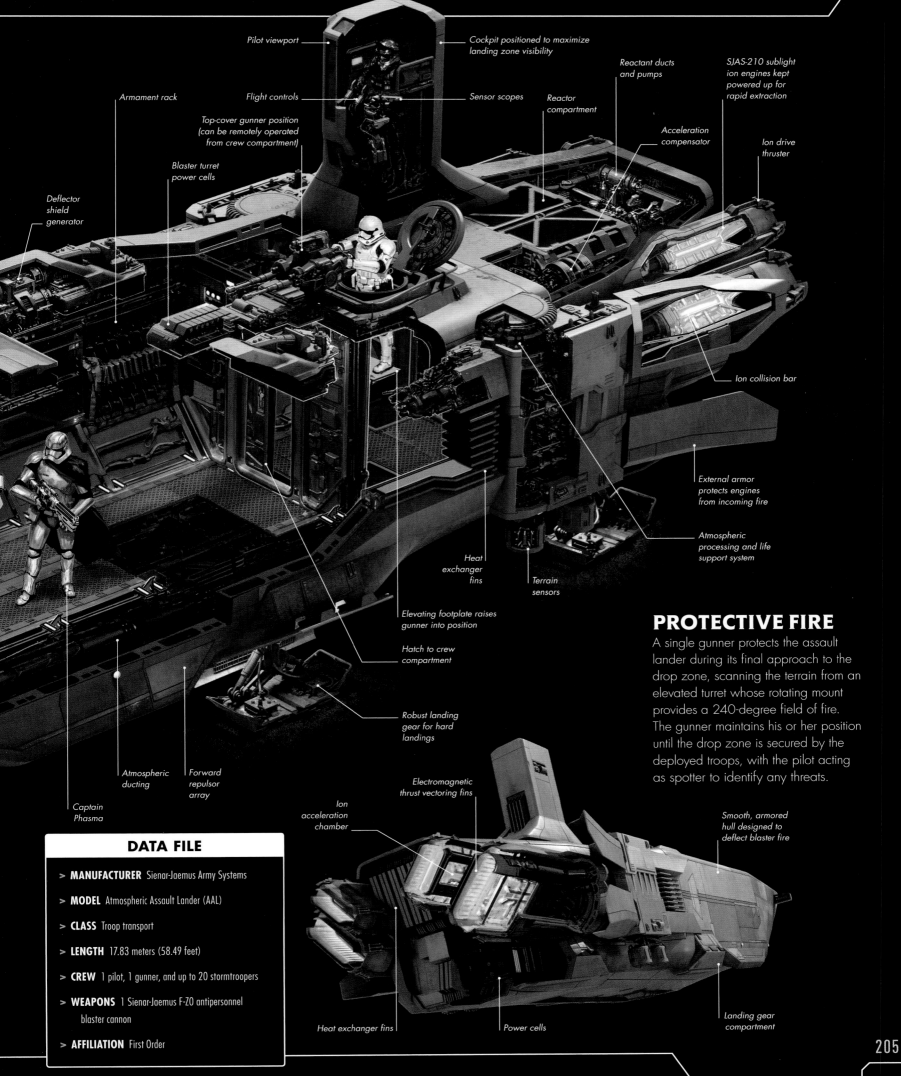

Pilot viewport

Cockpit positioned to maximize landing zone visibility

Reactant ducts and pumps

SJAS-210 sublight ion engines kept powered up for rapid extraction

Armament rack

Flight controls

Sensor scopes

Reactor compartment

Acceleration compensator

Ion drive thruster

Top-cover gunner position (can be remotely operated from crew compartment)

Blaster turret power cells

Deflector shield generator

Ion collision bar

External armor protects engines from incoming fire

Atmospheric processing and life support system

Heat exchanger fins

Terrain sensors

Elevating footplate raises gunner into position

Hatch to crew compartment

Robust landing gear for hard landings

Atmospheric ducting

Forward repulsor array

Captain Phasma

Electromagnetic thrust vectoring fins

Ion acceleration chamber

Smooth, armored hull designed to deflect blaster fire

PROTECTIVE FIRE

A single gunner protects the assault lander during its final approach to the drop zone, scanning the terrain from an elevated turret whose rotating mount provides a 240-degree field of fire. The gunner maintains his or her position until the drop zone is secured by the deployed troops, with the pilot acting as spotter to identify any threats.

Heat exchanger fins

Power cells

Landing gear compartment

DATA FILE

> **MANUFACTURER** Sienar-Jaemus Army Systems

> **MODEL** Atmospheric Assault Lander (AAL)

> **CLASS** Troop transport

> **LENGTH** 17.83 meters (58.49 feet)

> **CREW** 1 pilot, 1 gunner, and up to 20 stormtroopers

> **WEAPONS** 1 Sienar-Jaemus F-Z0 antipersonnel blaster cannon

> **AFFILIATION** First Order

POE'S X-WING

T he T-70 X-Wing is a favorite craft of Resistance pilots, including Poe Dameron, who flies a customized example codenamed *Black One*. The latest incarnation of the venerable X-wing family, the T-70 is faster than the ships that formed the backbone of the Alliance's starfighter corps during the Galactic Civil War and is equipped with more powerful weapons. X-wings are more expensive and complex than the First Order's TIE fighters, but much more versatile. They are nimble enough for dogfighting but powerful enough to slug it out with enemy capital ships.

Incom-FreiTek 5L5 fusial thrust engine

S-foil rear repulsor array

Centrifugal reactant fusion and ionization chamber

Hyperdrive

Life support system

Reactant injector

S-foil actuator

Turbo impeller

Static discharge coupling

Sensor-scattering ferrosphere paint

Deflector shield generator

Laser generator

Plasma combination injector

Laser cooling sleeve

Deflector shield projector

Laser blast condensing channel

Rear landing gear

Power coupling

Laser generator heat sink

Laser-blaster converter

Bottom-loading astromech droid

Proton torpedo firing rack

Laser cannon charge cells (accumulate energy for laser bolt)

Magnetic flashback suppressor (prevents feedback damage)

Miniaturized MG7-A proton torpedo

Proton warhead

PACKING A PUNCH

The original X-wing's designers envisioned a fighter with the speed and power to attack Imperial Star Destroyers, and delivered on that promise. Just like its predecessor, the T-70 has powerful wingtip cannons that can fire in single, dual, or quad mode, and it can punch through deflector shields with its eight proton torpedoes. Quick-change magazines allow pilots to swap torpedoes with other payloads, such as concussion missiles or mag-pulse warheads.

RESOURCE CRUNCH

The Rebellion built its T-65 X-wings in hangars and drydocks hidden from Imperial spies. The New Republic has no such constraints, but its demilitarization efforts and rampant corruption have steered the few remaining starfighter contracts to well-connected manufacturers. The Resistance can build few X-wings of its own, and instead must make do with fighters donated by local security forces or lent by senators who share General Leia Organa's fears about the First Order.

Lasers firing in alternating dual mode

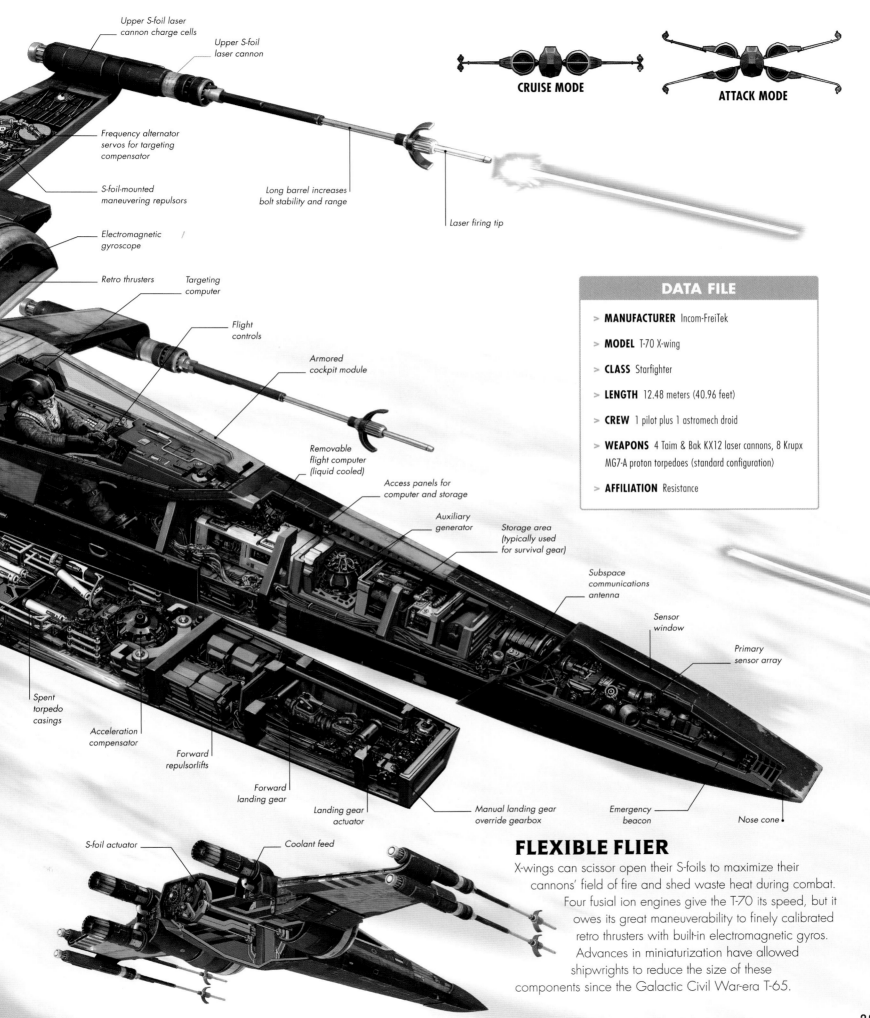

Upper S-foil laser
cannon charge cells

Upper S-foil
laser cannon

Frequency alternator
servos for targeting
compensator

S-foil-mounted
maneuvering repulsors

Long barrel increases
bolt stability and range

Laser firing tip

Electromagnetic
gyroscope

Retro thrusters

Targeting
computer

Flight
controls

Armored
cockpit module

Removable
flight computer
(liquid cooled)

Access panels for
computer and storage

Auxiliary
generator

Storage area
(typically used
for survival gear)

Subspace
communications
antenna

Sensor
window

Primary
sensor array

Spent
torpedo
casings

Acceleration
compensator

Forward
repulsorlifts

Forward
landing gear

Landing gear
actuator

Manual landing gear
override gearbox

Emergency
beacon

Nose cone

S-foil actuator

Coolant feed

CRUISE MODE

ATTACK MODE

DATA FILE

> **MANUFACTURER** Incom-FreiTek

> **MODEL** T-70 X-wing

> **CLASS** Starfighter

> **LENGTH** 12.48 meters (40.96 feet)

> **CREW** 1 pilot plus 1 astromech droid

> **WEAPONS** 4 Taim & Bak KX12 laser cannons, 8 Krupx
MG7-A proton torpedoes (standard configuration)

> **AFFILIATION** Resistance

FLEXIBLE FLIER

X-wings can scissor open their S-foils to maximize their
cannons' field of fire and shed waste heat during combat.
Four fusial ion engines give the T-70 its speed, but it
owes its great maneuverability to finely calibrated
retro thrusters with built-in electromagnetic gyros.
Advances in miniaturization have allowed
shipwrights to reduce the size of these
components since the Galactic Civil War-era T-65.

COMMAND SHUTTLE

The First Order's top officers and dignitaries travel in bat-winged command shuttles, heavily guarded by TIE fighter escorts. Looking like dark birds of prey, command shuttles have formidable heavy laser cannons, but their biggest asset is their defensive capabilities. Advanced sensor suites in the upper wings monitor communications and scan for potential enemies long before they reach firing range, while the lower wings are lined with efficient shield projectors and powerful jammers. These technologies are the products of secret research conducted in the First Order's hidden shipyards and laboratories. One of these shuttles ferries the dark side apprentice Kylo Ren from the Star Destroyer *Finalizer* to the forlorn desert world of Jakku, in search of a secret that could allow Kylo to fulfill his destiny.

IMPERIAL SECRETS

When the Empire collapsed, the Emperor's servants fled into the Unknown Regions with some of his regime's greatest secrets. For years, military scout ships had explored far beyond the galactic frontier, surveying star systems and blazing hyperspace routes known only to a select few. Far from the prying eyes of the New Republic, the remnants of the Empire established new bases, shipyards, and weapons labs, and began plotting a return to power.

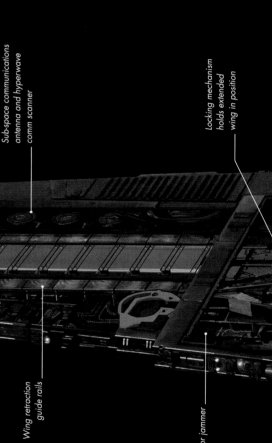

Wing shape draws on decades of Imperial shuttle design

Heat sink extends expected life of sensor systems

Jammer modulation node

Countermeasures system designed to deflect incoming guided projectiles

Primary sensor node

Sub-space communications antenna and hyperwave comm scanner

Locking mechanism holds extended wing in position

Static discharge vane

Long-range scan-mode sensor array

Passive-mode sensors

Wing retraction guide rails

Sensor jammer

DATA FILE

> **MANUFACTURER** Sienar-Jaemus Fleet Systems

> **MODEL** Upsilon-class shuttle

> **CLASS** Transport

> **HEIGHT** 37.2 meters (122.04 feet) with wings extended

> **CREW** 1–5 plus up to 10 passengers

> **WEAPONS** 2 twin laser cannons

> **AFFILIATION** First Order

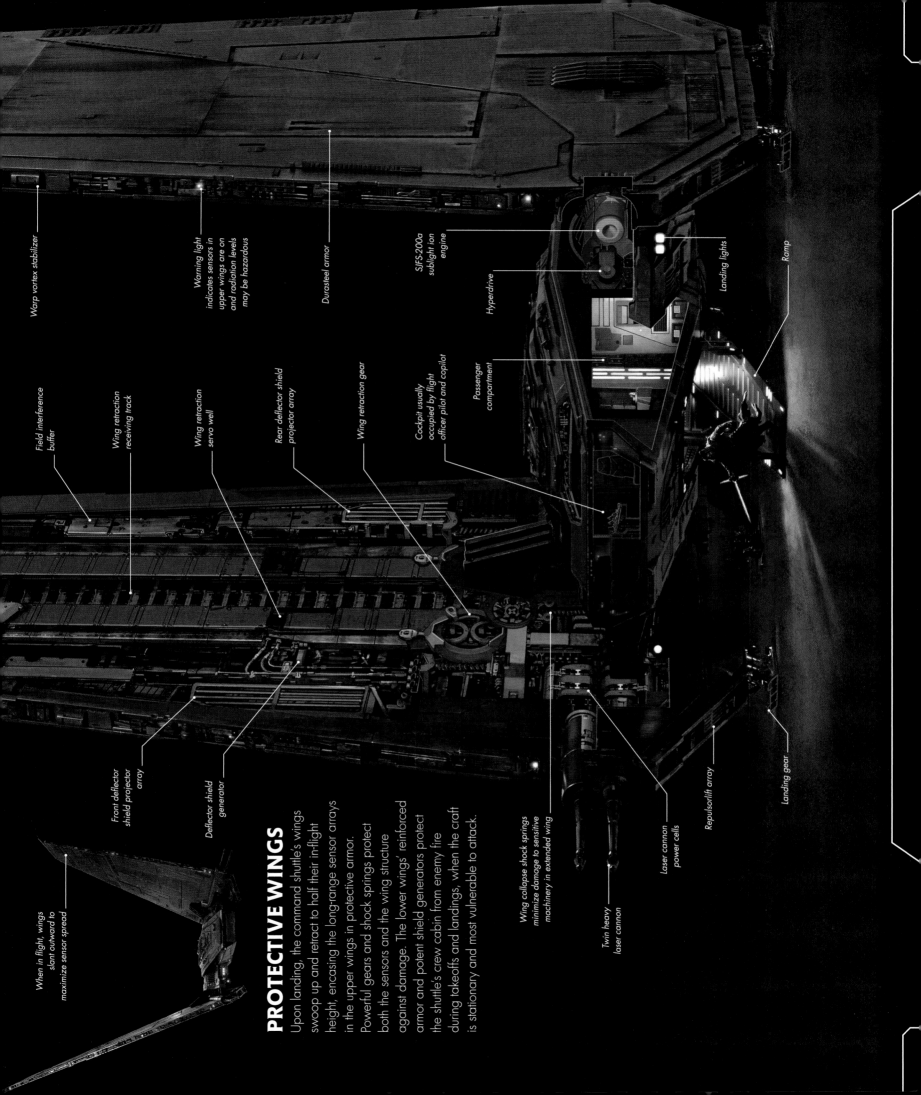

Warp vortex stabilizer

Warning light indicates sensors in upper wings are on and radiation levels may be hazardous

Durasteel armor

SJFS-200a sublight ion engine

Hyperdrive

Landing lights

Ramp

Field interference buffer

Wing retraction receiving track

Wing retraction servo well

Rear deflector shield projector array

Wing retraction gear

Cockpit usually occupied by flight officer, pilot and copilot

Passenger compartment

Front deflector shield projector array

Deflector shield generator

Wing collapse shock springs minimize damage to sensitive machinery in extended wing

Twin heavy laser cannon

Laser cannon power cells

Repulsorlift array

Landing gear

When in flight, wings slant outward to maximize sensor spread

PROTECTIVE WINGS

Upon landing, the command shuttle's wings swoop up and retract to half their in-flight height, encasing the long-range sensor arrays in the upper wings in protective armor. Powerful gears and shock springs protect both the sensors and the wing structure against damage. The lower wings' reinforced armor and potent shield generators protect the shuttle's crew cabin from enemy fire during takeoffs and landings, when the craft is stationary and most vulnerable to attack.

REY'S SPEEDER

Rey's pride and joy is her custom speeder, an ungainly but powerful vehicle created using parts unearthed in the junkpiles of Niima Outpost, reclaimed from the Starship Graveyard, or acquired from Teedo traders. Armed with welding torches, hydrospanners, and bonding tape, Rey built a vehicle combining aspects of a speeder and a swoop, making use of sophisticated military hardware and civilian machinery. Rey's speeder is fast and can carry heavy loads, making it ideal for scavenging trips. The top-heavy craft would be difficult for any other pilot to control, but Rey's skills as a pilot match her genius as a mechanic.

SCAVENGER SAFEGUARDS

Light-fingered scavengers are a fact of life on Jakku, and Rey knows that without her speeder she'd be even more trapped than she already is, unable to travel between the Starship Graveyard, her makeshift homestead, and Niima Outpost. Her speeder won't power up without a fingerprint scan, and she can electrify the chassis to give a powerful jolt to anyone who touches it while she's away.

HYBRID VEHICLE

At the heart of Rey's speeder are powerful twin turbojet engines reclaimed from a wrecked cargo-hauler. Rey mounted them in a stacked configuration instead of side by side, and bolted them to powered amplifier intakes from an Imperial gunship. She then customized them with racing-swoop afterburners, a modified combustion chamber, and an array of repulsorlifts taken from crashed X-wing starfighters.

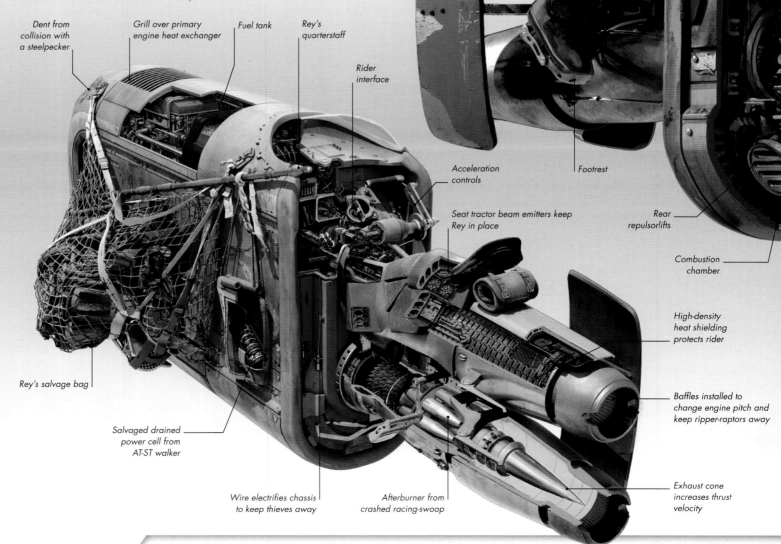

CPU housing

Rear stabilizer vane

Dent from collision with a steelpecker

Grill over primary engine heat exchanger

Fuel tank

Rey's quarterstaff

Rider interface

Acceleration controls

Footrest

Seat tractor beam emitters keep Rey in place

Rear repulsorlifts

Combustion chamber

High-density heat shielding protects rider

Rey's salvage bag

Salvaged drained power cell from AT-ST walker

Wire electrifies chassis to keep thieves away

Afterburner from crashed racing-swoop

Baffles installed to change engine pitch and keep ripper-raptors away

Exhaust cone increases thrust velocity

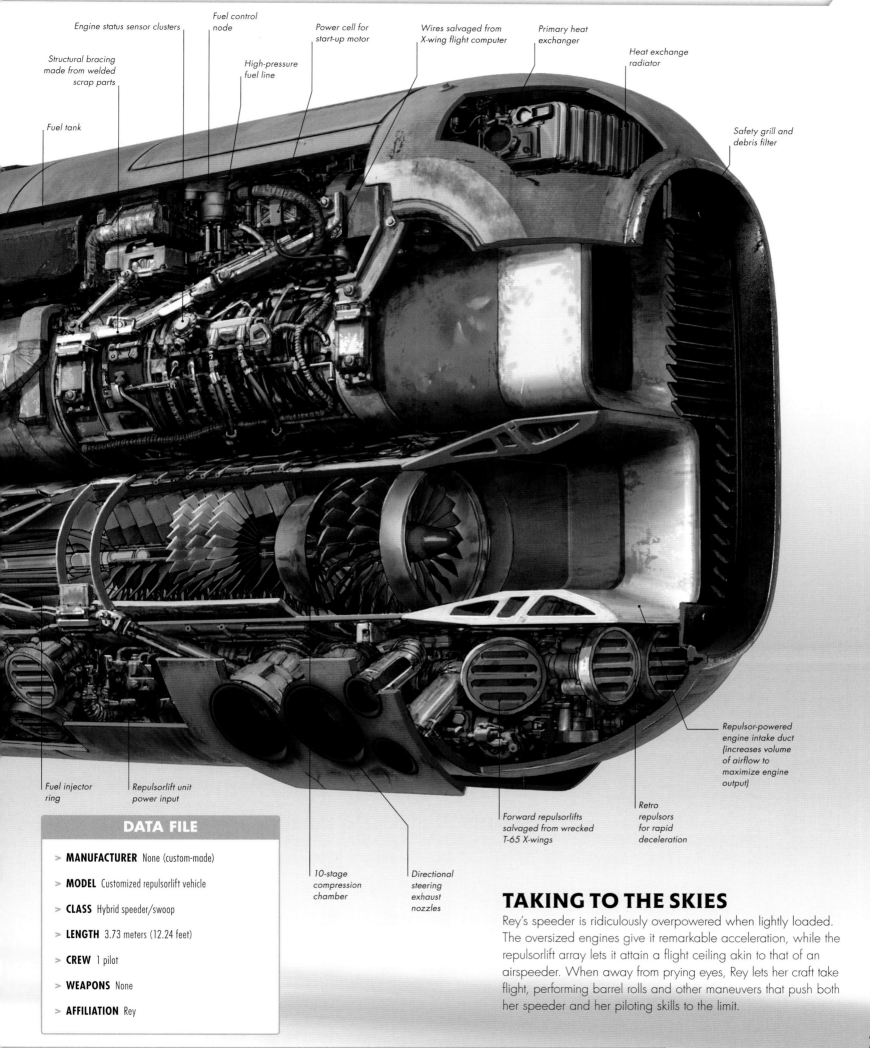

Fuel tank

Structural bracing
made from welded
scrap parts

Engine status sensor clusters

Fuel control
node

High-pressure
fuel line

Power cell for
start-up motor

Wires salvaged from
X-wing flight computer

Primary heat
exchanger

Heat exchange
radiator

Safety grill and
debris filter

Fuel injector
ring

Repulsorlift unit
power input

10-stage
compression
chamber

Directional
steering
exhaust
nozzles

Forward repulsorlifts
salvaged from wrecked
T-65 X-wings

Retro
repulsors
for rapid
deceleration

Repulsor-powered
engine intake duct
(increases volume
of airflow to
maximize engine
output)

DATA FILE

> **MANUFACTURER** None (custom-made)

> **MODEL** Customized repulsorlift vehicle

> **CLASS** Hybrid speeder/swoop

> **LENGTH** 3.73 meters (12.24 feet)

> **CREW** 1 pilot

> **WEAPONS** None

> **AFFILIATION** Rey

TAKING TO THE SKIES

Rey's speeder is ridiculously overpowered when lightly loaded.
The oversized engines give it remarkable acceleration, while the
repulsorlift array lets it attain a flight ceiling akin to that of an
airspeeder. When away from prying eyes, Rey lets her craft take
flight, performing barrel rolls and other maneuvers that push both
her speeder and her piloting skills to the limit.

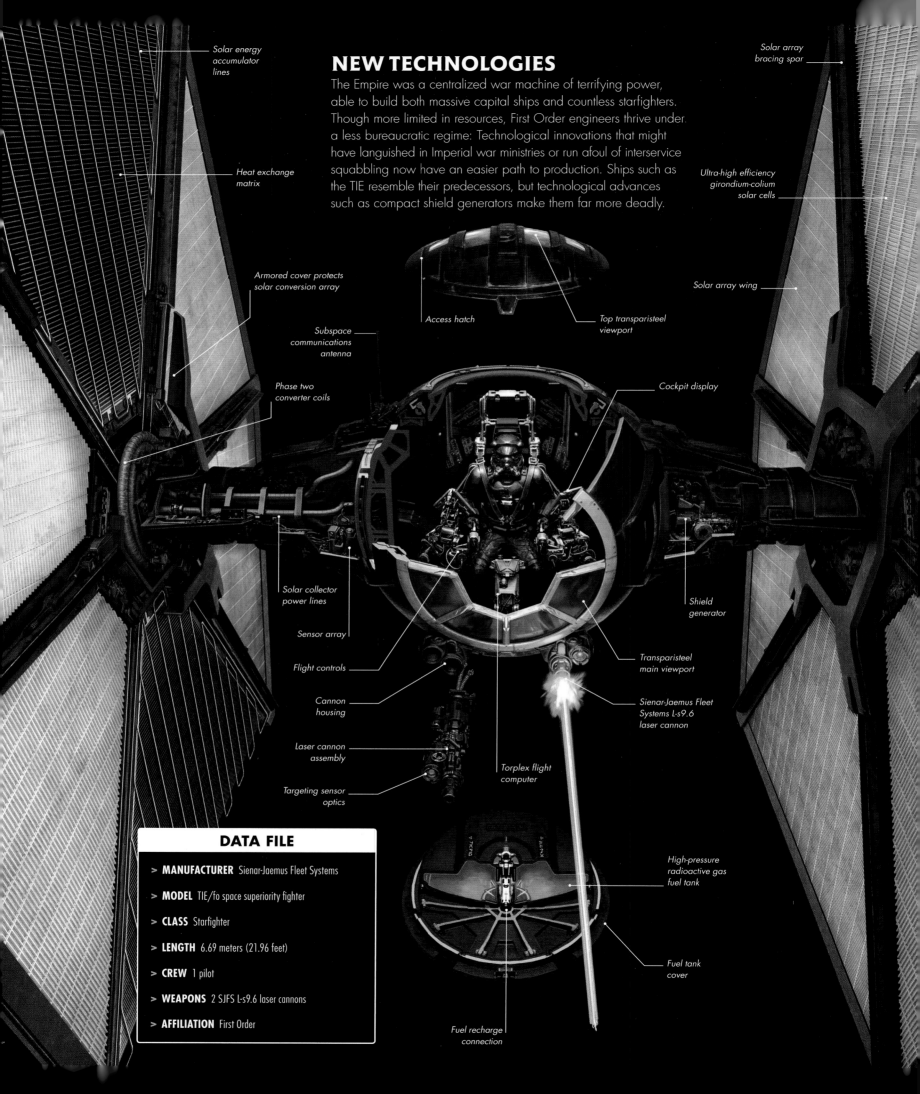

NEW TECHNOLOGIES

The Empire was a centralized war machine of terrifying power, able to build both massive capital ships and countless starfighters. Though more limited in resources, First Order engineers thrive under a less bureaucratic regime: Technological innovations that might have languished in Imperial war ministries or run afoul of interservice squabbling now have an easier path to production. Ships such as the TIE resemble their predecessors, but technological advances such as compact shield generators make them far more deadly.

Solar energy accumulator lines

Heat exchange matrix

Armored cover protects solar conversion array

Subspace communications antenna

Phase two converter coils

Solar collector power lines

Sensor array

Flight controls

Cannon housing

Laser cannon assembly

Targeting sensor optics

Solar array bracing spar

Ultra-high efficiency girondium-colium solar cells

Solar array wing

Access hatch

Top transparisteel viewport

Cockpit display

Shield generator

Transparisteel main viewport

Sienar-Jaemus Fleet Systems L-s9.6 laser cannon

Torplex flight computer

High-pressure radioactive gas fuel tank

Fuel tank cover

Fuel recharge connection

DATA FILE

> **MANUFACTURER** Sienar-Jaemus Fleet Systems

> **MODEL** TIE/fo space superiority fighter

> **CLASS** Starfighter

> **LENGTH** 6.69 meters (21.96 feet)

> **CREW** 1 pilot

> **WEAPONS** 2 SJFS L-s9.6 laser cannons

> **AFFILIATION** First Order

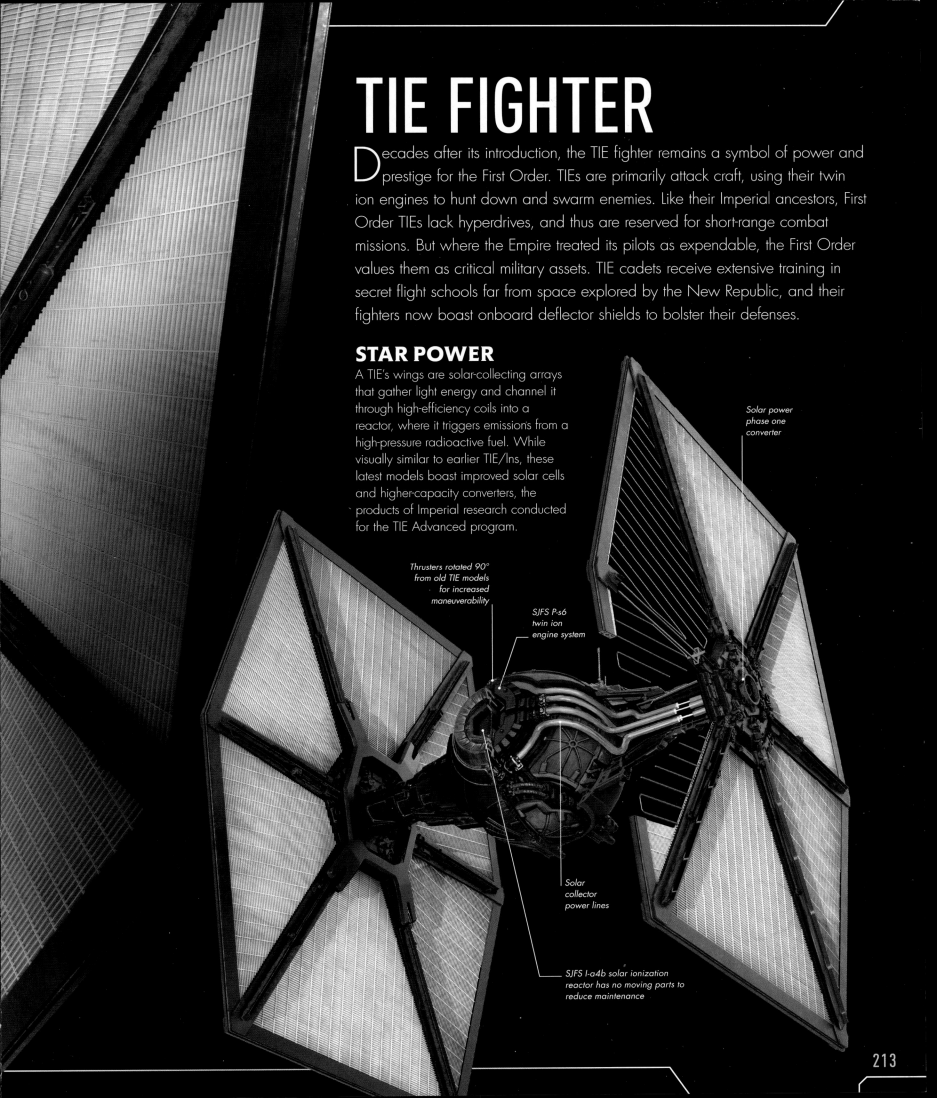

TIE FIGHTER

Decades after its introduction, the TIE fighter remains a symbol of power and prestige for the First Order. TIEs are primarily attack craft, using their twin ion engines to hunt down and swarm enemies. Like their Imperial ancestors, First Order TIEs lack hyperdrives, and thus are reserved for short-range combat missions. But where the Empire treated its pilots as expendable, the First Order values them as critical military assets. TIE cadets receive extensive training in secret flight schools far from space explored by the New Republic, and their fighters now boast onboard deflector shields to bolster their defenses.

STAR POWER

A TIE's wings are solar-collecting arrays that gather light energy and channel it through high-efficiency coils into a reactor, where it triggers emissions from a high-pressure radioactive fuel. While visually similar to earlier TIE/lns, these latest models boast improved solar cells and higher-capacity converters, the products of Imperial research conducted for the TIE Advanced program.

Solar power phase one converter

Thrusters rotated 90° from old TIE models for increased maneuverability

SJFS P-s6 twin ion engine system

Solar collector power lines

SJFS I-a4b solar ionization reactor has no moving parts to reduce maintenance

SF TIE FIGHTER

The First Order's feared Special Forces have considerable resources at their disposal. These include a specialized model of TIE fighter that packs additional armament into a craft designed for long-range operations away from a base or command ship. Special Forces TIEs are two-person fighters that carry a hyperdrive and deflector shields, as well as banks of high-yield deuterium cells that provide additional power to the engines, weapons, or shields and can be recharged from the TIE's solar panels. The TIE/sf's heavy weaponry and improved defensive capabilities make it a versatile attack ship suited to a range of mission profiles, from reconnaissance to combat operations.

WEAPONS PLATFORM

The Special Forces TIE's deuterium cells drive a weapons package far more powerful than that of a TIE/fo. The TIE/sf's primary weapons are its front-facing laser cannons, but a heavy weapon turret and warhead launcher gives it a 360-degree field of fire and the ability to deliver specialized ordnance. The pilot can fire all weapons, but the turret is ideally controlled by the TIE/sf's rear-facing gunner.

Twin reactors give greater redundancy and survivability

Thrust nozzle

Starboard ion reactor

Miniaturized hyperdrive

Rear gunner's seat

Power trunking

Ejector seat explosive booster

High-pressure radioactive gas fuel tank

Heavy weapon turret

DATA FILE

> **MANUFACTURER** Sienar-Jaemus Fleet Systems

> **MODEL** TIE/sf space superiority fighter

> **CLASS** Starfighter

> **LENGTH** 6.69 meters (21.96 feet)

> **CREW** 2 (pilot and gunner)

> **WEAPONS** 2 Sienar-Jaemus Fleet Systems L-s9.6 laser cannons, SJFS Lb-14 dual heavy laser turret, Kuat Drive Yards Arakyd ST7 concussion and mag-pulse warhead launcher

> **AFFILIATION** First Order

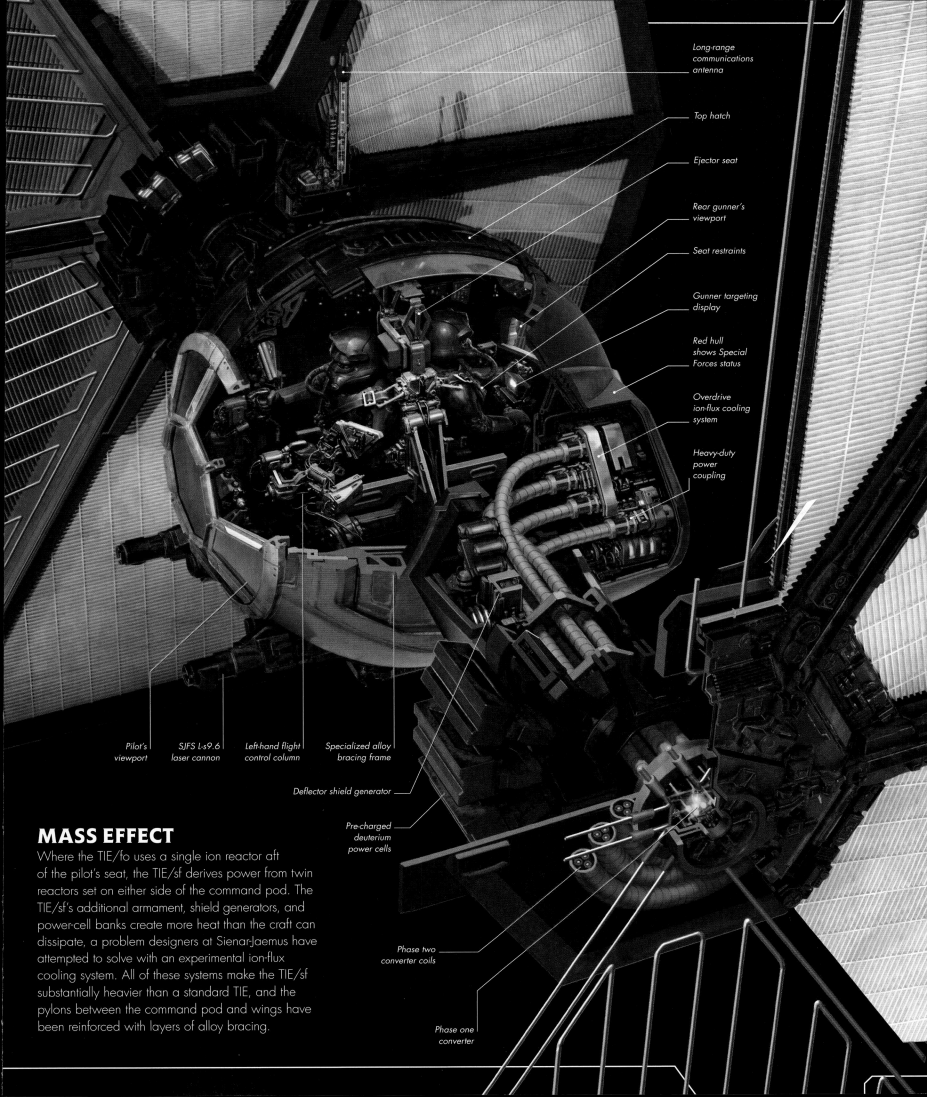

Long-range communications antenna

Top hatch

Ejector seat

Rear gunner's viewport

Seat restraints

Gunner targeting display

Red hull shows Special Forces status

Overdrive ion-flux cooling system

Heavy-duty power coupling

Pilot's viewport

SJFS L-s9.6 laser cannon

Left-hand flight control column

Specialized alloy bracing frame

Deflector shield generator

Pre-charged deuterium power cells

Phase two converter coils

Phase one converter

MASS EFFECT

Where the TIE/fo uses a single ion reactor aft of the pilot's seat, the TIE/sf derives power from twin reactors set on either side of the command pod. The TIE/sf's additional armament, shield generators, and power-cell banks create more heat than the craft can dissipate, a problem designers at Sienar-Jaemus have attempted to solve with an experimental ion-flux cooling system. All of these systems make the TIE/sf substantially heavier than a standard TIE, and the pylons between the command pod and wings have been reinforced with layers of alloy bracing.

MILLENNIUM FALCON

Once famous as one of the galaxy's fastest starships, the *Millennium Falcon* has fallen on hard times, languishing beneath a tarp in Jakku's dilapidated spaceport. Unkar Plutt won't say how he acquired the battered freighter and has refused to let Niima Outpost's scavengers strip her of useful components, insisting that the *Falcon* can still fly and that he has big plans for her. Beneath her shabby exterior, the old smuggler ship remains full of surprises: Her sublight engines are heavily modified for additional speed, her customized hyperdrive is twice the size of a stock YT-1300's, and her shields and weapons are more suited for a much larger warship.

NEW PARTS

The *Falcon's* military-grade rectenna snapped off during the Battle of Endor and has been replaced with a civilian model Corellian Engineering Corporation sensor dish, degrading the freighter's ability to detect and target hostile ships.

Water recycling unit

Quadex power core

Circuitry bay

Upper quad laser cannon

Crew quarters were reconfigured to include galley as wedding gift for Leia Organa

Vacuum suits in overhead locker

Storage lockers

Class 0.5 Isu-Sim SSP05 hyperdrive

Girodyne sublight engines

Thrust pressure manifold

Fuel intermixer

Inter-level conduits

Heat exhaust vent

Sublight drive exhaust

BREAKDOWN

Rey and Finn pay the price for Unkar Plutt's failure to maintain the *Falcon's* hyperdrive. An energy flux in the motivator bleeds back into the Quadex power core, causing a surge that sends a faulty signal to the fuel distributor. Liquid metal fuel overflows the distributor's propulsion tank and backs up into the ship's auxiliary systems, overheating components and rupturing a juncture. The liquid fuel sublimates into a poisonous gas that fills the freighter.

Fuel drive pressure stabilizer

Escape pod

Thrust vector plate

Hyperdrive tachyon venting

Landing gear

Engineering station

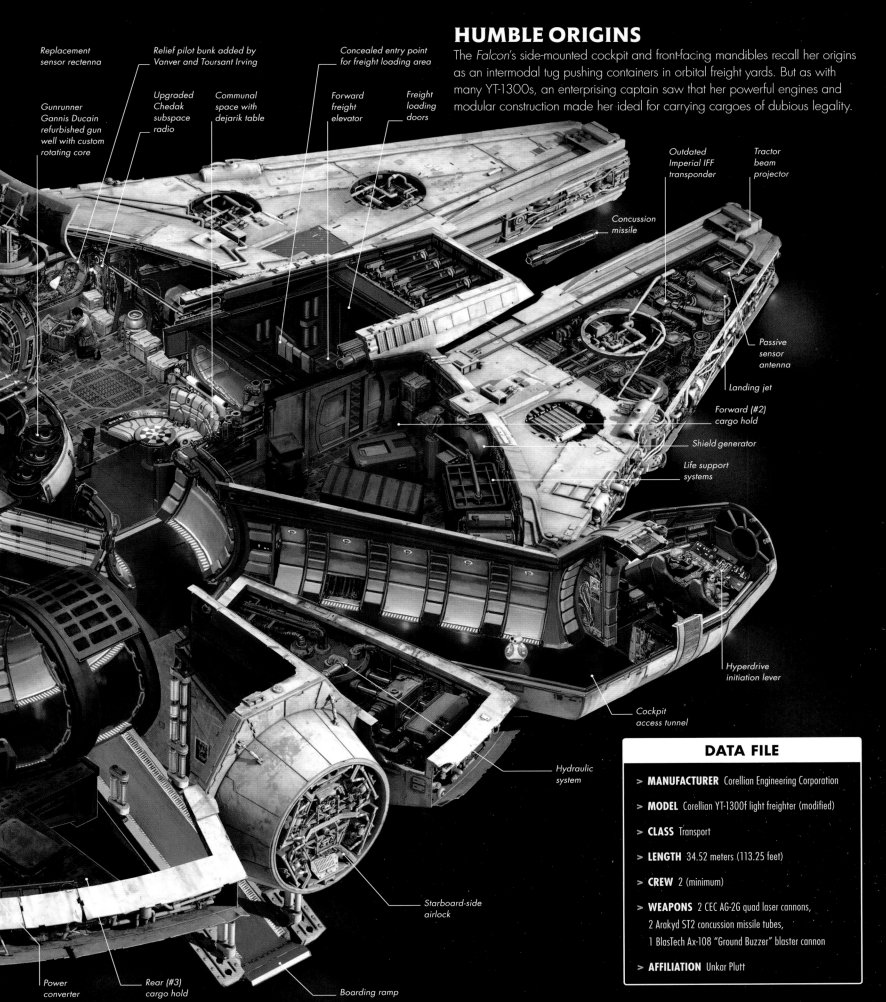

HUMBLE ORIGINS

The *Falcon*'s side-mounted cockpit and front-facing mandibles recall her origins as an intermodal tug pushing containers in orbital freight yards. But as with many YT-1300s, an enterprising captain saw that her powerful engines and modular construction made her ideal for carrying cargoes of dubious legality.

Replacement sensor rectenna

Relief pilot bunk added by Vanver and Toursant Irving

Concealed entry point for freight loading area

Gunrunner Gannis Ducain refurbished gun well with custom rotating core

Upgraded Chedak subspace radio

Communal space with dejarik table

Forward freight elevator

Freight loading doors

Outdated Imperial IFF transponder

Tractor beam projector

Concussion missile

Passive sensor antenna

Landing jet

Forward (#2) cargo hold

Shield generator

Life support systems

Hyperdrive initiation lever

Cockpit access tunnel

Hydraulic system

Starboard-side airlock

Power converter

Rear (#3) cargo hold

Boarding ramp

DATA FILE

> **MANUFACTURER** Corellian Engineering Corporation

> **MODEL** Corellian YT-1300f light freighter (modified)

> **CLASS** Transport

> **LENGTH** 34.52 meters (113.25 feet)

> **CREW** 2 (minimum)

> **WEAPONS** 2 CEC AG-2G quad laser cannons,
2 Arakyd ST2 concussion missile tubes,
1 BlasTech Ax-108 "Ground Buzzer" blaster cannon

> **AFFILIATION** Unkar Plutt

HAN'S FREIGHTER

The galaxy remembers Han Solo and Chewbacca as the daredevil pilots of the *Millennium Falcon*, equally legendary as smugglers and rebel heroes. But that was a long time ago. The Falcon is gone, and has eluded every attempt by her former owners to track her down. Han and Chewie now operate the *Eravana*, a massive bulk freighter that handles like a concussed bantha. The Corellian and the Wookiee have made a fair amount of credits with their new ship, criss-crossing the galaxy carrying everything from bulk consumables needed by remote colonies to exotic fauna desired by wealthy collectors. They have also made more than a few enemies—the inevitable consequence of Han's dubious business practices.

MOVING CARGO

Bulk freighters such as the *Baleen*-class move huge amounts of cargo across the galaxy every day, and are essential to commerce. Built in orbital shipyards, they almost never enter a planet's atmosphere, docking instead at space stations and transfer yards to load and unload cargo. Most bulk freighters are owned by corporations, as few independent captains have the credits to acquire and maintain these giant craft.

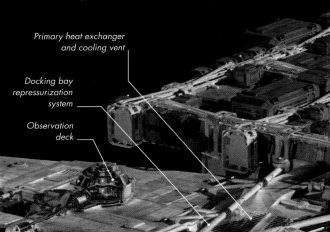

Primary heat exchanger and cooling vent

Docking bay repressurization system

Observation deck

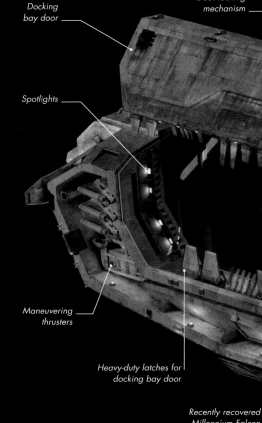

Docking bay door

Door locking mechanism

Force field projectors

Spotlights

Maneuvering thrusters

Heavy-duty latches for docking bay door

Recently recovered *Millennium Falcon*

Forward sensor array

Tractor beam projectors

Han's cabin

Long-range communications antenna

DATA FILE

> **MANUFACTURER** Corellian Engineering Corporation

> **MODEL** Baleen-class heavy freighter

> **CLASS** Bulk freighter

> **LENGTH** 425.99 meters (1397.59 feet)

> **CREW** 2 minimum, 6 recommended

> **WEAPONS** None

> **AFFILIATION** Han Solo and Chewbacca

FLYING LABYRINTH

The *Falcon* felt like home, but the *Eravana* is a means to an end, with Han and Chewie monitoring the giant ship's cargos and keeping her plodding along her course. The freighter's forward hold doubles as a docking bay, and is used for cargo that demands special handling. Everything else is housed in containers attached to the transport grid between the bow section and engines—a sprawling labyrinth of goods bound for distant starports.

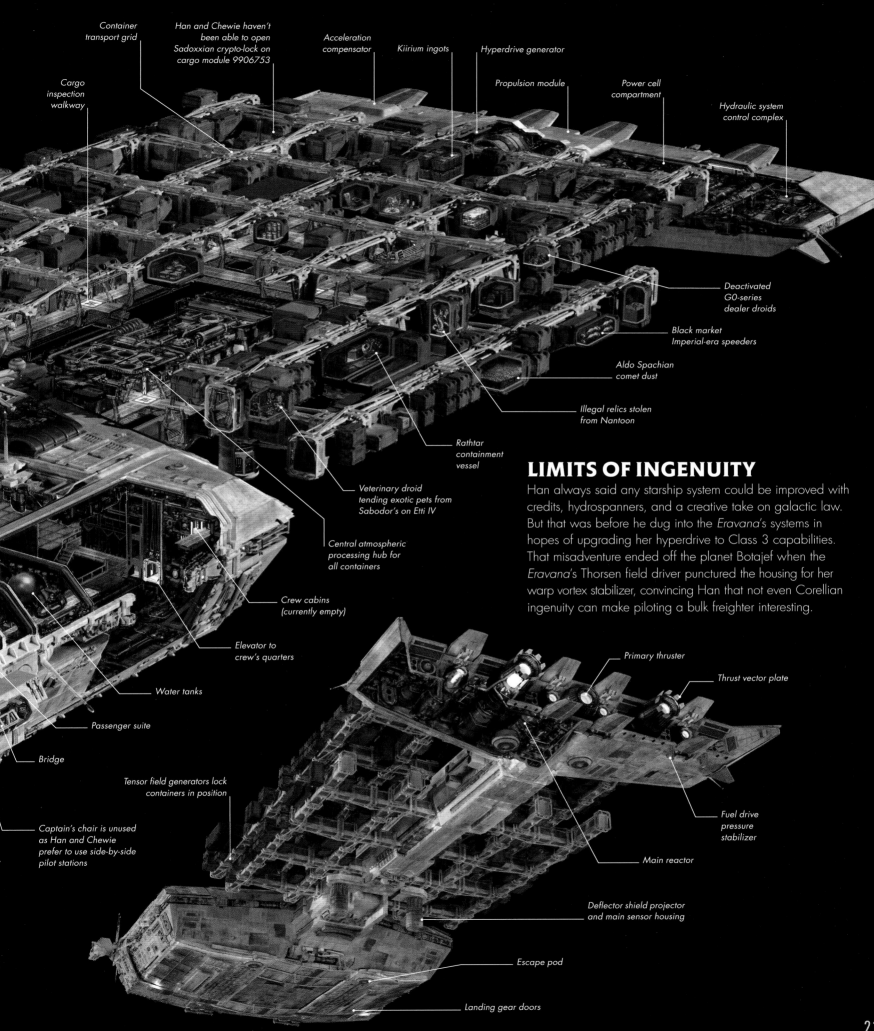

Container
transport grid

Han and Chewie haven't
been able to open
Sadoxxian crypto-lock on
cargo module 9906753

Acceleration
compensator

Kiirium ingots

Hyperdrive generator

Propulsion module

Power cell
compartment

Hydraulic system
control complex

Cargo
inspection
walkway

Deactivated
G0-series
dealer droids

Black market
Imperial-era speeders

Aldo Spachian
comet dust

Illegal relics stolen
from Nantoon

Rathtar
containment
vessel

Veterinary droid
tending exotic pets from
Sabodor's on Etti IV

Central atmospheric
processing hub for
all containers

Crew cabins
(currently empty)

Elevator to
crew's quarters

Water tanks

Passenger suite

Bridge

Tensor field generators lock
containers in position

Captain's chair is unused
as Han and Chewie
prefer to use side-by-side
pilot stations

LIMITS OF INGENUITY

Han always said any starship system could be improved with
credits, hydrospanners, and a creative take on galactic law.
But that was before he dug into the *Eravana*'s systems in
hopes of upgrading her hyperdrive to Class 3 capabilities.
That misadventure ended off the planet Botajef when the
Eravana's Thorsen field driver punctured the housing for her
warp vortex stabilizer, convincing Han that not even Corellian
ingenuity can make piloting a bulk freighter interesting.

Primary thruster

Thrust vector plate

Fuel drive
pressure
stabilizer

Main reactor

Deflector shield projector
and main sensor housing

Escape pod

Landing gear doors

THE *RADDUS*

The pride of the Resistance, the *Raddus* is a mobile command center for General Leia Organa and a symbol of the struggle for galactic freedom. Its name celebrates one of the Rebellion's earliest heroes, while its construction incorporates contributions from different shipyards and species. The *Raddus* serves as a carrier for the Resistance's hastily reconstituted starfighter corps. It is also the flagship of the ragged task force that flees D'Qar, just ahead of the First Order fleet bent on avenging the destruction of Starkiller Base. The fate of the Resistance and the dream of a free and peaceful galaxy both rest with this wounded warship. It races through space with an enigmatic commander at its helm and a restive crew desperately hoping that a safe haven can be found.

RAISED SHIELDS

The advanced deflector shields that cocoon the *Raddus* are an experimental design, capable of sustaining huge amounts of damage before failing. Though their heavy pummeling by the First Order makes structural damage inevitable, most other ships would have been destroyed long before this point.

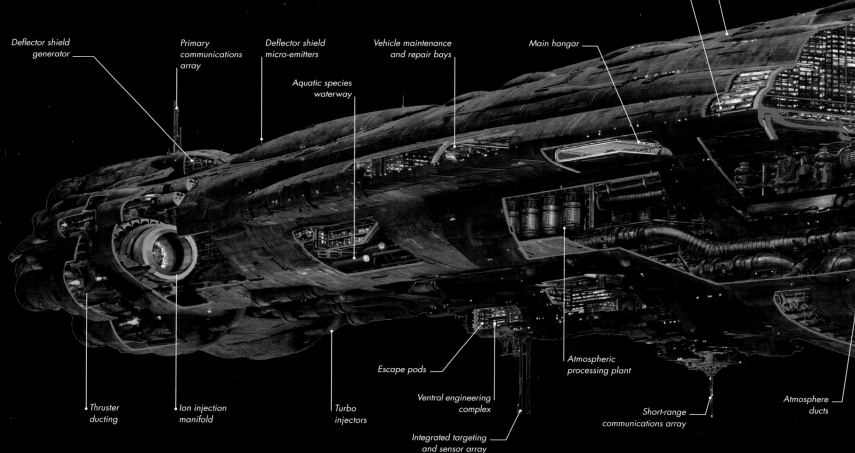

Durasteel hull plating

Concealed turbolaser battery

Crew accommodation levels

Deflector shield generator

Primary communications array

Deflector shield micro-emitters

Vehicle maintenance and repair bays

Main hangar

Aquatic species waterway

Thruster ducting

Ion injection manifold

Turbo injectors

Escape pods

Ventral engineering complex

Integrated targeting and sensor array

Atmospheric processing plant

Short-range communications array

Atmosphere ducts

MEMORY OF SACRIFICE

The *Raddus* was named in honor of the Mon Calamari admiral who defied the nascent Rebellion's political leaders and took a ragtag fleet to Scarif, sacrificing his star cruiser and his life to ensure the Alliance received the Death Star plans. The Mon Calamari species risked destruction at Imperial hands for their support of the Alliance, building the capital ships that formed the backbone of the fleet that triumphed at Endor. They remained loyal to the Resistance despite the disapproval of the New Republic, and when the Dawn of Tranquility found its way into Resistance hands, Admiral Ackbar petitioned to rename it in honor of a fellow Mon Calamari who had chosen to fight against seemingly insurmountable odds.

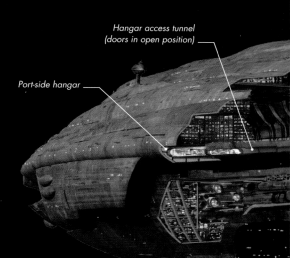

Hangar access tunnel (doors in open position)

Port-side hangar

Ventral crew decks

NEW OWNERSHIP

Originally named the *Dawn of Tranquility*, the *Raddus* once formed part of the New Republic's home fleet, but was decommissioned early—a move made with one eye on treaties limiting heavy warships and another on being able to reduce navy personnel. For the MC85 line, the Mon Calamari worked with the venerable Corellian Engineering Corporation to create interiors more amenable to non-amphibious crews. This has allowed the Resistance to avoid costly retrofits.

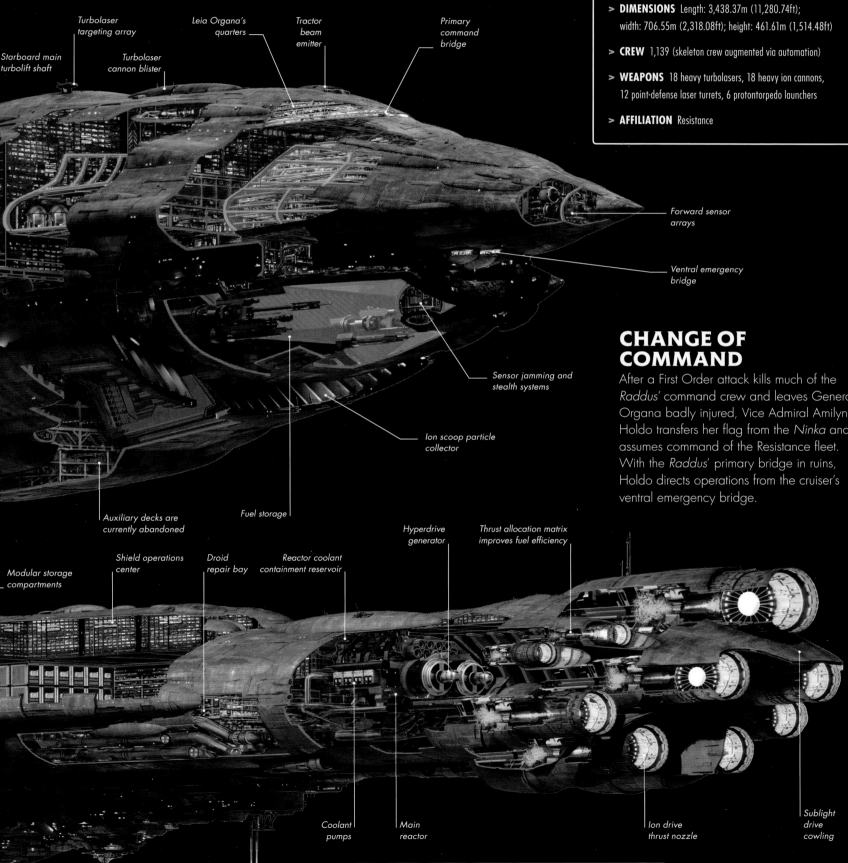

Turbolaser targeting array

Leia Organa's quarters

Tractor beam emitter

Primary command bridge

Starboard main turbolift shaft

Turbolaser cannon blister

Forward sensor arrays

Ventral emergency bridge

Sensor jamming and stealth systems

Ion scoop particle collector

Auxiliary decks are currently abandoned

Fuel storage

Modular storage compartments

Shield operations center

Droid repair bay

Reactor coolant containment reservoir

Hyperdrive generator

Thrust allocation matrix improves fuel efficiency

Coolant pumps

Main reactor

Ion drive thrust nozzle

Sublight drive cowling

DATA FILE

> **MANUFACTURER** Mon Calamari Shipyards/ Corellian Engineering Corporation

> **MODEL** MC85 Star Cruiser

> **CLASS** Star Cruiser

> **DIMENSIONS** Length: 3,438.37m (11,280.74ft); width: 706.55m (2,318.08ft); height: 461.61m (1,514.48ft)

> **CREW** 1,139 (skeleton crew augmented via automation)

> **WEAPONS** 18 heavy turbolasers, 18 heavy ion cannons, 12 point-defense laser turrets, 6 protontorpedo launchers

> **AFFILIATION** Resistance

CHANGE OF COMMAND

After a First Order attack kills much of the *Raddus'* command crew and leaves General Organa badly injured, Vice Admiral Amilyn Holdo transfers her flag from the *Ninka* and assumes command of the Resistance fleet. With the *Raddus'* primary bridge in ruins, Holdo directs operations from the cruiser's ventral emergency bridge.

RESISTANCE BOMBER

Pressing its war with the Empire's remnants, the New Republic contracted with Slayn & Korpil for the MG-100 StarFortress, a dedicated bomber that could deliver a far larger payload than starfighters. The Senate's subsequent demilitarization effort sent many of these bombers to the scrapyard, and some found their way into Resistance hands. A mercy mission to Atterra by D'Qar's Cobalt and Crimson Squadrons left the bombers unavailable for the assault on Starkiller Base, but the squadrons' survivors arrive in time to play a pivotal role in defending D'Qar from the First Order's assault. The brave crews' sacrifice allows Resistance leaders, including General Organa and Admiral Ackbar, to evacuate their besieged headquarters.

FLEXIBLE FLIER

Strapped for resources, the Resistance has improvised by using its StarFortresses on non-military missions. In the Atterra campaign, bombers delivered probes to spy on the First Order and ferried supplies to Atterra Bravo, eluding detection through power-baffling technology that hides energy emissions. Decommissioned MG-100s also see widespread civilian use. Mining companies use them to drop explosives that break up ice and rock; local governments deploy them as rescue ships, fuel tankers, and fire-fighting craft; and scout services rely on them for celestial mapping and exploration.

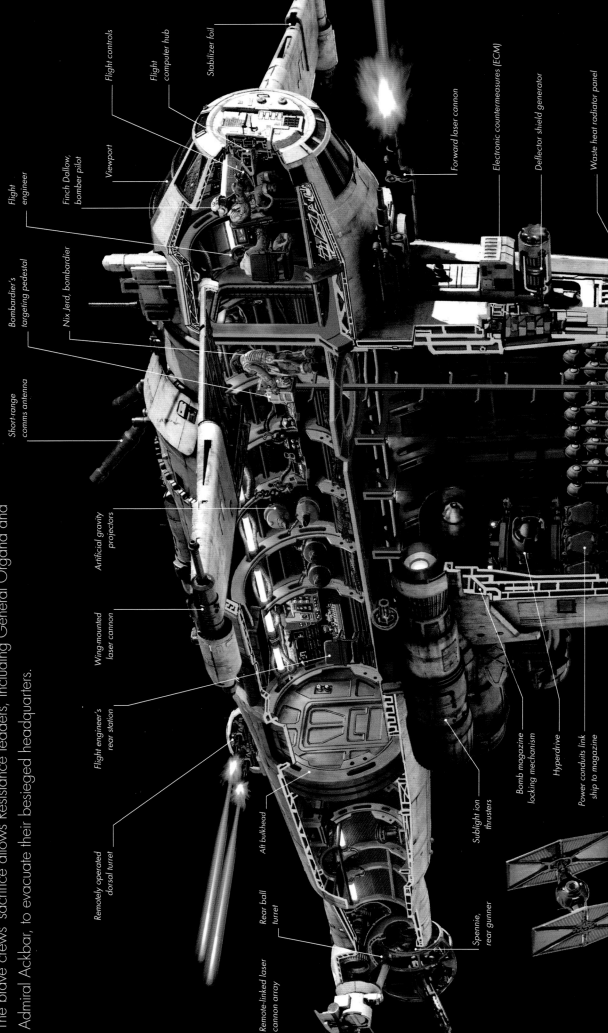

Flight controls

Flight computer hub

Stabilizer foil

Forward laser cannon

Electronic countermeasures (ECM)

Deflector shield generator

Waste heat radiator panel

Flight engineer

Finch Dallow, bomber pilot

Viewport

Bombardier's targeting pedestal

Nix Jerd, bombardier

Short-range comms antenna

Artificial gravity projectors

Wing-mounted laser cannon

Flight engineer's rear station

Bomb magazine locking mechanism

Hyperdrive

Power conduits link ship to magazine

Remotely operated dorsal turret

Rear ball turret

Aft bulkhead

Sublight ion thrusters

Spennie, rear gunner

Remote-linked laser cannon array

STRENGTH IN NUMBERS

Bombers are slow and ungainly, leaving them vulnerable to enemy starfighters during attack runs. For protection, they depend not just on fighter escorts but also on each other. Resistance flight instructors teach bomber pilots that it is essential to fly in a tight formation, opposing attacking fighters with overlapping fields of fire. The rear and ventral turrets offer a potent defense against attackers approaching from below or from the rear, but are less effective against threats from above or in front of the bomber squadron.

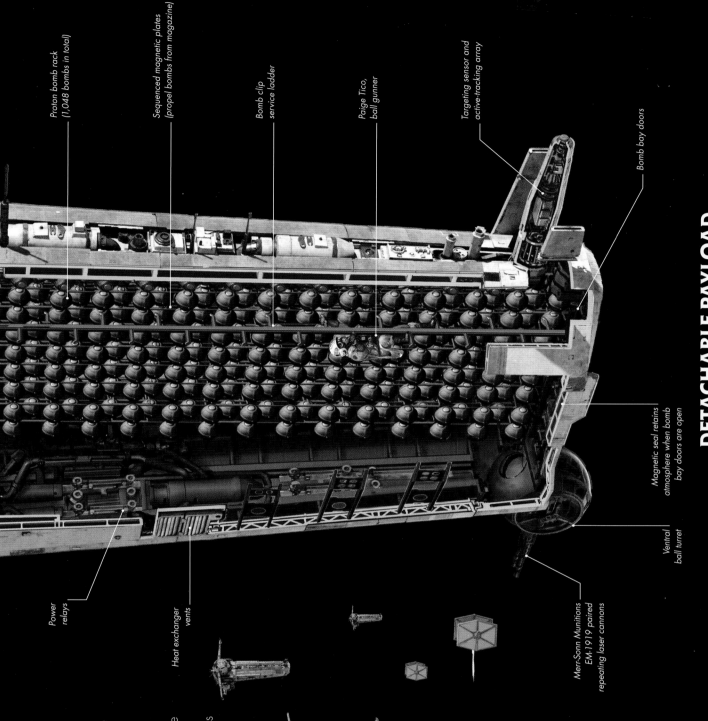

Proton bomb rack
(1,048 bombs in total)

Sequenced magnetic plates
(propel bombs from magazine)

Bomb clip
service ladder

Paige Tico,
ball gunner

Targeting sensor and
active-tracking array

Bomb bay doors

Power
relays

Heat exchanger
vents

Magnetic seal retains
atmosphere when bomb
bay doors are open

Ventral
ball turret

Merr-Sonn Munitions
EM-1919 paired
repeating laser cannons

DETACHABLE PAYLOAD

The bomb bay and ventral ball turret are housed within a separate magazine "clip" that slots into the fuselage, with the bombardier's targeting pedestal rising through a hatch in the flight deck. Separating the two components allows for more efficient stowage and easier post-flight maintenance. Resistance armorers load the bomb bay's payload while it is horizontal, then rotate the clip into position below a gantry used by the crew to enter the flight deck. When such facilities aren't available, the clip can be left coupled with the fuselage for docking at space wharves or orbital facilities.

DATA FILE

> **MANUFACTURER** Slayn & Korpil

> **MODEL** MG-100 StarFortress SF-17

> **CLASS** Bomber

> **DIMENSIONS** Length: 29.67m (97.34ft); width: 15.3m (50.2ft); height: 21.65m (71.03ft)

> **CREW** 5 (pilot, flight engineer, bombardier, and 2 gunners)

> **WEAPONS** 3 laser cannon turrets, 6 medium laser cannons, proton bombs

> **AFFILIATION** Resistance

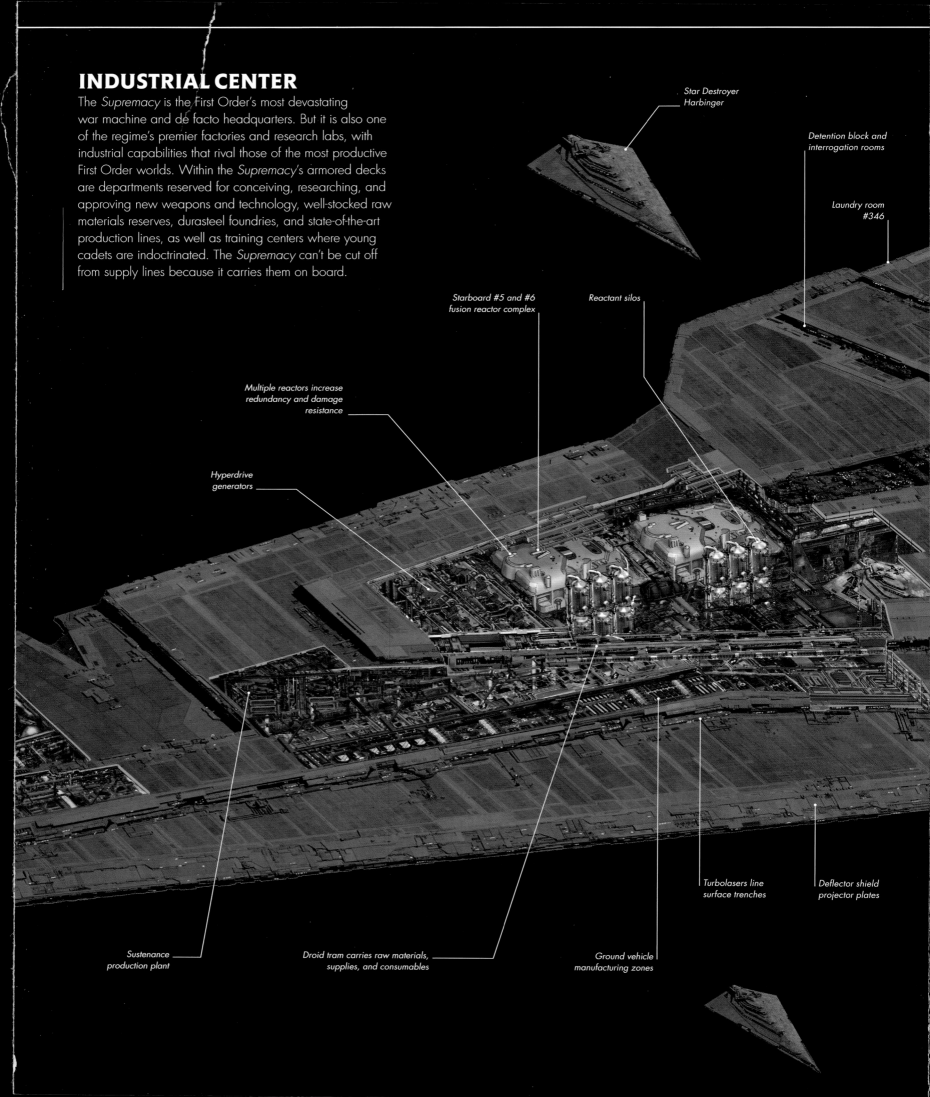

INDUSTRIAL CENTER

The *Supremacy* is the First Order's most devastating war machine and de facto headquarters. But it is also one of the regime's premier factories and research labs, with industrial capabilities that rival those of the most productive First Order worlds. Within the *Supremacy*'s armored decks are departments reserved for conceiving, researching, and approving new weapons and technology, well-stocked raw materials reserves, durasteel foundries, and state-of-the-art production lines, as well as training centers where young cadets are indoctrinated. The *Supremacy* can't be cut off from supply lines because it carries them on board.

Star Destroyer Harbinger

Detention block and interrogation rooms

Laundry room #346

Starboard #5 and #6 fusion reactor complex

Reactant silos

Multiple reactors increase redundancy and damage resistance

Hyperdrive generators

Turbolasers line surface trenches

Deflector shield projector plates

Sustenance production plant

Droid tram carries raw materials, supplies, and consumables

Ground vehicle manufacturing zones

THE *SUPREMACY*

A gigantic warship built on an unprecedented scale, the Mega-Destroyer *Supremacy* serves Supreme Leader Snoke as both throne room and mobile command center. Measuring more than 60 kilometers from wingtip to wingtip, this vast flying wing boasts the destructive power of a full fleet, has the industrial capability of a planet, and serves as a testbed for the First Order's newest military advances. From his sanctuary deep within the *Supremacy*, Snoke ponders the fate of the galaxy and the ripples in the awakened Force—and plots the dissolution of the New Republic, the destruction of the Resistance, and the downfall of the Jedi. The *Supremacy* was built at staggering cost at a secret birthplace in the Unknown Regions. With the First Order's day of destiny at hand, Snoke is finally ready to reveal it to the galaxy he intends to conquer.

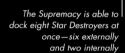

The *Supremacy* is able to dock eight Star Destroyers at once—six externally and two internally

A HUNTER'S SECRETS

The First Order tracks targets through hyperspace using a combination of technological advances and brute-force data crunching. The shipboard tracking control complex boasts the data-sifting power of a planetary intel hub, linking huge computer arrays to databanks loaded with centuries of combat reports and astrogation data. A static hyperspace field generated around the machines then accelerates their processing power to unheard-of levels. A target's last known trajectory yields trillions of potential destinations, but the system can assess them with terrifying speed.

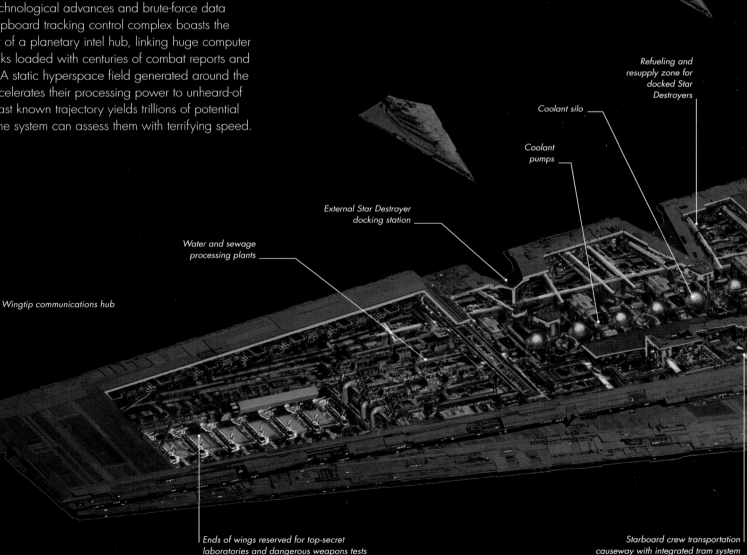

Refueling and resupply zone for docked Star Destroyers

Coolant silo

Coolant pumps

External Star Destroyer docking station

Water and sewage processing plants

Wingtip communications hub

Ends of wings reserved for top-secret laboratories and dangerous weapons tests

Starboard crew transportation causeway with integrated tram system

A-WING

The successor to an Alliance starfighter beloved for its speed but bemoaned for frequent breakdowns, the Resistance A-wing incorporates generations of improvements by rebel techs into a sleeker, longer frame delivering stability as well as speed. The New Republic has cut A-wing production to a minimum, but the Resistance uses these fighters for everything from reconnaissance patrols to bomber escort missions. As with a previous generation's rebels, Resistance pilots take pride in proving they have the skills and daring to master this ultra-fast, yet temperamental, starfighter.

SPEED AND STEALTH

Like its rebel predecessor, the Resistance A-wing is ideal for missions that require speed: hit-and-run raids, surgical strikes on capital ships, and intelligence-gathering missions. A capable pilot can emerge from hyperspace, engage the fighter's powerful suite of imagers and sensors, streak around an objective at top speed, and vanish back into hyperspace, all while enemy ground crews are still scrambling to get fighters airborne. The RZ-2 improves on its predecessors' capabilities, with more powerful sensors for faster data collection and upgraded jammers to impede detection.

FIGHTER'S FOREBEARS

Kuat designers developed the original R-22 prototype as a replacement for the Republic's *Aethersprite* starfighter, but sold the initial batch to the planet Tammuz-an after the Empire rejected mass production of the craft. Rebel cells acquired several R-22s and stripped them down to boost the fighter's speed and acceleration in an effort to counter the Empire's new TIE interceptors. After these so-called RZ-1s played a key role in the Alliance's victory at Endor, Kuat resurrected its forgotten prototype to create the RZ-2, standardizing years of field modifications and making the chassis slimmer and longer to yield even more speed.

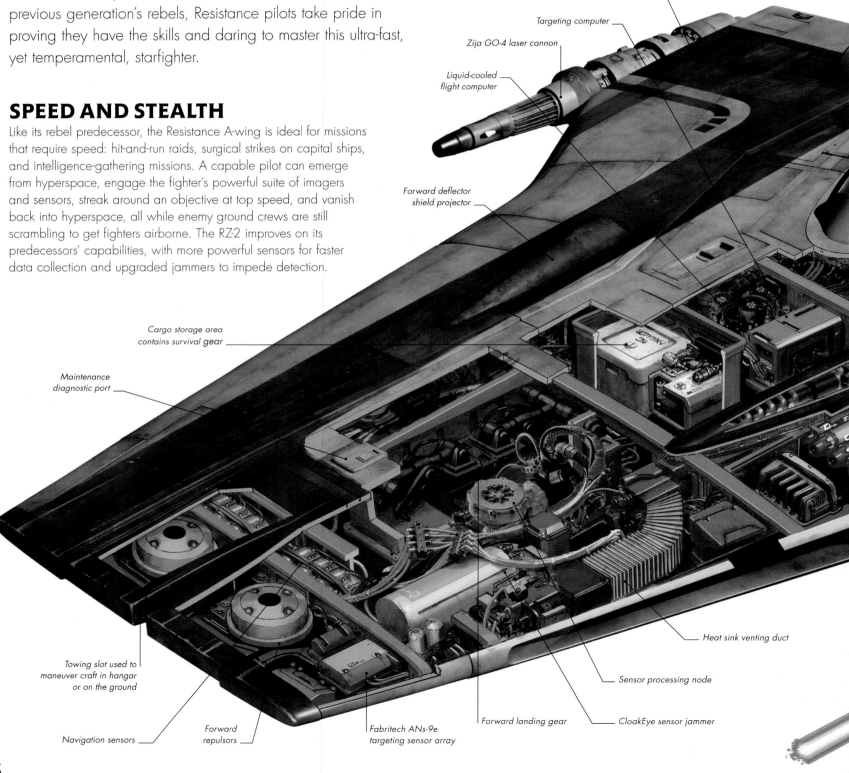

Squadron markings

Targeting computer

Zija GO-4 laser cannon

Liquid-cooled flight computer

Forward deflector shield projector

Cargo storage area contains survival gear

Maintenance diagnostic port

Towing slot used to maneuver craft in hangar or on the ground

Navigation sensors

Forward repulsors

Fabritech ANs-9e targeting sensor array

Forward landing gear

Heat sink venting duct

Sensor processing node

CloakEye sensor jammer

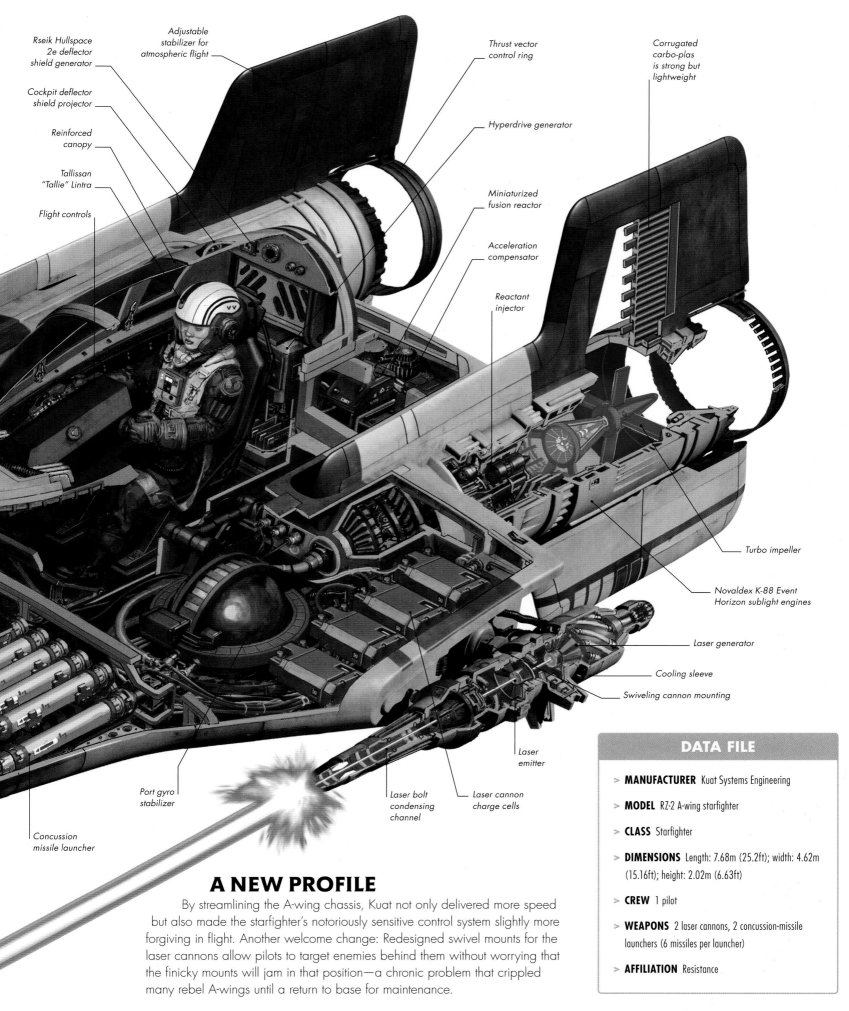

Rseik Hullspace
2e deflector
shield generator

Cockpit deflector
shield projector

Reinforced
canopy

Tallissan
"Tallie" Lintra

Flight controls

Adjustable
stabilizer for
atmospheric flight

Thrust vector
control ring

Hyperdrive generator

Corrugated
carbo-plas
is strong but
lightweight

Miniaturized
fusion reactor

Acceleration
compensator

Reactant
injector

Turbo impeller

Novaldex K-88 Event
Horizon sublight engines

Laser generator

Cooling sleeve

Swiveling cannon mounting

Laser
emitter

DATA FILE

Port gyro
stabilizer

Laser bolt
condensing
channel

Laser cannon
charge cells

Concussion
missile launcher

A NEW PROFILE

By streamlining the A-wing chassis, Kuat not only delivered more speed but also made the starfighter's notoriously sensitive control system slightly more forgiving in flight. Another welcome change: Redesigned swivel mounts for the laser cannons allow pilots to target enemies behind them without worrying that the finicky mounts will jam in that position—a chronic problem that crippled many rebel A-wings until a return to base for maintenance.

> **MANUFACTURER** Kuat Systems Engineering

> **MODEL** RZ-2 A-wing starfighter

> **CLASS** Starfighter

> **DIMENSIONS** Length: 7.68m (25.2ft); width: 4.62m (15.16ft); height: 2.02m (6.63ft)

> **CREW** 1 pilot

> **WEAPONS** 2 laser cannons, 2 concussion-missile launchers (6 missiles per launcher)

> **AFFILIATION** Resistance

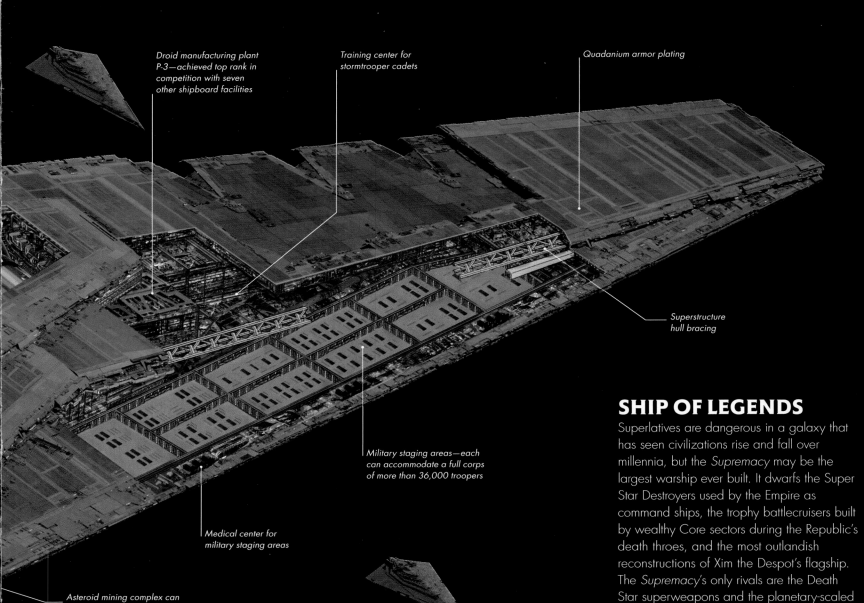

Droid manufacturing plant
P-3—achieved top rank in
competition with seven
other shipboard facilities

Training center for
stormtrooper cadets

Quadanium armor plating

Superstructure
hull bracing

Military staging areas—each
can accommodate a full corps
of more than 36,000 troopers

Medical center for
military staging areas

Asteroid mining complex can
harvest raw materials directly
from asteroid fields

SHIP OF LEGENDS

Superlatives are dangerous in a galaxy that has seen civilizations rise and fall over millennia, but the *Supremacy* may be the largest warship ever built. It dwarfs the Super Star Destroyers used by the Empire as command ships, the trophy battlecruisers built by wealthy Core sectors during the Republic's death throes, and the most outlandish reconstructions of Xim the Despot's flagship. The *Supremacy*'s only rivals are the Death Star superweapons and the planetary-scaled engineering project that created Starkiller Base.

Like Supreme Leader Snoke, Kylo Ren uses the *Supremacy* as his main base of operations and safe haven. After his defeat by Rey on Starkiller Base, Kylo returns to his quarters on the flagship to heal from his injuries and plan his next move on the path to power.

MOBILE CAPITAL

Despite entreaties from commanders and allies alike, Supreme Leader Snoke has refused to designate a world as his regime's capital, either in the sectors claimed by the First Order or the Unknown Regions. The First Order's future is not to dominate a lonely corner of the Outer Rim or rule worlds beyond the galactic frontier, but to restore the Empire's stolen domain and build upon its triumphs. Until that goal is achieved, the regime's capital will travel with its master.

DATA FILE

> **MANUFACTURER** Kuat-Entralla Engineering

> **MODEL** Mega-class Star Dreadnought

> **CLASS** Star Dreadnought

> **DIMENSIONS** Length: 13,239.68m (43,437.27ft); width: 60,542.68m (198,630.84ft); height: 3,975.35m (13,042.49ft)

> **CREW** 2,225,000 personnel including officers, stormtroopers, gunners, vehicle engineers, factory workers, technical specialists, and communications staff

> **WEAPONS** Thousands of heavy turbolasers, anti-ship missile batteries, heavy ion cannons, and tractor beam projectors

> **AFFILIATION** First Order

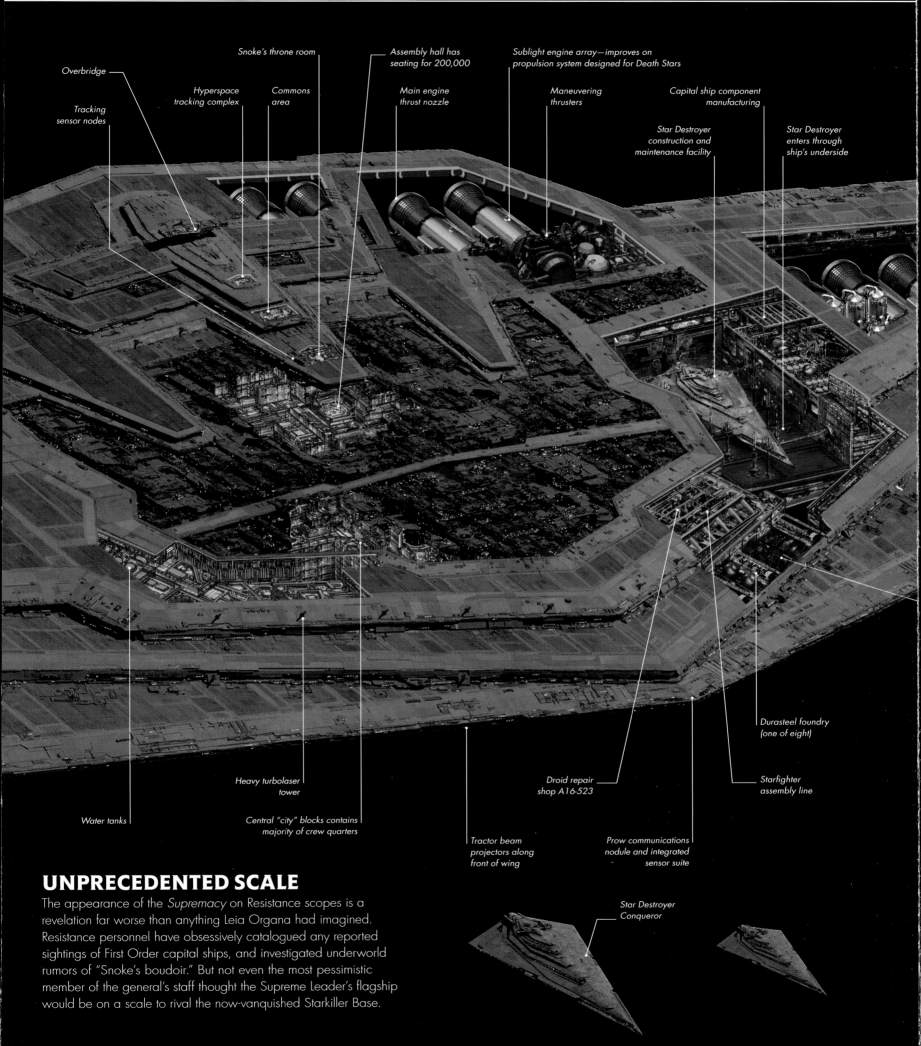

Overbridge

Tracking
sensor nodes

Hyperspace
tracking complex

Snoke's throne room

Commons
area

Assembly hall has
seating for 200,000

Main engine
thrust nozzle

Sublight engine array—improves on
propulsion system designed for Death Stars

Maneuvering
thrusters

Capital ship component
manufacturing

Star Destroyer
construction and
maintenance facility

Star Destroyer
enters through
ship's underside

Heavy turbolaser
tower

Water tanks

Central "city" blocks contains
majority of crew quarters

Droid repair
shop A16-523

Prow communications
nodule and integrated
sensor suite

Tractor beam
projectors along
front of wing

Durasteel foundry
(one of eight)

Starfighter
assembly line

UNPRECEDENTED SCALE

The appearance of the *Supremacy* on Resistance scopes is a
revelation far worse than anything Leia Organa had imagined.
Resistance personnel have obsessively catalogued any reported
sightings of First Order capital ships, and investigated underworld
rumors of "Snoke's boudoir." But not even the most pessimistic
member of the general's staff thought the Supreme Leader's flagship
would be on a scale to rival the now-vanquished Starkiller Base.

Star Destroyer
Conqueror

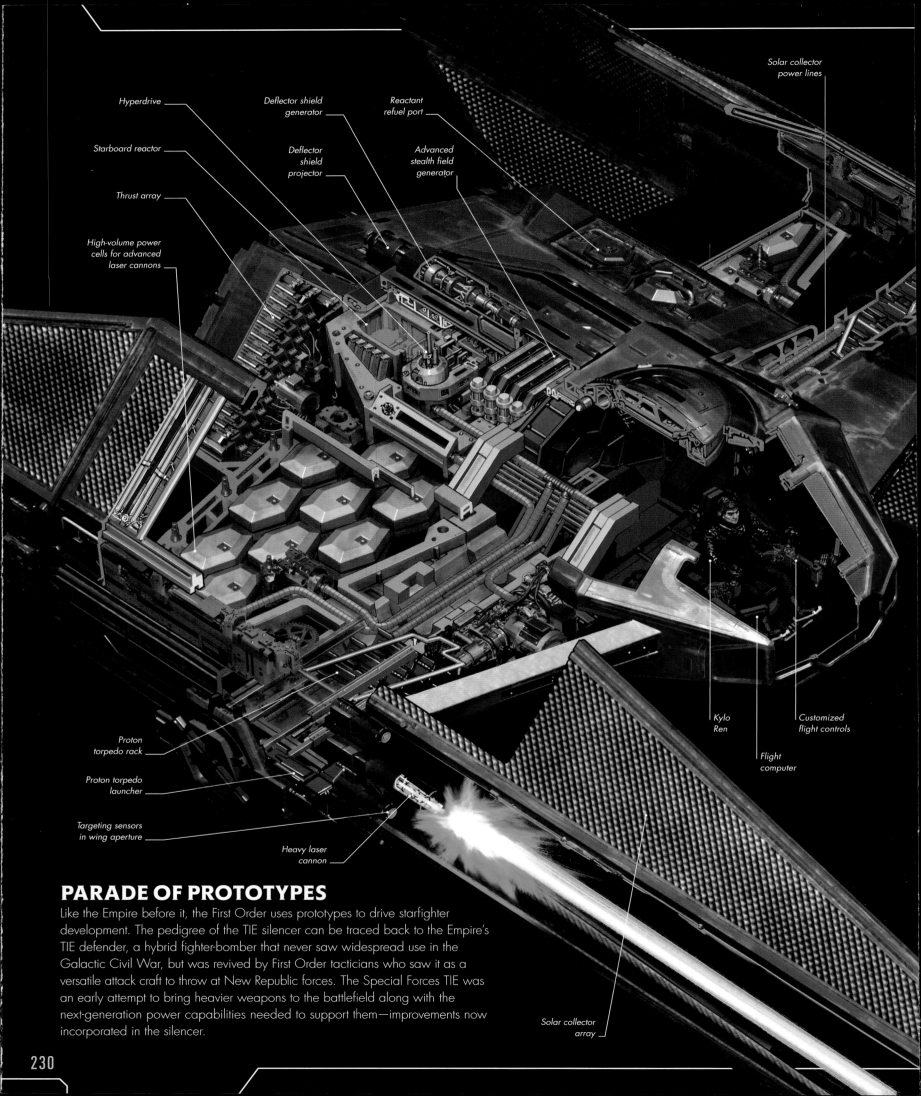

Solar collector
power lines

Hyperdrive

Deflector shield
generator

Reactant
refuel port

Starboard reactor

Deflector
shield
projector

Advanced
stealth field
generator

Thrust array

High-volume power
cells for advanced
laser cannons

Kylo
Ren

Customized
flight controls

Proton
torpedo rack

Flight
computer

Proton torpedo
launcher

Targeting sensors
in wing aperture

Heavy laser
cannon

Solar collector
array

PARADE OF PROTOTYPES

Like the Empire before it, the First Order uses prototypes to drive starfighter
development. The pedigree of the TIE silencer can be traced back to the Empire's
TIE defender, a hybrid fighter-bomber that never saw widespread use in the
Galactic Civil War, but was revived by First Order tacticians who saw it as a
versatile attack craft to throw at New Republic forces. The Special Forces TIE was
an early attempt to bring heavier weapons to the battlefield along with the
next-generation power capabilities needed to support them—improvements now
incorporated in the silencer.

TIE SILENCER

As the first order closes in on the Resistance fleet, Kylo Ren leads the attack in a prototype starfighter, the TIE silencer. With a hull as black as space, the silencer is a fearsome opponent—fast enough to engage rival fighters, yet packing heavy weapons that can crack the shields and armor of capital ships. The starfighter incorporates the latest First Order military innovations, and includes experimental stealth gear meant to foil sensors and tracking. Kylo's detailed post-flight reports allow Sienar-Jaemus techs to refine onboard systems, with an eye toward the day when shipyards begin mass-producing silencers for the regime's frontline units.

DATA FILE

> **MANUFACTURER** Sienar-Jaemus Fleet Systems

> **MODEL** TIE/vn space superiority fighter

> **CLASS** Starfighter

> **DIMENSIONS** Length: 17.43m (57.19ft); width: 7.62m (25ft); height: 3.76m (12.34ft)

> **CREW** 1 pilot

> **WEAPONS** 2 Sienar-Jaemus Fleet Systems L-s9.6 laser cannons, 2 SJFS L-7.5 heavy laser cannons, Arakyd ST7 concussion and mag-pulse warhead launchers

> **AFFILIATION** First Order

Laser bolt: highly energized plasma contained in magnetic field bubble

TWIN TRADITIONS

By flying the TIE silencer against the First Order's enemies, Kylo Ren continues two traditions. Firstly, that of prototype starfighters being tested by aces, with Kylo following in the footsteps of notable Imperials such as Vult Skerris and Darth Vader. Secondly, as the son of Han Solo and grandson of Anakin Skywalker, the former Ben Solo is a natural in the cockpit.

Corrugated surface maximizes energy absorption

Solar energy accumulator lines

Cabin access hatch

Heat exchange matrix

Twin ion thrust arrays

DEADLY IMPROVEMENTS

Working at hidden Sienar-Jaemus facilities, First Order designers reconfigured the weapons package of the Special Forces TIE to incorporate advances in power storage and energy conversion. The TIE/sf's power cell spokes have been replaced by a next-generation array protected beneath the hull, with shorter runs for trunk lines and converter coils. Rather than replicate the TIE/sf's ventral turret, the silencer relocates missiles and heavy cannons to the wing apertures, giving the pilot superior targeting and a wider field of fire.

CANTO BIGHT POLICE SPEEDER

Canto bight's winding alleys and promenades are difficult terrain for the heavy speeders favored by most police forces, so local law enforcement depends on nimble repulsorcraft known as jet-sticks. These craft are easy to control, with officers directing them by leaning one way or the other, and accelerating and braking with foot pedals and hand-held throttles. Their laser cannons are generally set for stun, but can kill a humanoid or disable a civilian vehicle at full power. While jet-sticks are not capable of true atmospheric flight, they can easily reach rooftop level or cross small stretches of water.

DATA FILE

- > **MANUFACTURER** Trochiliad Motors
- > **MODEL** Cantonica zephyr GB-134 jet-stick
- > **CLASS** Speeder bike
- > **DIMENSIONS** Length: 2.98m (9.78ft); width: 2.55m (8.37ft); height: 2.5m (8.2ft)
- > **CREW** 1 police officer
- > **WEAPONS** 2 anti-personnel laser cannons
- > **AFFILIATION** Canto Bight Police Department

QUICK RESPONSE

The whir of a jet-stick's rotors reassures visitors to Canto Bight that the police are keeping an eye out for shady characters drawn to the glitz and glamour of galactic high life. Officers use dash-mounted data displays to identify troublemakers and exchange information while hovering in the old city's graceful squares, or patrolling the labyrinth of ancient streets. In the event of trouble, an officer activates the jet-stick's sirens and speeds to the scene, ready to coordinate with foot patrols or call for backup from heavier units.

KEEPING THE PEACE

The Canto Bight Police Department is well equipped and its officers are well paid. This is all part of Cantonica's strategy to keep the wealthy engaged at gaming tables and racetracks, so credits flow freely from their pockets and into the coffers of the planet's entertainment barons. The police are trained to avoid deadly force if at all possible, keeping Canto Bight a sunny playground free of shadows cast by inequality and galactic unrest. The CBPD uses jet-sticks to contain trouble, responding quickly, firing stun bolts, and carting miscreants off to answer for their crimes at the convenience of a magistrate.

Repulsor projection grid

Repulsor field amplification node

Police light

Maneuvering repulsors

Power dynamos

Power distribution pylon

Power converters

Repulsor field generation frame

Canto Bight Mounted
Police officer

Data display

Flight
computer
chip boards

Searchlight

Pilot controls
direction by
leaning

Rear
power cell

Primary heat
exhaust

Structural
bracing

Cooling
sleeve

Power
trunking

Static
discharge
vanes

Altitude
controls

Forward light

Canto Bight Police
Department livery

Long-range comlink

Brake

Operator
pylon

Power
relays

Accelerator
pedal

Forward
power cells

Multi-setting
laser cannon
can be set from
stun to kill

Terrain sensor

JUMPSPEEDERS
AND AIRHOOKS

Jet-sticks and other personal repulsorlift
craft have proved popular with those
who must travel regularly within limited
areas, such as police officers and factory
workers. They also appeal to tourists
exploring the sights on exotic worlds.
Personal repulsorcraft operated
while sitting are often called
jumpspeeders, while those
driven in a standing position are
known as airhooks. An infamous
airhook model was the STAP, flown by
battle droids during the Clone Wars.

233

THE *LIBERTINE*

For the journey from Cantonica to the First Order fleet, DJ decides to travel in style, searching Canto Bight's spaceport for a ride worthy of the rich payday he is about to enjoy. For a practiced criminal, it is all too easy. He slips past the guards and uses a computer spike and key bypass to slice through the anti-theft defenses of the *Libertine*, a sleek and stylish star yacht belonging to a high-rolling executive turned arms dealer. The handsome yacht lacks weapons and robust defensive systems, which reflects its origins in a safer galactic era—as well as an aristocrat's certainty that wealth and breeding are safeguards against disaster and bad luck. DJ knows better; perhaps the *Libertine*'s owner will reach the same conclusion once he finds his prized yacht for sale in a black-market ship lot, stripped of its most valuable equipment and finest trappings.

STATUS SYMBOL

DJ grins at the sight of the staircase connecting the *Libertine*'s lounge with its flight deck. This seemingly out-of-place detail is a hallmark of a top-of-the-line yacht, one constructed with acceleration compensators and antishock fields to ensure a ride as smooth as a luxury airspeeder or groundcoach. Unfortunately, he'll have to ditch the yacht in short order. But that's all right—in an easy-come, easy-go galaxy, a wise being doesn't cling to possessions, but simply enjoys the ride.

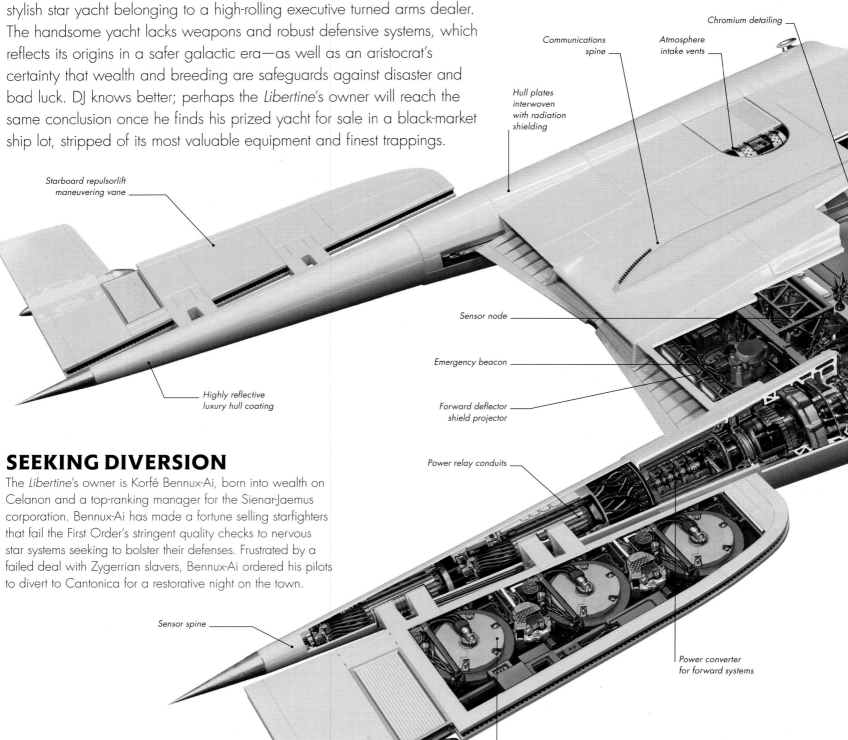

Starboard repulsorlift maneuvering vane

Highly reflective luxury hull coating

Communications spine

Atmosphere intake vents

Chromium detailing

Hull plates interwoven with radiation shielding

Sensor node

Emergency beacon

Forward deflector shield projector

Power relay conduits

Sensor spine

Power converter for forward systems

Overclocked forward repulsors allow for nimble micromaneuvers

SEEKING DIVERSION

The *Libertine*'s owner is Korfé Bennux-Ai, born into wealth on Celanon and a top-ranking manager for the Sienar-Jaemus corporation. Bennux-Ai has made a fortune selling starfighters that fail the First Order's stringent quality checks to nervous star systems seeking to bolster their defenses. Frustrated by a failed deal with Zygerrian slavers, Bennux-Ai ordered his pilots to divert to Cantonica for a restorative night on the town.

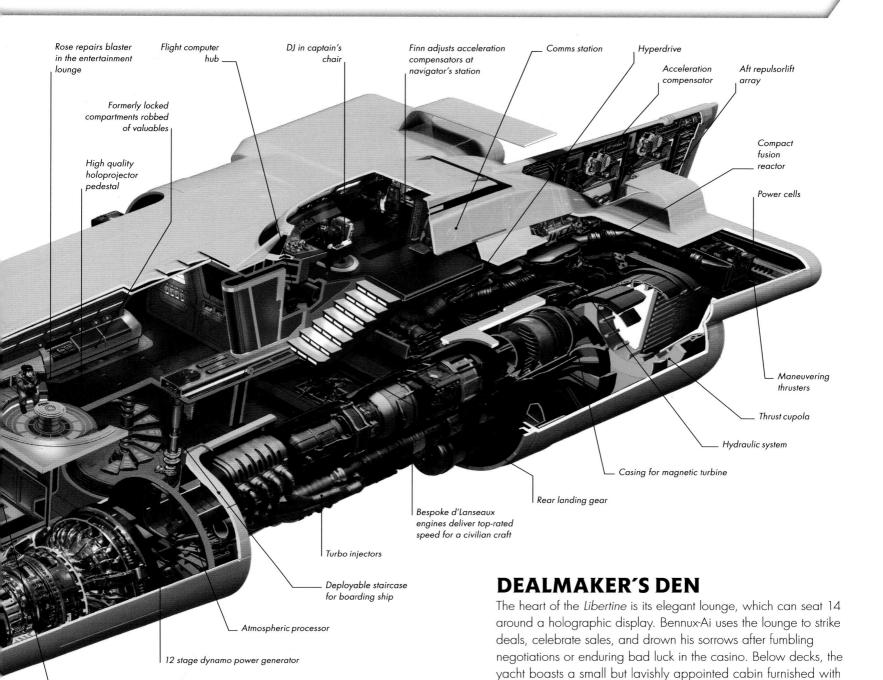

Rose repairs blaster in the entertainment lounge

Flight computer hub

DJ in captain's chair

Finn adjusts acceleration compensators at navigator's station

Comms station

Hyperdrive

Acceleration compensator

Aft repulsorlift array

Formerly locked compartments robbed of valuables

High quality holoprojector pedestal

Compact fusion reactor

Power cells

Maneuvering thrusters

Thrust cupola

Hydraulic system

Casing for magnetic turbine

Rear landing gear

Bespoke d'Lanseaux engines deliver top-rated speed for a civilian craft

Turbo injectors

Deployable staircase for boarding ship

Atmospheric processor

12 stage dynamo power generator

Deluxe sleeping cabin

DEALMAKER'S DEN

The heart of the *Libertine* is its elegant lounge, which can seat 14 around a holographic display. Bennux-Ai uses the lounge to strike deals, celebrate sales, and drown his sorrows after fumbling negotiations or enduring bad luck in the casino. Below decks, the yacht boasts a small but lavishly appointed cabin furnished with rare woods. Sizing up the lounge, DJ wastes no time breaking into Bennux-Ai's cabinets and safe, helping himself to hard currency, jewelry, spice, and valuable trinkets, before copying the executive's catalog of contraband starfighters for sale.

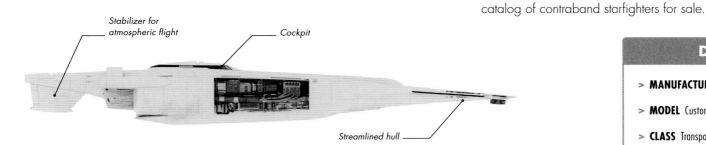

Stabilizer for atmospheric flight

Cockpit

Streamlined hull

ARTISANAL CRAFTWORK

In a galaxy where droid labor dominates industries from agriculture to manufacturing, nothing signals wealth and taste like a luxury item made by organic hands. The *Libertine* was built a century ago by the shipwrights of the Guild d'Lanseaux in the Chardaan Orbital Yards; like all d'Lanseaux yachts its design is unique. Registration data from the Bureau of Ships and Services indicates its first owner was the Kuati diplomat Valis of Kuhlvult, who christened the ship the *Steadfast*.

DATA FILE	
> **MANUFACTURER** Guild d'Lanseaux	
> **MODEL** Custom Star Yacht	
> **CLASS** Transport	
> **DIMENSIONS** Length: 52.92m (173.62ft); width: 26.13m (85.73ft); height: 7.03m (23.06ft)	
> **CREW** 2 (pilot and copilot) plus up to 14 passengers	
> **WEAPONS** None	
> **AFFILIATION** None	

AT-M6

A towering machine seemingly plucked from nightmares, the All Terrain MegaCaliber Six brings devastating firepower to the surface of Crait. Sheathed in state-of-the-art armor forged in secret facilities in the Unknown Regions, the massive AT-M6 is simultaneously a brutally effective siege engine and a fiendish example of psychological warfare. It is a menacing symbol of an emboldened First Order finally unleashed to wreak havoc on the galaxy that rejected its Imperial predecessors. The goal of such an obscene display of murderous power is to reduce enemies to abject terror, incapable of any course of action except total submission.

TOP GUN

The AT-M6 is fundamentally a platform for the MegaCaliber Six turbolaser cannon, which dominates the walker's massive fuselage. Intended to make siege warfare simple and short, the M6 is powerful enough to punch through shields rated to deflect bombardment from orbit. Bringing the destructive power of a battleship to ground engagements requires a dedicated power plant and a string of auxiliary fuel cells to reduce the cannon's recharge time.

DATA FILE

> **MANUFACTURER** Kuat-Entralla Drive Yards

> **MODEL** All Terrain MegaCaliber Six (AT-M6)

> **CLASS** Combat walker

> **DIMENSIONS** Length: 40.87m (134.09ft); width: 17.95m (58.89ft); height: 36.18m (118.7ft)

> **CREW** 5 (pilot, gunner, vehicle commander, and 2 weapon engineers) plus up to 12 passengers

> **WEAPONS** 1 MegaCaliber Six turbolaser cannon, 2 heavy fire-linked dual laser cannons, 2 medium anti-ship laser cannons

> **AFFILIATION** First Order

Heat exhaust

Gun deck access ladder

Turbolaser fuel cells

Auxiliary space can be customized depending on mission profile

Seats for small number of embarked infantry

Main fusion reactor

Reactor coil

Reactant fuel port

Weapon crew

Weapon diagnostics interface

Dedicated power plant for turbolaser

Recoil shock absorber

Targeting sensors

Main limb locomotion pistons

MegaCaliber Six turbolaser cannon

Anti-ship laser cannon

Fire control and targeting computer

Vehicle commander

Pilot and gunnery officer stations

Chin-mounted heavy laser cannons

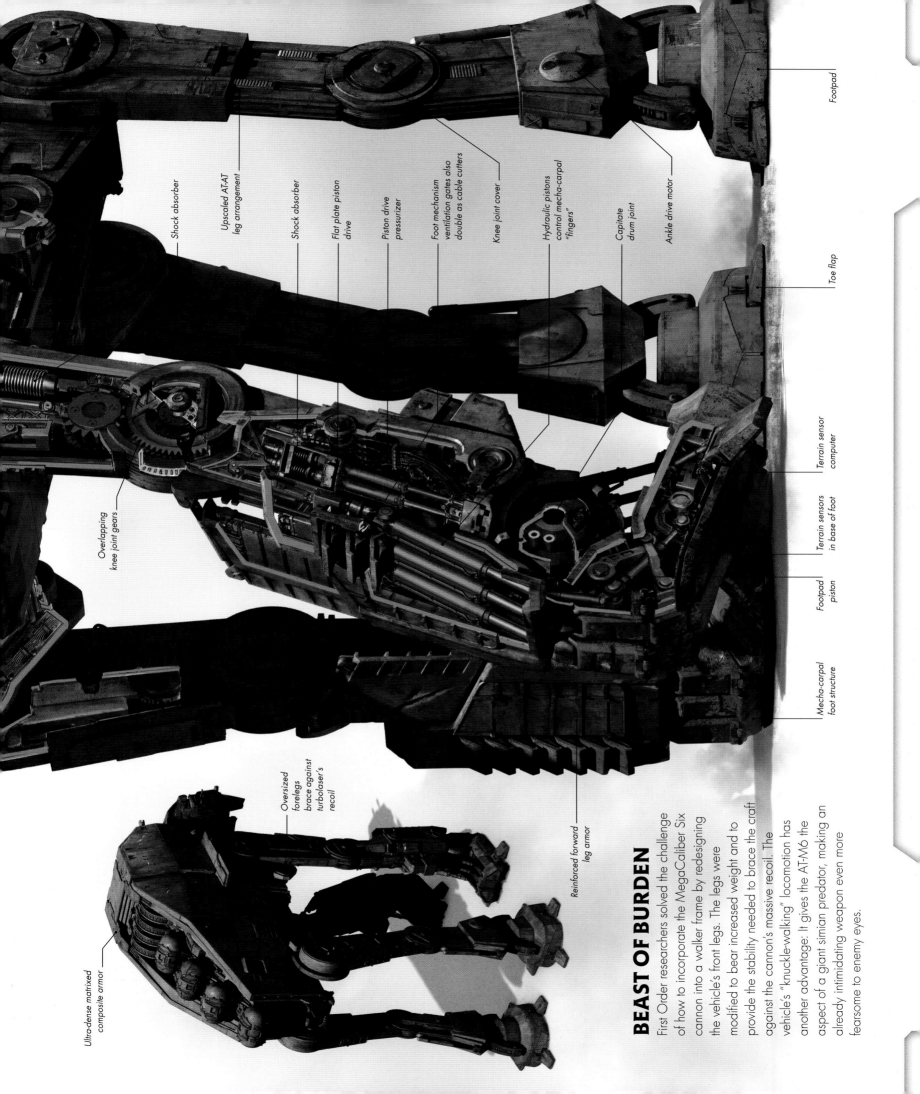

Footpad

Shock absorber

Upscaled AT-AT
leg arrangement

Shock absorber

Flat plate piston
drive

Piston drive
pressurizer

Foot mechanism
ventilation gates also
double as cable cutters

Knee joint cover

Hydraulic pistons
control mecha-carpal
"fingers"

Capitate
drum joint

Ankle drive motor

Toe flap

Overlapping
knee joint gears

Terrain sensor
computer

Terrain sensors
in base of foot

Footpad
piston

Mecha-carpal
foot structure

BEAST OF BURDEN

First Order researchers solved the challenge of how to incorporate the MegaCaliber Six cannon into a walker frame by redesigning the vehicle's front legs. The legs were modified to bear increased weight and to provide the stability needed to brace the craft against the cannon's massive recoil. The vehicle's "knuckle-walking" locomotion has another advantage: It gives the AT-M6 the aspect of a giant simian predator, making an already intimidating weapon even more fearsome to enemy eyes.

Oversized
forelegs
brace against
turbolaser's
recoil

Reinforced forward
leg armor

Ultra-dense matrixed
composite armor

SKI SPEEDER

The Resistance has a track record of making ends meet with surplus New Republic warships, supplies obtained on the black market, and carefully maintained equipment from the Rebellion era. But ingenuity gives way to desperation when a First Order strike force corners the Resistance on Crait. Frantic repairs to ancient, rickety ski speeders that predate the Alliance lead to the debut of Poe Dameron's "Reb" Squadron. The fragile-looking ski speeders were originally civilian sports repulsorcraft, up-armored by long-gone rebel techs for use as patrol vehicles. These lightweight craft were never intended to take on anything bigger than the speeder bikes and ground vehicles favored by smugglers and pirates—but they now stand as the Resistance's last line of defense.

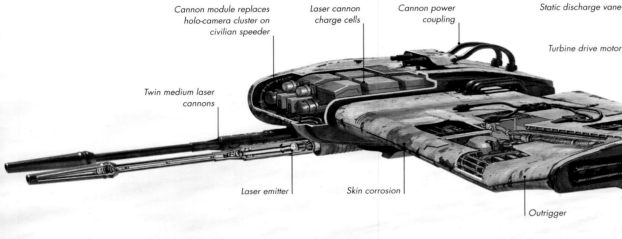

Insulated reactant fuel lines

Hybrid engine can also function in vacuum

Compressor

Fuel injector

Cannon module replaces holo-camera cluster on civilian speeder

Laser cannon charge cells

Cannon power coupling

Static discharge vane

Turbine drive motor

Twin medium laser cannons

Laser emitter

Skin corrosion

Outrigger

Turbine atmosphere intake

Heat exchanger grill

Terrain sensor

Halofoil shock absorber

RECREATIONAL VEHICLES

The early Empire witnessed a fad for asteroid slalom, a sport in which competitors sped along the surface of small asteroids, using them as springboards for high-speed turns and eye-catching stunts. The Verpine manufacturer Roche Machines produced the V-4 series of ski speeders, which boasted ventral mono-skis to keep the speeders anchored, and boom-mounted holo-cameras to record maneuvers. Unfortunately, an undetected stone-mite infestation led to the devouring of several racers and their craft in the Orleon Belt Grand Slalom Finals—a tragedy watched live by a horrified galaxy. As bookings plummeted, Roche Machines canceled production and sold off its inventory at slashed prices.

DATA FILE

> **MANUFACTURER** Roche Machines

> **MODEL** Modified V-4X-D Ski Speeder

> **CLASS** Airspeeder

> **DIMENSIONS** Length: 7.33m (24.05ft); width: 11.5m (37.73ft); height: 4.27m (14.01ft)

> **CREW** 1 pilot

> **WEAPONS** 2 medium laser cannons

> **AFFILIATION** Resistance

UNLIKELY BUYERS

With the asteroid slalom craze over, most of Roche Machines' ski speeders were scrapped. But a few found unlikely second lives thanks to tinkerers in asteroid settlements. Ski speeders were recast as exploration craft and transports, their outriggers adapted for mounting everything from scientific instruments to supply pods. Meanwhile, a rebel cell backed by Alderaanian credits adapted a number of ski speeders for use as patrol craft on Crait. The rebel techs attached laser cannons to the speeders' booms and added as much armor as the lightweight craft could accommodate.

CRIMSON CALLING CARD

Ski speeders were designed for use on asteroids, where there is enough gravity for repulsorlifts to engage, but not enough for true flight. They prove mildly terrifying to pilot in the heavier gravity of a planetary surface—the overcompensating repulsors threaten to launch the lightweight craft into the air with every bounce. The ventral mono-ski stabilizes the speeder, ensuring its powerful engine supplies thrust and not lift, and cuts a groove in Crait's bright white layer of saline crust. Crimson crystalline dust gouged out by the mono-ski is caught by the engine blast, giving each speeder a defiantly gaudy red tail.

FAMILY RESEMBLANCE

Sizing up his first ski speeder, Poe Dameron complains that it's "a B-wing that can't fly." The squadron leader is closer to the truth than he knows: The ski speeder's cockpit pod, central engine, and outrigger are mainstays of Verpine ship designs, which include the T-6 shuttle, the V-19 Torrent starfighter, and the production model of the B-wing fighter. The B-wing line began with a prototype built by the Mon Calamari engineer Quarrie, who sought to improve on designs conceived by Verpine shipwrights.

Repulsor field thrust vector ring and rudder

Duraboard construction

Anti-turbulence cowling

Hastily repaired control cables

Wing fuel cells

Reactant mixer fuel lines

Auxiliary power generator

Acceleration compensator

Cooling fan

Cooling vent

Throttle lever

Cooling air passage

Halofoil mono-ski

Rhodocrosite dust

Targeting sensors

Steering column

Navigation computer

Navigation sensor spine

Ablative armor plating

Pilot controls

Kinetic shield projector

GLOSSARY

ASTROMECH (DROID)
Multipurpose utility droid, designed primarily for use in spacecraft. Many starfighters incorporate an integral astromech droid to assist with astronavigation.

BLASTER CANNON
Limited-range, heavy artillery weapon fitted to starships for defensive use. Blasters utilize high-energy blaster gas to produce a visible beam of intense energy, which can cause tremendous damage to structures and organic tissue. Although their destructive power is considerable, blaster cannons are not as powerful as laser cannons.

CAPITAL SHIP
A large military starship designed for deep-space warfare, such as an Imperial Star Destroyer or Mon Calamari Star Cruiser. With crews numbering in the hundreds or even thousands, capital ships have numerous heavy weapons and shields. They often carry shuttles, starfighters, and other craft in their huge hangar bays.

Assault Ship –
***Acclamator* Class**

CLOAKING DEVICE
Used to render a starship invisible to electronic detection systems, a cloaking device disrupts the electronic signature normally emitted by a craft's various systems and sensors.

CONCUSSION MISSILE
A projectile that travels at sublight speed and causes destructive shockwaves on impact with its target. Concussion missiles are capable of penetrating the armor of a capital ship.

DROID
Generic term for any form of mobile robotic system that has at least some of the capabilities of locomotion, manipulation, logic, self-aware intelligence, communication, and sensory reception. Droids are usually fashioned in the likeness of their creators, or else are designed for functionality. Programmed with varying degrees of artificial intelligence and powered by internal rechargeable cells, droids are the workhorses of the galaxy. They are employed for an incredibly broad range of tasks, from field and manufacturing labor to use as soldiers, assassins, mechanics, diplomatic aides, and doctors. Many cultures treat droids as slaves or second-class beings. There are over fifty billion droids in current service in the galaxy.

Trade Federation
Droid Starfighter

ESCAPE POD
A space capsule used by passengers and crew to abandon starships in emergencies. Once launched, an escape pod uses its sensor systems to collect data on nearby planets, then utilizes its simple drive system to enter the atmosphere of the nearest hospitable world and achieve a safe landing. Pods have a limited fuel supply, but are equipped with up to two weeks' supplies to aid passenger survival.

HEAT SINKS & RADIATORS
Devices designed to draw away heat generated by spacecraft or vehicle systems and dissipate it into the surrounding environment. Removing this "waste heat" keeps the system's components within their normal operating temperature, preventing malfunctions and breakdowns.

Jedi Interceptor with
Hyperdrive Booster

HYPERDRIVE
The "faster-than-light" drive that allows a starship to enter the alternate dimension known as hyperspace, where the normal laws of space and time no longer apply. By traveling through hyperspace, vehicles can cross vast distances of space in an instant.

HYPERDRIVE CLASS
Hyperdrives are rated by "classes": the lower the class, the faster the hyperdrive. Most civilian ships use relatively slow hyperdrives rated at Class Three or higher. Government, diplomatic, and military vessels have Class Two or Class One hyperdrives, while some experimental or "rogue" craft, such as the *Millennium Falcon*, use even faster classes.

INERTIAL COMPENSATOR
A device that generates a type of artificial gravity, which helps to neutralize the effects of accelerating to high speeds aboard medium- and larger-sized spacecraft, such as the *Millennium Falcon*.

ION CANNON
A weapon that fires powerful bolts of ionized energy designed to overload a target's systems or fuse its mechanical components. It is used to disable an opposing starship without causing lasting damage.

Rebel Alliance
Snowspeeder

ION DRIVE
An extremely common form of sublight drive, employed to transport starships into orbit from planetary surfaces and through local space. Ion engines produce thrust by projecting a stream of charged particles. There are many ion engine configurations, but one of the most successful designs is the twin ion engine utilized in the TIE family of starfighters.

First Order TIE Fighter

LASER CANNON

The dominant weapon in the galaxy, found on both military and civilian spacecraft and vehicles. Laser cannons are a more powerful form of blaster, firing bolts of concentrated energy. They can range from low-grade models—which are only slightly more powerful than blaster rifles—to military versions capable of destroying starfighters with a single blast.

PROTON BOMB

A form of particle weapon that can be dropped onto spacecraft or planetary-surface installations. The bomb creates a cloud of high-velocity protons that can penetrate defensive shields. There are several types of proton bombs in the Imperial arsenal

PROTON TORPEDO

A high-speed projectile weapon that destroys its targets by releasing a wave of high-energy proton particles on impact. It can bypass standard deflector shielding but can be stopped by particle shielding.

Proton Torpedo

QUAD LASER

Laser weapon consisting of four linked laser cannons which fire alternately in pairs. Quad lasers are very powerful in comparison to many ship-mounted weapons, but more affordable than turbolasers. They are commonly used on small- to medium-sized starships.

REPULSORLIFT

Antigravity technology used by planet-based vehicles. Repulsorlifts create an antigravity field which repels a planet's gravity, providing lift that enables a craft to hover over the surface or fly in the atmosphere. Most starships also use repulsorlift technology for planetary landings and atmospheric flight.

**Battle Droid & STAP
(Single Trooper Aerial Platform)**

SENSOR ARRAY

A suite of information-gathering instruments fitted to a spacecraft or vehicle. A sensor array is composed of a number of different scanners and other detection instruments that provide data on the environment surrounding the craft.

SHIELDS

Also known as deflector shields, these protective energy fields absorb laser blasts and deflect physical projectiles. Almost all spacecraft and some vehicles are protected by shields. The strength, radius, and endurance depend upon the available power supply. There are two main types of shields: ray shields, which absorb radiation and raw energy; and particle shields, which repel solid objects, from proton particles to concussion and proton weapons.

**Republic ISP (Infantry
Support Platform)**

SPEEDER

Generic term for a ground vehicle that uses repulsorlift technology to hover and fly above a planet's surface. Variations for different environments include landspeeders, airspeeders, and snowspeeders.

SPEEDER BIKES & SWOOPS

Sith Speeder Bike

Personal ground-transport vehicles that use the same repulsorlift technology as speeders to travel across a planet's surface. Designed to carry one or two passengers, speeder bikes are in use throughout the galaxy for both civilian and military transportation. Swoops are high-powered versions of the speeder bike that are faster and more difficult to control. Swoop racing is a common sporting event throughout the galaxy.

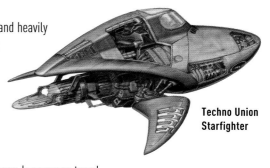

STARFIGHTER

A small, fast, maneuverable, and heavily armed starship used in direct confrontations between opposing forces. Most space battles are fought between squadrons of starfighters.

**Techno Union
Starfighter**

SUBLIGHT DRIVE

A form of propulsion used for non-hyperspace travel. Spacecraft use sublight drives to lift off from planetary surfaces and travel into orbit. They can also be used to travel into deep space, where a vessel can engage its hyperdrive if necessary. During space battles, all starships engage their sublight drives.

TRACTOR BEAM

Modified force field capable of immobilizing and moving objects in space. Tractor beams can be used by spacecraft and space stations to guide spacecraft into landing bays, move cargo or salvage, or capture enemy vessels for boarding or destruction.

TRANSPORT

A starship used to carry cargo or passengers. The term is usually applied to civilian vessels, but can also refer to a ship that ferries troops and military supplies.

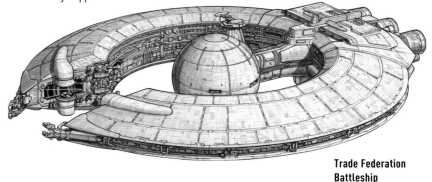

**Trade Federation
Battleship**

TURBOLASER

A high-powered form of laser cannon developed for use on capital ships. Turbolasers require large generators for power and multiperson crews to operate, but can penetrate the shields and armor of opposing capital ships. They are also effective against planetary targets.

**Republic Star Destroyer
Turbolaser Turret**

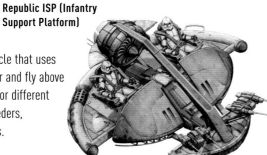

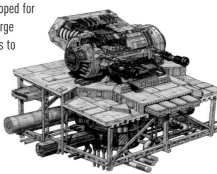

INDEX

Bold page numbers refer to main entries.

ACKNOWLEDGMENTS

Hans Jenssen would like to thank his good friend Tom Evans for helping with designing Luke's landspeeder, and his very tolerant family for their support over the years. Also all the top professionals whom he has been lucky enough to work with at DK and Lucasfilm, especially his brother in arms, Richard Chasemore.

Richard Chasemore would like to thank Lucasfilm for their kind words, support, and approval. DK for believing in a young artist and still calling with new projects! All the fans we meet at the conventions that push us to greater heights of detail. Of course my faithful dog Koco who sits with me in my studio into the early hours, and my art partner Hans Jenssen, Salute!

Kemp Remillard: First and foremost I'd like to thank Cameron Beck, Stacey Leong, Matthew Azeveda, and Chris Medley-Pole whose attention and help with Lucasfilm digital assets was indispensable in creating artwork for this book. Many thanks to J.W. Rinzler, Troy Alders, Pablo Hidalgo, Phil Szostak, Leland Chee, Newell Todd, Samantha Holland, Becca Friedman, Justin Chan, Mike Conte, Megan Matouzek, and everyone else on the 6th floor for their warm reception, hospitality, and help with *Star Wars* facts big and small. It's been a real pleasure working with such a great group here in San Francisco. And of course, I'd like to thank Owen Bennett, David Fentiman, Tom Morse, and the team at DK in London for having faith in my promised ability to complete an essentially impossible art task, and for striking fear into my heart when they first asked me if I wanted to do this. I would like to thank Jason Fry, whose collaboration on this book could not have been more enjoyable and for running with some of my crazy ideas.

I want to thank all of my good friends at Massive Black for teaching me the ways of the Force. I would also like to thank Hans Jenssen, Richard Chasemore and everyone who worked on the original *Star Wars: Incredible Cross-Sections* for all the inspiration. Lastly, I have to thank JJ Abrams, Kathleen Kennedy, and George Lucas for making it all possible.

Jason Fry: Thanks to Pablo Hidalgo, Phil Szostak, Leland Chee, Jonathan Rinzler, and all at Lucasfilm for showing us such cool new stuff; to Jeff Carlisle, Ryder Windham, Chris Reiff, and Chris Trevas for ace Falconology; to Joe Johnston for, well, everything; to David and Owen at DK for keeping us on track; and to all the previous DK writers upon whose shoulders we stood. And, as always, to Emily and Joshua for tolerating me.

DK Publishing: We would also like to thank Phil Szostak, Brian Miller, Natalie Kocekian, and Mike Siglain for their assistance with the creation of this book.

PROJECT EDITOR David Fentiman
ADDITIONAL EDITORIAL Alastair Dougall, Kathryn Hill, Lisa Stock, Matt Jones, Hannah Gulliver-Jones, and Clare Millar
SENIOR COVER DESIGNER Mark Penfound
SENIOR DESIGNERS Clive Savage, David McDonald
PROJECT ART EDITOR Owen Bennett
ADDITIONAL DESIGNERS Nick Avery, Mabel Chan, Ian Ebstein, Mary Lytle, Toby Truphet, and Ian Midson
CREATIVE TECHNICAL SUPPORT Tom Morse
PRE-PRODUCTION PRODUCER Kavita Varma
PRODUCER Isobel Reid
MANAGING EDITOR Sadie Smith
MANAGING ART EDITORS Ron Stobbart, Guy Harvey
CREATIVE MANAGER Sarah Harland
ART DIRECTOR Lisa Lanzarini
PUBLISHER Julie Ferris
PUBLISHING DIRECTOR Simon Beecroft

FOR LUCASFILM
SENIOR EDITOR Brett Rector
CREATIVE DIRECTOR OF PUBLISHING Michael Siglain
ART DIRECTOR Troy Alders
STORY GROUP James Waugh, Pablo Hidalgo, Leland Chee, and Matt Martin
ASSET MANAGEMENT Steve Newman, Gabrielle Levenson, Travis Murray, Tim Mapp, Erik Sanchez, Bryce Pinkos, and Nicole LaCoursiere

This edition published in 2018
First published in Great Britain in 2013
by Dorling Kindersley Limited
80 Strand, London WC2R ORL

In 2014 Lucasfilm reclassified what is considered canon in the *Star Wars* universe. *Star Wars: Complete Vehicles* (first published in 2013) draws mostly upon information from the Expanded Universe that Lucasfilm now considers to be "Legends"—that is, stories beyond the original six films and the TV shows *Star Wars: The Clone Wars* and *Star Wars Rebels*.

Page design copyright © 2018 Dorling Kindersley Limited
A Penguin Random House Company

001-313401-Sep/2018

Material in this book was previously published in:
Star Wars: Incredible Cross-Sections (1998), *Star Wars Episode I: Incredible Cross-Sections* (1999), *Star Wars Attack of the Clones: Incredible Cross-Sections* (2002), *Star Wars Revenge of the Sith: Incredible Cross-Sections* (2005), *Star Wars: Complete Cross-Sections* (2007), *Star Wars The Force Awakens: Incredible Cross-Sections* (2015), *Star Wars Rogue One: The Ultimate Visual Guide* (2016), and *Star Wars The Last Jedi: Incredible Cross-Sections* (2017)

© & ™ 2018 Lucasfilm Ltd.

ISBN: 978-0-2413-6983-8

Printed and bound in China

A WORLD OF IDEAS:
SEE ALL THERE IS TO KNOW
www.dk.com
www.starwars.com

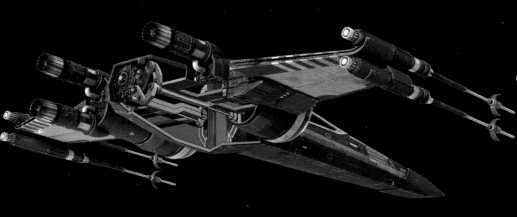